Court Jester:

The Making of a Comedian

By

Mark Sweeney
Professional Comedian

Sgt Mjr Gray -
Semper Fi -

This is dedicated to my parents and to those of us who have survived...so far.

ABOUT THE AUTHOR

Mark Sweeney is the oldest of six children born to your text book case of heavy breeding Irish Catholics. He found out early that funny gets attention. He spent most of his grade school years sitting in the hall alone, perfecting his craft to an imaginary crowd.

High school happened in the mid 70's. Rock and Roll, Marlboro's, flannel shirts and big bell blue jeans, it was a simple time. After high school, he joined the Marine Corps and spent four years adventuring and partying around the globe with unbridled enthusiasm.

After the Marines he embarked on a series of jobs that never completely satisfied. A four year gig in college, a waiter, bartender, sprinkler fitter, maintenance worker, security guard, copier repairman, shuttle driver, courier, traffic school instructor and real estate agent.

In 1989 he did open mic night in St. Louis and forever changed his destiny. He spent ten years on the road, and then spent six years in Los Angeles working periodically before heading back to his true love: stand-up comedy.

TABLE OF CONTENTS

CHAPTER 1
BEGINNINGS

I'm cold, wet, naked and covered in blood. I howl at the Gods as I try to claw my way through the shawl of skin that smothers me. Welcome to life, little one. It's a harsh beginning. I don't mean harsh like being born on the plains of Darfur in a mud hut with no running water, towels, soap or anything that resembles life as we know it, but it's not a pleasant hello. It's a slither and a squeeze and slap on the ass. Hi, dipshit. Welcome to the world.

I don't remember much of the early years. What I know, I learned from pictures, and from what I can tell, I was one snappy dresser. My outfits always seemed to match. From argyle socks to small fedoras, I was right on the cutting edge of child fashion. Keep in mind, this was way before Garanimals. We had no way of knowing which clothes went well together. We had to *feel*, it man. We just had to *feel* it.

Being the first born child of a newly married couple is a crap shoot. Most first children are lucky to have survived. First-time parents are clueless; they have no idea what they're doing. There's no text book, there's no test. Well, there was a book, *Dr. Spock's Baby and Child Care* book, but that was it. There was only one child-care expert in the old days. We didn't have pompous know-it-alls like Dr. Phil. There was Spock, and he was the man. One guy, one plan, take it or leave it. They were simple days my friends. It was basically learn as you go, and guess who was the test subject? That's right, the first born. It is a daily battle just to survive new parents. There is much celebrating, joy and cheer for the couple that just had a baby. I guess they're unaware that it's been done six billion times before. Why do new parents and their friends and family act like it's the first time anyone's had a baby? "It's a miracle." No, it's not. Something that happens a thousand times a day is not a miracle, it's an everyday occurrence.

A celebration of life, that's what it was, and nothing celebrates life like 20 germ ridden adults standing around drinking and smoking non-filtered cigarettes in front of the newborn. That's how much people cared about health back then. Oh how ignorance is bliss. There was usually a cigar thrown in as well. Uncle Larry just has to have his cigar, and he has to have it inside. Second-hand smoke is always a treat for the toddler. I was six months old and had developed a smokers' cough. Sweet. Maybe I can get a red handkerchief to keep close by for when I need to cough up a lung cookie. I know every man here has a handkerchief. All men used to carry them, little cloth rags full of snot tucked away in a back pocket. It could be whipped out at any time to service anything that may come up. Sneezes, coughs, they even caught tears from time to time. During a good snot releasing cry Dad could just reach down and wipe your nose. Never mind the crusty patch that you felt on the second sweep. It's just old snot, not to worry.

I had my first beer when I was five. What's up with that? People used to think it was cute when the baby had a beer, now they call the cops on you. Nothing makes a five-year-old take a nap faster than a cold can of Hamm's. People just didn't care then. I saw a commercial with a doctor advertising cigarettes. Hilarious. I miss the early 60's.

I've also noticed that I don't have a car seat. I imagine in about 35 years, you will be required by law to strap your child into a space-age, technologically advanced, booster rocket seat that will protect baby from everything from car accidents to R.P.G. attacks. But now, parents can feel free to just lay the kid on the four-foot-wide back seat and hope he doesn't roll off onto the floor when Dad slams on the brakes. Maybe you can hold me in your lap so I can cushion your body in case of an accident. I'm only 13 pounds, but I would gladly come between you and the dashboard, sweet mother. Let me cushion the blow so that you may survive to breed again, and I can become a footnote in the story of your lives. Later, my brothers and I used to stand on the back seat, lean over the front seat and encourage my dad to, "go faster." I guess people just didn't think about the safety of their kids. Kids used to be secondary citizens, nobody gave a shit as to what the kids thought or wanted. Why? Because we were kids. We did what we were told and there were no negotiations going on. Here's the deal, that's it. Safety was certainly never an issue. We knew as children, when we went out and played, that some of us may die. That's just the way it was, if you played by the train tracks long enough, guess what? Trains a' coming. We used to play by the train tracks a lot, we'd hang on to the fence as the trains went by and tried to keep ourselves from being sucked under the wheels. We would yell at the conductor when he went by and sometimes he would throw big hunks of railroad chalk to us. How's that for dangerous? Trying to catch a 5 lb. piece of chalk coming at you at 25 mph. We had a lot of concussions back then. I think that's why people used to have six, seven kids or more; they knew they might lose a few along the way. "Oh yeah, we lost two of them at the lake last year, but we've still got enough left to fill the infield, we'll be fine."

My journey has begun. I wonder where these roads shall take me. Let's find out.

CHAPTER 2
THE OLDEST CHILD

I'm the oldest of six children. I wasn't the oldest *when* I was born. It just turned out that way. I am the oldest child. Yes, I'm making a statement. It's a big one too. I am the oldest child. It wasn't easy being the oldest; ask anyone who is in that fraternity and you'll find that to be true. We are the ice breakers, the trend setters, the trail breakers, the pioneers for all the siblings that follow. We are up on the front lines, the people in charge of us have no idea what to do or how to take care of us. One day they're out with their friends, partying until all hours of the night, then all of a sudden they've got a puppy that doesn't come with an instruction manual. The oldest child is a human guinea pig, a lab rat to learn on. The oldest child is a recipient of a parent's first spanking. They don't know how hard, how long, etc. It's all trial and error. Every experiment a parent wants to try, they try on the oldest child. Oh look, he cries when we drop him down the stairs, that must not be good for him. If he screams until he's blue, there's something wrong. If he stops breathing, he's having oxygen problems. If you force him to eat food he doesn't like, he spits it back in your face. If you stick diaper pins in the wrong way, they puncture the skin. If he throws up blood, take him to the hospital. These are things we should remember. We'll do better with the second child. We have to, this first child is broken. He looks like a torn up doll you would find at the dump. Everything parents know about kids, they learned from the oldest child. So, every kid who is not the oldest child, remember to thank that oldest child. They made your life a whole lot easier.

Holidays at our house were always incredibly noisy. Well, every day at our house was noisy. It was bedlam most of the time. Holidays especially, Pictionary is not designed to be played by 24 people. Everyone's cheating and being sneaky. I don't even know if you can cheat at Pictionary, but if you can, then it was being done. I don't think there is a board game that can be played by 24 people. That's even too many for a football team. We have a tradition during the family gatherings called "let's reminisce about the horrible things Mark did as a child." Oh, it's a hoot. I wasn't the only one though, we had been discussing our various broken bones, concussions, burns, long falls, power tool accidents, electrocutions, firework incidents and the assorted knife wound that we had endured growing up, and we found out a very interesting fact. Almost all the injuries were caused by a brother or sister. Jimmy seemed to take the brunt of it. We (or I) knocked him off the swing set glider and he broke his arm. We were racing bikes up the street and ran him into a parked car and broke out his two front teeth. We (I) knocked him off a stack of cinder blocks one day and he fell against the fence and got 27 stitches in his hand, and this was all before he was ten. Phil kicked a tricycle out from underneath Kathleen and broke her collarbone. I broke mine when I was Batman and the Joker pushed me while running at full speed and crashed me into another parked car. What a sweet bunch of kids.

I didn't realize until later in life that my mother's secret to keeping her sanity was making us play outside, always. Smart chick. We used to get to play in the basement from time to time if it was raining outside. I still remember my mom coming downstairs, seeing the rain and saying "shit." Which I took to mean, yeah, we get to play inside! We often thought we were getting away with something by playing inside, and then somebody would blow it by yelling or some such, and then you would hear her footsteps, crossing the floor, coming to the top of the stairs and say, "Everyone outside." So we'd head outside and then hear the door being locked. It didn't matter what the weather was like, we were still outside. We would stand on the front porch wrapped up for an arctic storm, frozen tendrils of snot trying to ease their way out of our noses, pounding on the door going "mom, can we please come in? It's dark." My mom would just glance at the clock on the wall and slowly shake her head no. Sometimes we would take turns seeing how far we could get our spit to fly. Since it was frozen before it hit the ground, you could really get some distance. After an hour or so we had a nice little collection of frozen spit marbles at the end of the driveway.

My mother had a lot of patience. Her sister had three kids and when they would visit, the two of them would take the nine of us to the park. We'd be unleashed, and my mom and her sister would sit under the tree working on a thermos of gin and tonics. I'm not talking those little silver ones construction workers use, I'm talking the picnic thermos, it must've held two gallons. God bless 'em, now I understand.

We had a shotgun in the house, and only once did my mother actually chamber a round into that 12 gauge, just the once. Oh, she would whip it out from time to time, just to get her point across, but she wouldn't actually chamber a shell. After you see your mother, the

5

women who gave you life, your savior in those dark moments, standing there with tears rolling down her cheeks, a loaded shotgun in one hand and a bottle of Beefeater gin in the other, well, it just breaks your heart.

I don't know if I am the way I am because I was the oldest or if that's just how it turned out. I had it all for a while, then we had Jimmy, then Phil, then Kathleen, followed by Peter and then we finalized the group with Shannon. Up until I was 11 years old, all I heard was "Ssshh, the baby's sleeping." I just wondered when they were going to quite breeding so I could finally make some noise. We went through a lot of babysitters when I was a kid. Most of them never came back for second gig. One time I called the restaurant my parents were at to tell them I could wiggle my ears. That didn't go over well with the babysitter or my folks. Another lesson learned. Unless it's a life or death emergency, you better not pick up the phone and have your parents paged while at a restaurant. They're going to assume the worst.

We had this one sitter named Linda Hocking. I remember her because she came back more than once. I don't remember what I did when she was around, but according to the stories, I was not an easy child to sit for. If I misbehaved badly enough, my dad would make me walk over to her house the next day and apologize. She lived about three miles away, and my dad would follow me in the car the whole way there and back, never once offering a ride, just cruising behind me making sure I did what I was supposed to. He was a crafty devil. One January day we were in the middle of a deep arctic freeze, the entire city had been shut down, no services, no people out, no nothing. Animals were frozen into place on lawns everywhere, and he still made me go, just following behind me a snail's pace. By the time we got home, it was pitch dark, and frostbite had taken a finger and two toes. Oh the price we pay to misbehave for the babysitter.

By the time I hit ten, my parents were leaving the house with me in charge. I was ten years old and babysitting my brothers and sisters. Every time I sat for them, they would write down everything I did or said wrong, and the next day they would give those lists to my parents so they could deal with me. It seems I was tyrant. Who knew the power of the throne? I was in charge of whether they lived or died, and I took it seriously. I am in charge, I run the show, I am the king. For tonight, that is. My parents never really got on me about the lists. I guess getting lists from the younger children was better than paying a babysitter.

When my littlest sister Shannon was in kindergarten, she made a painting of her three wishes. The first? To be an only child. I believed her too. When we go back and look at family pictures from that era, Shannon is NEVER smiling, she didn't smile in one single family portrait. The pictures of her by herself, she's beaming. You never saw a happier child. She really did want to be an only child. I guess that didn't work out.

OK, let's get on with this.

CHAPTER 3
KINDERGARTEN

I remember kindergarten; some of it anyway. It was the first time I got suspended. Suspended from kindergarten, do you believe that? What kind of message were they trying to send me anyway? Throw a bird egg at your friend and get sent home for two days? It was during show and tell and we were passing a bird's nest around with each of us taking a gander. Well, when it came around to me, I picked up an egg and shook it. I could hear, or maybe feel, something sloshing around inside. I guess it just got too much for me, and this friend of mine, Matt Martini, (who had a fairly good size head for a kindergartner), was sitting straight across from me. When he turned to talk to the girl next to him, I saw the profile of his humongous head looming, just looming large on the horizon. It mesmerized me, and all I could think was "what a great target his head makes."

I'm staring at the side of his billboard-sized head, and finally, poor judgment and curiosity got the best of me, and I let her fly. That little egg was planted right, square on the side of his head and blew up all over. Maybe I shouldn't say all over, after all, it was a robin's egg and how "all over" can a robin's egg explode? It did crack open after hitting his head though, and it made a mess followed almost immediately by chaos. Who would've thought that a small bird's egg could cause such a commotion? Not me.

Relax, people, it isn't that big of a deal. Matt was screaming, girls were crying and screaming, and I couldn't figure out what all the panic was about. Sure, he had egg yolk and a preemie bird in his hair, but it wasn't like there were innards all over- the whole thing was the size of a quarter. I can see the panic if I would've thrown say...a rotted cat carcass at him, and when it hit him it split open and spewed stinky, decaying entrails everywhere, but I didn't. I didn't throw a rotted cat carcass. It was just a bird egg. I thought it was actually kind of clever, kind of funny. I just thought it would lighten up an otherwise boring session of show and tell. Later we found out that I was the only one entertained. Too bad they don't know funny. My mom picked me up for the first of what was to be many mid-day pickups from various schools. I wasn't allowed back until I could behave. How we, they or us were supposed to determine that, I have no idea.

Nap time was another problem area for me. I love a good nap now, but at five, I just couldn't appreciate that afternoon slumber. Maybe it was the green and maroon prison mats they made us sleep on. Hey, teach, maybe a little bread and water here for convict #4457. You could get better mats at the main prison in Stuttgart. The teacher leaving us unsupervised probably wasn't the best of choices either. For me it was like the curtain came up and my name was being announced. Ladies and Gentlemen, the teacher is gone, so will you please center your attention on mat #9, and put your hands together for Maaarrrrk Sweeeeeneyyyyy! I'd get up and do my little impressions of Mrs. T. That used to kill. Kids just love impressions. I had a few of the teachers and the principal down pat. It's the little mannerisms that make it work, and five-year-olds recognize that.

On the front of my kindergarten report card it says;

"The purpose of our Kindergarten is to socialize the child and to teach the essential habits and attitudes he will need in adjusting himself to school and community life."

That seems like pretty heady shit for five-year-old kids, doesn't it? Learning essential habits so we can adjust ourselves to school *and* community life? I'm carrying food in a Johnny Quest lunch box, I'm not ready to adjust to the community, as a matter of fact, I want a popsicle. On the report card itself, there are little stick figure drawings of the activities we did. Stick figures can only be so expressive. The one about following rules was hilarious, just a stick figure staring up at a sign that said "Rules." How informative. Each stick figure activity has a mark next to it. We didn't receive grades then, just marks. **S**ometimes, **A**lways and **N**ever, those were our choices. The following are my marks from my first schooling experience as a five-year-old.

I follow directions	**S**ometimes
I take care of school things	**A**lways
I keep trying and finish	**A**lways
I work and play well with others	**S**ometimes
I think of things to do by myself	**A**lways
I listen when others are speaking	**S**ometimes
I use my handkerchief	**A**lways

I work well with crayons	**Always**
I work well with scissors	**Never**
I try to be polite and not bother others	**Never**
I obey the rules	**Never**
I talk about things that happen	**Always**
I speak so others know what I'm saying	**Always**
I use my soft voice in school	**Never**
I rest quietly	**Never**

The last comment on the card says, *"**We must have a conference as soon as possible. When would it be convenient for you to come? Please call me anytime**."*

Apparently, I could color with crayons but couldn't cut with scissors, or maybe it was the *things* I was cutting with scissors. I put things away, but I was a loner. I didn't follow directions either, but they don't tell you what the directions were, do they? Maybe they weren't very good directions. Maybe they weren't directions I thought would benefit me. There are a lot of variables to be considered here. I sometimes played well with others, but who were the "others?" We don't know, and we may ever know. Maybe some of the "others" weren't worth playing with. Again, variables. Sometimes I would listen to what "others" were saying, and sometimes not. Again with the "others." Who were these "others," and how do we know they had anything to say? I didn't rest quietly, I didn't obey the rules, and once again, I was impolite to the "others." I didn't use my soft voice in school, but I spoke so others could understand me. "Hey, you crazy bitch, how I can speak so others can understand me, if I use my soft voice?" You have to be loud to be heard, lady. Take it from me. On the bright side, I took care of school property, found things to do on my own and blew my nose into a rag. That's not too shabby.

This report card actually turned out to quite prophetic. This was just a foreshadowing of things to come. At this point, I really can't say anything to defend myself, I was only five. Later though, after several moves by our family, I learned to blame my behavior on the fact I was always the new kid in school. Tough on a kid. Yeah. Tough. I don't think I would have ended up any different regardless. I was just plain rambunctious.

CHAPTER 4
FIRST GRADE

For first grade I had Mrs. Enke, and I have no idea who she was or what she looked like. I do know that she thought my handwriting needed a lot of improvement. She also thought I had a problem with respecting authority, following directions, listening effectively, completing assigned work and effectively using my work *and* free time. Let's peruse her comments about this particular first grader.

"Mark is overcoming his shyness. He seldom contributes at Share and Tell time or in Science or Social Studies. He seems to know his reading words quite well, but often refuses to share them."

Hey lady- the last time I contributed to Share and Tell was the egg incident. You may not want me to contribute, do your research. I REFUSED to share my reading words? How does a 1st grader refuse anything? Maybe I felt that reading was a personal matter not to be shared with classmates. Trust me, lady, I'll be sharing enough in the upcoming years. If you're still around, you'll get yours. You'll be praying for me to shut up.

"I feel that Mark is getting lazy. He has not been finishing his homework assignments. He has not been learning his reading words. He has the skills to be at the top of his class, but he's just not using them. He often fails to hand in his papers. I hope this will improve next semester."

I don't think I like this lady. I think she's coming down pretty hard on the ole' sweenzster. I'm lazy? What the hell does that mean? If I don't do "homework" I'm lazy? Hey, Mrs. Enke, that's why I go **to school**. I do my learning at school, not at home. You've got me all day long, so teach me what you want, but I'm not taking that shit home with me. I've got a full plate as soon as that bell rings, and doing "homework" isn't one of the things on that plate. Let's see if anything improved in the third quarter.

"Mark's reading comprehension is improving but there is room for further improvement. My main concern is Mark's attitude of being so defensive in most areas. He doesn't take interest in many things. He wastes so much time instead of doing constructive things. I marked him on respecting authority since he is defiant and disobedient most of the time. This hopefully will be changed the next quarter."

Well guess what, toots? Nothing did change. As a matter of fact, not much of this has changed in the last 40 years. Why should I feign interest in something that doesn't interest me? Have you an answer? I thought not. I love the way so many teachers "hoped for a change by next quarter." It's a phrase we'll see again and again. She also thought I "wasted time instead of doing constructive things?" Isn't that what I'm in school for? For you, my teacher, to give me constructive things to do? You want me to come up with constructive things to do during free time? Why are we even having free time? Aren't we supposed to be learning? If you're concerned about me doing something constructive, quit giving me free time. If my free time isn't mine to spend freely, then it's not really "free time" is it? This isn't the school for the arts, it's first grade. Give me something to do, and if it doesn't interest me I won't do it, but at least make the effort. Defiant *and* disobedient? What the hell? How does a 1st grader get to be defiant and disobedient? Was no one in control? What else happened?

"Mark will be ready for second grade next year. He should continue reading for his enjoyment and practice number facts through ten. He has been more cooperative this quarter. I hope Mark has a happy summer."

Whew! I'm glad I'm done with Mrs. Enke and she seemed glad to be rid of me.

CHAPTER 5
I SHIT MY PANTS

I shit in my pants once in second grade. I don't know why I'm even telling you. It's not something I'm proud of. I'm not sure there's ever been an instance when filling your shorts with poo is something to be proud of, unless there's some kind of bet involved. I'm not even really sure what happened. One minute I was sitting at my desk, the next minute I'm sitting at my desk in britches full of poop. I think I tried to fart and ended up shitting my pants. Either that or I just didn't want to raise my hand and ask for permission to use the bathroom. Was I ashamed that I had to poop? I don't know. Was I so embarrassed that I had to poop that I would rather shit in my own pants than ask permission to go? I don't know. What I do know is that I just shit in my pants. I didn't panic, even though I distinctly heard someone mention something about the smell of poop, as in, "did someone just shit their pants?"

I just sat there with undies full of poo and tried to play it cool. "Yeah, it stinks in here, who just shit?" I was forced to join the other children in chiding the offending party in order to cover my shame. There's nothing worse than having to sit at your desk in a pile of your own crap. I stayed that way the rest of the day too. Just sitting there with poo in my pants, and it was only morning so I had to sit there all day. I did eventually get to the bathroom and did some perfunctory cleaning, but it had to be done quickly and with a great deal of subterfuge. You don't want to raise any suspicions. I'm not sure what I did during recess, maybe feigned illness so I could just lie in the grass and watch the other children play.

"Are you going to play kick ball Mark?"

"No, I'm just going to sit here in my shit filled pants and try to get the smell to dissipate."

I guess I could've gone to the nurse's office and said I was sick, but the smell of shit was around me like a shadow. There was no mistaking it. At the end of the day I waited until everyone had left before I got up, you know, just in case the seat of my pants were stained by poo. I thought they had to be. After all, I just spent six hours sitting in my own waste. I had to walk home, I couldn't take the bus with the poo stench wrapped around me in its warm cloak. Somewhere on the way I stopped behind some bushes, took my underwear off and threw them down the sewer. What a relief. My poo pants were gone. I was still a mess, but the poo pants were gone. I've never forgotten that moment of throwing my poop-filled undies into that tunnel. To this day I can still see them lying in the bottom of that storm sewer. That wasn't such good times. I never did shit in my pants again. From that day forward, if I had to go, I raised my freakin' hand.

CHAPTER 6
CATHOLIC SCHOOL

I didn't last long in public school in the second grade. After the first two months, they called my parents in for a conference and suggested they put me into Catholic School. I'm not sure I remember why. I don't recall being so disruptive that I was being asked to leave. Maybe they knew about me pooping in my pants and didn't want that kind of element in their school. Maybe they thought it was contagious and they needed me to go before it spread to the other children. If they let me stay, who knows what could happen? Maybe the whole second grade starts to shit in their pants every day just because Sweeney did it. So they sent me to the Catholic school thinking that the nuns may have more luck curbing me and my activities. That, of course, was not to be. Sister Mary Charlotte and Sister Mary Henry, I'm sure never forgot me. I have certainly not forgotten them. Sister Mary Henry was the principal and Sister Mary Charlotte was my teacher. I lasted two years at St. Joe's. Then, it seems, my parents got called in for another conference. They wanted to put me back in the public schools. Let's take a look at why.

August 1966 - April 1967

I averaged all B's and C's except in handwriting where it was F's across the board. I never did do very well with the penmanship thing. I guess I figured if they couldn't read it, they would never know what I had written. It also becomes apparent I didn't have that much interest in Catholic Doctrine, Science, Social Studies or English either. The comments on the conduct were always the most interesting, anyway. My first real nemesis, Sister Mary Charlotte, she and I went toe to toe. Here are her remarks for Mark Sweeney, 2nd grader.

"Mark needs improvement in the following areas."
Plays well with others
Shows respect for authority
Follows directions
Listens effectively
Uses free time wisely

You know, that sounds strangely like my 1ˢᵗ grade teacher. How about something new? Can you do that for me? Again with these "others." Enough I say.

Quarter one
"Mark's energy is sometimes a handicap. He only contributes to Show and Tell when he wants to. He knows his reading words, but doesn't raise his hand to let me know it. He has a tendency to be disruptive. I hope this will improve next semester."

Maybe Sister, just maybe, I don't want to share my reading words. I find them personal and private. I'll share them when I'm ready. This also sounds like 1ˢᵗ grade. I didn't share my reading words then either, and I guess I really didn't like show and tell. Why? I have no idea; it seems like it would be a lot of fun. I don't know what it was with sharing reading words either. I don't really think I considered them personal and private; I just didn't want to do what they told me to. I honestly don't know where this defiance came from. My father was a fairly strict disciplinarian. Defiance at home would get you an ass whippin'. I didn't get away with much at home, but on the road, on the road, baby, I flourished.

Quarter Two
"I fear Mark isn't controlling his energy. He has not been doing well in his workbook. He only does the assignments he wants to. I feel he has the ability to be near the top of the class, if he just hands in his papers. He has no respect for authority, and can be very disruptive. I hope this will improve next semester."

Here's another teacher hoping that "this will improve next semester." It didn't. I don't really remember being that disrespectful; I mean, it was a long time ago. I just never liked having people tell me what to do. I'll survey the information, make my own decision and go from there. If I don't feel this assignment is necessary, let the "others" do it, I'm busy.

Quarter Three
"Mark has done much better this quarter with his comprehension and his reading words. He could be one of my best students. Mark's biggest obstacle is his attitude. Mark only participates in what interests him. He can be very hard to control and shows defiance to anyone in authority. I hope this will improve next semester."

Wow. I must have been a little shit. Showing defiance to anyone in authority? Even then. What a dickens. Am I really only in 2nd grade? I'm surprised at how many comments the good sister made that were also made by Mrs. Enke, maybe all teachers had a list of words to describe certain types of behavior. Hmm.

Quarter Four
"Mark will be ready for third grade next semester. I hope he has a good summer."

That was it for me and Sister Mary Charlotte. I find it interesting the way she refers to "my energy." It was a very PC way to say "I don't like this kid and can't wait to get rid of him." I'm still just like this sweet little guy. I'm still not participating in things that don't interest me.

Sister Mary Henry, the principal, used to have this weapon, (and it was a weapon, I don't care how many times she called it her "measuring stick") it was five or six yard sticks screwed together. Each yard stick was a different color. And when she swung that thing, you could see colored trails. She could move that thing impressively too. She had to have been 70 then. She was fast, but as it turns out, not quite fast enough. Her big thing was to have you hold your hands out, and she would try and smack them. The problem was I couldn't just leave them out there, and I kept yanking them back- a little game she never much cared for. She'd swing and I'd retreat my hands, she'd swing and I'd pull back. Oh we butted heads, Sister Mary Henry and I, she was indeed a worthy adversary. My parents sent me to Catholic School to be disciplined by nuns. At the beginning of third grade my parents received this letter from the Principal.

Dear Mr. and Mrs. Sweeney;

As you know, Sister Mary Charlotte was Mark's teacher last year. This year she is teaching third grade. Mark has again been assigned to Sister Mary Charlotte's class. Unfortunately, she has requested that Mark be assigned to another class. I realize that you know Sister Mary Charlotte and have become fond of her, but due to the circumstances, we feel it may be best that Mark attend Mrs. Johnson's class. If you have any questions, please feel free to call.

Sincerely;

Sister Mary Henry

How's that for a piece of work? I was only in the second grade and she wanted me transferred. That's just plumb mean. I was a child, for God's sake. What kind of scar did they think that would leave me with? Or did they even take that into consideration? Oh, this poor child, he's a wild one, let's ostracize him. Apparently he's not good enough for the nuns, let's send him off to Mrs. Johnson's class. I got sent to the one civilian teacher in the district. It was the class that met in the cellar with all the other mutants. We learned by candle light, were fed gruel, took time each day to clean each other of lice and other body mites and were let in and out of the school through the secret basement door. Nice.

Third grade was pretty much a repeat of second grade except it was the first time I saw puke in the hall. I was on my way to the principal's office and there was a circle of it on the floor with that sawdust shit the janitors threw on top of it. It masked what it was visually, but you could still smell it. Gross. I always think of that moment when I see a janitor, I picture him putting that sawdust shit on the puke pile of a second grader. I don't think I was cut out for the whole Catholic School thing. I never got off on the uniforms. It was a little too bizarre, all these kids walking around quietly through the halls, all wearing the same clothes. You could almost hear a smooth, heavy machine noise buried deep in the basement driving the whole thing. Like from Pink Floyd's *Wish You Were Here* Album. "Welcome my son, welcome to the machine."

Here are Mrs. Johnson's remarks for me in my third year of higher learning.

First Quarter 3rd Grade
"Mark makes minimum effort to achieve. He only seems to do enough to get by. He has been working and playing well with others. His biggest problem is he disobeys school regulations frequently, and disrupts the class on a daily basis."

Hey lady, maybe I just didn't think the school regulations were worth following. Unless I think a rule or regulation is a good one, I don't follow it. I'm still that way. I only obey the laws I think are good ones. In my opinion, rules and regulations are for "the others." And so it shall be.

Second Quarter
"Mark is still doing as little as possible. When he does the work, he does it very well, it's just infrequent. He seems to get along with others very well and he has many friends. He still disobeys anyone with authority, and seems to enjoy the disruption."

I don't remember much about this lady, but I know she had short hair. I'll always remember Sister Mary Charlotte and Mary Henry, but this lady didn't stick with me. Hmm.

Third Quarter
"Mark still doesn't seem to be fitting in with the regulations here at St. Joseph's. He disobeys school regulations constantly. He spends a great deal of time in Sister Mary Henry's office."

That's because Sister Mary Henry and I are buds and I like to visit her frequently to ensure that she's alright.

Fourth Quarter
"Marks' grades have improved greatly. His respect for authority has not. He disrupts class on a daily basis, and doesn't seem to mind. He tries very hard, but only when he's doing the things he likes to do. I truly hope that this improves over the summer. He is a very independent child."

As it turns out, I had a real problem remembering my prayers and remembering truths, which are two very important things in the Catholic Doctrine. We had to go to mass every day, which was actually just another arena for entertaining. You fill a large room with groups of first, second and third graders and discipline was hard to come by. There are just too many moments of quiet for me, almost uncomfortable quiet. A little fart noise was always a crowd pleaser. Plus, I could never figure out why we had to go to church every day. Didn't we just do this yesterday?

CHAPTER 7
FIRESTARTER

Here's a cute little story of mischief. I guess I was in second grade. My buddy and I decided to spend a day after school starting fires. I know that fire starting as a youth is sometimes a foreshadowing of bad things to come. Many serial killers started off lighting fires, but not me (I ended up a comedian) I was just a plain fire starter. Plus, it was only for that one day. We just cruised around and started little fires in sewers and ditches. We weren't out to burn anything down, we just liked watching things burn.

We started maybe four or five fires and watched them burn down. There was only one fire that we couldn't get started, and praise the Lord for that one. We spent 20 minutes trying to start a fire under a huge propane tank that someone had behind their garage. We didn't know it was a propane tank at the time, of course. I don't think we even knew what the hell a propane tank was. We didn't find out until the fire marshal got involved later that day. After a fruitful afternoon of burning shit, I headed home. My buddy, unbeknownst to me, was the child of a fireman. So, he goes home and tells his dad, which I couldn't figure out, because he was right there with me, side by side, Butch and Sundance, starting fires. So, I started my leisurely walk home, not a care in the world. Not a care in the world until I come walking through the back yard and see a police car parked behind the fire marshal's car in our driveway.

It didn't register at first, what the police and fire department were doing there, then I thought, "maybe they're here for me." I wonder if their presence has anything to do with the way I spent my afternoon? That may not be good. So I snuck in the basement door, slipped into the laundry room and hid behind the water softener. How's that for going back? A water softener. I was just sitting in the dark on 200 lbs. of salt, waiting. That laundry room we had in Iowa was a great hiding place for a long time until my dad found me there one day. Once your secret hiding place is discovered, it's no longer a good hiding place. It was a good one for a while, though. It was really a tight squeeze. That's why nobody ever thought to look for me there.

I've always been good and patient. If I know I'm in trouble, I can wait out anybody. So I spent the evening hiding in the basement. I was down there almost three hours before I scurried out to check the driveway. The cars were gone. Hah! I knew I could outlast them. Apparently, I had forgotten all about my parents. The police and fire department, as it turns out, were the least of my worries. I go wandering up the stairs like everything is right with the world. Wrong. First of all my folks had no idea where the hell I was. They thought I might have burned up in one of my little fires. My dad had been driving all over hell's half acre looking for my ass. According to the fire marshal, that propane tank held about 500 lbs. of propane, enough to "destroy the entire neighborhood." What the hell is propane? That was my next question. Needless to say, I didn't start any more fires, nor did I sit down for the next few days.

CHAPTER 8
A THIRD GRADE ESSAY

March 6th, 1967
by Mark Sweeney

Matt Martini was trying to beat me up again and would not leave me be. I should have stopped by the Hy-Vee and got a pack of cigarettes.

(For the life of me I don't know what that means. I was only seven. Matt must have still been pissed about the bird egg incident, and I don't know why I was turning to cigarettes for comfort)

Every Friday I watch the Green Hornet, Time Tunnel and Rango. My sister is a baby but in 27 years she will be a lady. A plane flew over our house last night. In school we write on paper. At night my mom reads me a story. At school I try very hard. We like to go swimming. Blue is my best color. Black is my favorite color. Green is a pretty color.

What is up with the colors? Jesus, son, pick one and move on. I remember Green Hornet and Rango, not so much Time Tunnel. I don't seem all that bright at this time.

CHAPTER 9
FOURTH GRADE

The year was 1969. We had just moved to Overland Park, Kansas, and I was just getting in to rock and roll. I bought my first album that year: Three Dog Night's *Golden Biscuits*, which, by the way, is still one of the greatest albums of all time. I also purchased my first Led Zeppelin album, *Led Zeppelin II*. *"The Immigrant Song"* changed my life. "Aaaaaaahhhhhhhaaaaaa Aaaaaaahhhhhhaaaaa, through the wind and the mud and the ice and snow…" That's powerful shit to a ten-year-old. Although I wanted to study abroad, I was continuing my studies at Katherine Carpenter grade school, Bill Dowden, principal.

Mr. Dowden was the only principal I ever had who was on a first name basis with my parents. That's how often they spoke. Bill, Mike and Jane all gathered in a conspiracy against the young lad. Mrs. Rea was my teacher, Dorothy Rea, or Dottie as she was called in the teacher's lounge. Remember the teacher's lounge? It was a daunting, unknown place where students weren't allowed. It was a place that was only talked about. We knew where it was, but nobody knew what went on in there. Sometimes, as you walked by, the door would open and for just a second you got a glimpse into the sanctuary. Once in a while, a student would have to go there for some reason (usually some kind of teacher's pet, a kiss ass, someone who could be trusted by the establishment) and they would have temporary access to the forbidden zone. They would see a place that no other student had ever seen. They would return with unimaginable tales. Tales of a land unknown, one that was shrouded in secrecy, like the Masons. They were like adventurers in a new land. They would tell us what went on in there and we'd be mesmerized.

"What do you mean Mr. Bennett and Miss Haines were holding hands?"

"I swear.

"No way."

"Yes way. They were sitting on the couch, holding hands."

"They have a couch in there?"

"There's two couches and some chairs, too."

"What? Why? Why are there couches and chairs?"

"I don't know, but there are."

"Are you sure?"

"Yes, I'm sure, I know what chairs are."

"I can't believe they were holding hands, I didn't even know they knew each other"

"What else is in there?"

"A fridge, a sink and a door that leads to outside."

"A fridge? What do they need a fridge for?"

"I don't know, but it's a big one."

"Cool."

"And guess what else?"

"What?"

"Mrs. Nuebecker was smoking."

"Bullshit, now I know you're lying."

"I swear to God, she was sitting in one of the chairs smoking a cigarette. Mr. Tartabull was smoking too."

That just blew us away, I think that was the first time I had thought of teachers as regular people, knowing that they held hands and smoked cigarettes. It was like the first time you saw a teacher outside of school. That was surreal. There, right there in the Hy-Vee, standing by the fruits and vegetables, was Mrs. Bax. Oh my God, what is she doing here? It can't be. That cannot be my teacher. In the store? Here? Now? What the hell is going on? Why is she buying food? Have I fallen into a fold in the time/space continuum? Not only was she there, she was there with her daughter! What? How can a teacher have kids? Isn't that illegal? And if it isn't, shouldn't it be? I never thought of teachers as being parents. Isn't that weird?

As a kid, you just never think of teachers as being normal people. They represent authority; they're "the man." They don't have time to be holding hands, smoking and shopping with their children. What in God's name is going on here? Has the world gone mad? The most important thing is evasion. I can't let her see us. I can't let her talk to my mom. My teacher and my mom having a chit chat? No good can come from that conversation. No good at all. They were two separate worlds, and they needed to stay that way. School and home overlapped, but not by much. There were plenty of things that happened at school that mumsy never knew about. But if these two worlds collide now, there could be an overlap of titanic proportions. If the home world and school world meet in the civilian world, it's bad mojo, man. Bad mojo.

It could literally effect the flow of magnetism around the planet. It may even disrupt the Earth's rotation. That's a major happening.

Due to my training as a toddler in the ways of counter espionage I received from a group of monks living as a counter culture sect in the sewers of Overland Park, KS, I was able to avoid a confrontation with Mrs. Bax. But it was close, very close. On future trips to the store, I ran a reconnaissance expedition before taking a cart. Just in case.

You couldn't do that now though, you know, sitting on school grounds, having a smoke. People would be in an uproar. I think kids are a lot more screwed up now than 20-30 years ago. We were subjected to second hand smoke and sugar and playing outside unsupervised and walking or riding your bike to school, fist fights with no police, getting injured at a friend's house with nobody's parents being sued, not to mention the occasional ass whipping you received for your misbehaving. Nobody called kids that misbehaved "dysfunctional." They were just assholes. They didn't need medication to fix their problem, they needed discipline. Plain and simple, it worked then, it can work now. Dysfunctional is a popular word these days. The establishment loves that word "dysfunctional." Well guess what? Everyone's dysfunctional; it's part of being a human being. It's part of the makeup; we're people, and people are dysfunctional.

Mrs. Dottie Rea, she was probably the only public school teacher that scared me a little. I didn't let her know it, but she frightened me. She had one of those huge bouffant hairdos, so she seemed about seven feet tall. That was very intimidating to a small, innocent, cherubic faced little boy. She didn't scare me enough to behave, but she made me uneasy. She was a tough old broad, and we had our battles. Fourth grade is where I really started to blossom. It's where I started spending a lot of time being punished by sitting in the hall, alone, perfecting and weaving my craft to an imaginary crowd. It never did any good though; many times I would just wander around the halls and find my friends so I could wave at them through that little window in the door. I would stand there and try to entertain them through that four-inch-wide window. The problem was that the window was so small you couldn't see the teacher in the class, and sometimes she would suddenly pop her head into view and scare the shit out of me. I mean how stupid was it to make me sit in the hall? I enjoyed it; I was out of class with no one to hassle me. It wasn't punishment, it was vacation. It was on one of these hall-sitting sessions when I found the janitor closet unlocked and hid up in the ceiling. I hid up there for hours. That was a fun day. Mrs. Rea didn't put me out into the hall after that.

Teacher's comments first nine weeks
"Mark needs to improve his self-control. He can be very disruptive. He has made a nice adjustment to his new school. Mark is reading in average material."

Little did she know I was reading way above average material. My parents read a ton and always had books on the shelves. My dad caught me reading *In Cold Blood* when I was ten, he took it away and told me, "this is not fourth grade reading material," which of course just made me want to read it more, so I did. He didn't hide it or anything; he just put it back on the bookshelf. I'm thinking, "well, that will be easy to find." It was just sitting there, so I read it when no one was around. Looking back, my father was right. *In Cold Blood* is not a book for a fourth grader. I read several other books I shouldn't have read, but read them I did. I read average material in school because that's all they had. Fuck *Black Beauty*, let the "others" read it. I'm reading *The Godfather*.

I should also note that the new school mention was because we moved a lot, and I was always the new kid in class, which probably explains some of my behavior. I guess I got used to being in front of a group of people while someone introduced me. Anyone who has been the "new kid" (I put that in quotes because that's how you're known for a while; until you make your mark so to speak) knows that it's a tough gig. The principal walks you down the hall in the middle of the day; stops everything and introduces you to the class. "Here's the new student; don't pick on him." You're standing there staring at the class and they're staring back at you. All you really want is to find a seat in the back row and get the hell off the stage. Then the teacher has to start the interrogation.

"What's your name?"

"Um, Mark."

"So, where are you from?"

"Um, Iowa."

"What do you like to do?"

"Make socks out of bunny pelts." That was the end of that interview.

It's the same thing I'm doing now except I get more time and I get paid. Up until about eighth grade, I used to get into fights a lot because of being the new kid. There's always someone who wants to pick on you to show off. By the time I got to fourth grade I was a pretty good pugilist, I mean, for being ten. There's a lot of anxiety that goes into fighting. I always found it best to just do it right there and get it over with, fights at school never lasted very long because a teacher would usually break it up. It was the scheduled fights after school that were the worst. You would have all day to let that tension and anxiety build up inside. I don't care who you are, knowing that you've got a fight after school was a stomach turner. You couldn't concentrate on shit. All you could think about was "the fight." Everyone knew about it too.

"I heard you're fighting Benton after school."

"Where did you hear that?"

"Everyone's talking about it; they think he'll kick your ass."

"Why?"

"Because you're the new kid and he's beaten up everyone he fights." Perfect. Not only do I have a fight, I've got to fight the badass of the school. You just don't need that ulcer causing anxiety at that age. Sometimes you just wanted to tell a teacher so she could stop it, but you can't. Like Brando said in *On the Waterfront*, "I ain't eatin' cheese for no cops that's for sure." I ended up winning that fight though, more or less. All you have to do at that age is start like a wild man and don't stop until someone cries. While he was taking off his jean jacket I punched him the stomach and then the side of his face, then I jumped on his back and start whaling on him. It was like one of those movies where the geek was on the back of the jock who was trying to kick his ass. I just held on tight and kept trying to punch him while he was reaching around trying to dislodge me. He never did get his jacket all the way off; that helped. All the while I was looking around wondering where the fuck the teachers were. As quickly as it started, it was all over. Teachers had seen the crowd forming and rushed in pretty quickly. We both got in trouble, but we were friends after that and nobody picked on the "new kid" anymore. So there.

I got suspended for a couple of days that year for getting caught TP'ing a house. I got caught because I did it during the day, on the way to school. Who TP's a house in the daylight? I do, that's who. It was a house where the guy had done something to piss us off, and we were seeking our revenge. I swiped a couple of rolls of toilet paper from the house, which was no easy feat. We didn't have backpacks or bags or anything to carry our shit in so it would've been fairly obvious I was up to no good walking out of the house carrying rolls of toilet paper. I had to throw them out the window into the bushes and grab them after I walked out. I had to leave a little early too because I had to walk. You can't just ask the bus driver to stop so you can TP a house. A little more covertness is required; apparently not enough covertness to do it at night, but still. So I walked to the guy's house and started throwing toilet paper into his trees. A neighbor must have called because he comes screaming out of the house and heads right towards me. I was only half way through the second roll, but I bolted anyway. There was no way he could catch me, I was fast; like a marsupial. By the second hour of school Mr. Dowden came to the class to get me. It seems I'd been identified and was brought in for questioning. It was my word against theirs, but an adult was always believed over a child, especially one with my history. It wasn't the smartest thing I've ever done, but I made my point, eh?

Teacher's comments second nine weeks
"Mark is doing nice work. He has fit in well and enjoys extra responsibilities. He has a delightful sense of humor, but usually displays it at the wrong time."

Hey listen, honey. When an idea hits you, you've got to share it. If you hold it in, it will fester and rot in your belly until it explodes or manifests itself in other, maybe more violent ways. If something funny strikes me, I feel it's only my duty to let my classmates in on it, so they can take a break from our cursive writing exercise for a nice little chuckle. I've always believed in spreading a little sunshine.

Teacher's comments third nine weeks
"Marks' reading level is increasing nicely. (yeah, well after reading the books I was reading, you pick up a lot) *He is very popular and has made many new friends, but still continues to disrupt class. He shares all his thoughts out loud. I would really like to see some improvement in this last grading period."*

Mrs. Rea didn't finish the school year. I'm not sure what happened to her. I think she had a nervous breakdown. The school called it an "illness." My mom thinks I drove her crazy. If that's true, then I'm sorry, but hell, if fourth graders are too much to handle maybe it's time she went into something more peaceful. She was replaced by Mrs. Willie. No shit. Mrs. Willie. Mrs. Willie and I didn't see eye to eye on many things. She wanted to be in charge. Hell, I'd been there all year, and now she wants to come in and rule the class. Good luck, bootsy.

Teacher's comments fourth nine weeks
"Mark and I have had several difficult times understanding each other. He is a very quick witted boy, but unfortunately by using that wit, he takes away time I can give to other students. I think he had a hard time adjusting to a new teacher. I hope Mark has a good summer and enjoys the 5th grade."

A good summer? Why the hell didn't I get a great summer wished upon me? I'm sure most of the other students got wished a great summer. But me, I just get the good summer. It didn't matter though; every summer is a great summer. I've always been a fan of summer. First of all, I'm a summer birthday, and I know birthdays aren't any big deal, but you always feel a little special on your birthday. It stays light until nine, there is just nothing negative about summer, except that it ends and it's off to Mrs. Bax's class.

CHAPTER 10
A CHRISTMAS ESSAY

January 15, 1969

A Good Holiday
by Mark Sweeney

On Christmas day my cousins came over and for Christmas I got two pairs of boxing gloves and I boxed my uncle and I beat him.

Then my dad and my uncle worked on my X-15 airplane that I got and then I got mad because they wouldn't let me play with it. While they were playing with it my mom and my aunt fixed turkey for dinner, of course I didn't like it so I didn't eat that night.

At 10 o'clock my aunt and uncle left and I had to go to bed. My little brother screamed his head off until 12 o'clock. I told my mom that it was the best holiday I ever had.

CHAPTER 11
SUMMER OF '70

The summer of 1970. Wow. What a great summer! It will always go down as one of the best. No, no, it was the best; it was just one of those summers that I never forgot. I turned eleven, between fourth and fifth grade. The first girl I fell in love with, as much as an 11-year-old can be in love. Debbie LaBonte; she blew me away. We had a song, or at least I had song for us. I'm pretty sure she knew nothing of it. I can actually guarantee it. "My Sweet Lord" by George Harrison, I still think of her every time I hear that song. I even bought an ID bracelet for $6, which was the way it was done back then: find a girl, fall in love, give her your ID bracelet and live happily ever after. My dad told me I was too young to be going steady and forbid me to give her my ID.

Love is a powerful thing, even as an 11-year-old. You couldn't tell me not to pursue the woman I'm going to marry. So I had my song, my ID and the nerve to go get her. Off I go. It may have been the most nervous I'd ever been; I was going to ask her to be my girlfriend. This was still back in the day when you called a girl and she answered, you hung up in sheer terror. I'm not sure why I thought I could talk to her in person when I couldn't do it on the phone. I was scared shitless, my heart was racing, my stomach was doing flip flops, I was sweating and in a panic. I'd practiced my lines, my moves, my thoughts, my actions.

I'm prepared, I'm shaking, but I'm prepared. I'm about to embark on an adventure of a lifetime, an adventure in love. Let's go. I got shot down out of the sky and was devastated. So I did the only thing I could do in that situation. I picked up the pieces of my shattered heart and went home. My heart was broken the way only an 11-year-old heart can be broken. Well, that was a waste of $6. My first experience with heartbreak, little did I know, it was just the start. There was plenty more where that came from. Just keep stepping up to the plate, boy, and the girls will continue to bombard you with bean balls. And we do, we just keep stepping up to the plate, because we LOVE you, don't you understand? I LOVE you; you have to go steady with me. Apparently she didn't. A note; in seventh grade she had a crush on me, but it was too late. I'd moved on. My trek as a lone wolf had started.

So Debbie LaBonte wouldn't go steady with me. I guess this means we're not getting married. I guess I'll just hang with my friends this summer, which prophetically enough, is pretty much the way it goes for your entire life. Find a girl, hang with her, break up, go back to your friends, find a girl, hang with her, break up, go back to the friends. I still have my whole summer. I'm going to have fun with or without my sweet Debbie.

The 4th of July is coming, the greatest of all holidays for a kid. It's the middle of the summer, no school in sight, it's hot so you don't have to wear shirts or shoes, and you get to play with explosives. It doesn't get much better than that for a young buck. We used to stock up on some fireworks. We had mostly Black Cat firecrackers, because nothing was cooler than Black Cat firecrackers. We would also get a hold of M-80's and bottle rockets. We didn't have much use for the shit that goes in the air and spews colors, we wanted something that exploded. We also had these things called "buzz bombs" which were pretty cool. They would fly up spewing sparks and such. We landed many of those things on various neighborhood roofs. That's a heart stopper when a buzz bomb lands on a dry, hot roof and it's still spinning and spewing. "Holy shit, grab the bag and run!" We did a lot of running on the 4th. It may have been the most runningest of all the Holidays.

Mainly on the 4th we wanted to blow shit up, and we did. During the year, my brothers and I would build model cars and airplanes and blow them up on the 4th of July. One of our delights was tying some fishing line to an airplane model, soak it in gas, light it on fire and then spin it around a leg on the swing set. The swing set turned out to be a launching point for many things that were on fire or about to explode. We had some cinder blocks next to the garage and we would sometimes put the airplane model on the block, fill it with cotton balls that were soaked with gasoline and throw bottle rockets and firecrackers at it until it was destroyed. Sometimes it would blow up and spray gas everywhere, you quickly found out it's best not to stand too close to the cinder block. Just ask Ricky Nelson, not *the* Ricky Nelson, the one from our neighborhood, it took almost six months for his eyebrows and hair to grow back. He smelled like burnt hair for a week.

Ricky had a little brother who was mentally retarded. I don't mean he was an idiot, he was actually retarded. Now they call it "mentally challenged," but back then it was OK to say "retarded." We always had to watch what we were doing around Ronny because he would mimic everything we did, and sometimes it was dangerous. My dad used to have these big rubber weights we could attach to our fishing rods, so we could practice our casting. One day we were practicing our casting in the street in front of their house and Ronny saw us doing that and went into the garage to get his own fishing rod. But Ronny, God love him, didn't use rubber weights, he grabbed a rod that had actual treble hooks attached. Treble hooks are three pronged hooks that do their job very well. So Ronny comes out with his fishing rod and his brother Ricky was unfortunate enough to be standing behind him on one of Ronny's monster casts and Ricky caught a treble hook right in the nostril, ouch. Ronny, of course, doesn't know this and thinks he's snagged, so he keeps yanking on that sumbitch until that hook was buried deep up his brother's nose.

Ronny had no idea what was happening because he wouldn't even turn around. He has no idea why he can't get his cast off and he doesn't seem to care. He was just going to keep yanking on that thing until it launched. Now, all hell is breaking loose, Ricky is screaming at the top of his lungs, and we're running into the yard to help. Ricky has blood flying everywhere, and Ronny is still trying to get his cast off. Mrs. Nelson comes running out and sees what's going on and flips out. Nothing freaks a mom out like seeing streams of blood flying off one of her children's faces while the other one is yanking a three-barbed fishing hook deeper into his face. She finally gets the fishing rod out of Ronny's hand and wants to know where he got the idea of casting in the yard.

Unfortunately, it's hard for us to say "not us" when we're standing there with fishing rods in our hands. Ronny stayed with us while his mom took Ricky to the hospital. They had to cut his nose all the way open to retrieve the hook. His nose was wrapped up for most of the summer. I don't think Ronny even knew what he did. We just sat on the porch eating Popsicles, and he seemed as content as could be. I say "popsicles" but they weren't actually "popsicles." They were ice cubes made out of Kool-Aid with toothpicks sticking out of them, and sometimes the toothpicks were crooked because my mom put them in too soon and they would fall over and stick out sideways; hard to hold is my point. We never got to buy popsicles; my mom "made" popsicles. We didn't really get in trouble or anything about the casting thing. My dad just told us to be careful what we do around Ronny because he didn't always know right from wrong. Like we did.

Ronny was almost like the mascot of our neighborhood. We would include him in most of our activities unless we had to go somewhere. Ronny's mom didn't like him wandering far from the house. He did participate in all the sports games though, which was a huge pain in the ass. Ronny always wanted the ball and when he would get it, he'd take off running. Every time. I don't mean he'd run down the field. No, he'd take off down the street with the ball. It didn't matter if we we're playing football, basketball or baseball; every single time he got a hold of the ball, he'd take off. I'm not sure we ever finished a game that Ronny was playing in because we would spend half our time chasing his ass down. I'm not sure what anyone else thought when they saw eight or nine kids chasing a retarded boy down the street. Ronny always laughed the entire time we were chasing him too. He just thought the whole thing was a delight. He was also deceptively fast; the only one who could really catch him was Tim. Timmy would catch him and grab hold and then we'd have to pry the ball away from him, because not only was he fast, he was strong as shit. It usually took a couple of us to get it away from him. We'd head back to continue play and Ronny would come with us and want the ball again. You'd eventually have to give it to him just to appease him and get him to settle down, but once he had it, boom, he was gone.

Back to the 4th. Here's something else to be careful about when gassing and exploding models. Keep them far away from the house. As we found out, wood burns, and so does paint. We scorched the side of the garage one day but good. It scared the hell out of us. As we're standing there, we can see the house actually starting to burn. We stood there for at least a minute, wondering what the hell to do. Go tell Mom or run. If we run, we'll have to come back, and then there will be hell to pay. Then my brother gets an idea, the hose! Get the hose! Good thinking. We can put the fire out and mom will never know. Well, she won't know if we cut out the burned wood, replace it, treat it and then paint it the right color. We got caught, no way around it really, a big, three-foot round black scorch mark on the side of the house, no real way to hide that. Inside if you broke something, sometimes you could just throw it away and hope that nobody ever noticed. You can't throw away a burn mark. But since we knew we were in trouble, we started blowing up everything we could get our hands on. We figured if we were going down, we might as well have fun.

Dad wouldn't be home for another four hours, and we can do some serious damage in four hours. Let's find some jars and coffee cans. Coffee cans we found out, can be treacherous, but the glass jars were fun, especially with the M-80's. We went over to Chris and Todd's house to get some peanut butter jars; their mom had plenty. We'd put them upside down on the driveway, slip an M-80 under it and watch the fun. We were a bit more careful with the glass, we stood behind a tree, all six of us, standing behind the same tree. When that M-80 went off, it sent shards of glass off in a huge circle of cutting, slicing, maiming death. But hey, nobody got cut, let's do another. We blew up about four or five jars when Chris and Todd's mom came storming out of the house. Apparently, the glass was bombarding the house as well, and she couldn't figure out what it was. The problem is, she's coming out just as one is going off and it peppers the front of the house with glass. It seemed to scare the hell out of her. Chris and Todd weren't allowed to play with us anymore. So it's off to the Sweeney's back yard and the coffee cans.

Our group is up to about eight, we lost Chris and Todd, but gained the Murray boys and two kids from one block over. I guess they came for the finale. I take this coffee can and drop two lit M-80's into it, put the lid back on and roll it out into the backyard, and we can't be more than twenty feet from this thing when it goes off. There are two incredible explosions and I feel crap hitting me in the face and arms. I look around and everyone is bleeding, the can blew up and sprayed us with shrapnel, no real deep cuts, but head wounds bleed a lot, so it looks pretty bad. Kids are crying and freaking out, the kids from the other block take off screaming, I don't ever remember seeing those boys again. Everyone's crying, and my mom runs out and there are eight kids standing in her back yard with blood streaming down our faces. It looked like some kind of war zone. If we would've been naked we could have made the cover of Time magazine. Jane kept her cool though, it was a little freaky at first, but she held it together, wasn't really new to it, she'd seen this kind of shit before, nobody needed stitches, so she got everyone cleaned up and sent home. And that, unfortunately, was the end of the 4th of July 1970 for us.

Those years of ages 9-12 were good ones; much mischief. Good years in Kansas City. As I said, I was at Katherine Carpenter grade school. We rode the bus to school, and most of the time I walked home. I set some kind of record for the most minutes spent after school in a three-year stretch. Every time you screwed off in class, you'd get five minutes after school, cleaning erasers or some shit. That's good for the kiddies, breathing chalk dust in the afternoon, nice way to catch some black lung disease, or in this case white lung. When you "misbehaved," your name went up on the board. Your name on the board equals five minutes you would have to stay after school. Each time after that, if you misbehaved, you got a slash mark, each slash mark was another five. I figured out I could get up to four slashes after my name and still run home before the bus got there. That way, no one would be the wiser.

On one of my "hall sessions," I found a storage locker unsecured; I slipped in and found an endless supply of inks and paints and other articles of artistry. Seeing as I had no place to carry such a load, I used a ladder to put my supply of trouble on top of a storage cabinet nearby. After class, a friend boosted me up and we get away with our supply of inks and paints and other things that make a mess in the hands of children. We had hours of fun hiding in the bushes, throwing those tubes of ink into the street and waiting for cars to drive over them. Oh, it would give a squirt and we'd giggle like school girls. I don't know what it is about young boys and breaking things, but we just love destruction. We went so far as to roll up pieces of bread and watched cars roll over them. Cars rolling over shit, now that's good clean fun. I don't know why bread being squashed by a car is entertaining, but damned if it isn't.

CHAPTER 12
BAD EATER

I've always been what you would call a picky eater. It's not a great word, but it's better than finicky. That's a lame word, isn't it? Finicky? "Oh he's a finicky eater, that one is." Shut up, lady. Picky wasn't really much better. Picky sounds like a guy that constantly has his finger up his nose, or digging his undies out of his ass.

"Where's Picky?"

"I'm not sure, I haven't seen him, but I hope he's washing his hands."

I preferred the word "selective." I was a selective eater. I don't eat just anything; I'm "selective." I was, and still am, frequently asked why I don't like something, and the answer is simple. "Because it tastes like shit, that's why."

I was very much aware of the taste and texture of what was going in my pie hole. That was a big thing for me: texture. If it had a bad texture I wasn't going to eat it. For me, food had to have a nice solid body to it. I want something I can chew, damn it. I didn't like gushy things, no soft stuff; I don't like my food soft. I also had a problem with anything that exploded its innards all over the inside of your mouth when you bit into it; that was too gross for me to eat. I don't want any explosions of grossness bombarding my taste buds with slimy, slippery particles of so-called "flavor." I never had an affinity for veggies for that reason, not so much the taste, but for that freakin' texture; veggies are too soft; a gag-inducer my entire life. That's how I knew I didn't like something; if it made me gag, I didn't like it. Seemed like a pretty simple gauge. Gag inducement wasn't the only criteria though. I also went by smell and sight and if it made it that far, taste. I could usually tell if I liked something right away just by looking at it. "Nope, not that, I'm not eating that."

People sometimes didn't understand how I could not like something when I hadn't even tried it. I could tell by looking at it most of the time; one look was all it took. One quick glance and I would know that it's not for me. I could go down a buffet line, "nope, nope, ok, ok, nope, nope," without any tasting going on. It was very existential, and very rarely would I be wrong. I never remember a time when I liked the look of something and it tasted bad. It was a skill I picked up early and it still works.

My father never cared that much for my "selectiveness." He would tell me, "Oh, you're going to eat that; your mother spent all day making that food." Really, Dad? How does one go about making peas? Seems to me I saw her take them out of a can. I think it took about 30 seconds. My father never cared much for my answers either. He always felt they were a little smart-alecky. When I gave an answer he didn't like, I had to hold my hand out. My father really liked the knife handle on the knuckles bit- seems his dad was a fan of it too, but I personally never cared much for it. I liked the game though; hold your hand out so he could whack it with a knife handle, never the blade, just the handle. I always pulled back, and we went on like that until my mom said to knock it off, and let's eat.

My dad's punishments were always what his dad did to him. I'm sorry, pa, but this ain't the forties anymore. He used to make me sit at the dinner table until bedtime or until I finished all my peas, or carrots or broccoli or asparagus or whatever the hell it was I didn't want to eat that particular evening. I would just sit there and sit there and sit there, every single time, and never once did I give in. Not once did I choke down a helping of something I didn't want. Not once. All those thousands of hours I sat there alone at the kitchen table, in the dark, forgotten by the rest of the family with a pile of cold, rotting, festering, decaying, disgusting peas in front of me. I guess I can thank my father for my resolve, my stubbornness. I think I learned a lot of patience from it as well. My mom would let me off early sometimes because she felt sorry for me. I didn't get dessert, but I never ate those fucking peas. Still don't. I always found peas to be the most disgusting of the garden vegetables, the most unattractive of the, "in-your-mouth" exploding vegetables. It makes me gag just thinking about it.

I remember once in grade school, I was in third grade (remember the smell of the cafeteria? Every single cafeteria in any school you went to had the same smell) and someone had dropped some peas on the floor in the lunch line and everyone had just walked all over them until they were smashed and smeared all over the place. It was absolutely horrific. There were dozens and dozens of peas, flattened and smeared like green guts on the highway. It was a slaughterhouse. You could hear the screams of the dying peas pleading to be put out of their misery while they lie there with their broken limbs all askew. It seemed that mayhem had run amok and laid waste to entire ladle full of peas. It was ghastly and disturbing. What I found even more terrifying was that some of these kids who trampled through the peas, had pea guts on the bottom of their shoes, and the guts were working their way into the crevices of the tread, hiding deep in the cracks so they can ferment and mutate into even larger peas with twice as many guts to be smashed and smeared along the vinyl floor tiles. Gaaacckk! At the time, it may have been the most disgusting thing I'd ever seen. You could almost smell the decomposing entrails of those massacred peas lying on that cafeteria floor with all those unknowing children grinding them into oblivion. That image has always haunted me. Haunted me, I tell you. I'm feeling queasy just thinking about it...hold on, I need to hurl.

I had a lot of tricks to ditch my food too because sometimes a boy wants to play after dinner in the summer, and you couldn't go out and play until you finished your food. There was very little negotiation at our house. My parents would tell us how it was going to be, and that was it. There were no ifs, ands or buts; the parents ruled the roost and that was the deal, Camille. It's kind of amusing now when you think about it. Parents used to never really care what the kids wanted; we didn't get to pick where we would eat or what we would eat. The parents made the decisions, not the four-year-old. Nowadays you often see people negotiating with their children.

"How about if we do this, then you can do that."

Are you shitting me? He's six, don't let him make decisions. When he pays for the meal he can have a say in where we dine; until then, "Knock it off and get in the car. If you keep it up, you can sit in the parking lot while we go in and eat and we'll get seats near the window so you can see us enjoying a delightful meal."

You had to be creative in hiding food; you couldn't just do it the same way every time. I would've shoved them up my ass if I could've gotten away with it, but that wouldn't pass the old man's strip searches. I would throw food on the floor underneath my brothers and then accuse them of dropping food because with six children eating, it's hard to get through a meal without a pound of food ending up on the floor.

It was great when there was a baby around because they've always got food around them. You had to be careful though; it's hard to explain why the one-year-old has a pile of corn underneath her when she didn't have corn to begin with. Hmmm. I used to put little pieces of food in my mouth, and then when I had a mouthful, I would spit it into my milk and just not finish the whole glass. I would just leave a small pile of food in the bottom. It worked a lot. I've stashed food in my pockets, rolled it up in napkins, stashed it in my socks, even held it in my hands as they slid under the plate to take to the sink. Oh, I was a crafty devil.

One time we were at my grandparents' house for dinner and we were having ham. I didn't like ham as a kid, nor did I like brisket or pot roast. I liked beef, just not in those formats. I never liked the smell of brisket or pot roast, I think it reminded me of Sunday, which means the next day is Monday and it's back to school. I like ham now; I just didn't like it as a kid. We were at my grandparents' house, and we were using cloth napkins, which is cool; you can hide a lot of food in a cloth napkin, and it doesn't break down due to carrot juice.

I'm sitting there with ham, carrots and mashed potatoes on my plate. Perfect, I don't like any of this shit. I like rolls, so perhaps I'll fill up on rolls today. I've got all this nasty shit on my plate and I start hiding. I'm using the "leave it in the glass" bit, I dropped some on the floor, I stuffed a roll with bits of ham, and I even lined up some ham on the chair next to the phone book my brother was sitting on right next to me. Mostly I stashed it in my napkin. The mashed potatoes the hardest to hide, you can't pocket them because anywhere you put mashed taters is going to get messy. What I would do is just spread them out flat on my plate and lay my silverware just so; that way it looked like my pile of taters had diminished. In retrospect, I don't know who I was kidding. My folks knew I didn't like this stuff, so how come my plate's clean? They know I didn't eat it. I've never eaten it before, why now? Why, all of sudden, had Mark eaten ham and carrots? Something's fishy.

I asked to be excused and my father reaches over, picks up my napkin, shakes it over my plate, and half of a pound of ham and carrots drops back on my plate, and now my plate is as full as it was when I sat down, except now there's mashed potatoes stuck to it. I remember my grandfather looking at me in amazement. I'm not sure he immediately grasped the concept of what was happening. How the hell did that boy get an entire dinner wrapped up in a napkin? My dad wanted me to sit there until I finished it, but my grandmother would have none of it. She said it was her house and if I didn't want to eat anything I didn't have to. She even gave me dessert; which is why people have grandmothers.

My whole life I've avoided having dinner at people's homes because I knew they would make something I didn't like. Every time a girlfriend would invite me over to her parents' house for dinner, I was doomed.

"You don't like corn on the cob? Who doesn't like corn on the cob?"

"I don't, that's who; it's gross, juicy, slimy and tastes like fucking corn." So everyone would be sitting at the table with plates piled high with food, and I'd sit there with nothing on my plate but meat and a roll. This went on my entire life, trying to tell new people how I didn't like corn or carrots or peas or cauliflower or broccoli or green beans or tomatoes or baked potatoes or cucumbers or celery or olives or eggs or onions or beets or spinach or squash or asparagus or brussel sprouts or dark meat on a chicken or any dark meat, for that matter, or fish or headcheese or goat balls or monkey brains. I just don't like them Sam I freakin' am, that's all. Now leave me alone. I'm going to make some hot dogs and mac and cheese. You just can't go wrong with ground up animal parts. Now, that's livin'.

CHAPTER 13
ROCK FIGHTS

We had some rock fights over the years. Boys like to throw rocks. It's all good, clean fun, that's all it is, just throwing rocks at your friends. I have a 15-year-old nephew that's never been in a rock fight. I think he's kind of a pussy. What kind of kid goes through his childhood and never gets into a rock fight? Maybe there's too much other stuff for them to do. Rock fights were a lot of fun. They usually started off slow, maybe tossing some dirt clods. No real harm getting hit by a dirt clod, they would usually break apart on impact. Usually. Sometimes they wouldn't disintegrate; sometimes they would hurt, and leave a lump and get you pissed off. That's when you reach for a bigger dirt clod; of course, once you hit an enemy combatant with a bigger dirt clod, he will now increase the size of his clod. As the size of the clods increases, the anxiety increases. Once a clod gets to the size where it can break glass, a young skull can be especially vulnerable. So you drop the regular clods and maybe look for one that has a rock in the middle of it, yeah, that's what we're looking for, a dirt clod with a rock center. Like a tootsie pop projectile, a nice dirt clod with a rock hard center, now we're talking some ammo.

Things never stay at one level; they always escalate. Once you've been hit with a dirt-covered rock, then you may move on to something that is rock only, no dirt, just pure rock. You start off small, of course; you don't want to kill anyone, yet. So you've moved on to small rocks, then to bigger rocks. Then you move on to hiding places. If you're having a strictly dirt clod fight, you just stand in the open and fire away. No worries. But as things get more dangerous, it's time to seek shelter. You can take a dirt clod to the head without too much worry, but rocks are another thing entirely. You do start out with small rocks, then the rocks get bigger and more dangerous. There's not as much laughing going on as before, things are little more intense. When a rock the size of an orange sails by your head, you realize you could die. That's no good. I'm just a kid, I don't want to suffer from blunt force trauma. That's a hell of a phrase isn't it? BLUNT FORCE TRAUMA. Scary. It's not something a child should have to worry about. Of course with no helmets, blunt force trauma was part of our daily lives.

Once the rocks get bigger, it's definitely time to hide. You can hear them sailing by. New construction sites were the best places for rock fights, lots of nooks and crannies to hide in. You could pop up in a window, rain rocks down upon the enemy and then disappear back into the shadows. Awesome. You have to back away quickly because the rocks are now the size of potatoes. They can do some damage. The only saving grace is that rocks that big are hard to throw; little arms can only get them going so fast.

One of our greatest battles was in Cedar Rapids, Iowa. It was epic. Our team was outside on the ground and the enemy combatants had taken refuge in a house that was being built. We had some good hiding places; well, we weren't hidden exactly, but we were sheltered behind a stack of plywood. Another benefit of being the outside team was an endless supply of ammo. If you were inside, you had to bring ammo with you. If you ran out of rocks, you would have to try and get outside, gather more ammo and scurry back inside before you got bombarded. The inside team had access to nails, but nails just don't sail as well as rocks. I mean they can be deadly too, if you get hit in the eye or something, but they're hard to throw accurately, so they didn't last long. They would lose a lot of steam on the flight. So, we're on the outside lobbing rocks into the semi-built house. The angles from the house were such that the boys inside couldn't hit us behind our stack of wood. This made them careless, which is what you want eventually from your enemy; carelessness. Once they get careless, the advantage is ours. They start moving into the living room or kitchen to get a better shot at you. They may even head to the upper floors so they can rain rocks on you from above. My buddy Mike Barnes was one such combatant that had headed to the top floor. My brother Phil tossed a nice one through the top floor window and just as he released it, Barnes stood up. That rock crashed right smack dab into the middle of his forehead. It was a killer, dead center shot. He dropped like he'd been hit with a bullet and disappeared from view. The battle ceased and a dead silence descended upon us. Nobody knew what to do. There was no noise coming from *anywhere*. Everyone was on pins and needles. I don't know why we were so freaked out just because Barnes got hit with a rock, I mean, after all, it's a rock fight! We were throwing rocks at each other trying to make contact, but when you do, it's a scary moment.

There were about ten seconds of silence and then Barnes starts wailing, stands up and we see blood gushing from his forehead. His entire face was covered in blood and we freaked. I doubt it was as bad as it seemed at the time, but that day it was a bloody mess. When something like that happens, as an eight-year-old, it's hard to decide what to do. Your first instinct is to run, I don't know why, it was always our first instinct. I guess when you've done so much shit that you had to run from, your first instinct is to always run again. "Spread out, they can't catch all of us." I don't know who "they" were since it was only us out there. As a kid you always thought that "they" would catch you. Just scatter, they can't catch all of us. That was a hell of an escape plan, the "just scatter-they can't catch all of us," plan. The only one who got caught was fat Bobby because he's wearing flip flops. Bless his little heart, but there's nothing slower or noisier than a chubby kid with sweaty feet, running down the street in rubber shoes. We kept telling him to take them off so he could run faster, "No, I've got soft feet" was what he told us. So he got caught a lot, but he never gave us up, he was a good friend. As a matter of fact, we only got to play with Bobby one weekend at a time because he was always grounded the following weekend for getting caught doing something with us.

We didn't scatter when Barnes got hit though. We all ran to his aid. I'm not sure what we thought we were going to do, but we're at his side. Not one of us has any first aid training, all we know how to do is hurt and be hurt. Most of his face was covered in blood, now what? That's the weird thing about head and scalp wounds, they bleed a lot. More so than you think they would. Even a small gash can unleash a fury of blood. Barnes is still groggy and wobbly on his feet, so we pick him up and start to carry him back to our house. We looked like a group of seven and eight-year-old war vets, carrying our wounded buddy to the evac area. We're carrying and dragging and he's screaming at the top of his lungs and his whole face and the front of his shirt is drenched in blood. Oh, it was quite a sight man. Moms are so cool in times of crisis. We're dragging this wounded, bloody soldier into her kitchen, and she calmly puts him on the counter and starts to wash the blood off. She cleans him up and realizes he needs stitches, so she sends him home. She'll clean him by God, but she's not going to take him to the hospital, she's got dinner cooking. So off he goes, and we sit down to dinner. He ended up getting nine stitches. No biggie. I think she had a little grudge against Barnes anyway because he was the one who told me that fuck was a bad word. That's always a bright spot for a parent, when their child comes home and asks "Mom, what's fuck mean?" I found out a few years later that Barnes had been killed when he tried to race his motorcycle against a train. Apparently, his timing was never right.

Eventually, as you grow older, you put away childish things like rock fights and move on to more mature things, like bottle rocket fights. Those were even more intense because now we're working with explosives. Yes indeedy. We used to use the paper tubes from the inside of a roll of aluminum foil or something like that. Then we started using Christmas paper wrapping tubes because the longer ones were more accurate. Plus, the longer ones let you reach around corners and launch without putting yourself on the firing line. If you practiced, you could time the rocket launch with a throwing motion and really get that sucker sailing.

The bottle rocket fights were always fun until someone got hurt. And someone always got hurt; it was inevitable. When you're pelting each other with bottle rockets, one's going to strike home eventually. The body shots aren't really dangerous, but it does give your heart a little jump. When one blows off as it hits your back, you can feel the small explosion through your shirt and it leaves a small burn mark. "Whew, that was close." Sometimes they would hit your hand and blow up, and that would numb you up for a while, half of your hand would be dead, and that too leaves a burn mark. When one goes off near your head and you can feel the paper shrapnel sting your face, you call "Time Out." It usually scares the shit out of you enough to quit for the day. I'm having fun and all, but I don't want to lose an eyeball from it. "He who fights and runs away, lives to launch bottle rockets at his friends another day."

Of course you outgrow bottle rockets fights eventually and move on to BB gun fights. Now we're talking. Now we're up to shooting projectiles at each other instead of just throwing them. BB gun fights were also fun...until someone got hurt, and they usually did. We would wear several layers of clothes and top it off with a heavy sweatshirt and a lined CPO jacket. Remember those? The CPO's? It was like a shirt, but it was a jacket! Wild stuff, man. But we never used anything to protect our eyes, and that, in retrospect was stupid. Of course when you think back in retrospect, almost everything we did was stupid. In the early days, we only BB guns that would only cock once so you couldn't increase your power. Then they came out with BB guns that you could pump and increase the pressure. That was sweet. We had a one pump rule when those came out. The rule was pretty steadfast until you got hit someplace that hurt, like inside the ear. Inside the ear is a lot more sensitive than you would think. Of course getting hit anywhere on the head with a BB is probably going to cause some discomfort. We found out that the one pump rule was quickly forgotten once pain/anger got tossed into the mix.

When we moved to St. Louis there were tons of farm fields around us and some of them had old, abandoned houses on them. Perfect places for BB gun fights. Some of us would fight from the barn and others would fight from the house. This one time I was in the barn and got hit in the head with a rifle shot from the second story. It pissed me off because we tried to avoid head shots. Most of us had a rifle and a pistol, you know, just in case we got involved in close combat. After getting hit in the head, I decide to rush the house, get inside and track down the party in question. I've got my rifle cocked and ready and I head up the stairs. Nobody went into the basement of this particular house because it was half-filled with water and was spooky as hell. We all thought the bodies of the former tenants were buried down there and were hiding under the water, so we rarely even opened the basement door. Too much chance there would be waterlogged zombies lurking on the steps. BB guns are weapons, but they won't stop the undead. I always thought that if I descended the stairs something would reach out from the murky depths, grab my ankle and drag me to hell. No thank you, sir, I'll stay upstairs. So, I'm tip toeing up the stairs listening for movement.

My heart is pounding because now we're in close contact. Things heat up a bit when you're shooting at each other *inside* the house. I've got my finger on the trigger and I'm about six steps from the top when I hear it, a shuffling noise and a whisper. Someone's near. It must be the enemy, I'm tense and sweating. Now I'm second guessing my decision to enter the house. I should've stayed outside and waited them out. Now I'm committed to taking my revenge on whoever shot me in the head. As I'm one step from the top I don't notice this twelve inch hole in the wall to my left, nor do I notice my friend Eric on the other side of that hole pointing a pistol at my head. Then, blam, he pulls the trigger and hits me right inside my ear. It hurts like a mofo and he immediately starts apologizing.

He said he was so freaked out he panicked and pulled the trigger. He's telling me this as I'm pumping up my rifle. He looks right at me pleading for mercy when I tell him to start running. I'm almost up to ten pumps when he bolts down the stairs and heads for his bike. I'm chasing him down the stairs while still pumping my rifle. By the time I got down the stairs, I can barely pump it anymore, I'm well over 25 and I've built up maximum pressure. I'm still yelling at him to run, but he's already a half of a mile down the road. He knew things were serious. I eventually calmed down, but we didn't have any more BB gun fights for awhile. Good stuff, good times.

CHAPTER 14
THE BIRDS AND THE BEES

Uncle Kurt. What can I tell you about Uncle Kurt? Well, he was the uncle of my friend Sammy. We were ten, still in the fourth grade. Uncle Kurt was 14. He taught us all about the birds and the bees. I mean, as much as a 14 year-old can teach anyone about anything. My father and I never had the "sex talk." I don't know how many fathers have actually had that conversation, but it seems like by the time they're ready to talk to the lad about sex, the kids know more than enough to get by. I learned a lot from the books I was reading. Ooohh yeah. Maybe it's just a thing about boys, we're sent out early on our own to learn, and it's just taken for granted that we'll accomplish this task. Out you go boys, hunt and gather the knowledge that you can. Uncle Kurt was where we ended up. He was our guru, our go-to-guy with any questions we had about life. A 14-year-old.

Our first lesson was on how babies were made. It was mind blowing, at first, it didn't seem feasible, "the man puts his thing where? That can't be right can it?" He assured us it was.

"Well, how does he get it inside?"

"His penis gets hard."

"Well, how does it get hard?"

"It just does, that's the only way it will work."

"Then what?"

"Then the man squirts inside her and it makes a baby."

"The man pees inside her?"

"No, it's not pee, its sperm."

"What's sperm?"

"It's the stuff that carries the man's half of the baby."

"How come it's in his pee?"

"It's not pee, it's white and it fertilizes the woman's egg and a baby grows."

"Your pee turns white?"

"No, it's not pee, its sperm."

"Well, why is it white?"

"I don't know, it just is."

"Well how does it get into the egg, isn't the egg hard?"

"No, it's not hard it's soft."

"Like soft boiled eggs?" we asked.

"No, I'm not sure what it looks like, but it doesn't look like a soft boiled egg."

We're sitting there in Sammy's basement dumbfounded. Eggs? Soft eggs? I know there are no eggs in there. That can't be right. Eggs come from chickens. Uncle Kurt is full of shit; there's no way this is true.

"How does the baby come out?" we asked.

"It comes out of the woman's vagina."

"What's a vagina?"

"It's a woman's part between her legs."

"She pees it out?"

"No, she doesn't pee it out, forget the pee, pee has nothing to do with it, pee never comes out when you're doing sex."

We were stunned. I don't think we grasped the fact that something besides pee could come out of our penises. It's a difficult concept for a ten-year-old to wrap his head around. That was the end of lesson one. I guess Uncle Kurt figured we'd had enough information to digest until his next visit. He didn't live near us, so we had to wait in breathless anticipation for his return.

When he did return, he came bearing pictures. Pictures of people having sex! Holy shit! Uncle Kurt was right. The man does put his thing in there! This was most exciting! And most interesting. Does anyone else know about this? So this is what you're supposed to do with girls?

"Hell no, you guys can't do this until you get your driver's license." He actually told us that we'd have to wait until we could drive. At the time it actually seemed reasonable. Something like this you need to prepare for. You can't just jump in and start banging away. So we thought he was serious about needing a driver's license; it seemed like you would need a license for something like that. That took a load off. I don't think any of us were ready to handle something like that anyway. We had all done some making out but getting naked and doing that stuff was a little much.

My earliest memory of making out with a girl was in second grade. My buddy Jeff and I, who had the same birthday, were over at a girl's house. Her name was Candy. We were watching TV in the basement and Jeff went upstairs, so Candy I went over and laid on the patio furniture that was stored in the corner and started kissing. We actually seemed to know what we were doing. I'm sure we had no idea how to perform properly, but it seemed right. Then Jeff comes back downstairs and says, "Hey, that's not fair." I have no idea what that meant, but that was his response. I think that he had a crush on Candy, and that's why we were over there in the first place. Apparently, my tendency towards being attracted to women already taken started early. He then mentions that we have the same birthday. That doesn't seem to make much difference to Candy. She didn't want to kiss him. He started to pout so we headed upstairs to have a snack of raw hot dogs. We must have had two or three apiece. I have no idea why, it doesn't really seem like a snack food, you know? Can you imagine that now? Knowing what we know about food processing. Eating a hot dog raw? Good way to get trichinosis. Enjoy.

I had a good time those grades 6-8. I had some good friends, mostly Brent and Sammy. Brent lived up the street and had older brothers and sisters, and Sammy had Uncle Kurt, so I learned a lot of shit early. I knew all about sex and hard-ons and ejaculations way before I should have. Of course once you find that shit out, you really want to try it. Once you tried masturbating, and succeeded, well, you want to keep on trying it. It's good stuff even though the first one was kind of spooky. I woke up with a stiffy but didn't know what to do with it. I was sitting in the bathroom and for some reason decided to put my penis in the roll of toilet paper, then pull it out then put it in, and before you know it, boom, my first orgasm. I thought it was pee at first but it sure didn't look like pee. Holy Shit, Uncle Kurt was right about this too. And so started my journey of putting my penis in anywhere it would fit.

It was unreal, and I can't speak for all men, but as for me, I spent many an hour looking for some type of cylindrical shape in which to insert my penis. When you're young you can fuck anything, and by anything, I mean any *thing*. I guess maybe your dick skin is tougher when you're young. Of course, as you get older, lubes and towels and fantasizing come into play, but when you first start, you will seriously put your dick into any cylindrical shape. It's a magical time I tell you, magical. There's also a gradual change over the years in what you need to complete the task. When you're young, all you have to do is basically touch it for a few minutes and bam! You're done. Then you work up to needing pictures of topless women, pics you can hold up with one hand, if you catch my drift. Then as you age a bit, you need pictures of completely naked women for it to work. As the years progress, you start to need pictures of people actually doing it. This of course was long before I knew of porno.

Pornography was around as I was growing up, but we just didn't have access to it, I mean beyond stealing dirty magazines from somebody's dad's secret stash he had in the garage, and Penthouse was about as risqué as we could get our hands on. Today you can find pornography anywhere, back in the day it was a rare commodity. Finally, in the masturbation evolution, you get to the point where you need porn videos to help. Then, after some years of videos, that doesn't work as well and you actually have to put yourself into the scene itself for it to work for you, a lot of mental games going on. Putting yourself into the scene isn't easy either because in your mind, you have to explain everything, like, how do I know this woman? Where did she come from? Whose yacht is this? It's not mine, is it hers? If not hers, then who's? Who's driving this yacht, or are we just floating around in the ocean? Where's the wife, who's watching the kids? Are they floating on a raft behind the boat? There are just too many things to account for, and it's like "fuck it, I'm just going to have cookies and go to bed."

I have a friend of mine who's pushing 50 and he said he's not masturbating anymore because he doesn't want to have a heart attack and die in the middle of it and have the kids find him that way in the morning. Funny.

We used to go sit at Brent's house and listen to his siblings' albums for hours on end. It was my first taste of Rock and Roll. It never left me. I remember finding a Herb Albert and the Tijuana Brass album that had a picture of a naked woman on the cover. No bush, but we saw titties, and titties are a big thing to a fifth grader.

By the time I got to seventh grade, I was fixated and infatuated with girls. We were still in Overland Park, Kansas. I attended Hillcrest Junior High School. There I found my next great love, Becky Daly. I don't think I handled this one very well; I think it was also my first obsession. It was that follow her home from school, walk down her street five or six or ten times a day just hoping she'd be out, leaving notes in her locker, asking all her friends about her, calling up to ask her out and hanging up kind of obsession. I decided to ask her to go steady with me.

This again, took weeks and weeks of preparation and anxiety. I bought another ID bracelet, and damned if she didn't want to go out with me either. I followed her home one day, caught up to her and asked her to go steady with me. She was crossing a field and I figured if I ran around to the other side, I could catch her by the big elm tree. I thought that would be the ideal place to start my courtin'. I'm not sure if she saw me running around the outside of the field, tucking and rolling and trying to stay out of sight. But if she did, she must've thought I was some kind of freak. I headed her off at the pass, so to speak, and gave her my speech I had so lovingly prepared. I asked her and she shot me down. Then she had one of her friends tell me that she wanted me to leave her alone. Bummer. I'm 0-2 on the going steady thing, both brunettes by the way. I'm not sure if that comes into play or not, but in my adult life it was mostly blondes. Hmm. I never thought about that before. Deep, man, that's real deep. I'm in seventh grade and I'm wondering if I'm ever going to be able to find a woman. Am I destined to spend my life alone? Will I ever find a girl to love me? I was devastated, but not for long as I quietly mended my broken heart and moved on. Again.

I'm not sure what was wrong with me, but I had crushes on half the girls in my grade. Looking back I feel like kind of a perv; how can you be interested in so many different girls? Here's who I had crushes on in one school year: Vicky Yanak, Serena Zimmerman, Terri Brooks, Becky Daly, Cindy Reel, Erin McGarrigle, Cindy Current, Diane Dickerson, Cindy Treaster and Ann Conyers. Big surprise that I didn't do that well in school. I wonder if I had some kind of disorder. I never went steady with any of them. I did carry that same philosophy on throughout my life. I just loved girls. Of course back then, I took no for an answer, but as I got older, I just kept at it until she mentally broke down and agreed to go out with me. "Co...stanza." (Seinfeld reference)

Break ups were inevitable, girls come and go. I usually got down after break ups. It's an emotional time and you've got to be careful about the decisions you make in the next few days. One time after a break up, I bought a car. I bought a car to spite a woman. Can you imagine such a stupid thing? A woman dumped me, and to get back at her I bought a fucking car. I didn't need a car, I wasn't looking for a car, I had stopped by to see a buddy who sold cars and suddenly decided to purchase an automobile so I could drive by later and go, "See? See? Look at this." I don't know what response I was expecting, I really don't. Thinking back I guess maybe she'd see my new car and scream with joy and take me back.

"You done did real good Mark, let's try it again."

That didn't happen and she didn't take me back. Oh, something else. It was a red car. A freakin' red car. Red is not my color, I've never thought about owning a red car, I never liked them before, but in order to show this woman who's in charge in my life, I'll take the red one. What a Dipshit.

I got dumped on Valentine's Day one year. That was cheerful. We were having lunch at a Pasta House (because I know how to treat a lady) and she dumped me over my pasta carbonara. It was purely symbolic though. We had been drifting apart a bit and one night I showed up at her apartment at 3 a.m., and if I'm not mistaken, I may have been drinking. Her bedroom door was locked and there were a pair of cowboy boots in the living room. Since I knew there were two girls living there and neither of them wore a size ten boot, my sharp as a razor's edge deductive skills kicked in, and I realized there must be a man somewhere. Then her roommate comes out and says that her new boyfriend is in there. Her new boyfriend? What? What new boyfriend? Why didn't I know about this? I'm out? Just like that? It's over? My first reaction was anger, I was ready to kick the door down and take some fucking names, but since that's not really my style, I opted out of that scenario. If she doesn't want me now, I doubt she's going to want me after I beat the shit out of her new boyfriend. Since there were no other options, I left my key on the table and boogied on home. Que Sara.

We had lunch together a couple of days later, and it happened to be Valentine's Day, and she made it official. It probably wasn't necessary; I get the picture. You're banging another guy. You don't have to hit me over the head, I get it. I then went to an "emergency meeting" at the bar I was working at and got news that I had been fired. Ouch. Double whammy, dumped and fired in the same afternoon. I got fired because I gave a fellow employee a free drink when he came in. They fired me, him and the waitress that gave it to him. Overkill? Sure. I guess it's time to move on, again.

You feel sorry for yourself when you get dumped, don't you?

"You're dumping me? Why? What's wrong with me? Have I done something wrong? Can I change? Oh Please, please. What can I do? Anything?"

"No, there's nothing you can do, I'm just sick of being with you."

Ok then, no need to sugarcoat it. I guess it's time we move on. Moving on is the only thing you can do. That's why I never understood these guys that kill their ex-wives or other women who don't want them. Get over it, she doesn't want you any more, now grow some balls and move on, you sackless douchebag. Why the hell would you want to stay with someone that doesn't want you around? There are over 6 billion people on this planet, and half of them are women. Find another one.

I've had some break ups where I just sat around and drank while listening to Bob Dylan and Neil Young for days and days. That's usually all it took, just a few days of drinking and downer music and I was right back up in the saddle looking for the next woman who would steal my heart, eat it, digest it, shit it out on the street and then step in it with her spiked heels as she walks off into the sunset.

CHAPTER 15
MY MOM'S LEAST FAVORITE STORY

One winter, my brothers and I were playing hockey on a lake about two miles from the house. My brother Phil got his skate caught in a crack and broke his ankle. Although none of us were doctors, we knew what we knew, and we knew his ankle was broken. It had that weird dangle to it. We were just about finished anyway because dark was rapidly enveloping the lake, and we were beginning to freeze our asses off. The nearest pay phone was about a quarter of a mile away, up by the school. Jimmy and I drug his ass all the way up to the school so it would be easier to pick us up. Even then, we thought only of others.

We called my mom and told her we needed a ride because Phil had broken his ankle. Her response was simple and to the point: "you kids get home right now, dinner is almost ready." No matter how much we pleaded, we couldn't get our point across that Phil had broken his ankle, was incapacitated, and couldn't walk. We needed help and we needed it right now. Her response again was, "it's getting dark and dinner is almost ready, get home right now." She wasn't going to come and get us, so we carried that boy two miles over icy roads, slipping and sliding, falling all over, holding on to him and our hockey equipment, which included sharp bladed skates hanging around our necks, coming ever so closer to slicing a jugular as they swished and swayed in the cold winter wind.

By the time we got home it was late, dark and foreboding, not to mention dinner was over. We put the injured lad in a chair downstairs and went up to eat. I think Jimmy and I felt that we had gotten him home so our job was done. When my dad went to check on him, his ankle had swollen up to the size of a cantaloupe, had turned a dark, purplish hue and he was sporting some massive, swollen toes. Well, that certainly got things in motion. My dad says "his ankle's broken, we need to take him to the emergency room." He ended up with a nice big cast along with some crutches. To this day my mother hates that story and has never truly gotten over it.

CHAPTER 16
KID SPORTS

I played sports as a kid; everyone did. Everyone I knew, at least; it was the thing to do. There really wasn't much else. We didn't have computers or video games or television. I mean, we had TV, but it was only three channels plus the UHF ones which were never watched by anyone, so we played sports. We certainly didn't start as young as they do now. I think parents start their kids in organized sports way too early. On MSNBC recently they did a show about sports injuries to children under the age of ten. There had been a 150% increase in kids having rotator cuff and various other shoulder and elbow surgeries from trying to throw baseballs. That's nice, isn't it? The kid is only a few years past crapping in his pants and dad's trying to teach him how to throw a curveball. Tiny little muscles aren't capable of moving like that; get a clue pops.

"Hey, Don, how's the boy?"

"The surgery went well but he's got a lot of rehab in front of him."

"That's too bad, he had a hell of a screwball."

"He sure did, now if I can only get him to ride that bike without training wheels, we may have something."

I saw this show on ESPN about this ten-year-old who was into bodybuilding. The kid was ripped and looked like some kind of freak. Do you need rippling biceps and a washboard stomach at ten? I think not. Do you ever? This kid had long hair and looked like a fourth grade girl when he was dressed. What a fucked-up life. His parents should have their asses kicked. Take the weights out of his hand, give him a Popsicle, and make him go play. If he keeps lifting weights, by the time he's 20 he'll look like the Michelin man, and I mean that in a bad way. He'll be an exiled, misshapen mutant, an outcast, a pariah, alone in the gym, grunting and groaning while lifting weights until something bursts. Poor bastard. He never had a chance.

Most of our playing was in a field or a yard or something. Organized sports didn't start until 4th grade or so, and before that we played by ourselves. You don't see that much anymore, kids playing football in someone's yard. Now they use the Playstation or Xbox, which doesn't feel like a real football. And I guess that's good for parents who are afraid their kids will get hurt; the only injury the gamers will suffer is carpal tunnel. We didn't have carpal tunnel, we had broken bones and bloody lips. Oh, the days.

I did the rounds: football, baseball and basketball; your standard sports for kids back then. We didn't have anything fancy. We played hockey too, it just wasn't organized. Plus, it was expensive. Baseball and basketball were cheap to get ready for, football you had to buy some equipment. My first year of football, we bought all my pads at a flea market. I guess we couldn't afford new stuff, so I had to play wearing pads that God knows how many people had sweated in. My shoulder pads were from the 40's, at least. They were these huge, red, rounded shoulder pads that looked like they were made before facemasks were invented. The pants themselves were made of canvas, I think; they were as sturdy as tent fabric. The helmet, oh my, the helmet. Again, big and bulbous like the shoulder pads, and I personally thought I looked ridiculous It made my head look cartoonish in size. But I digress, hockey was where we were.

We didn't play organized hockey; it was always on a pond, not a rink, and those are two different games. Rinks don't have roots sticking out all over or leaves frozen just under the surface waiting for some unsuspecting kid to fly to the net in the hopes of scoring the game winner only to be upended by the small bush sticking up from the bottom of the pond. Good way to lose some teeth. I was never that good at sports. I was OK, but I wasn't the one they went to in times of trouble. I was never the "go to guy." I did my part, but I knew sports weren't going to be my future.

Parents start too early on the sports thing is my original point. There are organized sporting events for five-year-olds. Have you ever watched a soccer game with five-year-olds? The field is almost actual size, which is stupid because it takes them almost two minutes to run from one end to the other. Not that they cover the whole field, they usually play the whole game in the patch of worn out grass at mid field. Each team takes turns kicking the ball two feet at a time. That's as far as they can kick it. One team kicks it two feet north, then the other team kicks it two feet south. It's like a pack of piranhas chasing a wounded, bloody animal around in a circle. I've seen games where the only goal scored was by a dog running across the field chasing a squirrel that accidentally knocked the ball in the net. That caused a huge brew ha ha.

"It's good, we win."

"No man, it doesn't count, the dog kicked it in."

"Oh, it counts, we win."

"No it doesn't count, the dog kicked it in, and you don't win."

"Fuck you, we win."

"Fuck me? Are you out of your mind?"

Then this huge brawl breaks out at a four and five-year-old boys' soccer game. I miss that church; they were a spunky, spirited bunch. The goalies are never really in the game. They're usually playing around behind the net, or drawing figures in the dirt with a stick. "Tucker, pay attention." Tucker is 40 yards from the field climbing a tree. Tucker doesn't really care anyway; there hasn't been a shot on goal in two years. The little football players are funny too. You can always tell when football players are too young; the crotch of the pants is down somewhere between the knee and ankle. It really slows them down too, they can only take baby steps, and when you're running, baby steps are hysterical. Their little legs are going 100 mph, but they can only move their feet nine inches at a time. Priceless.

Like I said, I was never great at sports. I spent a lot of time on the bench, "standing by" to join the game in the event of an emergency. The other non-starters and I sometimes had no idea what was going on because we're over in the corner jacking around, doing our own thing. When I was doing the kid sport thing there was no such thing as "everyone plays." Some kids stayed on the bench and only went in if we were losing by 30 points or something. Welcome to life, son. Not everybody gets to play. Sometimes during football warm ups on muddy days, the other non-starters and I would go nuts in the warm up session so that we would get nice and muddy and at the end of the game it looked like we had played our little hearts out. Covered in mud from head to toe and never played a down. I don't think anyone ever noticed that mud on our uniforms had dried and was beginning to flake off. We were warriors.

Let's not forget the girls. Seven-year-old girls' t-ball games, what the hell? Twenty-seven infielders and not one of these babes will catch a ball. "I got it, I got it," several gather around, it hits the dirt and is picked up with the bases empty then tossed to left field. Nice play, ladies. Who is coaching these chicks? Of course runs don't really matter because everyone bats. What's the point? Everyone bats and they don't keep score? "There are no losers." What a shitty thing to teach children- "there are no losers, everyone's a winner." Bullshit, the world is full of losers. We all can't be winners, and it's a lesson that should be learned early. Don't wait until your child is an adult and then let them find out that they're a loser, better they find out early. Let them keep score, make it worth something. I didn't come out here to watch everyone be a winner, I want some tears, damn it. Not to mention the fact that it's 96* out here with 99% humidity and I have air conditioning at home.

CHAPTER 17
STICKY FINGERS

When I was in grade school, I found I had an affinity for shoplifting. It's not something I'm proud of, I was just good at it. If I couldn't afford something I wanted, I always justified it by "beating the man." Good philosophy. I was good at being sneaky. I would take orders from kids at school, go do my "run" in the afternoon, and the next day I would sell the stuff to fill the orders. It was mostly candy and crap like that; not many third graders were asking for a kick ass stereo. I didn't get caught until high school.

I got caught twice. The first time was for stealing beer out of the grocery store. A friend (I was new in town, so I should say my "new friend") and I stashed three cans of Miller High Life Tall Boys a piece in our jackets at the local supermarket and headed for the door. As we reached the parking lot, the manager comes out and yells at us, so I take off running, because that's what you do when authority is calling your name, you run. I knew this and I knew most of my friends knew this, but apparently my "new friend" wasn't aware of RUN! My partner in crime stops and is captured, the idiot. I tell him to run and he tells me to stop or he'll tell the manager my name. Great crime partner. So I stop and turn around. There's 100 yards between me and my accomplice who is being restrained by "the man." Thirty seconds pass and nothing happens, I don't move, they don't move. It's like a standoff in the middle of the Kroger parking lot. I keep waiting for the music from the *The Good, The Bad and The Ugly* to start. We're just staring at each other, we both know that there is no way he can catch me if I take off.

The tension begins to mount, nothing is happening, I keep waiting for my partner to shake loose and run, but he just stands there like a dumb ass. It was obvious he had never been in a situation where you needed to run to get away; for me it was old school, but my new friend had never been in any trouble, ever, and had no idea how to handle it. What I was doing hanging around him was beyond me. Then he yells out my name. "Mark Sweeney." Busted. What a dick. Remind me to kick his ass later. That is why you should always do a background check on crime partners- you can weed out the ones with no balls. Now my options are few; if I bolt now, he'll just call the cops and they'll show up at my house. I decide to take my chances with the store manager. Better than the police, I always say. He drags us into the office and calls our mothers. Our respective moms came to pick us up and return us to our homes. My mom sends me to my room to wait for my father to get home and gives me the Boy Scout manual to read as punishment. What her reasoning was for this I'll never know. I was in the Boy Scouts about 15 minutes, just long enough to get a manual; I really don't think I'll be getting any life lessons from this tome. My crime partner and I never hung out after that; he pretty much avoided me for the next two years. I never did kick his ass for that, but he was always expecting it, and that seemed good enough.

The second capture was later in high school, this time we were going for cigarettes. Black market smokes in high school was a profitable business. We'd steal a couple of cartons of smokes and then sell them to our friends. Easy money. For our next caper we would strike out of our neighborhood. It was me and a buddy and his little brother. His little brother was the lookout, I was the lead man, and my buddy was the driver because we had gone back to his old neighborhood.

I entered the store. This was when the cigarettes were in the aisles and not behind the customer service counter. You had access to them. I was wearing a huge down jacket, plenty of room. I could get six cartons of cigs in that puppy. I've got five in and I pick up number six and start to walk down the aisle, and as I'm putting that last carton in my jacket, an employee walks by the end of the aisle and looks straight at me. Our eyes meet. He knows. I know he knows, and I know that he knows that I know he knows. My first thought is to drop them all and leave, or hell, even put them back. That's the smart move, but then again, anyone who tries to steal six cartons of cigarettes can only be so intelligent.

I'm big and I'm ballsy, so I turn and head for the door. There are three employees standing by the door waiting for me. There is still time to abort the mission, but I'm no quitter, even against unbeatable odds. I continue to walk, and as soon as I hit the mat the door opens and I took off. I took off because they are chasing me; and as I'm running, I was pulling the cartons out of my jacket and tossing them. I have no idea why I was throwing them away. If I was going to do that, I should've never taken them in the first place. The cartons are hitting the ground, breaking open and there are cigarettes sliding all over the place. It's pandemonium, people are staring at the scene then racing to pick up the free cigs! It's chaos. I hope they pick up all the evidence and take it home. I stole cigarettes? What cigarettes? There's nothing in this parking lot but *empty* cigarette cartons.

So I was tossing these things and trying to cut and dodge so nobody could grab onto my coat. I felt like Jim Brown at the end of *The Dirty Dozen* when he's dodging the machine gun fire while throwing grenades down the air shafts. I was just like that. Yeah, that's how I remember it. I would have outrun them too except I was wearing hiking boots, not the light weight jobs they have now, I'm talking the old Colorado's, which weighed about eight pounds apiece. It's like running with a toddler strapped to each foot. By the time they grab me I'm clean, no more smokes.

"I'm innocent," I proclaim, just as one of the employees cracks me in the face, uh oh. That was unexpected. I take a lunge at him and try to get a swing in but the other two grab me and drag me back inside. One guy has me in a headlock, one has me in an arm bar, and one keeps telling me, "we got you good now, we got you good now." The other guy is picking up stray packs of cigarettes in the parking lot. As we head for the door I see my buddy and his brother sitting in the car, one in the front seat the other in the back, and they have these looks on their faces that I can't describe. Horror, shock, confusion, fear and I think, maybe, just a little uncertainty. I look at them as if to say "be cool, everything is under control," as I'm escorted in a headlock, back into enemy territory.

The stock boys bring me back to the storeroom, and make me sit on a pile of potato bags. The one guy keeps telling me how much trouble I was in and how they "had me now." Then they head to the office to discuss the situation: a couple of pea brains trying to figure out what to do with the renegade. I remembered that I have a couple of joints in my wallet so I toss them behind the potato sacks. No sense in taking a pot bust along with shoplifting. I sat there kicked back on those potato sacks for almost 30 minutes before they came back, took my money out of my wallet, all nine dollars of it and told me "never come back to this store." I didn't bother telling them I lived about 30 miles away and had no intention of coming back. I was free, and my ride was still there. Good stuff, good times.

CHAPTER 18
HIGH SCHOOL

We've moved to Hoffman Estates, IL, or what people in Chicago call the Northwest Suburbs. Helen Keller Junior High School. I loved going to that school, I made friends faster there than anywhere. I really blossomed at Helen Keller Junior High School. I learned how to work the room; it was so much easier than fighting. I made friends in my neighborhood, on the bus, at school. I had never known so many people. My first year of high school was at Hoffman Estates High School. We were the first class to attend because it was a brand new school. It was cool being in a new school, everything was so clean, and our dirt was the first dirt ever tracked in. Hoffman Estates was the first place that I ever smoked and drank. It was also the last year of organized sports for me. No more football, basketball or baseball. The off-field activities proved to be much more fun than the on-field ones. That first beer was a Pabst Blue Ribbon we stole from my friends' dad. I think that's true for most people; your first drink was from stolen liquor. In retrospect, that may not be completely true, my folks have plenty of pictures of me as four or five-year-old drinking beer. In one pic, I'm one-handing the can, that's a cool skill for a toddler to have isn't it? Drinking one handed? Sure. It was usually a can of Hamm's; that was a biggie back then. Parents used to give their kids sips of liquor all the time. Now you can go to jail for it. There's a lot to be said of a simpler time, when alcohol was used to put a fussy child to bed. "Here, drink this, now good night."

How else can a ninth grader get liquor except to steal it? It's all part of the game. Later, we used to steal beer from people's garages. Six o'clock in the evening and we would walk up to someone's garage and run out with a case of beer, split it up on the curb and take off. One guy couldn't carry all that beer so you had to divvy up the load. It had to be done quickly though, before some neighbor called to tell Mr. Reynolds that "some kids just walked out of your garage with a case of beer, and they're still on the street." Mr. Reynolds comes running out of the house with his grandaddy's 12 gauge, ready to blow some holes in the bastards stealing his beer. We'd be running down the street dropping a few stray beers as we ran for our lives. Good times people, good times.

I had a pretty good time in high school. First at Hoffman and then on to St. Louis and Parkway West. When we moved to St. Louis , I went back to Junior High and I was pissed. I felt like I had moved on and now I was being dragged kicking and screaming back to school with seventh and eighth graders. Bollocks. At that point, I wasn't bringing my lunch anymore; I bought my lunch at school. Well, we bought some of it. It was so easy to steal lunch that I only paid for milk and Suzy Q's. Weren't those delightful? The Suzy Q's? I used to love them, now I find them a little spongy, but back in the day? Fantabulous. They had just come out with soybean burgers and I did love them, I know that much. We used to stuff two or three of them down our pants and walk right out, you did have to walk quickly though, they were hot and the plastic wrapping would burn you if you weren't careful. It's hard trying to explain to the nurse why your lower stomach had a burn mark on it the size of a soybean burger. I'm not sure what the cashiers thought, we'd come in grab a few things, pay for them, go sit down, a few minutes later we'd come back, walk around and then scurry past with an unusual walk like our balls are on fire and buy nothing, hmm, strange. So we'd sit there and eat our stolen burgers and paid-for Suzy Q's and wash them down with milk, now that's a party.

I know a lot of people say that high school was the worst time of their lives. Not for me. I had fun. Of course, I didn't attend school on a regular basis, and maybe that was part of it. Back in the day...we had a smoking area at school. I say "back in the day" for comic effect, it makes you sound old, don't you think? I think the older you get, the more you start off a sentence with "remember?" or the worse, "back in the day." Thanks, Pa Kettle.

Anyway, back in the day, we had a smoking area outside the lunch room of the school. We had this little square, defined by a yellow stripe outlining the box. We had to stand inside the box to smoke. Outside the box and trouble would brew. Inside the box, you could puff away. Seems unreal eh? Smoking at high school. What a concept. Of course, many of us had just come up from the woods. Ah, the woods. The woods were great. It was this little circle of trees right outside the back door of the school. Just go to the smoking box, turn right and head down the hill. We used to hang around in there and smoke pot. Right on the school property, 30 yards from the back door. What a crazy bunch of kids. If it was cold we'd sit in the car and smoke. Five or six of us sitting in the station wagon smoking joints the size of pinkie fingers rolled up in strawberry papers.

The assistant principal was the disciplinarian at our school, and he would sometimes try and sneak up on us in the woods, or wherever we had slithered off to. One morning I was sitting in the station wagon (brown with wood paneling- a classic) and four of my buddies were in the car and we were sharing a doobie, a spleef, a jay, a number, a jibby, if you will. It was cold so we had the windows closed, and after five or six minutes the car is so full of smoke that we can't even see. It is literally a fog out. We're laughing and smoking and lighting up a second joint, music is jamming (Rory Gallagher) and we are having a great time getting ready for school. Suddenly, and I do mean suddenly, there is a knock on the window. We freeze. Was that a knock on the window? Sssshhhh. Don't make a sound. Oh shit! Turn off the music! Maybe if we're quiet he won't know we're in here.

It must have been pretty good pot for us to think that the sudden silence will hide the fact there are five high school boys sitting in a car with plenty of windows, or that a second ago the music was playing, and now it's not. The smoke will dissipate eventually and then he'll see us. We'll be sitting there slowly coming into view, with this incredibly stupid look on our faces saying "who me?" Knock, knock again on the window. Someone says something; "shut up" is my reply. Maybe whoever's knocking on my window will go away. Knock, knock. Or maybe they won't go away.

"Open the window please," I hear a voice say. I'm stuck, there is nothing I can do, I must open this window and see what's up. I opened the window and this massive cloud of pot smoke billows out and right into the face of the assistant principal. Oops. There is nothing for me to say, nothing. Nothing in the world can explain this huge cloud of very mediocre Mexican pot smoke that envelops his entire head. We can't run away, we can't drive away, there is no escape. Why the fuck did we do this here? We could've moved around the corner, anything, anywhere, we could've gone anywhere. Time's up boys, we've got to face the music. The cloud dissipates.

"Morning fellas, whatcha doing?"

"Getting ready to head up for class sir."

"I suggest that's exactly what you do."

And that was it. He chased us up to class, and that was the end of it. Of course we spent the day freaking out over what was going to happen. We thought that letting us go was just to mess with our minds. Make us squirm all day, wondering. Did he call our folks? Is he going to call the cops? Are we going to be suspended? Expelled? WHAT THE HELL IS GOING TO HAPPEN? It was maddening. Our pot-riddled minds had come up with all kinds of torturous punishments that he may dole out, but he never did anything. Maybe it was a psychological game he was playing. We kept to the woods after that. Sometimes we would just go for a drive and then come back to go to class. Just skip an hour of school to go burn one. What balls.

After school it was more of the same, wandering the streets, sharing doobies. I hung out with a different crowd after school. I lived in a different district, so my neighborhood friends went to a different high school, so I had two sets of friends. They were all stoners; almost everyone I knew was a stoner. In the mid 70's that's just the way it was. At home it was Louie, or Sweet Lou as he was known, (whom I still hang with) Wills, Riggs, Bird, Nico, Hobbit, Moosehair, Charles and Buddha. My neighborhood friends all had nicknames. My school friends did not. Weird. We spent a lot of time stoned in high school. I'm actually surprised we graduated. My senior year, I spent more time outside of class than I did in it. Parties, pot, drinking, classic rock, big bells, dingo boots, Marlboros. Those were the things of my high school.

The night I graduated, I almost got laid. I had my Dad's car, and it was actually pretty cool, no wagon this time. He had a dark blue, 1976 Ford Gran Torino, just like the Starsky and Hutch car. No shit, it was the coolest car I ever saw my Dad in. After the ceremony we went to some parties, and I ran into a girl I had some classes with and we started partying together and ended up doing shots of Southern Comfort. I had one previous experience with Southern Comfort on a float trip, and it did not end well. I don't know how Joplin drank that shit, it's too sweet. It's sweet coming back out too, I will give it that.

So we're pounding shots and hitting from the keg, then she wants to go for a ride, so OK, let's motor. I'm thinking pretty positive thoughts by now. Sweenz is getting laid tonight. We head down the outer road of the highway and park off this gravel side street and start to get busy. I immediately feel dizzy and the spins are starting. That's not a good sign, getting the spins just from kissing? Uh-oh. We take a break and then get back to it, but no go, because along with the spins, I now feel my tummy gurgling. I excuse myself, thinking I just need some air, so I step outside and then throw up all over my dingo boots.

Oh, it was a good body wrencher; it felt like it came up from my toes. All I can taste and smell is Southern Comfort as it splashes all around me. And you know what? It's still sweet. As I'm wondering if I'll recover enough to get this thing done, another round exits me and I know that tonight's not going to happen. Even if I start to feel better, there's no way she'll kiss me after 20 minutes of heaving right outside the car door. What a Romeo. I was Rico Suave before Rico Suave was. Somehow, I got her home and myself as well. A drunk-ass 17-year-old driving around town; if I was my kid, I would've given me a good pummeling.

Most of the guys I knew had jobs, which means we always had money, which is crucial for a good time. Without cash, you've got nothing to do, nobody to do it with and no way to get there. I was what you call a "freak" in high school. In the mid 70's in suburban St. Louis, we had your three basic groups of peoples. We had the freaks, the jocks and the soshes. That pretty much covered everyone. There were some small splinter groups of people that didn't fit into the big three, but they kept to themselves and never infiltrated the main body. The jocks were the jocks, they're the same everywhere. They played sports, dated the cheerleaders and had short hair. They would drink, maybe smoke a little dope at weekend party, but they weren't out at the park with a half barrel of beer, tossing a Frisbee around at 1 o'clock on a Tuesday afternoon.

The freaks, oh the freaks. The party people, the long hairs, the rock and rollers, the wood hippies. What a sight. We were some snappy dressers too. Big bell blue jeans. Can you imagine? We wore fucking big bell blue jeans! Hard to believe when you think back. Those big ass pants dragging behind you getting all ratty and torn up until they were just right. We thought we were so cool. They had to be long too, there's nothing worse than big bell high waters. They would flop and sway and swing all around the boot tops making the person wearing them look ridiculous. You had to wonder if they knew, can't you tell that you're wearing high waters? Nobody wears high waters on purpose, do they? If all I had to wear to school were high waters, I'd call in sick. High water big bell jeans- there's nothing worse.

The soshes, if I recall, were mostly girls. I think to be male sosh you had to be a cheerleader or on the dance squad or do pom poms or some shit. If there were a lot of male soshes, I wasn't aware of them.

The soshes knew people from both groups and often brought them together, kind of like Charlie Manson.

We had a lot of keg parties in high school, usually outside in the spring. School was almost out, and the weather's perfect, a little too perfect to waste it inside a classroom. We'd gather some friends, snag a half barrel and head to the park. We could buy beer because I had a buddy who used his older brother's ID for about six months until the people at the liquor store knew him and quit carding him. Sweet. You had to remember to call him Matt though.

Now, the thought of a group of 17-year-olds skipping school, picking up keg and then hitting the road makes my blood run cold. It seemed alright when we were doing it. I guess it's because everyone feels that they're mature at that age, and when you get older you realize that you weren't mature and didn't know shit. I'm sure that's true for past generations as well. Of course, they didn't have access to the things we did and we didn't have access to the shit kids today have. In our wildest dreams we had beer, pot, acid, maybe some mushrooms and the video game Pong. That's about it. The youngins today can get a hold of just about anything they can imagine through the internet. Lucky bastards. They even have better prescription meds as close as grandma's medicine cabinet. They have access to the World Wide Web; wow, if we had that, some of us may not have made it. Acid to Zoloft, animal porn to zipper necks. I don't know what a zipper neck is, but it started with a z.

Yeah, we had keg parties when we were supposed to be in school. I can't actually believe we got away with it. We should've been in Geometry, and instead we're at Babler Park drinking, playing Frisbee and grilling hot dogs. What the hell? Who did we think we were? It was always tricky getting home though. You can't just show up at the house at four in the afternoon and pretend you just got home from school, timing was everything. You'd stalk the house, wait until mom came out for something and then scurry past feigning "illness." Can't let her smell the beer, pot and cigarettes on you; no kid is supposed to come home from school smelling like a tavern. I guess our moms just thought we were working so hard at school that we needed a nap upon returning home. I'm not sure what she thought of those naps sometimes lasting 14 hours. "That boy studies so hard, he comes home from school and sleeps 14 hours." Good times, my friends, good times.

Unfortunately, high school will be over soon and then what? First, I can keep smoking pot, drinking beer, hanging around with my buddies and going to rock concerts. Not much pay in that job. Most people wouldn't even consider those activities an actual career; too bad. It's fun. Not to say that's *all* I did in high school, but that was the basic plan. You could show up late to a job like that and no one would care, and maybe, just maybe, no one would even notice. But to finance a job like that I would have to keep working at Sam Wilson's restaurant. Sure, it's a lot of fun, but it's hard to picture myself at 40, still dumping dishes into a bus tub and chasing after waitresses, all while wearing an apron. Plus, after years of working in a restaurant, you begin to take on the smell of the restaurant, and it never leaves you.

It's not necessarily a bad smell, but it's a restaurant kitchen, dish room smell. If you've been there you know. It's a wet, foody, soapy smell and it attaches onto your clothes and skin like a fine layer of grease. You transfer the smell as well. (the smell as well- how do I do it?) The smell, oh Lordy, the smell. I think most of it clings to the shoes; your clothes can be laundered, but the shoes man, the shoes. Your footwear absorbs those odors and brings them to the very root of the fibers where it dwells and ferments and grows horrible lesions of pulsating stinky sacks, and each time you take a step and bend those fibers, they unleash the undead. Yeah, that's what it's like. Just like that. The undead. I'm sure most people wouldn't refer to restaurant smells as the "undead" but I'm not most people. Your car will always retain the odor as well. Anyone who rides in your car will know you work in a restaurant, and if they're really good, they may be able to tell which one. It takes a special skill to be able to pinpoint a dining establishment by the way the employee's car smells. There are many different odors that will always stay with you. For the rest of your life, you'll remember. The locker room in high school. It's a musky smell that refuses to be washed away with simple earthly materials like bleach and high pressure fire hoses.

If you walk into a locker room when you're 50, it will still have the same smell as when you were 15. All those pubescent boys who only took their gym clothes home once every month or two. Nicely done, fellas, what a bunch of pigs. Vomit is another smell. I know what you're thinking "vomit is another smell? This guy is brilliant." Nonetheless, puke was the worst. Many times I was the second kid who threw up. It was the smell. As soon as that smell hit me, I was gone. Well, that and the sight of it, along with the sound and the very idea, that's right; the very idea of puking made me want to puke. To this day when I walk through a grade school (not once in the last 38 years), I keep my eyes peeled for the piles of sawdust in the hall. If I happen to see it, I make a wide, sometimes, adventurous path around it, and I may even use a whip to wrap around the water pipes and swing myself over. I don't want it anywhere near me; I don't even want to take a chance that a little droplet had flown out of the inner circle and I may step in it. I had to make a conscious effort not to look at it, like a car accident. You know you shouldn't but you can't help it. You know it's puke on the floor, you know what it is, you know what it can do to you, don't look! Don't look! Too late, I snuck a peek and now I'm gagging. The horror, the horror. As a kid I couldn't imagine how the janitors could clean that stuff up. I was in awe. Of course, moms clean up puke like it's spilled kool-aid, and I never did get that either. I've seen my mom clean up puke while talking on the phone! How is that possible? Has she no soul? Is she not human? Doesn't she know where that stuff came from? Vomit still grosses me out, don't know why, that's just the way God made me. I'm not a big blood and guts fan, but that stuff is nothing compared to the bodily fluids brought up from the inner sanctum. When I was six, my little brother threw up on me. I had no other choice but to throw up right back on him. It was during Christmas time and my brothers and I had just finished our eggnog. We were wrestling at the bottom of the stairs, and apparently, the eggnog was getting sloshed around in our stomachs and bluey, puke everywhere, then the chain reaction starts and bam, bam, all three of us had puked all over the floor. Well done boys. I still think about that every time I have eggnog. Happy Holidays.

Oddly enough, I never got thrown up on again until my sister did it to me at a party. We had a gathering at the house one weekend, and my little sister, who was 16, had been drinking strawberry daiquiris, which is an appropriate drink for a 16-year-old girl. At least that's how we thought of it at the time. My parents had finished the basement of our house, and we had some legendary parties. We had a foosball table, a pool table, a bumper pool table, a dart board, a huge poker table, a bar and we were wired for sound. Heaven. My folks were at home for every one of them, and most of the time they had a blast. My mother was always a hit. Someone would be out back sparking a joint and my mom would pop up and ask if anyone's hungry. "Not yet Mrs. Sweeney, but soon, very soon." This was back in the day when underage people could have a keg party. It's hard to believe now, but it's true. Seventeen and eighteen year-old people standing around a half barrel, just pumping that handle to their hearts content. We had those parties until our early twenties, then everyone started drifting off into their new lives, but for most of a decade, the Sweeney parties rocked.

Back to my sister vomiting on me. I was sitting behind the bar with my sister standing next to me, and she starts to say something then spews strawberry daiquiri all over my left side. From the shoulder on down I'm drenched in strawberry daiquiri. Nice. Thank God it smelled like strawberries or there would have been two of us blowing lunch. I went upstairs to get cleaned up and my youngest brother, who I guess was about 14, was puking in the upstairs bathroom. Well done, Mark, your two littlest siblings have consumed enough alcohol to regurgitate. My parents found out and understandably were quite pissed off. We didn't have any more parties for a while.

Throwing up at school was the worst. I only did it once. That was enough of an emotional scar to last a lifetime. It happened in seventh grade. I was in Spanish class and it was right after lunch. It came upon me fairly quickly. I started getting sweaty, and my stomach was gurgling, and then wham, I leaned over and let her go. I thought at first it was going to be a big burp, but I was wrong. I launched myself out of the class and to the restroom. I was humiliated, embarrassed, degraded, mortified, horrified and downright tortured about what I had done. Should I go back and apologize? Should I tell the class how sorry I was for ruining the class by drenching it with puke? What should I do? I'm in quandary. This has never happened before so I don't know the protocol. Am I supposed to go to the nurse? Get a note? Go home? I feel fine now. What should I do? Go get my books and have to face the class? I don't think so. I headed down to woods to wait for my friends. I never did go back to that class. Never. I just stopped attending. As far as I was concerned, I was never there, I never attended that class. There was no way I could face those people again. No freakin' way.

So yeah, I had a good time in high school. I got my driver's license, that's always a big step for a young lady. I failed it the first time because I rolled a stop sign. Five minutes into the test he says "we can head back; you just failed." I thought I was doing pretty well, but apparently, if you break a law, it counts against you.

We went to a ton of concerts in high school as well. All the bands of the 70's came through town twice or three times a year. And we went every time. Lynyrd Skynyrd, Aerosmith, Jethro Tull, REO, Marshall Tucker, Charlie Daniels, Poco, The Allman Brothers, Black Sabbath, Journey. Man, we saw all those guys a dozen times in high school, many times on a school night. Yeah, life was sweet and everything was all right, but now what?

CHAPTER 19
HIGH SCHOOL IS OVER

Uh Oh, two more months and I'm out of high school. What to do? What to do? Now I realize that a little prior planning would've come in handy. That's a good idea, isn't it? Figure out what you're going to do with your future before it shows up. High school is over; you can't just keep showing up to visit with your friends. The vice principal will come down to the smoking area and ask you to leave. "You fellas graduated, go home."

My first option was college. Please. I had no intention of continuing my education. I'd had my fill of educational institutions. Too much authority involved in the school system; I'm tired of people telling me what to do. Maybe I could join the military. Hmm, the military. You know, that just doesn't sound like my thing, a little too much regimentation, and again, authority for sweet poppa. I like my thing flowing a little more in the breeze, if you know what I mean. Then, at a party one weekend, I met the cousin of a friend of mine who had just gotten out of Marine Corps Boot Camp. He said it was the most horrible thing he had ever experienced. He hated every second of every minute of every day. It was as bad as he had imagined and worse, but it was worth it because when it was over he was a Marine. Three months of being tortured, beaten and tested to the limits by United States Marine Corps Drill Instructors. He started giving me a synopsis of his time. Getting up at 5 a.m. Eating breakfast in the dark. Marching, running, sweating, crying, screaming, shooting rifles, climbing mountains, fighting with pugil sticks, running obstacle courses, throwing grenades, learning HOW TO KILL.

"That is, if you make it; most don't, we lost almost half our guys." Bells and whistles are going off in my head as I was thinking, "that sounds like something." I bet nobody else will do it. I think that really appealed to me. I think that's what appealed to me the most. I bet nobody else will do it. I've always been that way- I just have to do it different than everyone else. If I joined the Marines, I'm sure I'd be the only one. That would be cool. I decided right then I was going into the Marine Corps. Standing at a party, with hair hanging in my face, a beer and cigarette in one hand and passing a joint with the other, I decided I will join the Marines. I guess you could call it an epiphany, though I wasn't familiar with either the word or the concept at the time, but I distinctly remember at that moment, I knew what I was going to do. No question, I had finally made some plans for my future. Right out of the blue, I decided my fate. I liked that, no him-hawing around, no weighing the pros and cons, no thinking of the consequences or the long term, just think of it, make the decision and die by the sword. Rock on, Sweenz, I'm proud of you. Of course, when I mentioned this to my companions, they all had a good laugh and told me I'd never make it. Really? That's how you feel?

"It's the Marines man, the fucking Marines. You'd never make it."

Well, now I have to go. These clowns don't think I have the stones to get through Marine Corps boot camp. Well, I do have the stones and I'm going to prove you dipshits wrong. Thanks, fellas. Any chance I had of changing my mind had just dissipated. I was going to join the Marines. As it turned out, I was the only one from my class that joined the Marines. See? I was right, I knew I'd be the only one.

I was the easiest recruitment that guy ever had. I went in knowing I was going to join. You don't have to convince me, I'm sold, sir. I want to join the Marines. Where do I sign? The problem was that I was only 17 and a minor so I needed my parents' signature. I had this whole speech prepared for my dad. I had already talked to the recruiter, and I thought I knew what I was getting into. I went downstairs to my dad's office and told him I wanted to join the Marines and needed his signature. It was a pretty short conversation.

"Hey Dad, I want to join the Marines."

"The Marines, huh? You sure you wouldn't be more comfortable in the
Army?"

"No, I want to be a Marine."

"OK, give me the papers."

Without any more hesitation he had that puppy signed and was telling my mother to set one less place for supper. Whoa, hold on, pappy, I'm not leaving yet, I still have my summer. The ink isn't dry on the paper and he's converting my bedroom into a sauna. That summer was a great one. I ran, did sit-ups and push-ups, and it was party central. The only thing that put a damper on it was the Marine Corps thing hanging over my head. Sometimes I wish I had just joined and gone, because the anticipation and dread was on my mind all the time. It just hung in front of my face, all dark and disturbing. On September

18, it's all over, the Marines will own my ass. I had three months of people saying to me "are you insane?" or "man, you're fucked" or "what did you join the Marines for? Don't you know they're crazy? They'll kill you." That of course, just furthered my resolve. I **knew** I would make it; there wasn't a doubt in my mind. There was no way I could come back if I didn't make it. I would've been banished from the village to scavenge a meager, sad existence, living on the outskirts of town, just rummaging through the town's refuse pile looking for my next meal. So just keep it up you civilian scum, I'll show your ass.

By the time August came around, I was a wreck. I was getting these feelings of regret, fear and overwhelming doom. All I could think of was what a horrible mistake I had made. The Marines, the fucking Marines. What the hell was I thinking? I was a beer drinking, pot smoking hippie. I didn't want to take on a huge challenge like that. I like things quiet. I'm a peaceful, loving man. I don't want to know how to kill somebody. Don't they have like, Marines for that kind of stuff? Viet Nam was over, but there are plenty of other places where they might need Marines to go and kill people. But the closer I got to leaving and the more anxious I became, it was almost like "come and get me damn it, let's get it on." The friends that I had who were going to college didn't seem to be worried or scared or nervous or anything negative, they seemed excited. They were worry free, after all, it was just school. What kind of maniac joins the Marines? Tick, Tock.

CHAPTER 20
I JOIN THE MARINES

Well, the time has come. I'm off to the Marines. My dad has to drop me off at the recruiter's at 5 a.m. The Marines love 0500- a lot of shit starts right at 0500. My mom was in tears as I left, her oldest baby is flying the coop. I somehow think that after she closed the front door, she immediately broke out into song, "One down, five to go." She must have been thinking, "now we've got extra room, more food for the rest of us, and just a little more peace and quiet." The rest of you kids take note and hurry up and get the hell out of here. Let's go people, grow up and go. My father didn't have a big speech prepared for me or anything before the Marines took me away, but he did tell me something I thought profound. All he said was, "Just be a man." Poignant and simple. "Just be a man." Thanks, Dad, I will.

The recruiter takes me downtown to the government building to do our final paperwork. All the guys who are leaving for the military that day are down there as well. The different branches are all represented in their respective areas of a large meeting room. My recruiter sits me down to fill out my paperwork. As I'm doing it, I notice that the Army and Navy each have at least 100 guys doing paperwork in preparation for their departure, the Air Force has about 80 in their group and the Marines area has three of us sitting there. Hmm. When my recruiter comes to check on us I inquire as to the whereabouts of the rest of the Marine guys are, he says,

"What other guys?"

"Um, the rest of the guys going into the Marines?"

"There isn't anybody else; it's just you three."

Well, now that's interesting, three of us. The three musketeers, the three amigos, the three stooges. "What do you mean there's only three of us?" Does everybody else know something that I don't? How does a city the size of St. Louis have only three guys going into the Marines? Three? That right there should have told us something. I'm no math expert, but that seems like an awful small percentage. Three? There must be some mistake. I know there are more than three guys in St. Louis who want to be Marines. No, there weren't. I guess "The Few, The Proud, The Marines" isn't just a recruiting slogan; it's really taken to heart. One of the other three, who I had been chatting with earlier, had an older brother in the Marines, and we were going over some of the tips his brother had given him about getting through boot camp. The number one tip? Remain anonymous. The single most important thing to remember is: DO NOT STICK OUT. Do your shit, keep your head down and your mouth shut. OK, I'll remember that. When he noticed that I was little concerned about the lack of people joining us, he just kind of leaned in close.

"Do you know why there are only three of us?"

"No, I don't." I replied. Then he said something that changed everything.

"Because it only takes three Marines."

It gave me goosebumps man, my whole attitude changed right there. I didn't dread it after that, I looked forward to it. It made me excited. Holy shit man, I'm going to be in an elite group. I was going to be a Marine. Now I was pumped, primed and ready. It was almost another epiphany, "it only takes three Marines." Wow, that blew me away. I've never forgotten it.

After what can only be described as a long and torturous day, we land in San Diego. There is a Marine in his dress uniform waiting on us, impressive sight. Nobody looks as good in the dress uniform as the Marines. The dress blues are by far the sharpest looking uniforms of all the services. The Navy dress whites are almost comical. What do you guys do, work on a cruise ship? Or maybe a waiter somewhere, a good waiter too; I'm guessing from all the pins and ribbons. I think that's actually where TGIF got the idea for pins and other "flair" on their uniforms, from the Navy. It's not just me either, I had friends in the Navy, and they hated the whites as well, too disco. The Army or Air Force? Fuggetaboutit. Not in the same class as Marine dress blues. Of course, I may be biased. So we followed this Marine to a check-in area. I don't think anyone had any luggage. I had the clothes on my back and a toothbrush, that's it, and I didn't need the toothbrush. Travel light, that's my deal. Everyone at the airport knows where we're going. They've seen it before. A little pack of puppies following the Marine, straggling behind him in single file, dragging our blankies and binkies as he leads us to our future. A trek into the unknown, a future of things we can't anticipate or understand. A future of things we shouldn't anticipate or understand. Sympathetic looks abound. They know what's up, they know where we're headed, and they know what we're headed for and there's nothing they can do to help us. Boo hoo, it's too late now anyway. We're beyond the reach of mere mortals. We stop briefly do some more paperwork; apparently, they wanted to make sure that we hadn't disappeared at some time during the day. Now it's off to the bus.

It's approximately 6 p.m. We sit on the bus and wait. We have to wait for the rest of our platoon to arrive from their parts of the country. Nothing builds apprehension like sitting on a bus with a group of strangers all getting ready to embark on Marine Boot Camp. Tension is mounting; the bus is beginning to smell like a locker room, it's the reek of stale sweat, fear and uncertainty. Nice combo. Finally, after four hours, everyone is accounted for and we're off to the base. In order to confuse us, we took a long, circuitous route to the base, winding around the town so we don't know how to get back to airport if we decide to go AWOL. Military logic at its finest.

The base is right next door to the airport; you can see planes taking off from the depot. If I bolt, I'm not taking the streets, I'd hop the fence. It's literally a five minute drive, but it took us 45 minutes to get there. Are we lost? Haven't you ever taken this route before? Are you new? It's a five minute drive, what the hell is going on? I'm ready to start this thing and then we stop. As we crane our necks to see what's out there; we see the wall. It's a tall, dark, gray wall, dripping with moisture. Wow, there it is: MCRD San Diego, where they train Marines. It's foggy, damp and dark. Then we look up and see the Marine Corps emblem under the words UNITED STATES MARINE CORPS RECRUIT DEPOT. Dead fucking silence. You can barely hear people breathing, it's like we've gone into a vacuum and all the sound has been sucked away. There were no engine noises, no plane sounds, no other vehicles around, no birds chirping. It was actually kind of eerie. Holy shit! Well I guess it's real now. Our time has come; signing the paper wasn't really being a Marine. Just wanting to be a Marine wasn't real. Telling people you joined the Marines wasn't real. This? This is real, we're here. I can pretty much speak for the entire bus when I say the common thought was "Dear God in Heaven, what were we thinking? We should've all joined the Coast Guard, we could be cruising the waterways pulling big bales of pot out of the ocean." Strangely enough, the bus now smells like a dirty diaper. Great, someone just shit in their pants, nice start. We continue. As we drive on base, you can't see a thing. I think that's for a reason. They don't want anyone planning escape routes. We stop.

Our bus driver kills the engine, turns and gives us a look that was part sympathy, part paternal love. It almost seemed like he wanted to say something profound, to say something of encouragement, to say something to ease our minds. But no, he gave us a look of pity and despair, a look that said, "You fellas have no idea what's coming. You'll find out shortly, but right now, you have no idea of the shit that's about to hit the fan." He paused before stepping out and said, "Good luck boys, Godspeed," and he was gone.

I will say this; if I would have known that his was the last friendly face I was going see for three months, I would've hugged that man. I would have hugged him long and hard. But in a flash, he was out of our lives forever. He left the bus and headed into the darkness. The silence was almost too foreboding; all you can hear is your own heart beating. The predominant smell is poop and underarms; it's a smell that we'll experience more than once. If you look out the left side of the bus, you can see the yellow footprints. The infamous yellow footprints. Oh sure, we've all heard of them, but to actually see them was, well, I'm not sure what it was, maybe unsettling is the word I'm looking for. Yes, unsettling is the word. I never actually thought I would see them, but there they are right outside the bus, the famous yellow footprints, the historic yellow footprints of the Marine Corps and in a few minutes, I'll be standing on them.

Ten minutes roll by, nothing is happening, and we don't know what the hell is going on. It's completely dark except for one light shining on the yellow footprints. Those damn footprints! They haunt me! I'm becoming frightened! Sweet Jesus, what have I done? Why do the footprints torture me? It's just paint, yellow paint, in the shape of footprints, nothing to be afraid of. "But we are, we are afraid, Blanche." Release the demons, release the hounds! We know once we stand on those footprints it will begin. Each minute that rolls by increases the tension tenfold, and after 20 minutes we can barely breathe, the air is so thick with tension; it's like trying to breathe through a wet towel.

Then we hear it. A door slams. Someone's coming! We can see four figures walking towards us. One goes to the back, two go to the sides of the bus, so now we're surrounded. Everyone's head is on a swivel as we're all trying to get a peek at what's out there, but it's too dark to see clearly. All we can make out are shadows, and they're shadows of guys wearing uniforms. We see a body walk in front of the bus. Who is it? Do you know? Do you? Is it our drill instructor? Is it a highway patrolman? Is it a cook just playing with us? Is it Jack Webb? Is it Satan? Who the fuck is coming? Uh Oh. It's a Marine and he looks serious. He gets on the bus takes a quick look around and says "You've got ten seconds to get off my fucking bus and eight of them are gone."

We sit and stare. "What did he say? Is he talking to us? Are we supposed to leave?" Then he reaches down towards this kid sitting in the front row (just one more reason you NEVER sit in front, not in class, not at the movies, not on the bus on the way to boot camp) grabs him by the shirt with one hand and throws him down the stairs of the bus. The other three start rocking the bus and yelling. Oh, I get it. He wants us to get off the bus. What follows can only be called anarchy. I've never been a part of a wild mob, but that's what I'm in the middle of now. It was my first experience with group fear. There are guys going out the windows, the emergency exit, I think some kid ripped a hole in the top of the bus with his toothbrush. I never imagined that one guy could cause so much disturbance.

We get off the bus and take our place on the yellow footprints. I know now why the footprints are yellow, it's because they're soaked in urine; the urine of fear. These guys seemed pissed off. Now it's getting interesting, there are confrontations going on everywhere, well, not confrontations really, because those require two people, we're not confronting, we're being confronted. What's up, fellas? Lighten up a tad. We just got here and these guys are nose to nose with us screaming at the top of their lungs calling us all kinds of names. Excuse me, sir, I think you can tell by looking at me that I'm not a lady. Civilian scum maybe, but I'm no lady. Nor am I a cock-sucking piece of shit. That seemed a little harsh.

These witty thoughts were created in retrospect of course, at the time I was quite frightened and had no clever retorts. Another name they seemed to love was that of whale shit. Whale shit of course lies at the bottom of the ocean, so nothing is lower. I can't believe these guys don't have headaches with all the straining their head goes through. I almost expected to see someone's head exploding like in the movie *Scanners*. There is a long-hair in front of me and they zero in on him. Poor sap, he should've followed my lead and gotten it cut first. I didn't know exactly what was coming during boot camp, but I knew enough to cut my freakin' hair before I showed up.

The chaos continues. I really have no idea how long this verbal assault went on. I will say it was long enough to become

81

uncomfortable. First stop, haircuts. Six chairs, there will be waiting. Thirty or so guys can fit into this room, so you can stand there and watch every one in front of you get their heads shaved. They kept yelling at us to make the line shorter. "Get your toes on his heels." Really? How are we supposed to stand with our toes on his heels? What if he has a huge ass? I can't get close enough to touch his heels with my toes. Even if I could, I don't think I'd want to stand that close to a man, especially one I haven't been formally introduced to.

The barbers are good; they can shear a head in about 60 seconds. At the foot of the chair this mound of hair started to grow, and you can see it becoming larger and larger. Weird. They told us if we had a mole or some type protuberance on our heads, we should point to it. I thought it was so they could shave around it, turns out it's so they can apply more pressure to shave it off. There were about 10 guys walking around with blood streaming down the backs of their heads. It's weird to have your head shaved. For the first two weeks you can't keep your hands off it; you just rub, rub, rub. I have never had a shaved head, and as a matter of fact, my neck and ears hadn't seen the sun in several years, and it's just not the most attractive look for a white guy. Just about any black guy in the world can shave his head and still look pretty good; even the Mexican guys looked pretty good with shaved heads. White men just look like skinheads. Not fair, but there you go.

Next stop is to make our phone call home. Thirty seconds to tell our loved ones we made it. A parent's worst nightmare is that phone call in the middle of the night. Nothing good ever comes from a phone call at 1 am. "Hi mom, it's me, I made it here ok. Hey to dad, I'll talk to you soon. Bye." There, that should make her rest easy. Now it's off to get our new clothes. Ahh, military clothing, nothing quite like it. Heavy denim, dyed green. We were issued white boxer shorts and T-shirts, a couple of pairs of green sateen uniforms and the socks, man, the socks. Green, wool socks. Comfort from heaven. There is nothing quite like a wool sock, especially in San Diego. I think if you find a survival guide to southern California, the first thing it would tell you to get is wool socks; itchy, sweaty, non-breathable wool socks. I'm almost certain that prisoners aren't issued wool socks, not to mention the fact that after several washings there's no elastic left and they just hang off your calves.

We got issued our little shaving bags of stuff, and it's off to orientation. I was actually ready for bed because now it's well after 1 a.m., but apparently we have more shit to do. By the time we get our showers and get in our racks and after a rather lengthy lesson of bed making I might add, it's close to 2:30 a.m. The process is amazingly smooth. There were a total of 290 of us in our series. A series is made up of four platoons. There are about 70 guys in each platoon. They get us dressed, initiated, shaved, checked out in just about one hour. If only all the military were run that efficiently. We're broken up into our platoons and sent to a barracks. How to describe one large room with 70 guys living in it? Hmmm. The interesting thing is the smell. Distinct. Memorable. The smell of thousands and thousands of previous recruits, all experiencing the fear. Heady.

It's pushing 3 a.m. and it's time for bed. Your heart pounds, and it's hard to sleep when you can actually see your chest moving from your heart beat. Comforting. I hope my heart doesn't explode. It's been a big day but there isn't a sound in the barracks. I grew up sharing a room with three brothers and it was noisy every night. Seventy-two guys in this room and not a peep. You just lay there for a while, a lot of things going through your mind. Mostly it's, "What have I done? Could this have been the biggest mistake of my life?" I hope not. I hope to see the sun again. I hope to see my family again. I hope I can see my friends once more. I'm not sure that I will, but I hope. It has begun.

First morning; 5 a.m., and its reveille. I'm sure most people have heard the reveille song, but it's a whole different animal when it's your alarm clock. There is no way you're going to have a nice day when reveille is what gets you up in the morning. A bugle is just not what you're looking for as a wake-up call. It's loud, brash and long. Reveille doesn't stop just because you're up; it keeps going until the record is over.

After a while you get adjusted to waking early; I started waking up right before reveille came on, and I would lay there and cuss knowing that any minute reveille was coming. "Please, please don't go off again," knowing full well it was only a matter of seconds. Just lying in your rack literally begging for anything but another day to start. How about a fire? Or an earthquake? This is southern California, why can't we have an earthquake that brings this place to its knees. Anything Lord, anything at all. Then you'd hear it, bup bup bup da bup bup bup bup da bup bup bup bup da.......

You could actually hear the p.a. system being turned on, and reveille was played on a 45 record, so you could hear the needle drop on the record and then the dust being amplified all over base. Those were the worst feelings I've ever had, lying in bed in boot camp, listening to the amplified dust, day after day. Morning after morning; catchy tune. The very first day was the worst. September 19, 1977 was the worst wake up I've ever had; the very first morning of boot camp.

I'll never forget that feeling, 0500, reveille goes off, the lights come on, there's screaming and trash cans being tossed, and I wake up and have no idea where I am. None, not a clue to my whereabouts. My first thought is, "what the fuck is all the noise about?" I look around and see all these shaved heads jumping off the racks and lining up and it hits me, I'm in boot camp. Noooooooooooooooooooooooooo! To this very day, I have never experienced a more deflating feeling than waking up and completely forgetting where I was; then realizing I'm in boot camp.

Each morning we'd line up and count off, "one sir, two sir"...until all 72 guys were accounted for. Those first couple of days we screwed up several times. I'm not sure how you screw up a count off, but we did. That didn't go over very well. This was done to ensure that nobody had run off in the night. I'm not sure where anyone would go; there didn't seem to be that many escape options. An 18-year-old with a shaved head, green pants and a gray sweatshirt with his name written across the back is going to have a hard time blending in anywhere. We were actually told that the civilians were given $200 if they turned in any runaways. The base is right next to the San Diego airport, which sucks because every night we would be lying there listening to planes taking off, knowing that there were people on them going somewhere, anywhere, it didn't matter where, they were going somewhere. There were actually people who weren't in boot camp. Oh how we envied them. We were told that one time a recruit ran on to the tarmac after jumping the fence and got hit by a plane. True? Who knows, but we believed though, we believed.

The first two weeks were spent in processing. That surprised us because we thought those guys who we first saw were our Drill Instructors. Not so, those guys were the gentle ones. Now I'm really excited! We learn how to make our bunks, shine our shoes, stand in formation and march together. Marching in formation at first seemed like a really stupid thing to do. Stand in a group and march around the parade ground. Not much of a resume booster. Mr. Sweeney, it says here you can march in formation. "Yes, sir, I can," would be my reply; "That I can do. I can do obliques and flanks and the whole nine yards."

"Well, we don't have much need here at Microsoft for a formation marcher, but if a position does come available, we will keep you on file."

Once you grasp the idea of close order drill, which is to get a group of Marine recruits to work as a unit, it doesn't seem that farfetched. Although, I've known plenty of Marines who served in Nam and WWII, and not one of them got into formation during a firefight and marched around. That strategy was phased out years ago. It's hard to believe that during the Revolutionary War, someone's "brilliant" war strategy was to line everyone up, shoulder to shoulder, forty deep and march straight into a wall of flying lead. They used some serious hunks of steel in those days. Some of those rounds were the size of a persimmons fruit; that will take some shit off a body. Marching straight in, no ducking, no hiding behind a bush, not one of those knuckleheads even laid down. The safest place to be in that battle is the BACK row; y'all can have the front row.

Just work as a unit. That's the whole key to boot camp; break you down to build you back up as one of them. The few, the proud, the Marines. Bring it on, baby. Those first few days were the worst of all, getting up at 5 a.m. and going to the chow hall in the dark. Everybody on the outside of the formation had to carry flashlights. The saddest thing you've ever seen. A bunch of young punks wearing baggy green pants, baggy sweatshirts, brand new hats, and freshly shaved heads, many with tears rolling down their cheeks, thinking only about their sweet mamas and Suzy Rottencrotch back home. Suzy Rottencrotch was they called the girls back home, as in "you're not going to be finger banging Suzy Rottencrotch anytime soon." I didn't understand that- if we're the finest fighting force on the planet, wouldn't we have the best girls? I doubt any of them would have what you would call a "rotten crotch." Suzy Rottencrotch- how do they come up with this shit? If your girl's name was Suzy, then it was all over. We used to sing songs about Suzy Rottencrotch, just a platoon of guys running along singing finger banging songs on a Tuesday morning. Any guy that had a picture of his girlfriend was forced to put it on a bulletin board called "the hog board." That way everyone in the platoon could look at the pics of guys' girlfriends. I'm not sure of the reasoning behind it either, but I knew it was not a positive thing to have your girl on the "hog board."

Being the newbies on the block, we had to eat first. It's too early to eat. It's fucking dark outside. Even animals aren't up yet, why are we?

We filed in for our first taste of Marine Corps food. It's almost robotic the way you have to stand in line for food. Eyes front, tray held out in front of you like you're deflecting incoming blows from some unknown assailant. One side step at a time. It was amazing to me how fast they got rid of our individuality. Yesterday we were all at home doing our thing, long hairs, short hairs, Blacks, Whites, Hispanics, and now we're moving through this chow line like automatons. We're all wearing the same clothes and haircuts. I'm looking around, well, not actually looking, doing more like what they call "eyeballing." That was really the only way to check things out, you don't move your head, just your eyes. God help you if you got caught "eyeballing." It was verboten, and there would hell to pay. Can you imagine that? Getting punished for looking around your new environment? It actually takes a while to get good enough so you can eyeball without being caught. It is a skill that very rarely comes in handy, but it's a skill I acquired nonetheless.

I was literally without thought on that first march to our first meal, on our first day. My mind was in a daze, all these new sounds and sights and smells. Hmmm, curious. Then, just when your mind is fading out, it hits you. The smell of the chow hall. We were ½ mile from the place when we smelled it, you could almost *feel* it. It's in the air. For those who have never experienced it, you probably never will, but those who have, will never forget it. It stays with you. Mass quantities of military-style prepared food, especially the breakfast. The heavy, slippery smell of grease. Real meaty grease type of greasiness. It hangs heavy in the air like a misty wall of canola oil. The smell of eggs, not that eggs really have a smell, but they put something in the air. Marine eggs were green. I don't know if that's intentional or not, but they were green. If I remember correctly, it was only in boot camp that they were that color. They may have even had a touch of gray to them; yeah, green/gray eggs for breakfast. Ooh rah. I've been on Naval bases and ships, as well as Air Force bases and only Marine Corps eggs are green. I was never a big egg man myself, but when I pointed and asked for an ID and he said "eggs," I knew I would probably never become and egg man.

We started with 72 guys on day one, and 32 graduated. I'm not really sure what happened to the rest of them. We had heart attack, a couple of suicide attempts, some runaways and some that just plain disappeared. Those were the strangest of them all. Sometimes we would get up in the morning and someone's rack would be empty and all their shit would be gone. Well, that's odd, what happened to Martinez? Even his sheets are gone, what the hell?

Even the firewatches never knew, or if they did they had been scared silent. Every night, there would be two guys each hour walking firewatch. I never had to do firewatch, because I was a squad leader. The four squad leaders and the guide don't have to walk the watch. We caught a lot of shit daily because of what some numb nuts in our squad did, and in exchange for getting punished for someone else's deeds, we got to sleep the night through and not get stuck on firewatch. I'll get back to the Squad leader/guide thing shortly.

So, we lost about forty guys. I don't really know if that's good or bad. Sometimes we would be in chow and see some guy that used to be in our platoon, "a runner," as they were called. He'd been recycled. The ultimate terror in boot camp, being "recycled." That means you had to start over from the beginning, doesn't matter how far you've gone, it's back to the beginning. Day 1, no questions asked. That was plenty of motivation, there's no way I'm starting over. Each day ended with Taps, which is a beautiful song. It meant that peace and quiet was here. We were being left alone for the next seven hours. Taps would play, we would say the "my rifle" prayer and then would receive a "good night ladies, now sleep." Like some kind of hypnotist, "now sleep." Hey kiss my ass, sleep on this you bastard, I says to myself.

CHAPTER 21
BOOT CAMP

During my time in boot camp I wrote letters to my folks. They kept all the letters and they are reproduced in this chapter. Remember that? People writing letters? Some people have never written a letter, but we used to, back in the old days. We wrote letters to people far away. We had phones, that line of communication was available to us; we just opted to write letters. Plus, I think that then, long-distance phone calls were about $5 a minute. At least that how it seemed. Making a long-distance phone call was a big deal. You didn't just pick up the phone and call long distance, something like that had to be planned days in advance. "We'll call on Sunday at 7, that's the plan; it will be right after supper, before everyone goes back out to play." We'd all sit around the table in a circle like they used to gather around the radio. Everyone had to be present before the call could be made, that way no one would have to be searched for when it was their turn to talk to Grandma; a search wasted precious time, and at that rate, time is money. So this is what my parents learned about boot camp and what I was doing at the time.

September 27, 1977
Dear Folks,
Today is Sunday and I just got back from church, a lot of people went because it's the only time we can sit. We get until 11 to write or just sit. We got off the plane on Wednesday and then sat on the Marine bus for 3 hours. We got on base and off the bus and right away we were running for our lives. We stood on the footprints waiting for our haircuts, and there was a lot of yelling and screaming going on. Then we got our clothes and sea bags and then stood at attention for about 20 minutes. Then we got our shaving stuff and writing things and other necessities. We finally got in our racks all shaved and showered in 10 minutes. 70 something privates in 10 minutes, we were cruising. At 5 am the lights came on and some Sgt. started yelling. We went to chow and it was more yelling, these guys swear more than anyone I've ever heard.

Friday afternoon we switched barracks and started marching drills. We had dental exams and learned how to brush our teeth. They tell you how to shower, shave, sleep, walk, talk and go to the bathroom. We have to ask permission to go the bathroom and to get a drink of water. We get three real good meals a day at 5:15, 11:00, and 5:00. We hit racks at 9:00 and are up at five, six on Sunday. Tuesday we take our medical exams and Wednesday we get our Drill Instructors. Some of the guys are already hoping they fail the medical exam so they can go home. I can't believe that, we just got here. We're in processing now, we start boot camp next week. Well, I've got to go, I've had my combat boots on since yesterday and it's time to polish them. Our Sgt. said it will take a while for us to receive mail, but I'll write again soon.
Love, Mark.

This was all during processing, of which I knew nothing about. I thought we'd get off the bus, meet our Drill Instructors and get busy. Wrong. We had to spend two weeks "un-fucking ourselves" of our civilian ways so that we had some clue when our Drill Instructors picked us up. It was just general knowledge, ranks and insignia's etc. We also learned not to use the words "I, me, or you." It was "this private" or "that private," and it took a while to get used to. The guys we had in processing told us that if we used those forbidden words with a Drill Instructor, it would be a bad day. We all went to church every Sunday. It was air-conditioned and quiet. It's amazing how many people find God in boot camp, just like in prison. It didn't matter if you were praying to your God or not. It was somewhere peaceful to go. The Drill Instructors had no authority in church, and they didn't like that so we paid for it physically.

September 27, 1977 pt.2
Dear Folks;
You're probably wondering why you're getting 2 letters at once from me. Today is Monday and I haven't been able to send my 1st one yet. Today we were told to write another letter home to say if there was a family emergency that the only way we could be reached is if you

contact the Red Cross and then they would get in touch with me. If there was an emergency I could get a leave but only if it was cleared through the Red Cross of St. Louis. All of our names have to be processed on 4 rosters so it will be awhile before I get any mail. Everything is pretty good except my ears got sunburned, they started to bleed last night and when I woke up this morning I was stuck to the pillow. It didn't hurt at first but the pillow pulled off some skin. The Sgt. gave me stuff for my ears. It comes in a little green can and is like ear wax, we're supposed to put it on top of our ears to stop sunburn. We'll see. Yesterday afternoon we saw John Wayne in THE SANDS OF IWO JIMA, it was supposed to be a motivational thing. I don't think anyone got too motivated though, there were about 400 of us sitting shoulder to shoulder in a 100* warehouse, sitting up straight with our hands on our knees for 2 hours. We just sat there and got soaked in sweat. It was all we could do to keep from wiping sweat from our faces. You can never wipe away the sweat, never. It just runs down your body and drives you nuts. Most of the guys here are looking forward to Wed. so we can get our Drill Instructor's. This processing is a drag. All we do is march and read our knowledge (Marine books). Today we took a 6 hour test, I think I did pretty well. Tonight I have firewatch from 2200-2300 which is 10-11, everything is military lingo now.

I'll write again soon.

Love, Mark

P.S. Don't ever send food, even on holidays. They said the Marine Corps chow was the best in the world and we didn't need anything else.

Getting packages was dangerous business. Food was the worst because if you didn't receive enough for everyone (no one did) you had to eat it all. You may think that would be all right, except after eating a pound of brownies if you still didn't puke, the Drill Instructors would thrash your ass until you did. So if you got anything edible in the mail, it usually meant you'd be vomiting later.

Picking up our Drill Instructors was an anxiety riddled day. You go to sleep the night before knowing tomorrow is the day. We'd seen Drill Instructors out and about, marching around with their respective platoons, but we weren't the center of their attention yet. The platoons that are marching around or getting close to graduation give you looks when they go by. They know what you're about to get into.

So we packed our trash and marched over to a different building to meet our Drill Instructors. They stood us at attention, and the Marines that have been guiding us through processing quickly disappear. They don't say anything; they just get us into position and take off like they know the bomb's about to go off and don't want to be around for the detonation. Uh oh. So we stand, and stand and stand and after about two hours, I'm start to think if these sumbitches don't come out and get us pretty soon, I'm leaving. I am about as baked as I can be. We're just standing underneath the Southern California sun and frying in our boots with pools of sweat gathering at our feet.

Then we see one of them walk by a window in the building in front of us, just a glimpse, mind you, but that's all it took for your heart to start racing in anticipation. Is that him? Is he coming? Is it time? Are we starting? Then...nothing; we stand in the sun. Another five minutes rolls by, and we stand and wait, nothing. Then we see another Marine walk by the window. Is that him? Is he coming now? Is it time? No, it's nothing; we stand in the sun. Now they wait only two minutes before another one walks by, teasing us, taunting us, then nothing; we stand in the sun. This is bullshit. Stop fucking around and let's gets this dance started, we didn't come here to stand around and be tormented. Or did we?

The anticipation is brutal. We know why we're here, they know why we're here, let's meet. Nothing; we stand in the sun. Another one walks by the window and stops in the doorway. He stares at us... it's time. We know it's time. They know it's time. The time is here, the time is now. We're ready. Are we? I think so. Maybe. Shouldn't I be? I don't know. I felt ready, now I'm not so sure. I hope I'm ready. I felt ready yesterday, now I have no idea if I'm ready. I don't think anyone knew. Does it even matter if we're ready? No, it doesn't. We stand in the sun.

Another Marine walks by the window, the door opens, and out walk our Drill Instructors. The Senior Drill Instructor comes out first and stands on the top step checking us out. Staff Sergeant Houston. Immediately your breath hitches, maybe a little gasp escapes. He is impressive. Not big, not really formidable, but impressive. He's standing on that top step with his hands on his hips, that Marine Corps uniform and the Smokey the Bear hat (campaign cover). You can tell the Senior Drill Instructor by his thick, black belt. I don't care how much of a badass you think you are, you know this guy could suck out your eye ball and pee in the empty socket while eating a cookie. He does not look like a man to be trifled with.

I think I've changed my mind. I am scared. I'm not ready. I think I'd like to go home now, please. Then the other two come out: Staff Sergeant Brice and Sergeant Sanchez. Again, impressive. Why aren't they sweating? Our uniforms are wet to the nipples and they look freshly pressed and cool as cucumbers. They just stand there and stare. We stare at the wall, and they're staring at us, just a giant stare down. Even though they're out-numbered by about 70, it seemingly doesn't matter. Trouble is a-brewing. After what seems like an eternity, they move. What do you get when you mix 72 young men right out of high school and three Marine Corps Drill Instructors? Bloody freakin' chaos, that's what you get. I thought the madness we experienced earlier was something. Now I'm in the middle of utter pandemonium; there is nothing going on but sheer panic.

They're screaming and yelling at us to grab our sea bags and start running. They don't tell us where to run, just run. Our sea bags weigh about 60 lbs., and they're awkward, un-balanced and hard to carry. Guys are falling and other guys are trampling the ones that fall, which is tripping other guys. Soon there are piles of recruits all over the place and our Drill Instructors are screaming at us to help our fallen comrades, but no one pays attention. We're just trying to get out of the way, fuck our fallen comrades (that changes later). I'm running for my life.

Dust is flying along with assholes and elbows. Help our comrades? My comrades had best get up on their own. I've got shit to do. I need to find out where we're going and get there first. If I want to remain anonymous, I need to get to the back of the squad bay. I need to be a long way from the bosses. I want to be a long way away from the hustle and bustle of everyday life, back where I can kick back and soak my feet. By the time September rolls into San Diego, it hasn't rained in ten months. Oklahoma wasn't this dirty in the Dust Bowl years. We're sucking in big lungfuls of sand and dirt and we're covered in sweat, which is forming into a lovely little paste; all-in-all, a nice comfy feeling.

Hearts are jack hammering, we're running in circles, freaking out, nobody knows where we're going, we're just running around in this huge cloud of dust. You'd be running through this cloud of dust and bam, a Drill Instructor would pop out of the sand wall and get up in your face. We never did figure out how they could see us in all that dust, but they did. Run, you motherfuckers, run. Where? Where do we run to? Does anyone here know where we're going? Anyone? Bueller? Anyone? Nobody knows where we're going. We're like a herd of wildebeests on the run from a pack of wild dogs. Nobody knows where we're going, why we're going there or how to get there. They finally corral us in the direction of our new home. We hit the squad bay running, followed by a giant cloud of sand and dirt. I'm in my new home. Maybe I'll get a nap in today, here in my new home. I always found taking a nap in new home a real nice way to feel comfortable. I go to the back, pick the last rack and stand at attention in front of it. I'm frozen, not moving, I'm invisible, no one knows I'm here. I'm a grain of sand on the beach, blending, just blending into my surroundings. I've become one with my universe. No one knows I'm here. I'm a statue. Perfect. Everyone is in front of a rack.

Something is happening up front. They are going off on some poor bastard, what an idiot, I wonder what he did? I can hear screaming and some type of disturbance about 40 yards from where I'm at. Who is in trouble? I don't know, should I look? Are you crazy? Maybe I won't look, maybe I'll just glance. Should I? No. Let that poor bastard get his; he shouldn't have fucked up. He shouldn't have drawn attention to himself. What a dumbass; he got what was coming to him. I shouldn't look. But I want to. I'm curious, one little peek, that won't hurt anything will it? I've never seen a Marine Drill Instructor going off on someone. I won't even move my head, just my eyes, just a quick peek, glance. OK, that's enough. I really couldn't see anything anyway. Whew! That was close. Uh oh, I hear footsteps, not walking footsteps, running footsteps that were purposeful and quick.

Some other dumb bastard did something to attract attention to himself, poor sap, he's going to get his. When will these fools learn? What an idiot; he should've known better. You can't mess with these guys. I realize that the screw up is near me because here comes Brice, barreling down on some unsuspecting fool. I can see him out of the corner of my eye- he's going after the guy next to me! Holy shit, I wonder what he did? I didn't see him do anything. Wow, this is really going to suck for someone. I feel bad for him. Dumbass. Then SSgt Brice stops is front of me. "What the fuck are you looking at?" he bellows, as spittle flies around my head in a mist. I know he can't be talking to me. There is no way he saw my move. He had his back to me. There is a mistake. I can't be the dumbass that brought this attention to me. It can't be! I was going to do good. It can't be me that screwed up. But yet, here he is.

We are toe to toe, nipple to nipple, nose to nose. All of his attention focused on me. He wants to know what my malfunction is. I don't know how to tell him that I just shit in my pants. I'm not sure if that's a malfunction or not. I'm new here. I do know that I need some personal time and a clean pair of shorts. He unleashes a fury of expletives directed right at me. He's going off full throat, full tilt, right in my face. I can feel the wind of his breath moving my eyebrows. I was in another world. Everything I knew about life and the world is moot. None of that shit from the real world matters anymore and won't matter for the next three months. I've got a United States Marine Corps Drill Instructor in my face, and he's pissed-off, at me. I think I was literally shaking.

How could I have brought down his wrath already? I was playing it cool, blending in, doing my thing and now my life will never be the same. He ends his tirade with the words, "I can tell I'm not going to like you, grab your trash and move up front so I can keep an eye on you." Nice job, Mark, you've managed to remain anonymous for exactly 37 seconds. I guess each Drill Instructor has his pet projects in each platoon. I just happen to be Brice's project. Yippee.

Personal time in boot camp was of short duration. We'd usually get from 2000-2100. (8 p.m. - 9 p.m.) During free time we'd shower, shave, clean our rifles, shine our boots, clean and organize anything that needed it and write letters home...all in an hour. You really had to be efficient with your duties. First off, personal hygiene. They would split us up in half. Squads 1 and 2 would "get in the land of sky blue water" which was the showers, and Squads 3 and 4 would "go scrape your face and brush your fangs" which was shaving and brushing teeth. Simple. They tried to keep it simple. Sometimes it seemed they were making it too simple. I was thinking "how dumb do they think we are?"

but after being there a week or so, you met a few guys, who you realized needed things explained to them in simple terms.

The Head (bathroom) was split into two big areas, split by a wall. Showers on the left, sinks on the right. You had two walls in the sink area with about 10 sinks on a side facing each other. We usually shaved two to a sink, which was cozy. Most of us didn't really need to shave, but we did. A large percentage of us were 18, and you only have a scraggly beard at that age, but we were told to shave, and by God, we shaved. You get to know your fellow recruits when you stand asshole to elbow with someone wrapped in a towel. I'm a white boy from the 'burbs, man. I only had known about ten black people in my whole life, and I don't think I had known that many Mexicans either, and I call them Mexicans because that's what they called themselves, but there we were, standing half naked next to each other while shaving imaginary beards and sharing a mirror.

Then came the showers. I had taken group showers once in a while in gym class or something, but not often, my friends and I, for the most part, didn't participate enough in gym activities to get sweaty. But again, white boy from the suburbs, we didn't have many different races or creeds in my schools; it was mostly young, white boys. I was unprepared for group showers with MEN. Most people are also under the impression that all black men have big penises, and it's not true. Some do, but not all. We had such a fella in our platoon, Ray Robbins, from Austin, TX. Ray had what I can only describe as a freakin' schlong. It was, without a doubt, the biggest penis I've ever seen, and I've seen hundreds.

There is, of course, an unwritten law that you don't check out another man's package, but we all do, even though we're not supposed to. But when you see one that size, you have to look, and when you do, it takes your breath away. You're first thought is, Holy shit, Ray, how do you run with that thing? Doesn't it get in the way? We better talk to Sgt. Sanchez and get you another boot, there's no way you want that thing getting damaged climbing a rope or something. That penis, my friend, belongs on a mantel somewhere; cast it in bronze and hang it from the wall, like a trophy. "What the hell is that?" Someone may ask. "That? That's my monster penis, cast in bronze, isn't it pretty?"

I think that may be the problem some people have with gays in the military. When I was in, there was never any talk of gays in the military. There were gays in the military back then, it's just that we called them "sailors." Ha. It's an old Marine joke. Being gay and taking showers with 72 naked men is like being at a smorgasbord. I mean I think; I don't know if that's how they feel. But if you compare it with a hetero man getting to take showers with 72 naked women, yikes! Nirvana. Again, I'm not sure if that's how gay men view it, but I would. I've had gay friends over the years and they're bigger horndogs than straight guys. I know, I know, it seems weird, but I've found it to be true. The group showers were quite a transition, that's my point. One day you're walking the neighborhood with your friends, hair down the middle of your back, smoking pot, drinking beer and the next day you're standing in the land of sky blue water with a room full of naked men, just trying to maintain eye contact. Culture shock indeed.

In the beginning we had hygiene inspections every night after our showers. That's right, they would inspect us to make sure we were clean! No shit, we would stand on our foot lockers at attention and when a Drill Instructor came by, you would hold your arms out at 90*, palms down and they would check you over for missed spots of dirt or grime. Like a bunch of five year-olds after taking their first bath unsupervised, we had to be inspected to be sure we still didn't have mud in our ears. It's weird, as a grown man to stand there with a Drill Instructor looking you over so closely with a flash light. Hey mofo, I know how to take a shower, back off, I may not know all my general orders yet, but I know how to bathe. I'm thinking this, of course. I never *said* a word unless requested to. You think a lot of things in boot camp that you don't actually verbalize, like everything.

This the letter parents of new recruits receive.

Dear Friends;

To meet the standards set by the Marine Corps, a recruit must undergo a rigorous military training program in which emphasis is placed on developing discipline, physical fitness, rifle marksmanship and instilling in the individual the qualities of a Marine: self-confidence, pride, determination, a sense of duty and responsibility, and a love of Corps and Country. The purpose of this letter is to provide you with the information which I hope will enable you to better understand what your recruit is now going through.

For most young men the process of changing from civilian to military life is a challenge and often even the most mature recruits do not adjust immediately. Unfortunately, many recruits arriving here have not experienced the type of discipline or strict routine found in a military organization and require several weeks before they can cope with recruit training. As a result of this stress, it is not uncommon for some recruits to become discouraged, un-happy or to attempt actions which they hope will get them out of training. A recruit may express his dissatisfaction in letters complaining about the rigid routine, discipline, or training methods used by his Drill Instructors. It has been our experience that often a recruit in this mental state will write home expressing any or all of these thoughts in exaggerated accusations concerning his experiences. Since most wives or parents are not familiar with the Marine Corps or its philosophy and methods, I can readily understand a person's concern about what his recruit may have written.

It is the policy of the Commandant of the Marine Corps that recruit training be conducted with firmness, fairness, dignity and compassion. (I always got a kick out of that phrase because it seemed so contrary to what we were experiencing) *I do not condone nor will I tolerate any treatment or training of recruits which is not authorized by our strict training regulations and the Uniform Code of Military Justice. If questions arise, or if you should become concerned for the welfare of your recruit, I urge you to write to me and a prompt reply will be made. I have also attached a letter from our Chaplain for your information.*

You may assist your recruit by writing cheerful letters frequently and asking his friends to do the same. Your support and assurance will do much to help him adjust. News from home has, throughout the years, been found to be the single most important factor in a Marine's morale.

Isn't that lovely? Your recruit is going to be under so much stress that you can't believe a single word he says. "Some recruits have never experienced the discipline or strict routine found in a military organization." Yeah, like everyone, none of us had experienced a military organization. Duh. When I read some of the letters I had sent home, I couldn't believe that they had been edited. There were whole sentences blacked out, and some had actual paragraphs cut out. Late at night someone was reading all our letters and taking an exacto knife to the parts our parents weren't supposed to know. I just picture a guy wearing one of those green plastic visors, hunched over a little table, with a goose-neck lamp, blade in hand, muttering to himself, "those little bastards, I'll show them, each time they try to send for help, I'll squash their hopes, dreams and everything else they've got going for them."

> *October 2, 1977*
> *Dear Folks;*
> *Today is Sunday, we just got done washing our clothes outside. We have to scrub them ourselves. It really stretches out the t-shirts. We scrub them with Wisk and a nylon brush on a concrete platform. Our platoon has 3 Drill Instructors, but you never call them DI's. They are SSgt Houston, SSgt Brice and Sgt. Sanchez, one guy called Brice a DI and almost got his head chewed off. We got our Drill Instructor's Wednesday night and by Thursday afternoon two guys passed out and one guy got taken off on a stretcher. Today another guy passed out and two guys got taken away on stretchers. But we're supposed to tell you not to worry. We've had guys throwing up all over the place, a lot of them are sick and everything else. I'm sure glad I got myself in shape over the summer, because I'm not hurting as much as most of them. There were seven of us who took a special test the other day, I guess we scored really well on the six hour test so they wanted to see how we did on the special test. It was to see if we're qualified for special jobs. I don't know what kind of jobs, they just said special.* (The special job turned out to be Recon school, which is Special Forces of the Marine Corps, like the Green Berets or Navy Seals. We were told that only the smartest Marines could be Recons. I didn't fall for that one though. I had no desire to graduate from boot camp only to turn around and go back to another boot camp that was

not only longer, but ten times worse. Special Forces training is way beyond what I had in store for myself. Not that I actually had anything planned, but being a trained killer wasn't in my cards. I politely turned them down and said I'll stick with my electronics job. The only guy who took the offer was the smallest guy there, about 5'7" and I guess he wanted to prove something. Adios muchacho, Godspeed, where's my volt meter?)

Yesterday we had our initial Physical Fitness Test, I scored 186 out of 200. Only 12 people failed, we take it again at the end of phase 1, our DI's said nobody fails that one, nobody. Two days ago we got our rifles, M16 A1 is what they are. They're awesome. We're supposed to name them, so I'm calling mine Roxanne. In two weeks on T-14 we go to Camp Pendleton, to the rifle range and learn how to shoot. Friday was T-1, which is training day 1, we graduate on T-78, those of us who make it. We've already lost 4 guys, I don't know where they went, but they're not here anymore. Our Drill Instructors are sweet guys, ha, they are probably the meanest, scariest people I've ever met. You can never look at them, ever. I made that mistake and ended up doing bends and thrusts, jumping jacks, sit-ups and other assorted exercises. When we come to attention in the classroom and the Drill Instructor says, "ready," we slam our chests and say "Loyalty Sir," and when he says, "seats," we say "Discipline Sir," and when he says "at ease," we say "Sir, platoon 2090 ooh-ra." Our Drill Instructor said when we scream it is to be bloodthirsty, savage and animalistic, and it is. He says their goal is to make us total blood hungry animals in 78 days. And it seems like they're succeeding, I can't believe how much noise we can make. My hair is now about 1/4 inch. They told us today that are going to be people recycled on T-14. That means they have to go back and start over. There is no way I'm going back, I'm doing what I'm told and I'm doing it as fast as I can. If all goes well, I'll be a Marine on December 16. Gotta go, I have to clean Roxy. Love, Mark

Chow was an interesting time. It was time that you basically had to yourself, but you had to be constantly on guard. It wasn't peaceful time to yourself; it was a tense "me time." If you relaxed even for a minute and let your guard down you could do something stupid. Even something like accidentally mumbling, "hmm, this is pretty good," could light off a firestorm of biblical proportions. "Who the fuck said that?" Uh oh, shit, he heard me. Then louder "Who the fuck is talking at my Marine Corps table." Damn, man, all I was doing was complimenting my delicious Marine Corps food and now I've got to pay the piper. "Sir it was Pvt. Sweeney Sir." Then he'd walk over make me stand up and he'd say those dreadful words "Sweeney, fucking begin."

That's right, everyone else is eating chow and Brice has got me in the corner thrashing my ass off while my food gets cold. Other platoons are filing past on their way out, and I'm rolling around in a pool of my own sweat and drool. I don't know what SSgt Brice had against me, but we did not become pen pals. I wasn't a screw-up either. I did everything right. I understood everything. I knew what to do and how to do it. Houston and Sanchez NEVER got on me about anything (except the Armory incident), but Brice was on my shit every day. I never figured it out; I guess he just didn't like my face. So although chow was "our" time, it didn't feel like it.

Eyes front, mouth shut, side step down the line, get your seat, sit up straight as a board, eat mechanically while some Drill Instructor walked down the middle of the table just waiting for someone to splash food or gravy, or milk or freakin' anything on their shoes, and they would lose their shit. Yelling about a drop of something "ruining my Marine Corps shoes." And then he'd kick the offending recruit's tray all over his lap. Lunch is over for you numbskull. Bummer. Everything on that base belonged to the Marine Corps, and we were reminded of it on a daily basis. "Who got mud on my Marine Corps floor" or "dirt on my Marine Corps window" or "breathing my Marine Corps air?" "Bullshit, man, the Marine Corps doesn't own the air," I once again, says to myself. Those guys really seemed to love the Marine Corps.

There were only two rules in the chow hall: eat everything you take and don't say a word. OK, seems simple enough. It wasn't. It turned out to be a problem. About the third week in, during lunch, I grabbed what I thought to be chicken fried steak, turned out to be chicken fried liver. Suffice it to say, I'm not a big liver eater. I got sloppy and it was going to cost me. I didn't even know what the hell it was at first. I took a bite and cried out "gggggkkkkkk, what the hell is that?" It's liver, dude, be cool. Liver? Uh oh, that's going to be trouble. I'm not eating that. Now I have to figure out how to sneak this into the trash can. I try to mask it as well as possible with napkins and milk cartons and silverware, and then head off to the dump station. If I hold it at just this angle, the shadows will hide it. I'll hold my arm like so, yes, it looks unnatural, but I need it to cover this angle. Stealth must be used at all costs. The last thing you want in your life is to get caught throwing food away. Dark clouds it will draw, my friends, dark clouds it will draw.

I haven't seen anyone suffer the wrath of getting caught, and I don't want to. They make a pretty strong point about it "THERE WILL BE ABSOLUTELY NO FOOD THROWN AWAY" said the big sign near the dump window. I believed them too, very adamant about it. There was always a Drill Instructor standing at the trash to make sure you didn't toss anything they deemed edible. It's made pretty clear, but apparently there's not much trust yet. As I moved down the line, he's looking right at me, and of course it's SSgt Brice, my nemesis, and I must look guilty as hell. Our eyes meet and I'm trying to play it cool; I almost nod to him in acknowledgement, as if to say, "hey, I see you and you see me," but I quickly defer that thought. Nodding to a Drill Instructor?! What the fuck was I thinking? That's a smooth move there, ex-lax. I can't imagine the tsunami of shit that would come down on your ass for doing something like that. Nodding to a Drill Instructor. The relationship between Drill Instructor and recruit is not one that involves nodding in acknowledgement. It involves only fear and trepidation. I gingerly approach the dump off. Closer, closer still, I'm almost there, I might just make it. I'm inching, I'm inching, 20 feet, getting closer, 15 feet, inching closer still, "I'm going to get away with this," 12 feet, then I sense that time has stopped. I can feel the sweat on my brow, but I can't let him see it. If I move my arm up to brush the sweat away, the napkins may move and expose my plan. I can't believe I'm this nervous about throwing away food; excuse me, I meant to say "My Marine Corps Food." It's just food after all. I mean if you consider liver to be food, which I don't. I'm now 10 feet away and my heart is beating out of my chest. I'm absolutely terrified of getting caught; now I know how Billy Hayes felt in *Midnight Express*, but I'm not smuggling hash out of Turkey, I'm just trying to throw some deep-fried liver into a trash can. Five feet, I'm actually starting to dump my tray. It's going to work. I'm getting away with it. I swear, I will never accept food if I don't know what it is. Thank you, thank you, thank you.

"Private Sweeney, come here."

Shit. I was so close. Brice walks over, lifts up my napkins, and spies the liver. Busted. How did he know? There's no way he can see my liver stash. Maybe it was previous experience with recruits, I don't know, but he knew, the mofo knew. His beady little eyes burrow into my soul and he looks like he's going to explode. I thought it was a bit of an overreaction, but again, I'm new here. He walks me outside (while still carrying my tray full of evidence) to where the rest of my platoon is lining up to head back to the squad bay and says,

"Platoon 2090, back inside."

He makes the whole platoon return to the chow hall and sits me down in the middle of the table. The rest of the platoon has circled around me. Staff Sergeant Brice is standing on the table in front of me with his feet on either side of my tray. "2090- I want you to see what happens when you try to throw away my Marine Corps chow, the best chow in all the land. Sweeney, eat." For the next 30 minutes the whole platoon has to sit there and see and hear me gagging and choking my way through 78 ounces of liver. I got it all down, but it took awhile. My milk was gone so I had no fluid to help wash it down; it was just a dry, deep-fried hunk of shit that I choked down in front of my fellow recruits. It was an unpleasant lesson for everyone. It was definitely not good times. That was my only food incident, which wasn't as bad as this dude named Randy. This poor bastard threw up every day after breakfast for two weeks. After every single breakfast for two whole weeks he would dump his tray, run outside and toss his meal. Then of course he would catch hell for wasting food, a total no win situation for him. Lunch and dinner was no problem. Breakfast? Yak city.

We had inspections on a pretty frequent basis. Anything we did got inspected, from rifle cleaning to toilet cleaning. Uniform inspections were the worst; you could never get a uniform perfect, ever. At least to the inspectors, we thought we had our shit wired, only to be torn up by the eagle eyes of SSgt Brice. "Is that pledge pin? On your uniform?" I tease, of course- that's from *Animal House*, but he always tore me up, mostly for what they called "Irish pennants," which were loose threads on your fatigues. I think they were called that because they were green and stuck out of your uniform like flags, that's all I can figure, it was never explained to us.

The uniforms were new, so there were a ton of threads coming loose and you could never get them all. You could go over it with a magnifying glass and find nothing, get into formation and Brice is all up in your shit. "Sweeney is that an Irish pennant on your sleeve?" he would ask with his nose brushing mine. "What? No. Where? No, it's not, it couldn't be, there is no way, this bitch is clean sir, no Irish pennants on this private." But there it was; the lone thread that was going to cost me, right there at the cuff, how did I miss that? You stupid motherfucker, now you've done it, you've woken the bull. At least I wasn't the only one who ended up in the pit; there were about 12 of us thrashing around in the hot sand for 20 minutes, the whole time knowing that more pennants were springing out all over like porcupine quills.

October 15, 1977
Dear Folks;
I have gotten all your letters. Today is Friday T-15 and we are sitting in the sun frying away waiting for the bus to take us to Camp Pendleton. We got our 1st check today, a whole $20 and I spent $12 at the PX for stuff I needed, as you can see, I've got new writing material. Thursday we had a drill competition, and since this is our Senior Drill Instructors last platoon, we were told it would be very painful on our bodies if we didn't win. I guess the fear of pain is a great motivator because we won. To celebrate the smokers got to have a smoke and the non-smokers got a piece of candy. I'm glad I'm a smoker, because the non-smokers have to suck a big red one. We lost a couple of more people, we're down to 55, I'm still not sure where they go, sometimes we wake up in the morning and someone's rack is empty, the sheets are gone and so is all their stuff. We also recycled three guys. Nobody has the nerve to ask where these people keep disappearing to. The other day a guy went UA, which is unauthorized absence, they caught him 1/2 hour later so now he has to go to CCP Platoon and break rocks with a 16 lb sledgehammer all day, for a month, then he has to start over. He should have just stayed. I've been appointed as the guide of the platoon, he is the head honcho of the recruits, which is good to be except if someone screws up they punish the guide and squad leaders, it doesn't seem fair. There are 4 squads in a platoon and each squad has a squad leader. Each squad leader is

responsible for everyone in his squad and the guide is responsible for everybody. Our last guide got fired because he couldn't finish a run. I thought I had a stress fracture in my foot, but turns out it's just a sprain. While I was waiting for x-rays I heard on the radio that Lynyrd Skynyrd's plane had crashed. That's too bad. I have light duty for three days and I hope I don't get fired as guide because everyone says I'm the best guide so far, and I'm the 5th one. I thought I might lose my job after the light duty, but not yet. After the rifle range we go to I.T.S. which is Infantry Training School. We learn how to fight wars, we get to play war games and shoot bazookas and rocket launchers and all kinds of cool shit. We also have to go on a 3 day force march with 50 lb packs on. We're also going to a place called Mount Mother Fucker. I'm not sure what it is yet, but all the Drill Instructor's think it's funny. They have been threatening us with it for a couple of weeks. They promise it will be torture. The other day some idiot lost his rifle and the drill instructors went ballistic. We came back to the barracks and it had been destroyed, all the racks were turned over, sheets torn off and thrown on the floor, mud, dirt, sand and all of our footlockers thrown all over and then covered in liquid laundry detergent. It looked like a bomb had gone off. They had us rolling around in all that sticky mess and we're being thrashed and it was total bedlam. It was pretty wild. Then we had to make our racks with the dirty sheets that had liquid Wisk all over them. We slept in those sticky, sandy sheets for three more days before they were washed. I think our Drill Instructors are crazy because they seem to enjoy this. A couple of guys ended up puking and then had to keep going, rolling around in their own mess. I'm glad it wasn't me. As usual we're supposed to tell you we're fine, everything is great, we're having the time of our lives. I might be able to call soon.
Love, Mark

Our trips to the PX were fun, like little shopping sprees. Again, anything to get into some air conditioning. The smokers always had to buy smokes, but we never got to keep them. We always turned them in as soon as we got back to the barracks. They usually told you what brand to buy as well, because the DI's smoked most of them. I bought 10 packs of smokes in boot camp and smoked five single cigarettes.

I've mentioned several times about guys puking. The Drill Instructors seemed to get a kick out of that. Each time someone blew lunch, they would have a subtle look of satisfaction on their faces. Thrashing is what usually caused the vomiting. When a Drill Instructor said "begin," as in "Sweeney, motherfucking begin" you would start with bends and thrusts, which was bending over, putting your hands on the ground, shoot your legs out behind you, bring them back, stand up and start over, that was "begin." From there he would shout commands like "hops" (jumping jacks) or "push-ups" or "sit ups" or "on your back, on your belly, on your feet, on your side." All done at a furious speed until you were two or three steps behind, and you were so tired you couldn't translate the commands into execution. It was madness.

That's what usually made guys puke. Running caused a lot of it too, and there was no sympathy for the pukers either; they usually caught a lot of shit for it because it slowed down the platoon. I never puked, but I did get tired enough from thrashing a couple of times where I almost said "fuck you, I'm done." Just lying there on the floor or parade deck or sand pit in a pool of sweat and tears and drying vomit thinking "I cannot do one more push-up or sit-up or pull-up or anything that makes me go up, you win, I lose, I need to leave, thanks though." But you wouldn't quit. Somehow, we would drag our asses off the ground and get back in formation. Why? I guess we just wanted to be Marines.

October 30, 1977
Dear Folks:
Today is Sunday and it's another free time. Today is T-31, only 47 days left. Time is going by pretty quick. We're out at the firing range now. Since I'm the guide, I get to be in charge of the ammo. 48,840 rounds, and if even one of them is unaccounted for, it's my ass. I'd have to be recycled. We get up a 4 am here, and it's freezing out, so I've got a cold. I hope it goes away before I have to qualify. If you don't qualify at the range, you can't move forward, and I'm not going back. No way.

Well, it's now almost a week later and I still haven't finished this letter. I qualified; as a matter of fact I was one of only 9 guys in my platoon who qualified as a rifle expert, which is the best. The first day I didn't shoot well enough to even qualify, the second day, I shot marksmen and the third day I shot expert, so I was pretty proud about doing better. Last week, I'd never fired a gun before, this week I qualified expert. I needed 216 pts. for expert and I shot a 217, close. Everyone else was either sharpshooter or marksman. I almost got fired as the guide. The guy I assigned to armory guard duty (where our weapons are stored) left his post and went to chow. Our series commander came by, saw that the armory was unsecured and our DI's got in trouble, which means I got in trouble. I'm not supposed to say anything about what happened so I'll tell you all later. Now I'm a seven day trial, if I screw up again, I'm gone. Next we go to Infantry Training School for 2 weeks, and then back to MCRD for the final weeks and Phase 3. Have a Happy Halloween, I'm sure mine will be a real humdinger.
Love, Mark

What actually happened concerning the Armory incident: I got my ass kicked. Sgt Sanchez brought me into the DI's hooch, dragged me into the head, closed the door, picked me up by the throat and gut punched me a couple of times. No place that would leave marks though. Even then they weren't allowed to physically attack us, although nobody seemed to be enforcing that particular rule. It seems that our Drill Instructors don't like being chewed out by their superiors. I mean, I didn't like it either, but I didn't have anyone I could take it out on. Lesson learned. Halloween wasn't anything special, we didn't dress up and we didn't trick or treat.

November 2, 1977
Dear Folks;
I know I've answered all your questions so far, so either you aren't getting my letters or you're not reading them. I got a letter from my recruiter the other day saying my mother would like to hear from me? I've written about

15 letters already. I got my rifle expert badge, one of the few that had actually fired expert. There were a lot of marksmen and sharpshooters, but only about nine of us made expert. Last night we were wakened at about 2 a.m. because some kid tried to kill himself. He tried to cut his wrists with a disposable razor. The Drill Instructors were pissed, they made everyone come into the classroom and showed us the proper way to cut your wrists. Apparently you have to open the plastic cover and cut from the elbow down, not across the wrists. We learn something new every day. Now we're down to about 45 guys. I can't believe that some of these guys are such pussies. I don't know what they expected, it's the Marines. We had 2 more go UA too, they caught one at the airport but they're still looking for the other guy. I hope you guys can come in for graduation.

Love, Mark

A note about the suicide attempts. It's not something that pleases the Drill Instructors. They are of the mind: If we want you dead, we'll kill you. They take it as an insult, trying to kill yourself instead of becoming a Marine. The first night it happened (there were three attempts total), they made us all sit in a circle in the classroom while the corpsmen (medical personnel) were working on the suicide attempt in the head. They showed us how to open the safety blade with a fingernail clipper, get the blade out without cutting ourselves and then how to drag the blade, along your arm, not across it. As the corpsmen were wheeling out this guy on a stretcher, you could see the blood soaking through the wraps on his wrists, and one of our Drill Instructors said, "there goes a coward, and we've got no room in the Marine Corps for cowards, now back to your racks." Not much sympathy for that particular recruit.

November 18, 1977
Dear Folks;
Well, today was T-48, 30 more to go. Today was the final day of the 3 day war. Our Drill Instructors said if Marines were in charge of wars, every war would be a 3 day war. Last night we sat in fox holes in the rain until 4 am, we were totally soaked and tired and hungry but we

got to fire blanks and flares at each other, so it was fun. We spend most of our days humping mountains, the Drill Instructors called them hills, but they were mountains. We'd hike all day, go to a class on grenades, or heavy artillery then we would hump some more. I had no idea there was this much hiking in war. We've been living off of C-rats (combat rations) for over a week, we ran out of heat tabs a couple of days ago, so all our meals are eaten cold. Cold beef, cold turkey or cold spaghetti. It doesn't really matter though, we're so tired and hungry, we'd probably eat anything. It's kind of gross though, you always have to pour a layer of grease off the top before eating. We hump all day at full speed. We learn about different types of assaults and all kinds of combat knowledge. We also finished the Death March, 3 days we humped. We hiked and hiked and I think most of us felt like quitting, it was the sorest and most tired I've ever felt. We thought we had done a great job, because we thought it was over, we're all sitting around going, we made it, we made it. Then our series commander says this is where everyone else stops. Not us though, we've got 4 more miles. We all said ooh-ra let's do it, but most of us were thinking "Fuck this." But we got up and kept going. We also lost another 5 guys, down to 40, we started with 72, I'm wondering how many will be left. I know I will be. See you next month at graduation.
    Love, Mark

    During I.T.S. we got to go to the gas chamber. What fun that was. They wanted us to experience C.S. gas so we would know what to expect if we got gassed. We went into this gas filled shed wearing our gas masks. Once we got into proper formation we would take off our masks and show that we could get them back on and cleared in just a few seconds. Then a Drill Instructor would stand in front of you, make you take off your mask again and say, "Private Sweeney wants to be a United States Marine, platoon 2090, ooh ra." Then we could leave. It seems simple but by the time I got to Pri, I was choking my ass off. It's almost impossible to say anything when you're breathing in C.S. gas. It burns your lungs and makes you cough. It burns your eyes and ears and makes you cry. You staggered through the chamber scrounging for the outside. It was worse when you get outside and the clean air hits you. Every ounce of fluid in your head leaves through your nostrils; we literally had rivers of snot hanging from our faces. Some of it may have even been the brain liquefying and leaving your skull. You can't see, you can't smell, you still can't breathe, and then some numb nuts would throw up right next to you. A lot of guys tossed lunch from the gas. Disgusting. It would take about 20 minutes before you could see again. Then you had to walk around the rest of the day with all that snot drying on your shirt. Charming.

November 23, 1977
Dear Folks;
Today was T-54, 24 more days, OOH FUCKING RA. Third phase is alright so far. Today we went over and gave blood at the Squid Hospital. Dad, sorry to hear about your cousin who joined the Navy, oh well, to each his own. We're down to about 34 guys, I don't think we'll lose anyone else, if you made it this far, you're pretty much in. Not too much new to report, all we ever talk about is leaving. Every night we lie in bed hearing the planes take off, and dream about being on one. 3 more weeks, 3 more weeks. Then it's over. I look forward to seeing you guys again. When you fly in you can see the depot on your left as you land. It has yellow buildings with red roofs. (red for blood) Tell Jimmy to keep his nose clean or I'm going crack his skull. When I get back that boy's going to be using some common sense.
Happy Thanksgiving
Love, Mark

November 27, 1977
T-59, I'm almost home, we picked up our tailored uniforms today, we can't wear them until graduation because until then we're not Marines, and only Marines can wear the uniform. We've had a blast this week, we got to use the pugil sticks. It was a lot of fun, getting out some of your aggression. I lost my first match, but in the second one he dropped his guard and I flattened him with 2 nice shots. Winners get extra ice cream at chow. We spent 2 days doing that so I had extra dessert both days. We also had our

swimming qualifications. There's 3rd class, 2nd class, 1st class and Water Survival Qualified. Out of the 200+ left in our series, me and 5 other guys are the only ones to make it to WSQ. Pretty impressive NO? Not one of the black guys in my platoon can swim. Ty told me it's because they have denser muscles, I've never heard of such a thing, but sure enough every one of them jumped off the platform and sank to the bottom. Weird. I'm scoring 190's on all my PFT's and scored in the top 5% on all my written tests. Not too shabby. For Thanksgiving we had to go the Protestant mass, the Catholics didn't have one for some reason. This will be my last letter, they told us there won't be time to write any more. Hope everything is well. I'll see you soon.
Love, Mark

My parents came out for the graduation ceremony. Later that day we went to the San Diego Zoo where I said "fuck" for the first time in front of my parents. They didn't say a word. Cool. Things have definitely changed. It was weird being back in the civilian world, and even though I was just visiting, I was much more critical of people. I thought everyone lacked discipline. I went back to St. Louis for a month on leave before heading to my first duty station in Twenty-nine Palms, CA. I never thought about duty stations and what I'd be doing after boot camp. All most of us were concerned with was getting through that three months. I pretty much thought it was over, back to the real world, but, apparently, the Marine Corps had different thoughts.

I had three years and nine months to go. Oops. Everybody back home thought I was weirded out. I did feel weird. I thought everyone was a non-hacker and civilian scum, even my friends. College was for pussies. What the hell is wrong with you people? Are you all losers? You all need a little Marine training. That will get you back on track. Get some focus in your life. I went to a party one night with some old high school buddies and I ran into a guy who used to give me a lot of shit. Well, he was just as nice as can be now. I'm thinking "this dipshit is afraid of me." I liked it. I didn't realize it at the time, but all my friends were a little freaked out by me. I actually felt a little freaked out. I didn't feel like I fit in anymore, and I liked it. I never really fit in anyway, but now it was official. Thank you, Marine Corps for making me an outsider in my own neighborhood. That changed after a while, after boot camp wore off. That mentality sticks with you for a while. It takes a couple of months for a lot of the boot camp shit to leave you. For some guys it never leaves. My buddy Sweet Lou was still wondering what to so with his life and after seeing me get through boot camp, he decided that becoming a Marine was what he wanted to do to. That was the start of him following my ass all over the globe. That was 1978 and we're still hanging out. We ended up having a couple of duty stations together, so that was cool. After 30 days at home on leave, it was off to Twenty-nine Palms. The Stumps.

CHAPTER 22
SUPER BOWL 1978

29 Palms, a.k.a. "The Stumps," was where the electronic students and tankers were stationed, and I was in electronics. I originally enlisted to fly helicopters, but my eyesight wasn't 20/20, and back then you had to have perfect vision in order to fly, so I worked on the electronics that communicated with the helicopters.

They call it "The Stumps" because there is nothing there, literally nothing. Just a base and 29 palm trees. 29 Palms was my first experience with living in a barracks with no Drill Instructors in your face. Everybody's a Marine now, and we're off to do our jobs. It was noisy though, with just about 50 or so guys living in one room. Friendly. Sweet Lou made it out of boot camp and got stationed at the Stumps as well, cool. We used to party pretty hardy in those early days and sometimes in the early, mid days and even sometimes in the early, mid, late days. Once in awhile we'd even party hardy in the mid, late, early days or the mid, early, late days. We got the job done, is what I'm saying.

One night we had been drinking and started some type of chase game, I don't know why or what, but we were chasing a guy named Don, and he bolted out of the barracks in the dark and smack dab into the open end of a metal t-shaped clothesline pole and tore his ear off. I shouldn't actually say "off." The last ½ inch of his lobe was still intact, but the rest had been shorn off. Wild shit, man. I had never seen an ear just hanging like that. Wow, this whole life will be an experience, eh? I've only been here two weeks and look at this. He ended up with more than 40 stitches, and we didn't do anymore chase games. Lesson learned. There wasn't much in the mid desert. They did have an enlisted men's club. The E club is where you could go and drink. Eighteen and we could drink, even if it was only on base. We thought we were the shit. Eighteen years old, Marines, and we could get liquor. How much better could our lives have been?

Unfortunately, the club didn't stay open the whole time I was there. The tankers and electronics people didn't get along, maybe because the tankers spent all day in a tank in 100* weather and we were in an air conditioned building. Tanks are horrible; they're claustrophobic, hot and stinky. Nice way to spend four years. One night at the E club, a fight breaks out and it turns into a rumble. It's a fight with 100 people, but it was kind of fun, just like the movies where there is a huge fight, like in *The Great Race* with Tony Curtis and Jack Lemmon, an absolute classic; tables being thrown, bottles tossed, just smacking anyone that came near you, complete and utter chaos It was a gas. The result was club closure. The closure notice on the door said something about the lack of maturity of the Marines involved, so the club was closed until further notice. No more drinking on base. Oh well, it's off to other travels.

For the Super Bowl that year, Louie, myself and a guy named Greg, decided to go into L.A. to watch the Super Bowl. We wanted to do something different, something special, something we'd remember forever; after all, it was the Super Bowl. We decided to road trip to L.A. Between the three of us, we don't know shit about L.A. We don't know the beach from Riverside from the Valley from Orange County. We didn't know where to go or where not to go, but we didn't want to watch the game in the barracks on a little black and white TV. We wanted a little space, a little room to move. We figured we would cruise into L.A., get a nice hotel room, order some room service and watch the game on a nice big color TV. Good plan. Friday was payday, and Saturday morning we left. No inkling, no visions, no sign whatsoever of what was to come.

We get our bus tickets, bum a ride into town and get on the bus to the city. The bus. I had never ridden a bus. Interesting ride. Interesting group. If you've ridden a bus, you know from where I speak. It's an unusual ride. Just about anyone can afford a bus ticket. I mean, why else would someone pay for a ride that takes twelve hours to go 200 miles? The trip from 29 Palms to L.A. was about 80 miles and it took us four hours. We were making stops in the middle of the desert. Someone would just say "Stop here," and Paco would get off the bus. Apparently, he and his brother ran a fruit stand somewhere in the area. There was an older couple in back that were very dirty. I don't mean they swore a lot, I mean they were covered in dirt. Strange. I don't if they were homeless or what, but we gave them a couple of bucks anyway. We had no real plans- we were just going with the wind. As soon as the bus stops in the city, we get off.

Where are we? East L.A. is where we're at. For those of you unfamiliar with Los Angeles, East L.A. is predominately black and Hispanic. Not many white people at the time living in East L.A. We disembark, and our journey has begun. Off we go looking for our hotel. The three of us, waltzing down the street, white as can be, wearing Marine Corps t-shirts. Louie had a high and tight, which is like a mohawk, but wider across the top, and I'm sporting a mohawk, for the one and only time. I actually was written up on a charge sheet for having a non-regulation haircut. Greg has your regulation Marine Corps cut.

I imagine we cut quite a picture, the three of us wandering the streets of East L.A., clueless as hell with our lily white skin and red and yellow shirts, carrying our sea bags on our shoulders. Idiots. We're looking for a Hilton, or a Holiday Inn, or even a Howard Johnson's, but we get nothing of the sort. There's nothing remotely resembling a hotel like that around the bus station in East L.A. No sir. We end up at this place about three blocks from the bus station. I call it a place because it wasn't a hotel per se, it was more of a flophouse/dive of death kind of thing. But at eighteen and right out of Marine Boot Camp, we were about as invincible as we could be. We check into this place, and it's $20 for the three of us. That probably should have been a red flag.

We get a room on the fifth floor of a five-story building with a broken elevator. As we're hauling our shit up the stairs we notice that the higher we climb, the rattier it's getting. The condition of the stairs was deteriorating with each step, and the variety and intensity of the odors were increasing. By the time we hit the top, we should've seen the next red flag. The carpeting in the hall is all torn up, the wall paper is hanging in shreds on parts of the wall, and then Louie points out something on the wall that appears to be a rather large blood stain. Hmm. I wonder why there are blood stains on the wall? Shouldn't they be on the floor? Might there have been some kind of trouble? Some kind of tussle perhaps? A couple of guys rough housing maybe? Playing a little slap and tickle that got out of hand?

We also found what appeared to be bullet holes. No shit, bullet holes in the wall and in the trim around one of the doors. Wow, this place has some character. Oh well, not to worry. Our door opens onto a tiny little room with one bed, one dresser, a desk, or at least it resembled a desk, two chairs, a six-inch television bolted to the dresser and a bathroom, and it became understandable why it was $20. We decide to make the best of it and have a good time; it's Saturday afternoon, we decided to go out exploring.

Now we're back on the streets, wandering around east L.A. without a clue. We stroll into this little tavern, which is exactly like you would imagine a tavern in East L.A. may look like, or any city tavern in the country. It's dark, dank and dismal even on the brightest days. Inside a tavern, you don't know day from night, night from day. We go in. There was a long bar on the left, smudgy smoke-smeared windows, so thick with dust that no sunlight could filter through, 15 shitty little tables scattered along the right. There's one pool table in the back and one old black man sitting at the bar and another behind it. We went in and belly up to the bar. We do some shots, drink some beers and smoke our cigarettes. After a while the old guy at the end calls out, "hey, Marines." I don't know how he knew. Maybe he used to be a detective. We go down to chat. Rufus Murphy was his name. I'll never forget this guy. I don't know if Rufus Murphy was his real name, but that's the nome de plume he laid on us. Rufus was in his seventies, where in his seventies he didn't say, but that was our guess. He was wearing a black fedora with a red feather in the band, he had on a red sport coat over matching black pants and t-shirt, along with a red pair of what I would call "Beatle boots." Rufus was in the Navy years ago and lived in the neighborhood.

We do some more shots and drink some more beers and are having a great time with our new friend Rufus. We're telling stories, he's telling stories, we love this guy and he loves us. We do another shot in celebration of our new friendship. As the sun was setting on our afternoon, Rufus asks us if we'd like to meet some girls. Well that's a silly question. Yes, my new friend Rufus, we would like to meet some girls. If you know any girls, by God, bring them out. He asks where we're staying, we tell him and he goes to the back to use the phone. He returns shortly with good news, the girls are going to meet us at our "hotel." Things are looking promising; we are set to have a rip-snorting Saturday night in East L.A. Go get 'em, tiger.

We stop at the liquor store to stock up on libations. We got two cases of Bud, a bottle of Jack, one of Wild Turkey, one of Southern Comfort and a bottle of Canadian Mist for Rufus. It's his favorite, and nothing is too good for our new friend Rufus. In retrospect, we may have over purchased. There we are, the three Marine boots, our new friend Rufus and enough liquor to throw an Oscar party, waltzing down the street. We arrive at the hotel and there are the girls, two Latina lovelies and a black chick with red hair. No shit, red hair. All of them dressed rather sassily. Oh yes sir, We's gonna have a good time tonight, oh yes we is.

Into the hotel we go, and up the stairs with our little entourage. Nobody mentions the conditions of the stairs or the hallway, another red flag missed by the clueless brigade. Good thing we weren't on a mission of some sort, with the observational skills we're displaying, we'd all be dead. Not one of these girls said, "nice place," or "what's that smell," or "are those bloodstains?" We're just bounding up the stairs with our little group. I think, actually, we were bounding, the way that only youthful exuberance can bound. Once inside the room, we spread out, get situated and start partying. We're doing shots of Turkey, Jack, chugging beers and passing joints. It is quite the festive atmosphere. It's definitely good times. We're about to have an orgy. Oh, I'd heard about them, read about them in Penthouse, but experience one? Never. Of course at eighteen, what have you experienced? Getting a driver's license? Graduating high school? We're getting fucked up and then getting laid. How can life get any better?

The last thing I remember is doing a shot of Wild Turkey and slamming my glass down. I woke up on the bed with absolutely no idea where I was. Every drinker has had one or two or however many times like that, when you wake up and it takes you awhile to figure out where the hell you are. I've had a few where I had to walk around for ten minutes, finally ending up outside to get a look at the house and see if that jogged any memories. That's not too good.

I wake up on Super Bowl Sunday and have no idea where I am. I arise from the bed and realize I'm down to just my skivvies. That's odd; I don't remember getting undressed. Then I realize that the door to the room is wide open; hmm, now that's not a very secure way to sleep in a hotel. That's when I see feet, the feet of someone laying in the hall. I'll be darned if it's not Sweet Lou, and he's down to just his skivvies as well, and he's passed out in the hall. Sound asleep on a floor that I didn't like walking on when I was wearing shoes. Not to mention, he's sleeping like a baby. What hell is going on here? I'm a little pissed off I missed the party, and where is Greg? I go in to use the bathroom only to find Greg asleep in the tub, again, wearing nothing but his skivvies.

Man, this is bullshit. I passed out and didn't get laid; shit. As we roust, I'm standing in the doorway looking around the room trying to figure out what's different. Something seems a little off, I'm not sure what it is, but there's something different in here today than last night. Oh, that's it. All of our shit is gone. And I mean all of it. Rufus and those chicks ripped us off! But, but, they were our friends! Our wallets, our sea bags, the boom box, all the tapes, every watch, ring, nickel, dime, every piece of clothing; they even took the rest of liquor and pot. Everything. Well, everything it seems but our bus tickets back to Twenty-nine Palms. Those they left us. They left them neatly laid out on the dresser, side by side. I realized later how poignant that was, "we took your shit, now go back home."

Well, we have no money for food, no clothes to wear home, and no liquor to drink or pot to smoke, so we might as well head home. Louie is pissed; he wants to go looking for them. To do what, I don't know. Beat up a guy in his seventies and try to track down a hooker at 7 a.m. on a Sunday? I reminded him that we're wearing nothing but our underwear and it would probably be best if we just went back to the base. Now the three of us start walking to bus the station in nothing but our skivvies. Oh, we drew some attention. Nothing serious. It seemed like everyone was in on it. It was almost like they all knew what had happened.

We get to the bus station and the bus driver doesn't want to let us on without being properly dressed. After we told him our tale, he let us on; he actually seemed to be entertained by our story. Big surprise, we didn't stick out on the bus. We rode back into the Stumps without a word. Not much to say really. We got as far as the front gate but couldn't get back on base with no ID, so they had to call our C.O, (Commanding Officer) at home to come to base and vouch for us, and that didn't go well. By the time we got back to the barracks, the game was just ending. What a great game; we didn't see a play. Boy oh boy did we raise some questions. We never told anyone what happened. How can we tell anybody that three young strapping Marines were rolled by an old man and three girls? Somewhere, those four were laughing their asses off. Dumb ass Marines, standing over our passed out bodies, filling their pockets with goodies. No sir, nobody in that unit ever found out what happened on Super Bowl Sunday 1978. Good stuff, Good times.

CHAPTER 23
BARS AND BROTHELS

Socrates once said, "Without prostitution, man would be at constant war." You know something? I believe him. Granted, most people wouldn't consider being with a prostitute "lovin," but nonetheless. A man's pressure release valve is his penis. All his problems, all his tensions, all his worries leave his body during an orgasm. They come back eventually, of course, but the procedure just has to be repeated. It's not wrong or right, it just is. Prostitution has been around as long as mankind has been. It's always been a part of society. During the Olympics in Greece, there was a 70% increase in applications for a brothel license. Those darn Greeks, they love to hold on to tradition. The first brothel was actually in Greece. It was opened in 600 B.C. That was a long time ago, my friends. It was even legal in the States until about 1915 when the women from the Women's Christian Temperance Union decided that drinking, smoking, doing drugs and getting laid were "bad" and fought like hell to get them banned. Sounds like an uptight group of ladies to me.

I don't even know why prostitution is illegal. I won't go so far as to say it's a "victimless" crime, but it's a consensual one. A hooker's life isn't a pretty one, but if legalized, it would get better. Those girls who work in Nevada have insurance plans, retirement plans and can make $300,000 a year, at least according to the show *Cathouse* on HBO, and that's where I'm getting that information from. You can have sex with your wife or girlfriend, give her $100 for whatever and nobody thinks twice. Give money to a woman on the street, and you're busted and headed up the river to be gang raped by white supremacists. What the hell? Being with a hooker is a little weird. It's not something you do in the 'burbs. You know about hookers, but you've never seen one. You've heard the stories, you know the legends, you've read things. But in real life, face to face with a real live prostitute is surreal. You can't believe you're standing there with a woman who is going to have sex with you for money. Is this a great country or what? Oops, I'm in Mexico...Oh hell, it's still a great country. If a man has been in the military and is single, most likely, he's been with a hooker. Not everyone did, but almost everyone I knew did. It was just something to do on the weekend. A little drinking, a little whoring, a little fun.

My actual first time was in Tijuana. What a toddling town, that TJ. If you're looking for anything, you can find it there. It's a little scary the first time you go. There's a lot of activity. There are a lot of people. It's fast, noisy, dirty, wet, dry, hot, sticky, smelly, overwhelming and scary, I mean, boo man. But you have to go; as an 18-year-old, you have to go to TJ. You can drink in TJ. Did I mention the bars? Hundreds of them, all over the place. Hookers and bars. Nirvana to some, Hell to others. To us, just a weekend getaway from the base. Believe it or not, I wasn't down on prostitutes, even though my first encounter with one was the Super Bowl weekend fiasco in L.A. I figured they can't all be bad. Louie and I decided to give them another try.

The bars and brothels were different entities; the brothels had bars, but the bars weren't necessarily brothels. Once you decide you're "ready" you head inside. You order a drink and the girls walk around. I use the term "girls" loosely, very loosely. None of them had been girls for quite some time. Those women hadn't been "girls" since before I was born. I guess if you're hot, you wouldn't be turning tricks in some dive in Tijuana. So you make your pick, and if I remember correctly, it took us an hour; I think we kept waiting for the better ones, like they were holding out on us or something, like there was a secret stash of hotties, but they were being saved for the high rollers. If we just wait a little longer there will be better ones coming out. Turns out, there were no "better" ones. This is it, this is our pick.

A group hookers in their forties on a Saturday afternoon in some hell hole in Tijuana. Does life get any sweeter? That's my question to you. Let's do this. By the time we decide on our pick, we're trashed; it's already been a long day. Mine was at least 40, had to be, maybe older. She led me to one of the back rooms. There was a hallway in the back, just to the right of the bar. This hallway led to the inner sanctum, the pleasure palace, Nirvana, if indeed Nirvana can be found in a seedy, dumpy little bar in TJ. We head down the hall, again dingy. What is it with all these dingy hallways I've walked down lately? Can't I find a hobby or something that doesn't require a walk down a badly lit, weirdly smelling hallway? Is that too much to ask? Yes, apparently, is the answer. I remember the heavy red fabric lining the wall and many bead strings being used as walls and/or decoration.

She leads me into the room, and it looks lived in, so maybe she crashes here as well as works here. The headboard is also made of beads. There must be many bead makers in this part of the world. The

bedspread is a patchwork quilt that is strangely calming. She begins to
undress me, and she was just wearing this robe-type thing, so it was
easy for me to remove, thank goodness. She doesn't speak English very
well, but I don't think I cared. I don't know what I would've talked to
her about anyway; I didn't see that we had much in common. "Hey,
some weather we're having, eh?"

Or "What are your likes and dislikes?"

Or, "Do you come here often?" no pun intended. She strips us both
and drags us down on the bed. Then I have a thought; I'm going to
impress this 40-year-old Mexican hooker, yes, sir, I'm going to get her
off.

You heard me; I was going to get this chick off. She always does
the pleasing, and now it's time someone pleased her. Keep in mind of
course, I'm 18, I don't know shit about how to please a woman yet.
Still, I'm going to take all my love-making knowledge and put it to
work on this woman, this goddess, this voluptuous temptress, this
whore. I figured I would go down on her. WHAT... did you just say?
Yes, my plan was to go down on her. I don't how drunk you have to be
to want to go down on some old Mexican hooker, but apparently I had
reached that point. To think of it now, it boggles the mind. Going down
on a hooker. Who would've thunk it? That's depraved, outrageous, sick,
twisted. And yet...

Was I actually going to do that? Yes, by God I was. I'm the master
love maker. I am the king. I am a great lover. I am a man amongst
mens, to quote Muddy Waters. I am what this woman has been waiting
for: someone to please her, like man should please a woman. I will
bring her to the edge of ecstasy, but just for a moment, bring her down
and then back to the top, just play and please her all afternoon. Oh
yeah, I'm going to get her off in a big way. Fortunately, she wasn't
having any of it. She stopped me cold, grabbed me by the ears, pulled
me up and put me in. She tossed me around for a couple of minutes,
finished me, wiped me off, and sent me on my way. The total
professional. She was too good, too experienced, too caring to let a
young Marine lose his way. She could have said yes, yes to a life of love,
a life of sexual experimentation, of wild, untamed passion. A life of
dirt and heat in the desert, a life of sharing a tin shack with no
plumbing on the outskirts of Tijuana, but no, it was not to be. Fare thee
well, my sweet maiden until I return. I will get by on your scent which

will forever linger in my memory. I will be back. No matter what happens, I will return, I will find you. I never saw her again.

Most of the Mexican brothels were the same. Same look, same smell, same hookers. I don't know how that was possible, maybe they had a tour bus and were one step ahead of us on the road. We had us some fun in TJ, Nogales, Ciudad Juarez and Matamoros. Matamoros, Mexico, wow. It's just on the border of Brownsville, Texas. Brownsville is aptly named. I've been in some dismal places in my time, but Brownsville was brutal. Dry and dirty, that's how I remember it. If you're from Brownsville, or know anyone who is, my apologies, but come on. Its only purpose is a place to get supplies before heading out to Padre Island. Matamoros is on the Mexican side. People leave Brownsville to go to Matamoros, it's further south so they have a better breeze; oh yeah, it comes off the Rio Grande River, which by the way, is some kind of majestic. Well, maybe not majestic, maybe muddy, slow and ugly. It looks like people have been crossing that thing with all their possessions for decades. I didn't see one jet ski. Not one boat filled with mom, dad and the kids slathered in sunscreen heading out for a day of water fun on the Rio Grande, tubing and having picnics on a "river island." I guess if the water is shallow enough to walk across, it's probably too shallow to water ski. Not to mention the fact you'd be dodging people hoofing across the border all day long.

Matamoros is where those college kids disappeared and were found buried in a field somewhere after being kidnapped by some satanic cult. Oh, it's a toddling town. My impression of Matamoros was that it was a good place to get murdered. Maybe we should go over with a wallet full of money, get drunk and find some hookers. What could happen? Turns out, if you leave before sundown, things are cool. After dark is what my dad called "the time when the crazies come out," and he was right about that. You had to travel in a pack, had to. There were guys who didn't, but they learned their lesson. Groups of at least four, five preferably, that way almost nobody would fuck with you. Still, the nighttime was scary. Lots of alleys with weird noises coming out, that kind of shit. But I digress.

Our year at the Stumps came to a close. Sweet Lou got sent to Cuba and I was off to Okinawa. I don't know if they split us up intentionally, but we had to go our separate ways for a year, we met up again in Cherry Point, so no worries. I just couldn't shake that boy. Okinawa, Oh boy. The Rock. Oki. Trouble. Forty Marines living in one barracks. Okinawa ended up being one of those places where if you ran into a buddy from there years later, and he said something like, "remember that time we...," you would have to stop him and say, "sssh, man my wife doesn't know about any of that."

Okinawa, Japan. Wow. What a year. Sept '78- Sept '79. I turned 19 that year. We had some fun. I've covered some of the drinking escapades in another chapter, so let's talk about BC street. BC street was lined with bars and brothels. Seems to be a common thread. Bars and brothels. Brothels and bars. Drinking and whoring, whoring and drinking. BC street was a weekly thing, we didn't often go during the week because you never came home "early" from BC street. If I remember correctly, the honchos quit running at midnight. The honchos were the cab drivers. I don't know why they were called honchos, but if you said, "hubba, hubba honcho;" that sumbitch would take off, and race to your destination, scaring the shit out of you the entire trip. If you missed the honchos, it was a long walk back to base. Something like four or five miles. While that may not seem too long, try it at 2 a.m. after a night of drinking.

My buddy Mikey and I had to walk home one night. We came to the conclusion that if we went to the back gate of the base we could save some time. The problem is that, of course, the back gate is locked. We decide to climb over it; can you imagine such a thing? Two drunk, dumbass Marines trying to climb over the fence of a military installation at three in the morning. Seems to me like a good way to get shot. We did tear our pants up pretty good climbing over the concertina wire, but we saved 30 minutes. What's a little blood if you can save that kind of time? Apparently security wasn't as much of an issue then. We just climbed over the back fence and got on base.

BC street was like a wild west town. You could get anything on BC street. Anything your young heart desired. They had a little black market thing going on, and they loved American stuff: cigarettes, whiskey, whatever, and they would trade for it. What would they trade? Well...the pharmacies in town sold things over the counter that aren't sold over the counter in the U.S. Little pills and whatnot that were rather tasty. Nothing too radical, some ups, some downs, just pleasant things. No hallucination generating meds, but fun stuff. U.S. Military personnel weren't allowed in the pharmacies in town. Hmmm. I wonder why? If we traded them Marlboros or Jack Daniel's, they would give us the blue pills and we'd all go off and have our parties. Very amicable. I wish that's how our leaders would deal with each other today. Give them some of our good shit, they give us some of their good shit, and we all sit down and have a good time. Lots of laughing. Wouldn't that be great? Our leaders, Iraq's leaders and the leaders of every other country that has issues, sitting down in the desert at night, drink some wine, eat some mushrooms and talk about the stupid shit that we're all doing. Anywho... we'd trade and party. It was all so very innocent, but I'm glad the general public didn't know.

There was a bar on BC street called Sgt. Peppers, and they served a drink called a "purple haze." I can't remember what was in it, but you could only drink two of them; well you *could* drink more, but it wasn't advisable. Unfortunately, that is one of those lessons you learn the hard way, like many of life's lessons. Another lesson learned the hard way? Don't get drunk on sake. Oh you can drink it, but don't make it all you drink. It's like walking around with a belly full of nitro. Nitro doesn't mix well with many things like, for example, a full load of Okinawan buffet.

It was my first meal on the town, I was with a bunch of guys that had been on the rock for awhile, so they did the ordering. Needless to say, as a picky eater, nothing looked appetizing, or even edible for that matter. I couldn't identify anything. From what I understood from my brethren, I didn't want any I.D. We ate and ate and drank sake and then more sake, no beers, no waters, just sake. Well, that went fine for the early part of the evening and even into the later evening; actually everything went well until about an hour after I fell asleep. I woke up and knew something was wrong. For one thing, I didn't know where I was; I had only been in the barracks for three days and had no idea where the hell I was. Freaky feeling, surreal, disorienting, terrifying. Then I realize that my dinner feast wants out, and it wants out now. I bolt out of bed and run to the bathroom, but being new, I ran the wrong way, and I don't mean I ran knock-kneed or like a spaz or anything, I mean I ran the wrong direction and ended up on the second floor fire escape. Not exactly the place I was looking for. With no other options, I let it fly over the railing. It took me ten minutes to finish; nice job Marine, hanging over the railing with drool and puke running down my face and out of my nose. Welcome to the rock, newbie.

You almost had to be with a hooker in Oki. Living in a barracks with 40 other Marines really limits the time you can take care of your personal, private business. There's no privacy. You can't take care of business in the shower; it's an open place, and if you get caught jacking off in the shower, there will be hell to pay. It's an unspoken rule. We all have to shower in here, so don't whack it in here. It's just not done. This isn't prison. You can't do it in your rack because there are people walking around all the time. Plus, you're in a bunk bed and there's someone above or below you. If you're in bed and the guy above or below you starts shaking the rack, you have to go, "hey, dude, I'm still awake up here." So you have to go out and get laid. If you can find an 18-year-old male that can go a year without ejaculating, I'd like to meet him. Well maybe not; he would be one messed up cat. I don't think I would want to be anywhere near a guy who hasn't ejaculated in over a year. Talk about a dangerous, explosive situation. So, it's go to a hooker or spend the year with blue balls. Big ole blue balls banging around between your legs like a couple of grapefruits. You can't run, walk or do anything properly. It's almost a necessity that you visit a hooker simply to survive, for your health, for your sanity.

You didn't have to look hard to get laid. The girls would usually stand out front and solicit. "Come on, Joe, $10 for a short time, $20 and me love you long time." They always called us "Joe." I guess it's from WWII where everyone in the military was called Joe. Ten dollars to get laid, now that's a bargain. You won't find a deal like that at Wal-Mart. You could get laid for $5 if you were a cherry. A cherry being someone whose never been with a hooker. The girls loved that, getting their hands on a cherry, and we even had a couple of guys that were virgins. I don't know about losing your cherry to a hooker, but it worked for some. Most guys want to remember their first time with a certain fondness, either for the girl or the moment. Losing your cherry in Okinawa would leave a different kind of memory; a memory deeply clouded, a memory of nervous, drunken fumblings on a threadbare mattress sprawled on a shaky cot in a seedy room in the back of a dilapidated building at the far dark end of a dismal alleyway, just lying there while some little Asian hooker squeals delightfully as she bounces up and down on you. Good times, damn good times.

I've never done the hooker thing in this country. Well, there was the one time in East L.A., but we all know how that ended up. In 1980 we headed to Norway. We were doing this fake war thing with the Norwegians. Team Spirit '80 was what is was called. The military love coming up with names for things, like "Operation American Eagle," or

"Operation Enduring Freedom," or "Operation Iraqi Freedom." I bet the military calls medical procedures "Operation Operation."

"Hey, who's supposed to take out this trash?"

"Me, Sarge, I'm in charge of Operation Dumpster Run."

We spent two weeks on the ship going over. The U.S.S Saginaw. It was a tank carrier, so it had a flat bottom. We were warned about the flat bottom, but we didn't care. Flat bottom, round bottom, what the hell's the difference? Well, the difference my dear boy is negligible...in calm water. In calm water the bottom doesn't make much difference, but in stormy weather it's a whole different ride.

Out of the two week trip over, five days of it were spent in a storm. Not a spring shower, a North Atlantic Ocean Storm. It was a NAOS. That's what it was. That's not an official name. I came up with all on my own. That's something, eh? Close to 80% of the guys on the ship were sick, the sailors too. It was unbelievable. They issued us these little plastic bags to clip onto your belt so you had something to throw up in. It's an odd thing seeing someone realize they're about to lose lunch. You can see it in their face, that recognition that something bad is about to happen, the deep breath taken, the look of disillusionment that crawls across their features, the dropping of the lower lip, the glassy eyes, the little sliver of drool, the knowledge that whatever is down in their tummy is starting to travel. You see that look on their face and bam, they're gone, off on a race to the toilet, bobbing and weaving around obstacles and people, plastic bag in hand flapping in the breeze, there as a back-up "just in case."

I never actually threw up, but I didn't feel very good. I felt nauseous the entire time, five days walking around feeling like I need to puke. Cool. It is a constant swaying motion 24 hours a day for five days. You could barely travel through the ship. Everything you do is done like you're on a balance ball and people are trying to knock you off. Eating was fun, what you could eat. You had to eat one handed because your other hand was holding on to your drink and your arm was holding down your tray. Jello and crackers were the biggest meal I kept down. It's hard to eat when you're riding the swells of a North Atlantic storm. You kept your eyes focused on your food. If you looked up and saw all that movement it sent off a queasy attack. The only time your stomach settled was in the rack.

We slept on what were basically hammocks. The rooms we slept in were cozy, to say the least. It was about fifteen feet long and eight feet wide. Fifteen us were in there. Snug, tight, confining, claustrophobic. Like a thong on a fat European guy with hairy shoulders. We slept three tall, stacked up like cordwood lining the walls three high and about three feet wide. Two weeks we slept in that room on the way in and three weeks on the way back. I didn't spend much time there. I volunteered for a job on the signal bridge; it's on the top of the ship, and it's outside and has a great view. It does move a lot, but still, it's the best place to be. I couldn't believe how cramped it was below decks. I could never be on a ship full-time. The thought of being on a submarine gives me the night sweats. I think that's why I'll never be buried; I'm too claustrophobic. If you aren't friends with your bunkies when you start, you'll be so at the end. Either that, or you're on trial for their murders.

Norway was fun. We didn't really do much. Most of it was spent in a muddy field, living in a tent with a wooden floor, and it was cold, wet and overcast for two weeks. We had two days of liberty, and we walked around Hammerfest. Most of the people in Norway don't speak English. How rude. All we really did was drink and eat reindeer. It was quite tasty. If you entered a drinking establishment with a black guy, you got extra attention. There aren't many blacks in Norway, and I don't think there were any in Hammerfest, which is one of the northernmost cities in the world. When you entered with a black guy, people were curious; it was odd. I'm sure they'd seen black people on TV, hadn't they? Why all the fuss? But all the girls approached right away.

I was with my buddy Bobby, who wasn't just black, he was really black, the blackest guy I've ever known. He referred to himself as "African Black." He giggled a lot, and I haven't known many men who giggled, but Bobby did, and the girls liked it. They kept touching his face and hands. They were enthralled. Two days in Hammerfest was plenty. Time to head to Germany. After the war games were over we made some European stops on the way home, as a treat I guess. We went to Scotland and saw Loch Ness. It was cold and rainy. We never saw Nessie. Totally bogus. Of course, when you find out people have spent 30 years looking for her every day, the fact that we didn't see her during our 15 minute visit, shouldn't upset. That was about all we stayed. After a while, there's not much to do but look at the water. Hell, I've seen water, and it's getting cold, so let's head back to the ship. We wanted to stop in Amsterdam, but they wouldn't let us. Drugs and prostitution are legal. I wonder why we couldn't go? Next stop: Germany.

Our stop is Germany was about four days, if I remember. We stayed in the port in Hamburg, Germany. Oddly enough, the blocks surrounding the port were full of bars and brothels. Again, with the bars and brothels, like soup and nuts. I don't know why soup and nuts go together, I never got that one. I've had soup in my life, and not once have I put nuts in it. The brothels in Germany were different than in Japan. For the most part they were like underground parking garages. You would walk down the ramp and it opened up to a huge area with girls walking around. They were all dressed up in their sexy, revealing, whore outfits. Yummy. You could just walk around, find one you wanted and take her to one of the rooms lining the far wall. I picked this brunette with dominatrix clothes; I'm not into being dominated, but it's a great look. We go into this room and get down to business, and I finish but just keep going, I tried to hide the fact I was finished. Remember those days? When you could come and just keep going? Yowza. During a position shift, she checked the condom and says, "oh, you're finished." What the hell, shouldn't I be able to continue? Apparently not; you get your one shot and then it's off to party. We spent four days in Hamburg and never got further away from the ship than three blocks. I'm sure Hamburg and the surrounding areas are beautiful, but we didn't see any of it. Stupid, yes, but we were busy drinking and whoring. A young man must do what a young man does. I can see architecture in books.

It's not easy for a man to become a hooker. I wish it were. If it were as easy for a man to make money turning tricks as it is for a woman, every man I know would be out hustling on the weekends.

"Where are you going?"

"I'm off to work."

"But it's Friday night."

"I know, honey, but if you want to go to Jamaica this year, I need to make some extra cash. I'll be back late."

I think the problem with a man becoming a hooker is that we're so horny, we'd end up being cheap hookers. We would be banging away in the back of the minivan for $10 a pop. It's hard to make a lot of money $10 at a time. Not that we wouldn't try hard, but it would be slow going. We may have to even work on Sunday. Men as hookers, only in Nirvana.

CHAPTER 24
STRIP CLUBS AND SUCH

I've been to a few strip clubs in my life. Some have been nice. Some haven't been so nice. They are bizarre things, these strip clubs. It's not really an odd concept, women dancing for men; it's been going on for thousands of years. Some people don't like strip clubs, some do. Men just love titties; that's the way it is. Many days it's the only thing that gets us out of bed; the chance to see some titties today. That's what was truly amazing about the whole Janet Jackson fiasco. 300,000 people picked up the phone and called the FCC to complain that she had flashed her breast at the halftime show of the Super Bowl one year. They actually picked up the phone and made the call. I wonder what kind of priorities someone like that has in their life. I wonder if they've ever watched television. It's nothing but murder, violence and sexual situations with adult themes, and that doesn't seem to bother them; it's all ok. Then flash a titty at a football game and they lose their minds. "Titties?! I'm outraged," was their battle cry.

Outrage, oh it's very popular these days. People don't just get pissed off anymore; they have to be "outraged." One viewer was quoted as saying, "I was offended by this breast flashing and my children were traumatized." Don't you just want to give them a good slap? First of all, if your child was *traumatized* by a female breast, he's a freakin' moron and you should have him put down because he's never going to make it in the real world. Secondly, if your children have been brought up to be traumatized by the human body, then shame on you for being a shitty parent; maybe you should be put down for being an uptight douchebag. Jesus, get a clue; it was a titty, not a public decapitation. Kids see murders everywhere and on everything today. The average child sees 20,000 murders on TV by the time they reach 18 and the news is nothing but real-life violence and death. They're downstairs right now playing video games where they're buying drugs, picking up scantily dressed hookers and shooting policeman. I seriously doubt that the titties are going to push them over the edge.

Back to where we were. Strip clubs are harmless. A man watching titties; big deal. There are other fish to fry. I understand if you don't want a strip club across the street from the school, cool, but keeping it out of the town? A bit extreme. Strip clubs have such a bad rap, which is wrong; they're not all drug dens and places that degenerates hang out. First of all, degenerates can't afford to go to titty bars- only a certain class of people can and will pay $8 for a bottle of beer and a $10 cover charge. See, strip clubs are visited by people with jobs, contributors to society. They just want a peek at some naked girls. Anyway...strip clubs. Nice ones and icky ones. Let's cover some of those, because I've been in both.

I do believe I've covered, or will cover some of my excursions into Mexico, so I won't replay them here. What I haven't told you about are some of the clubs in the Far East. Japan, Korea, Thailand, The Philippines. A year in Asia. A strange and frightening world. Even the name...Asia. Seems far away doesn't it? No place I've ever been makes you feel more like an outsider than Asia. You're a foot taller than everyone, and you're white. Hard to blend in. You may or may not have heard stories, tales, yarns, fables, poems or songs about these so called "donkey shows" or "snake shows" or any other type of show that you may conjure up. Well, whatever you've heard is true. Yes, I know. Please, Mister, tell us more. Tell us of the bad places. The dark places. The scary places. The places of wetness and slime. The places of sin and moving shadows. The places that burrow into a man's heart refusing to release him back into the light. The places where sounds of unknown origin echo through the hall, reverberating in your head like the screams of a thousand tortured souls. The places of scents and emotions, both unidentifiable. The places where only a select few even know you were there. The places you don't talk about, except late at night when you're all alone. Tell us of those places; tell us of the things you've seen in these places. Tell us.

BC street, Okinawa, Japan: a one-mile stretch of bars, brothels and "clubs." The Asians always made me uneasy. Not individually, but when you're really outnumbered. I think a lot of it is because of the language; some of it's kind of scary, and they speak it so fast, but not so much the Japanese, more so the Laotians or the Vietnamese or the Thai's. They scared me. It always sounds like they're angry or like they're giving the order for somebody to lop off your head. Hey, man, I just wanted a banana, chill out a little.

So we strolled BC street and took in some shows. The donkey shows were bizarre to say the least. A chick actually comes out and blows the donkey and then bangs him. Nice. Does your mother know what you're doing for a living? There's got to be a better way; I mean damn, honey, you just fucked a donkey. Where do you go from there? I'm not sure I even want to know, but I'm guessing it's up. You're at the bottom of the entertainment ladder. It's the same for the snake shows, except it's a snake, not a donkey. I guess she never really blew him either, I'm not sure snakes have penises, or peni. But same kind of thing. The people would go nuts too. It's unreal; this girl's putting a snake inside her and the crowd is losing its mind. When I say the "crowd" I mean the guys who would see something like that and cheer it on. Not what you would call a "normal" crowd. I don't think I would've invited many of these fellows into my home, but there they were. I think my buddies and I just stood there with our mouths hanging open. I was dumbfounded. Two weeks ago, I was home on leave, sleeping in my own bed, hanging with my friends and bopping around St. Louis, and now I'm in an underground bar watching some Filipino chick banging a snake. Heaven help us.

Of course to see these kinds of shows you had to go "off street." Not always a wise decision. You couldn't get too carried away with the drinking, or you might get your shit rolled, and that's a long walk back to the base. Trust me from where I speak. The off street journeys weren't just in Okinawa, they were in all the places we went: the Philippines, Thailand, Korea, mainland Japan. Off street was where you went to see the weird shit. They weren't advertised in the paper; they didn't have store fronts or signs. They weren't that hard to find though because they all had barkers on the street. I call them barkers because they barked at you to come into a certain club. Hey, Joe, Joe, Joe, come on in, Joe, we got good shows, Joe. It must have been cool if your name was really Joe; then it would be like everybody over there would know your name. "Hey, Joe." Cool.

Many times you'd have to follow him somewhere. OK, not many times, every time. It's not the kind of place you have in the mall. It was always an anxiety-ridden walk. You're actually preparing for someone to jump out and try to rob you. Again, you always travel in a pack. Safety in numbers was never more apparent. We'd walk through these alleys and follow him down some outside stairs. We'd cross another alley, maybe head up a flight of stairs, come back down, cross another alley and then start heading down. Down into the bowels of late night entertainment.

More than once it crossed my mind that this is dangerous, but what the hell, it's Saturday. Let's party. We would go down the stairs and he'd bang on a door, a slot would open up, they would threaten each other, or at least that how it sounded to me, then we would be allowed in. When I use the word "seedy" you have a pretty good idea of what I mean. I wish seedy would be useful here. This place made it seem like "seedy" would be an upgrade. It was like that scene from *Deerhunter,* where you expected to see the Russian Roulette game going on. Doesn't anyone here have a mop or a sponge or some paper towels? What's on the floor? What is that on the wall? Are those real stuffed zebra feet? Why is that dwarf carrying a machete? What is that sound? Is that a real mummy? What the fuck is that smell? Is somebody cooking something? Don't tell me they serve appetizers. Where are the white people? Do I want something to drink? Fuck yes I want a drink. I *need* a drink, but only something in a bottle please. I don't want to drink out of a glass from this place. I was a little uncertain about the bottle to be honest, but alcohol was definitely needed for this night. I had a buddy who in these situations would say, "you've got to experience life if you're going to experience life." Yeah, well I'm a 19-year-old suburban boy in an underground sex bar somewhere in the Philippines, so I think I'm experiencing life. I'm also trying to experience tomorrow, so behave yourself and don't start any shit. That was the only bar I've ever been to that I was hesitant to even pee in. That's a dirty place.

I've seen some strange things, and I've seen some funny things in these bars. One night I was out with the boys and we headed to a club, and if I'm not mistaken this was in Okinawa. Sometimes it's hard to remember exactly where you were when these particular sights etched themselves into the memory banks. This was another "downstairs" club. I don't know what it is about going downstairs to enter a bar, but it never seems to be a positive I'm moving forward with my life kind of thing. You should be going "up" the stairs, not heading "down" into the bowels of dank, stinky clubs with naked girls. But once again, there we were.

A crowd had already started collecting around the stage, there seemed to be anticipation in the air. The club had your standard bar off to the right and the stage on the far left wall. The stage was bathed in a pale yellow spotlight. I'm not sure if there's there a more unflattering spotlight color than yellow, but there it was, soaking the stage in its amber glow. A murmur ran through the crowd, and since most of the people in there weren't speaking English, I'm not sure what the murmur was about, but it was there. A single chair stood on the stage. I wasn't sure what the show was going to be. I don't think the barker mentioned it; he just grabbed us and told us we were in for a treat. Thinking back to that area, I'm not so sure you could've found anything anywhere that could be referred to as a "treat." There were girls over there that had some very talented vaginas. I don't mean in a sexual way, I mean in a show business way.

The place was filling up fast. Locals, Marines and even a few Flyboys from Kadena Air Force Base were in attendance. Beer and shots were flowing, and a party atmosphere was forming. As we're cradling our mead and sipping our grog, the mood changes. The lights remain the same, but a guy comes on stage and puts a soda bottle on the chair. That lonely, dirty, wooden chair now has a companion; a soda bottle. Dear God, what's going to happen here tonight? The air fills with the stench of sweat, spilled beer and sticky floors. I realize that using "sticky floors" right there may not have been applicable, but it seemed like the phrase to use in this particular situation. Sticky floors, you can appreciate the feel of that can't you? You can associate the smell that may come from the sticky floor in a basement bar in a foreign land...can't you?

So we wait. Tension mounts, almost palpable now. Something's going to happen. She appears from behind the curtain...a girl...a dancer... a gyrating sexual goddess. Keep in mind that as I'm thinking this, I'm 19, a product of the suburbs, I've got no wife, no girlfriend, a head full of liquor, cash in my pocket, and I'm also about 8,000 miles from home. To me at that time, she was a gyrating sexual goddess. She dances, she sashays, she glides across the stage and sidles up to the chair. She then places a quarter on top of the bottle. Hmm, that's interesting, I wonder what she's going to do? She does a little more dancing and then straddles the chair/bottle. As she's lowering herself, I'm trying to figure out what the hell she's doing. In my little pea brain, I can't seem to wrap my thoughts around what I'm seeing. As she gets closer the crowd starts getting vocal, again cheering on. I've got to pee, but I can't leave this scene, I'm mesmerized by what's happening on the stage.

She gets to just a crack above the bottle (pun intended, ha ha) she closes the gap, and bam. SHE PICKS THE QUARTER OFF THE BOTTLE! What!? Did I just see that? Did this chick just pick up a coin off a soda bottle with her coozy? By God she did, and the crowd goes wild! Success! It was like we scored a touchdown on the final play. How exciting. We waited almost an hour to see this babe picking up change with no hands or feet, and it was worth it. I'm embarrassed to say it, but it was worth the wait. You don't get to see that kind of shit in Missouri. I'm not sure you could find that kind of shit anywhere in the U.S. Wow. She's got skills. What we didn't know at the time was that she was just getting started- that's just the warm up trick.

Her closer was something altogether different. She leaves the stage to a thunderous round of applause, shortly to return. We can't wait. What next? This is entertainment. What kind of craziness can we see next? When she returns it's to a monstrous round of applause. Whoa, what's that in her hand? A banana? Really? What can she possibly do with a banana? Like I said, I'm just a kid. She sits on the chair shoots her legs in the air and starts to pleasure herself with the banana! Holy shit! Is she really banging herself with a banana and not breaking it? That's incredible! Now that's something we should've seen on that Kathy Lee Crosby show. Can't you just see it? A clip of some Asian chick pounding away at herself with a 'nanner and not breaking it and Kathy Lee going "now, that's incredible." I'm taping that show. A banana's for heaven's sake, what next? She finishes off the thing and then disappears again. I guess she needed a break to regain her composure.

When she returns, it's to a standing ovation. I doubt there was anyone left sitting after act two, but you never know. The spot turns back on, and she returns. We don't know what kind of madness is coming, we just know it's coming. This time she has a cloth bag in her hand. What's in the bag? Oh my God, what does she have in the bag? The crowd is whipped up in anticipation. We want to know what she's got in the bag, and we want to know right fucking now. She reaches in a pulls out a ping pong ball. That's right, a ping pong ball. I have no idea what she's planning on doing with it, but I'm as excited as everyone else. She sits on the chair and puts a ping pong ball in her mouth and then slips it in her womanhood. I'm not shitting you, she put the ping pong ball inside her. Wild, wacky shit man. Everybody is losing their minds. The crowd is at a frenzied peak. They're (we're) jumping up and down and throwing yen all over and doing toasts and cheers and just reveling in the moment. How much better or how much weirder can this get? Once again she sits on the chair pulls her legs up around her head and SPOINGGGG! She shoots a ping pong ball across the top of the crowd. Yes, that's right, she shot a ping pong ball out of her coozy, and it flew at least twenty feet. Hilarious.

I'd never seen anything like it or even imagined anything like this could even happen. I'm flabbergasted and dumbfounded, but I want more, oh yes, I want so much more. Something else I'd never seen is these drunken idiots trying to catch them in their mouths. Oh yeah, as she's shooting these ping pong balls out of her, a lot of these guys are trying to catch them. They're running all over the place on a sticky, slimy floor with unsure footing. Even if they hit the ground they're scrambling after them like there's some kind of prize involved. There actually may have been; I just didn't know about it. It wouldn't have mattered. Even if there were gifts and prizes involved, I'm not touching that ping pong ball. I couldn't believe it, I've been drunk before, and I'm sure I was that night, but never drunk enough to catch, in my mouth mind you, a ping pong ball that was coming out of this particular kind of woman. Just too weird, even for me.

It was some kind of show. It was amazing how far she could shoot those things. During each launch, you could almost hear the little "pop." I wish I had had a cell phone camera back then. The show ended and we headed back up to the street. Well, that was something. I think we were all a little speechless for a while. It's hard to even comment on something like that. Words don't really do it justice, so perhaps we'll just bask in our own thoughts for awhile. I'm not even sure we should tell anyone; maybe it should be our little secret. I think I know what's in order. Corn Dogs. BC Street had street vendors all over, and some of them sold some mean corn dogs. Not the best food to eat after a night of drinking, but when else would one eat a corn dog? Standing on a corner of BC Street at 3 a.m. nice buzz on, hanging with your friends, eating corn dogs after watching some chick shoot ping pong balls out of her puss. Good stuff, Good times.

CHAPTER 25
COLLEGE

I'm not sure where in the book to put this little story. It doesn't really tie into any of the chapters of the book. It doesn't really fit into any sub-chapters either, so I guess I'll just tell it.

I went to school at Southeast Missouri and at the time was living with Ted and Louie. The year was probably 1984 and topsider shoes were all the craze. OK, maybe "all the craze" isn't the right wording, but a lot of people had them. I didn't have a pair, but I was thinking about getting some. I wanted to try a pair out first, just to see if they would be something I would wear. I felt that I had reached a certain level of cool and wasn't sure if I could maintain my present position if I was wearing Topsiders- they were a bit too preppy for me. I came up with this idea of buying a cheap pair, wearing them for a couple of days, then, if it seemed like I could wear them, I would get a good pair. I headed up to the discount shoe store to see what was what. I found a pair that fit and off I went. These shoes were called Coasters. I'm not sure where they got the name, but that's what they were called, Coasters.

I went out, purchased the Coasters and headed home. For some reason, I didn't want my roommates to find out. To this day I can't explain why I felt the need to keep this secret, but I did. The Coasters were cheap. I think I paid about $10 for them. I soon found out why. First of all, they were made of vinyl, not leather. I mean, what do you expect for $10? Vinyl does not wear well, especially in summer. So I slip them on and head out for a walk. Ten minutes into this walk my feet are so sweaty the shoes are sliding and slopping all over my feet. It was ridiculous. I guess vinyl doesn't breathe. As I'm walking down the road, test driving my new Coasters, my roommates drive by, lean out the window and yell out "nice shoes." I can't believe they noticed I was wearing my new Coasters, but they did. I had explained my whole theory to them, which in retrospect, I should've just kept to myself, so they were on the lookout for some new treads. I can't tell you why they were so obsessed with my new foot wear, but I knew they couldn't wait to get home and make fun of me and my new shoes. Keep in mind, these are grown men.

When I got home, my feet were soaked and the shoes stunk. I mean stunk with all capitals. I think the vinyl must have been bad or something; maybe they were assembled inside out. I only had them on my feet for about 20 minutes, so how could they make my feet smell so bad? It wasn't just my feet either, the shoes themselves stunk. What the hell? They reeked up the living room. I knew the boys would be home soon, so I had to make a decision, toss the shoes and pretend I never purchased them, or admit my error in buying a $10 pair of deck shoes. I decided to toss them and deny everything. I slipped them back into the box and hid them in the trash. I didn't just hide them in the trash. I stuffed them down deep and covered them up with as much nasty trash as I could. I knew when they came home they'd be searching for these shoes. I don't know how I knew, but I did. Those goofballs will search high and low until they find something to give me shit about. Roomies, eh? So the shoes are stashed and I head off to work. As I'm leaving, they return.

"Where are your new shoes?" they ask as soon as they enter.

"What new shoes?"

"The new shoes we saw you walking down the street in."

"I don't know what you're talking about, I didn't buy any new shoes."

"We saw you giving them a test drive, where are they?"

"I didn't buy new shoes and I didn't test drive any shoes, the shoes I was test driving were yours."

I thought the information about me wearing Ted's shoes would throw them off the trail. I mean wouldn't you be pissed if someone was wearing your shoes? I headed to work with the solid knowledge that they will never find the Coasters stashed in the trash. A half hour later, my phone at work rings.

"Hello."

"Nice Coasters."

Then they hung up. Damn them, they found my shoes. How in the world did they find them? And why? What in the world could be so important that you would dig through the trash? Are their lives so empty that they have to tear the house apart board by board until they found something to give me shit about? Are these two obsessed with me or what? This wasn't your run of the mill kitchen garbage can; this was an industrial-sized trash receptacle. You could've gutted a cow in our house and had plenty of room in the trash can for the remnants. If you have a really big trash can, you don't have to empty it as much, that's our philosophy. So there they were, digging through the trash, just looking for my Coasters. Mission accomplished. Those bastards rode me hard for weeks about the Coaster episode. I don't who was more fucked up, me for hiding them, or those two for digging through the trash.

We had some good times in college. Weird times as well. We used to have parties at the house. One time we had some people over and some of the girls were looking through some pictures my roommate had taken. Then this girl asks, "what's this?" I take a look at it and have no idea. We're flipping this pic upside down and right side up and nothing is assisting us in deciphering its origin. I know something about it looks familiar; wait, isn't that our bathroom floor? And finally I realize what the picture is of.

"Oh, Ted, could you come here and explain this please?"

Maybe people get a little weird when they are at college, or maybe they're just weird in general. What the girls were looking at was a picture of a turd. It seems that Ted had left a long snake turd in the bowl that had come out in one piece. He must have been proud of it because he went and got a camera and snapped a picture of it. Some people take pictures of their friends, and some take pictures of their cars or homes or families or anything. Few take a picture of a huge turd sitting in a toilet bowl. And even fewer still leave it in the pile of other pictures for people to browse through. I don't want to say it was the highlight of the party, but we got some serious chuckles from it. I may have purchased a vinyl pair of shoes, but I've never taken a picture of a turd. At least not yet.

One night around Halloween we had a few people over to do some blow and carve pumpkins. I'm not sure why we thought cocaine and carving pumpkins would go together, but we did. We were also drinking Bailey's and coffee because we were very sophisticated. Who in their right minds would mix cocaine, coffee and sharp knives digging into pulpy, flesh-like substances? This group, that's who. We just locked ourselves in and began wielding knives. The lines were going down, the coffee was hot, and it was like a slaughterhouse in there. We had pumpkin guts everywhere. Pumpkin entrails were flying and then piling up on the floor. We had four guys carving the shit out of some pumpkins, man. I was amazed at the pile of orange, stringy sinew we had around us when over in the corner was this huge trash can. We were slashing and cutting and carving both sides of the pumpkin. Some guys carved three sides, so we had faces everywhere. In retrospect, I don't remember many of the resembling faces. I think we were satisfied with a couple of eye holes and a mouth.

"There, I'm done."

"Oh, that's nice, what is it?"

"I don't know."

We ran out twice and got more pumpkins; we went through about 25-30 or them. We couldn't stop. Most of what we ended up with was unidentifiable and therefore unusable, but we didn't care; we just wanted to carve.

I stayed down at school during summer breaks. We had a house, so we didn't get kicked out every summer. I just worked and partied and hung by the pool. We did a lot of that, hanging by the pool. Sometimes we had tanning contests. I know, it sounds kind of lame, but they weren't really verbal contests, but the strive to be the brownest was there. There was this one guy named John who hung out at the pool a lot but would only lie on his back and tan his front. Hilarious, his face and front were tan as hell, but his back and his legs were white as the dickens, goofy look. Louie would often get so hot, he'd just lean-sit in the shade with only his feet in the sun- he always won the tannest feet segment. Nobody showed the dedication to tanning feet like Sweet Lou. Contrary to Ted's belief, I usually got tanner. He may have spent more time in the sun due to the unemployment, but I had better browning genes.

The parties at the pool would get carried away from time to time. That happens when you tap the keg at 10 a.m. poolside. One day we decided to eat some mushrooms, which is nice. A nice little chuckle buzz for a Tuesday. The pool was at an apartment complex that none of us lived at. We knew the manager, and he'd let us hang around. The building was four stories with the pool at one end. After the mushrooms have taken effect, someone suggests we climb up on the roof and jump into the pool. I know, I know. Crazy kids.

The only real way to get to the roof was to enter a top floor apartment, go to the balcony, and climb onto the railing and then climb to the roof using the metal trellis. OK, no sweat, the mushrooms should help. In the end, only three of us went up. Me, Larry and a dude named Freddy all lean over the edge and look down to the pool. Seems a lot higher from this angle. You can tell second thoughts are running rampant. Nobody really wants to jump off now, despite the mushrooms. We all walk back over to the trellis and realize it's more dangerous to climb back down than it is to jump. If we fall here, it's a long way to the parking lot. At least the other option gives us the pool to hit. We walk back over to look at the pool again, then once more to the trellis. Strangely enough, jumping the four stories into to the pool seemed the safest way down. Oh, we got ourselves into a pickle.

I decide I'm not waiting anymore, so I lean over, judge my trajectory and go. I went a little far, but hit the water, bumped the bottom and shot to surface of the water like a champion. I was smiling and waving to the crowd (about 11 people) and just basked in their warm felt applause. Then Larry goes, he's a little bigger, so he made quite a splash, but his jump was successful as well. Freddy wasn't quite ready yet. He's just leaning over and getting a good look. We didn't want to pressure him; after all, it is over 40 feet and he's got a head full of mushrooms, so take your time, Freddy, take your time. We'll get a beer in the meantime.

We sit at the table and enjoy our beers and talk of the stupidity of jumping off a building while eating mushrooms. Clever. An hour rolls by and we forget about Freddy. We had all moved on with our lives, completely forgetting our loved one, tripping his balls off, stranded on the roof of an apartment building in Cape Girardeau. I realized he was still up there when I looked down and saw the shadow of his head leaning over the edge yet again to gauge his jump. "What the hell?" We all look up and sure enough, he's still up there. He had to be thirsty by now. After a few more minutes of cajoling, he leaps. It was the most frightened, terrified look I have ever seen on someone. He did a fine job on all aspects and hit the water with a nice splash. The most amazing thing at the end of the day was the fact that we had forgotten him on the roof. Good thing the sun was just right to cast his shadow or he may still be up there.

I didn't join a fraternity when I went to college. It just didn't seem like me. A couple of fraternities tried to get me to join. I just wasn't a fraternity kind of guy. I guess the Marines are a fraternity or sorts, but a college fraternity didn't seem like a place I would fit in. I could be a Sig Ep if I made it through rush week. Make it through rush week? Whoa, that's a challenge. After making it through three months of Marine Corps boot camp, something tells me I could make it through rush week. I didn't though. Join a frat I mean. I went to college in the 80's, so a lot of the frat fellas wore the izod shirts with the collar turned up. Biggest douchebag look ever. Even worse were the ones that wore TWO shirts, both with the collar up. Where were tasers then, I ask you; where were tasers then? A few of the recruiters were tenacious. They really wanted me to become a member. One guy asked if I was afraid of rush week.

"Yes, I am, boy. I'm terrified of some college punk giving me shit. The Marine Corps didn't frighten me, but the Phi Sigs do."

I told one of the guys who was trying to get me to join that if someone tried to hit me with a wooden paddle I would take it away from him and shove it up his ass. "Ok, maybe you're not Phi Sig material." You've got that right, Howard.

I was on an ultimate Frisbee team for a couple of years. Our team was called the Zig-Zags. I think you can get the picture. We were the only independent team; the rest were fraternity teams, and we loved to play them. It's like an arch-rival type of thing. Before the game the other teams were going over strategy and whatnot, and we'd be on the other side of the field smoking a couple of jays. You would think that with the amount of running involved we wouldn't be smoking pot right before the game, but that's what they all thought. But we fooled 'em, we fooled 'em all. It helped us, no...really, it did. We were some diving, leaping, gallivanting, trotting and Frisbee throwing sons of bitches. The pot didn't affect us at all. We won "the cup" one year, maybe twice, I don't remember.

I had fun in college, even though it was basically a way for me to avoid going out in to the real world and be one of "them." I never considered myself one of the masses who get up and go to work each day. I'm not sure why, it's just the way I felt. I didn't belong in the "work force." I belonged on the fringes of society, on the outside looking in. That's the way I liked it. You know, keeping an eye on society, without actually becoming a part of it. Just keep eyeballing things, making sure one of the "normals" didn't make a break for it and try to get out on the fringes. I started school when I was 22. A good age to start college. Everyone else starts at 18, having just left home and doesn't know jack. I had been around the world, been in the Marines and knew a few things about things that it's good to know things about. I knew that college would be a blast. I was going to party, have fun and get laid as often as possible. I was going to go through every girl in this school if possible. I'll be an uncontrollable love-making machine. I'll be monster, a hound, a savage, if you will. I had just spent four years around mostly men and it was time to cut loose. Do my thing. Forget classes, I've got women to chase. I started school in January and by March I had fallen in love with a girl and now had a girlfriend. Wait... wasn't I supposed to be out bird-dogging chicks and banging beaver? The hound, the monster, the savage? We ended up together for two years. Well done, lover boy.

My first experience with a beer bong was in college. You learn a lot of stuff in college that has nothing to do with classes, like how to make bongs out of...well, anything. Pot smokers are very ingenious people when it comes to making smoking paraphernalia. Straws, wood, old pipes, anything cylindrical will work. You can find a screen in any window in the house. If you don't want to tear up your screens, you can use your neighbors'. We even used the screens in the dryer filter. Oh, we were crafty devils. Anyway, my roommates and I had gone to a party, a keg party. As if there's any other kind in college. A few of the lads were doing beer bongs and I wandered over and inquired as to what they were doing.

"A beer bong huh?"

"Yeah, you take a large funnel, attach a rubber hose, fill up the funnel with your finger over the end of the hose, and when all the air is out, you put it in your mouth, pull your finger away and all that beer shoots down your gullet." Hmm, that looks interesting.

"What's the point?"

"Well, you can slam two full beers in about five seconds."

I'm not sure what the attraction was in slamming beers that fast, but I'll admit I was curious. An hour later, I've done about five of them and didn't want any more. I'm full. When I say I'm full, I mean I've got no room left at the inn, my stomach is literally bursting at the seams. I couldn't have eaten a piece of rice without it absorbing moisture and then exploding out my front side. I feel like I've got this huge ball of beer gas in my belly. I now have to pee. There is a huge line for the bathroom, and being a guy, I just go out to the yard. As I'm leaning against a tree for support, getting ready to do my business, I feel this huge belch coming on, which I gladly welcome, anything to relieve this feeling of fullness I've got. As I'm peeing, I burp and this huge ball of foam comes out of my innards. When I say huge ball, I mean a HUGE ball of foam comes flying out and it stays in one piece. It was almost the consistency of shaving cream. I was dumbfounded. I've never seen anything like it. It even came out in a near perfect circle about three feet across. I don't know if it was some kind of record, or if they even keep track of records like that. Big piles of beer foam, in first place...Mark Sweeney. I just stood there staring at it. I had to redirect my urine stream so as not to destroy this beautiful foam thingy. I went inside to get my roommates to come and check it out. They didn't want to come out and see my puke. "But it isn't puke, its foam." So they followed me out to the tree and sure enough, it was still there, I'm not sure it had even started breaking down yet. It was just a huge circle of beer bong foam sitting in the yard with three drunken idiots marveling at its very existence. It was amazing, at least at the time. I ended up walking home because I guess I had more beers now that I wasn't full anymore. That really was Good stuff, Good times.

CHAPTER 26
JOBS

It seems like I've always had a job. Not that I'm complaining, it just seems like I've always had work to do. It started young, cutting grass, shoveling snow, etc. I'm not sure many kids have jobs anymore. I miss those days, when you could use children as cheap labor, it's good for them, keeps them out of trouble. My friends and I used to cut grass for money, which, by the way, makes it work. We used to get $5 for a regular yard and $8 for a corner lot and that included the trimming. We always had money to buy stuff; granted, we stole a lot of things, but the option to pay for it was there. We didn't have rides to the work, so we had to push our mowers and other implements of destruction ourselves, blocks and blocks. Oh, the horror.

Of course, we didn't have rides to anything when I was a kid. Don't you hate that phrase? "When I was a kid" it seems we heard it from our parents when we were children and now we're saying it. It's true though; things are always different after you grow. But by God, if we didn't have rides, we walked, ran or rode our bikes wherever we went. That's why there weren't really any fat kids when I was little. Armour Hot Dogs could have never gotten away with the ads they ran then. "Fat kids, skinny kids, kids who climb on rocks..." you can't call kids fat anymore, it's politically incorrect. He's endomorphically challenged. Please. Mom's watching TV, "Oh my God, Bobby, they're calling you fat." Bobby looks up, but doesn't say anything because he's elbow deep in a bag of Cheetos. We played outside all the time and ran and played and played and ran. When you play outside, you don't have time to get fat.

Granted, we didn't have as many distractions as kids do now. We didn't have computers or video games or 500 channels on TV; we had three channels and of course the UHF station which never aired anything that was ever watched by anyone. If we had stayed inside we were put to work. I think that's one of the reasons my mom stayed sane. She'd put us to work if we were inside. So outside it was. Sometimes if the chores were horrendous enough, we'd just go outside to be outside. Even if we were just standing there doing nothing it was better than working.

In our house, if you wanted something, you went out and earned it. We had chores to do, but there were no allowances being handed out. Our allowances were being allowed to live in the house, eat the food and wear the clothes. Seems barbaric now, doesn't it? No special treatment, no dropping everything and rushing to the needs of the children; we used to be secondary citizens. It was the parents' life; the kids were part of it, but they didn't run the show. Kids could do stuff if it was convenient for the parents, not vice versa. It was a beautiful and simple time. My nephew recently asked his mother for a $100 pair of tennis shoes and nobody told him to learn how to start the lawnmower. What the hell?

My work career was fairly spotty until I was 14 or so, then I worked at a condo complex, cutting grass, cleaning up, etc. It was a pretty good gig. We got to work outside, smell cut grass all day, and to top it all off, we got to play with hoses. I don't know why it's so much fun to use a hose, but it is. Always has been. It's cool to wash down the driveway. Maybe it's the phallic thing, whipping that big hose all over, moving things around with "your water." It was a kick. Plus, you could take a long time when using the hose; it can be a great time killer. At lunch we would ride our bikes up to Rinkel's market and buy sodas and bags of lunch meat. We'd sit in the cool of the garage and drink our Cokes and eat four or five bags of meat. Oh, it was a simple time. I did that for a while, then I got into a fist fight with my co-worker and we both got fired, I think we were fighting over the hose. Oh well.

I guess my first "real job" was in high school, I was a bus boy. It was a great gig. It was at Sam Wilson's restaurant, and we had a blast. Three of my best friends worked there as well, Mike, John and Sweet Lou, and we ran that place. Well, as far as we were concerned we ran it; the four of us, ten lbs of hair a piece, running through the restaurant with full bus tubs stacked three high. Oh, we were badass. A lot of first experiences came from that place. I've spoken of, or will speak about the restaurant workers; they are a special breed of cat, man. I love restaurant/bar people, or as we refer to ourselves "the industry."

It was the first time I did downers. We stayed after work eating reds and scrubbing the floors. Apparently, you have to use barbiturates and beer to get high school kids to scrub kitchen floors with scratchy pads. Good times. As a 15/16 year old, being exposed to people in their twenties was fantastic. They knew so much more than we did. Each night after work, we'd sit around the cars in the parking lot, drink beer, smoke pot and learn stuff. I'm still surprised my folks let me work at night. Sometimes we wouldn't get home until after 1 a.m., then get up the next morning and go to school. Well, go to school as we saw fit; we probably didn't attend as much class as the other students, but we had jobs, and by God, sometimes a day at the park was what was needed more than "edjewcashun."

We loved that job too. On our nights off, sometimes we'd go up to the restaurant and see if anyone wanted off. The dishwashers always did. So we'd smoke a joint with our heads inside the dish machine so the vent would suck up the smoke and then proceed to slinging dishes. Soaking wet from nipples to toes and we couldn't have been happier. Hard to believe isn't it? We had a good time at work. We'd hang with our friends, make some money. I don't think I could've washed dishes full-time though. It takes a while for the stink to leave you. Your shoes were never the same after spending an evening in the dish room. That odor of wet restaurant never really leaves you. I talk of the odor as if it were alive, real. In a way it was. It was an entity of sorts. It took on a life of its own. Powerful stuff, baby. The stink of the dish room. As busboys though, we couldn't just stand in front of the dish machine. It may have looked suspicious. A couple of dish dogs and a few busboys all huddled around the dish machine with our heads stuck inside, burning a jibby. Sure giveaway. You don't see something like that and not realize something's amiss. We used to "take the trash out," which was code for taking a doobie break. We'd take a trash can out back and torch up along the way, just a couple of crazy kids standing out back at work, smoking a little jay, and then go in and bus tables like madmen.

We'd get stoned, but it didn't interfere with work. That place had a two to three hour wait on the weekends, and we never got behind; we had the greatest bus staff in the world, and we were also the hairiest and the most stoned. We thrived on it. The wait staff loved us and we made a ton of money, at least it seemed like a ton at the time.

That was the job I had through high school. By the time I graduated, I had joined the Marines, which is covered in detail in other chapters so we'll move on. After I got out of the Corps, I still didn't know what I wanted to do, so I got a job as a security guard. It is a job that any former Marine can get. I got the idea from a buddy of mine who became a prison guard. I couldn't see working in a prison, so I got a job as a guard. That was in October, and by December I was gone. One night someone took a shot at me while I was sitting at my desk, so

I quit that job. That was interesting, getting shot at. I didn't even know it at the time; it took a minute to figure it out. I was just sitting there reading and someone shot at me. I still remember the book: *By Reason of Insanity* by Shane Stevens, it's still one of my favorite books of all time. I quit that job the next morning on my way home; there had to be a better way. I tried to think of the place with the most women. College. That's where I need to go.

I worked my way through college. I had asked my father for money to go to college, he just smiled, patted me on the back and said, "I would, but you're a grown-up." That was the end of that conversation. I was a bartender for most of my college career, great job. I started off working the door, which is a great way to meet girls, as well as finding out their names, birthdays and addresses, if of course, that information should ever become handy. You get to know a lot of people working the door, which comes in handy while breaking up fisticuffs. It's a lot easier to stop a fight if both of the guys know you. When you first start breaking up fights, it's kind of fun; you get to smack some people around while "calming the situation." After a couple of years and receiving some smacks of your own, you don't hop over the bar very often- maybe if girls are fighting, but then, only maybe.

I also had another security job while in college, again the former Marine shit helped. It was a good job, except for the fact it was in a hospital, a place I'm not fond of. You don't go to the hospital for anything good. Ever. If you're there, it's because something's wrong. It smells funny too. It's a mixture of sickness, weird food, death and disinfectant. Nice, huh? I worked the 11 p.m. to 7 a.m. shift. Just the way I like it. Not much going on at that time. I used to get most of my studying done and then be so far ahead I could skip class for a week. I did have some interesting nights though.

A lot of the behind-the-scenes stuff happens at night. The people from the funeral homes would always pick up the bodies at night. Creepy. They would come to the basement door, and I'd let them in and unlock the morgue. The problem was the guys who worked the midnight shift at the funeral home were all in their seventies, which, of course, meant they needed help moving bodies. I won't go into detail out of respect, but God bless the people who can handle doing funeral stuff. It was usually uneventful. Surreal, but uneventful.

It's an odd thing, moving cadavers. You know what it is you're doing, you're just not paying attention to the fact. Too morbid. One night the lady in the cooler was a 300+ pounder, and Earl and I had quite a time trying to move ole Bessie. If it weren't for the circumstances, it may have been quite amusing. Moving around the room trying to figure out how we're going to do this, like it's some structural problem at a construction site. All that was missing were hard hats and us leaning over a table looking at blueprints. We were walking around looking at angles, figuring out lines of attack, what's possible, and what's not. We're thinking about gurney tire tread and slickness of the floor. We're figuring density factors and weight distribution. We're looking at the windage factor and temperature change. We're looking at door width and ease of hinges. We're keeping an eye on the barometric to make damn sure a nor'easter doesn't blow us off track. All these things are being checked along with numerous other variables that are being considered and discounted with alarming frequency. We're looking at this from everywhere until we realize that no one else is coming and we have to do it ourselves.

We're going from feet to head, head to feet, the gurney's moving, we're trying to slide her, pick her up, shift her, move her, and there was some kind of fumes coming out of a rather odiferous nature, and then the noises started, noises like I've never heard before and hope to never hear again. Gurgles and gaggles and burbling noises that came from somewhere dark, terrifying and foreboding. A place where there is no light, no joy, no love. A place where dark, wet, slippery things move slowly across the tiled floor, looking for your bare skin, take purchase, start climbing and begin to burrow. God help us. I had bad dreams for a month.

Hospitals can be eerie places at night. The top floor of the hospital I worked at was vacant. Well, not exactly vacant. They used it as storage. There were "things" up there. They just weren't normal things. No. Not the things you and I would put in a storage room. Hospital type of things. Lifeless things. Unsettling things. The top floor was only five stories high, but it was still like an attic. Even the phrase "fifth floor" had serious connotations. As in; "you're going up to the fifth floor? Godspeed, little one."

They had disconnected the lights on the top floor, so the rooms were lit by the street lights shining up from below. The streets lights had a yellow glow to them so the effect was haunting. One of the things that were stored up there were body parts. Why? I don't know. I'm sure they were kept for scientific reasons and not just to freak me out. They had jars and jars of things suspended in fluid with tendrils of horror reaching out through the murk to wrap around my neck. It was damn freaky. Plus, the street lights would shine up from the ground and throw weird shadows up on the wall, and they would dance and move and ...aaaiiieeeee. I used to go up there all the time. Again, I don't know why, the place gave me the willies, but once a month, I'd go to the top floor and look at the mutants. You'd think with all the depraved shit I read, I would stay away from creepy places where men with hideous deformities, erections and sharp knives hide in the corner with puddles of urine at their feet just waiting for me to inch closer.

I'd try to stay as long as possible, but after ten minutes I'd be scurrying back to the elevator and go back down to the light. When those doors open up on the ground floor, I'd walk out, grab a handful of the warm light and rub it all over me. "I'm alive, I'm alive." It was a huge relief. What a dipshit.

One night I saw someone get shot and killed in the ER. That was a first. It turns out that most people haven't actually seen someone get killed. Crazy night that was. I got paged to get to the ER for some disturbance. An ambulance had brought in a girl who had overdosed and her boyfriend and another couple were there and had obviously been partying. When an overdose comes in with people in attendance, chances are, they were in on the festivities as well. The OD's boyfriend was pretty drunk and wanted to be in the treatment room, which of course is not allowed. I went in and talked to him in my best "I'm cool too, dude" voice and got him to go back to the waiting room.

Shortly after, the police show up. These two were quite a match, the one guy was a reservist who was in his late 60's, and the other one was about 15; at least he looked 15, couldn't have been out of the academy two weeks. It seems that the OD's boyfriend had a history with the law, and things start to escalate as they tried to throw him out. The next thing I know the four of us are in the entryway to the ER, along with the other couple, a knife gets pulled, people are screaming, the tension is thickening quickly and bam, bam. The old cop shoots him twice in the chest. He hits the wall and slides to the ground.

I'm speechless. I can't believe what I just saw. I know it's real though, you can see the two red spots growing larger on his chest. I'm literally dumbfounded. I didn't know what the hell to do. Bedlam ensues and things get kicked up a notch. The ER doc comes running out from the back, sees the dude on the ground and tells me to grab an arm. We start dragging this guy through the middle of the ER, with a huge trail of blood behind us; apparently one of the rounds went through him and he was bleeding out the back. It was absolutely incredible. It was like a scene in a movie where the bank robbers are pulling their buddy back inside and he leaves a trail of blood in his wake. You know how they say a lot of blood smells like wet pennies? It does. I don't know if you've ever heard that, but I have, and it really does. I remember thinking, "Wow, a lot of blood really does smell like wet pennies, hmmm." Then I remember thinking, "you need to pay attention mi amigo, there is a lot at stake here."

Then I'm thinking about the fact that I'm not a Doctor and there is really little I can do for this guy. The doc and I put him on the gurney in back and doc goes to work. I'm standing there while he splits this guy's chest open and starts digging for the bullets. I'm literally standing there with my mouth wide open (this was before I'd seen an autopsy) looking into his chest cavity. What the hell? It was very messy. My heart was going a thousand miles an hour. When someone dies in the ER, they really do go TOD (time of death) 3:13, I'll always remember that time: 3:13.

My shift was over at 7 a.m. I had done my talking and made my statements and so on and was ready to go home. One of the things the night shift guard does is log in everything that happened and fill the boss in on what went on during the night. I almost told him, "Nothing, it was pretty quiet," but I knew he'd find out eventually, so I spent the next two hours going over things with the boss man. But I did use the whole thing to be excused from class for a couple of days. I'm so crafty.

The dead guy's family ended up suing the city and the cops who shot him. I received a subpoena to appear in court. That was nerve-racking. I don't care how cool you are, or think you are, all that disappears when you sit on the witness stand. I was actually shaking before I walked in to the court room. I was shaking with anxiety. All I was doing was telling what happened, I wasn't on trial, I had done nothing wrong, nobody was questioning my behavior, but my voice quivered through the whole thing. I was on the stand about 10-15 minutes, and I was shaking the whole time. Maybe even a little pee came out. I can see why it's so hard to lie on the stand. I couldn't have done it, and I consider myself a pretty cool customer.

Court Jester

Court is the most authoritative place I've ever been in. With the flag, the judge, the courtroom, yikes, get me the hell out of here. It was an impressive display of power, order and conformity. I've never had a "problem" with authority, I've just never felt in sync with authority figures, and therefore, never felt the need to obey them. I myself will deem whether a law is worth following or not, and if not, I'll pass. I do obey the "big laws," but for the most part, I feel that laws are for everyone else. It's only the other people who need to be governed. Me, I can figure out what do on my own. Maybe it's because I've never been in a position of authority, or maybe people of authority have been trying to tell me what to do since forever, and that has always disagreed with me. It was very uncomfortable. I've never been back in a courtroom. Praise the Lord.

I hung sprinkler pipe for a year, you know, installing sprinkler systems in new construction. It was a good-paying job, even though I didn't know shit about it. A friend of mine, who's a fitter, got me the gig. I was mostly a gofer for the more experienced fitters. The guys I worked with all drank at lunch, so to be part of the gang, I joined them. By the time we got back to the site after that first time, I knew I had made a mistake. We were working in the atrium of a soon-to-be church, and as I'm standing on the top of four stories of scaffolding, I realize I shouldn't be drinking at lunch. Being that high up in the air is not where you want to be if you've got a six pack in you. They didn't have any safety equipment back then, or if they did, it was still in storage. There was a railing around it, but that's it, nothing to keep my dumb ass from going over. I don't care how good scaffolding is, it's on wheels and it always wobbles. An un-sturdy feeling indeed. All I can think of is falling. I'm taking baby steps all over the place. I figure if I fall four stories, I'll die. I knew I was in trouble as I was climbing. I remember thinking, "I'm fucked up, there's no way I should be climbing this thing, if I fall I'll die." That's a comforting thought to have in your head all day. "If I fall, I'll die." Almost like a song that's stuck in your head. "If I fall I'll die, if I fall I'll die, if I fall I'll die, die, die oh yeah." What an idiot. I quit drinking at lunch.

After I graduated from college, I stuck around for the summer. It's summer vacation man. I still can't get that feeling out of my system. Once summer rolls around I feel like I should be off until September. Wouldn't that be great? Even as adults, we get summer off. Yeah, baby. Instead of "getting a job" after college, I went back to bartending.

Nicely done, a four year degree and I'm back pouring cocktails. It was too much fun to do anything else. That's what it should be about, eh? Having fun. I wish everyone could have fun at their jobs. I know it's naïve, but I'm an immature man. Oh well, let's get this party started. I better move back to St. Louis and find a job, a "real job." I never liked that phrase. To me, if you're doing something and getting paid for it, and you take that money and support yourself, you've got a "real job." A "suit and tie job," is what you mean. Bullshit- if you're getting paid, it's real.

I moved back to St. Louis to find a job with my new degree and a desire to become an adult. At 27, I was ready to become a grown up. But first, I'll need a job to support myself until I find a "suit and tie" job. Maybe I'll get a part-time bartending gig. That's a good idea. Yeah, I'll just get a part time gig behind the bar. I got a job at the Flashback Café. It was a 50's bar. I ended up loving the 50's music. It was such a simple and happy time. It was great gig too. The only real drawback was the dancing. Every once in a while the employee's would have to go out and do a little choreographed dance number. Totally lame obviously. We actually had to practice. What is this bullshit? I'm a bartender, not a chorus girl. Let me pour some cocktails and leave the dancing to the customers. It got to the point where if I heard "Bend over and shake your tail feathers" somewhere, I would break into the little dance that had been drilled and pounded into my head over the last six months. Oh yeah, I spent six months doing my "part-time" gig. I was having too much fun to go into the world of men wearing ties.

I just didn't want to go on the job search. It was such an adult thing to do, going on job interviews. I just didn't consider myself one of those people, you know, the people who put on suits and sit there and tell someone what they can do for their company.

"What are your strengths?" What are my strengths?

"Well, I'm strong enough to fight the temptation to fly over this desk and smack that stupid look off your face. That's my strength."

The questions man, the questions. I've never liked being questioned. If I want to tell you something, I will. But I don't want to answer any questions. Don't you get it? I never liked being called on in school, even when I knew the answer. I didn't want to be asked about it. "Explain yourself."

"No."

They want to know about your weaknesses. "Well, I don't have any, that's probably by biggest weakness." You jackass. I love the advice you can find about job interviews and how to respond to certain questions. "My weaknesses are...I'm too dedicated, I've been known to put too many hours into a project. I'm overly ambitious. I have too many ideas." What a crock of shit. If those were truly your weaknesses, you'd be a hell of a lot more successful by now and certainly wouldn't be interviewing for this job. I would almost like to be a job interviewer so I could hear someone say that and then shoot them on the inner thigh with a staple gun.

It seems odd that I would complain about talking about myself when I'm a comedian, which for me is talking about myself, and I'm writing a book about myself; a little self-indulgent for someone who didn't want to talk about himself. Make up your mind, man.

I had some friends who had been searching for jobs for months. They were exasperated and disheartened. Six months out of school and still no job. I was dreading the job search with every fiber of my being. It was the last thing I wanted to do, leave the life I was leading and enter the forbidden zone. I don't belong out there. Why am I being forced to cross the line? Can't I just stay here where it's warm and safe and fun and I can wear t-shirts every day? Heaven help me!

My first interview for a real job was with a Computer/Copier company. I had to take a test and scored 98/100. They said that was the best score they ever had. I was baffled. The test was on basic electronics and not that hard. If I was the best score they ever had, what kind of dumb shits do they have working here? If I'm going to be one of the smartest people here, what chance does this company have to make through the year? I'm supposed to be one of the bright ones? I just wanted to tend a little bar and head to the lake. They offered me a job and I took it. My job search was complete. That wasn't so bad. One interview, one job. I don't know what's wrong with my friends, but they're doing something wrong. What's the big complaint about? I was reluctant to start this thing, and now it's over already. The job was as a copier technician. I would go people's offices and fix their copiers. I had to wear a coat and tie. To fix copiers, what the hell? Anyone who has seen the inside of a copier can attest to the fact they are messy, dirty things with toner that gets everywhere. I was never so dirty in my life. That lasted about nine months. So endeth my foray into the world of people with day jobs. I went back to bartending.

By the time I was 29, I started thinking about what I should do with my life career-wise. I can't keep tending bar my whole life. I was always told that I should do sales of some kind. So I got a job selling real estate. Ouch. I took the class, passed the test, got the job and was off on a new career. The office was full of women in their forties, me and another guy my age. I guess they were trying to even out the playing field. Those women had been doing this job for years and were all great at it. They would be at their desks, pagers going off, phones ringing, faxes flying out, contracts to be signed, houses to show, houses to list, and Jay and I would be sitting around discussing the fact that I had recently purchased some colored paper clips. We were out of our league. The boss actually had us out doing cold calls. I've never heard of a realtor that did cold calls. "Hi, I'm a new real estate agent and if you'd like to sell your house, give me a call." If I remember correctly, I made exactly one cold call and decided that I had to do something else with my life. This wasn't it. I did not like that job. I had a girlfriend at the time and when her father passed away, *I* took a week off work.

Now I was bartending at a place called Menage, yes like the sex act. I was looking for a job and now I've got two. The bar was at Union Station in St. Louis. It was a rocking place, good crowds, but unfortunately, it was open when the Tom Cruise movie *Cocktail* came out, so everyone wanted to see bartenders throwing bottles and glasses around. Well, easier said than done. You have to practice that shit, and we all had other things to do. But we practiced and got good at it. We still thought it was stupid and showy. Every time I went to a bar and the tender was throwing bottles around, all I thought was "quit tossing bottles in the air and get my beer, and quit spinning my beer on your palm, I don't want it foamy."

What you don't notice in the movie is that all those bottles being tossed around were almost empty, much easier to throw, don't you know. You can't just flip a full bottle of vodka, you can tear wrist and elbow tendons and what not. You'd have seven bartenders with carpal tunnel. Not to mention, if you throw a full bottle in the air, an ounce or more of liquor is being sprayed out as well. Liquor costs went through the roof, and bottle tossing was forbidden. Thank you, Jesus; thank you, Lord.

It was great place for about a year. It could've been longer, but that's all it was open. There had been some type of corporate thing going on and Menage was on the chopping block. Management, of course, didn't tell us that we were closing until the last night. "Oh by the way, this is the last night we're going to be open." Well, how courteous of you, thank you for giving us time to look for other jobs. We were packed that night and we only rang up one out of every five or six drinks. We'd sell someone five beers and ring up $2.75, the rest went into the tip jar. I think we all walked with about $4-500, not bad. Later, while the management was in back, we boxed up all the liquor and glasses and stashed them out front in the bushes to be picked up later. We literally cleaned them out, we took anything that wasn't part of the building. It was pretty funny; we had a near assembly line of guys just passing out boxes of stuff from the bar. We figured it was the least they owed us. I had a bottle of Midori Melon liqueur for almost 15 years before I finally tossed it- not many drinks at our house that call for Midori. I still have some of the glasses.

When I moved to Los Angeles I found out that everyone in L.A. has "another job." It's a matter of survival. It's not possible to act everyday unless you're a regular on a show. That is rare; not many actors get to work a lot. You don't know that going in. How many actors can there be? Turns out there are tens of thousands of them. They're everywhere. Everyone in L.A. is an actor, or wants to be an actor, or was an actor or will be an actor or is writing a screenplay for actors. The only problem is they don't act. They do their day jobs for years and then give up and go home. Fewer than 3% of the people in the Screen Actors Guild make over $100,000 a year. That's not many, especially considering what the wages are.

I had some crappy jobs when I was there. The first was as a traffic school instructor. In California, if you get a traffic ticket, you can attend an eight-hour traffic school course and have the points taken off your record. I taught for the Improv traffic school because I thought it would be a good way to get in the back door of the club and get some stage time. I was mistaken. Eight hours of traffic school. I'm supposed to talk about traffic for eight hours. That should be interesting. I got bored with that quickly. After a couple months, I was talking less about traffic and just telling stories. I'd spend the first half of the class working the room and the second half telling party stories. You'd be surprised how long it takes to ask 40 people their names and what their tickets were for. I turned into quite a time killer. This is really boring, let's move on.

I had a couple of driving jobs in L.A. Good place to get a driving job. The most traffic congested city in the west, and I got a driving job. One was a shuttle van driver at LAX. The horror, the horror. It was me and about 50 Armenians, who, at least to me, seemed related. Needless to say, the new white boy didn't get very good fares. I was last in line for the most part. I started at 3 a.m. and drove until noon. I shouldn't say drive actually, more like waiting to drive. I may have had five fares the time I worked there. Granted, I only lasted a week, but still.

I also had a job as a courier; taking packages and whatnot to various places in town. I thought it would be a good way to get in to see casting people. Again, I was mistaken. We were forbidden to slip our headshots into submission piles. I still did it, but we were forbidden. But again, who the hell gets a driving job in L.A? I was using my own car to boot. I had that job until I totaled my car. Nice. I broadsided some knuckle head from England driving in the wrong lane. Maybe I should go back to bartending.

I also did some acting jobs. Acting was kind of fun, certainly not as fun as I thought it would be. It's just too repetitive. That's one of the things I like about being a comedian- the spontaneity. You do your shit once, it's done, and you move on. There's no "back to one people." No do-over's. No different angles, it's done, it's out there and nothing can bring it back.

I booked a couple of gigs doing extra work. Those are the people that walk around in the background or sit at table or whatever, which is also why they're called "background." The number one rule of extra work is "don't look at the camera." But, as an extra, your only concern is getting ON camera, which means you have to look to see where it's at. If you don't look around for the camera, how are you going to know where it is? That is your one goal. To get on camera, so when you watch the show, you can see yourself. It's quite a kick. The director doesn't care about you getting screen time; you're background, just sit at that table and pretend like you're talking. You can't actually talk because the microphones pick it up and then the sound guy wants to know why he can hear people talking. I didn't really like doing extra work; I always felt that I should be a principal character. Well, too bad, you're background, now step aside and let the principals and crew get their food first.

I also did some commercials. My first one was for Freeway Insurance. I got the part because I was playing with my bare feet during the audition and the casting director thought it was hilarious. The problem with that commercial is that we had to wear masks. Not actual masks, but nylons over our heads. We were supposed to be shady insurance dealers, dealing over the phone wearing nylons. Funny idea, but you can't tell it's me. I guess that's why criminals sometimes put nylons over their heads. It's a creepy look.

I did a commercial for Sony music once. It was the Christmas campaign for Celine Dion. She wasn't actually at our shoot; she shot her part in N.Y. I played the father of a 16-year-old girl. When I went to the audition, there were about 20 guys all with gray hair and looking at least 50. So I know right away that I was not going to get the part. I do my audition anyway; they just wanted me to ad lib a line to an imaginary daughter and see how it went. I opened my "daughter's" door and said, "I'm going up to 7-11 to finish my Christmas shopping, what do you want?" It got a big laugh from the casting people. The next day, I got a call back for the part, and again, it's me and a bunch of older guys with gray hair. Again I'm thinking, there's no way I'll book this part. I "do my line" again, and the next day I found out I booked it. What the hell? Do I even look old enough to have a 16-year-old-daughter? Apparently to Hollywood I do.

As I'm going over my lines before shooting starts, I meet "my daughter." She's smoking hot and looks about 21. We go over our lines together and get ready to roll camera. My line is something about not knowing what she wants for Christmas. I changed it up a bit and added a "baby." After the first two takes the director asks me to do the line like I'm her father, not like I want to bang her. "I'm sorry?" He tells me that the way I'm saying the line sounds like I want to get into her pants, and he reminds me that I'm playing her father and to keep that in mind. "OK, gotcha." We shoot for a couple of hours and it all turns out well. I toned down my line, said it a little less sexy, and then became a huge star.

The first movie I did was called *Bicycle ER*. It was a student film, which means you don't get paid for it. Everybody has to start somewhere, and student films are where new actors, writers, directors, assistants, directors of photography, and everyone else affiliated with making a film start off. You rent equipment, find a crew, find a spot, do some auditions and start shooting. It's quite a blast. Like many jobs, you've got to get some OJT baby.

Bicycle ER was a take-off of the show *ER*, but it was set in a bicycle repair shop. Funny. I was Doug Boss, the George Clooney character. We filmed one night in a bike store. The story was: a guy comes in with his bike on a stretcher and we have to make a "life and death call" about saving the bike. Rules are broken and careers are jeopardized in the decisions made by me and the other docs. It was very funny shit, I thought; one of the nurses even throws up when she sees the bike grease smeared all over. At the end I was sitting on the stairs after we had saved the bike and I was talking about how I hated seeing the little ones come in, you know, the tricycles. He didn't use much of it in the final edit, but we had a good time doing it. It was actually played at a small film festival in Santa Monica and got a good response. It's weird watching yourself like that though. I'm uncomfortable watching myself act because I suck. That's hard to take. I did notice that I had a whole new appreciation for good acting; it's an incredibly difficult thing to do well.

One day I got a call from my agent, and he has an audition for me for a Playboy Channel movie. It's a union film. It was a little soft-core porn. I did it to get my SAG (Screen Actors Guild) card, which is what every actor strives for. You can't get a SAG card until you've been in a union movie, and you can't get a part in a union movie until you get a SAG card. Nice catch-22. I would explain the particulars, but they are not very interesting, so I'll move on. I was very excited, my first feature film. After reading the script, I realized that I was the only one in the movie that didn't get laid. Ten characters in this film and the comedian is the only one not getting any. Which is fine, I'm a comedian, not Ron Jeremy.

My characters name was Pokoloff, and I had my own trailer, which was most righteous. My first movie and I've got my own trailer and I'm in a bunch of scenes. Most of them, turns out, didn't make it to the final edit. Que Sera Sera. We shoot for two weeks, 10 hours a day, and I spent about 30 minutes a day in front of the camera. It takes a long time to shoot a movie. Everything must be discussed, dissected, tested, re-lit, etc., etc. It's a wonder anything gets done. I spent a great deal of my time taking naps in my trailer. They closed the set when doing sex scenes, so anyone not in the scene had to scram. Apparently they don't want a bunch of looky loos hanging around the set watching these actors having fake sex.

The director was also in charge of casting, so he knows this is my first film. After a couple of days of shooting, he tells me that I'm doing such a good job that they're going to write a sex scene for me, and they're going to shoot it the next day. I'm flabbergasted. First of all, I'm a hairy man, my chest is covered in hair. Normally not a problem, but I've noticed that the guys in this flick have no body hair. None. No chest hair, no leg hair, no arm hair. It's a cast of hairless men...and me, Troglodyte man. It should be visually stimulating. The entire day, I'm riddled with anxiety; I have to have simulated sex in front of cast and crew. I told him they will have to shave me down, a prospect I'm not that fond of. I'm proud of my testosterone levels. I also realize that I will have to inform my Mrs. of the new developments. Keep in mind, we've been out in L.A. for over a year and I've done some acting, but it was all for free. So, I go home to tell her that I have to do a love scene and ask if that bothers her. "I don't care if you've got to bang somebody, just bring home a paycheck." Okey doke.

The next day I'm a wreck, I haven't slept, I'm worried about my love scene, getting naked, good breath, no b.o. etc., and I realize it's part of acting, but I really didn't consider myself an actor at this point. I'm still a comedian, which turns out, is what I will always be. All day long I'm being egged on by the director, "your scene will be the last of the day." Good God, I have to wait all day for my scene; I can't even concentrate on my regular scenes knowing that at the end of the day I'll be dry humping someone on camera. As the day winds down, anxiety level is at an all-time high. I'm running out of time. The director then tells me that we won't get to my love scene until tomorrow. What? Are you out of your mind? I'm not putting this off another day. But time has run out for today.

They decide to light me for the scene and check positioning, etc. So I go over to the bed and drop my pants so they can see what kind of makeup, lights etc. they will need for tomorrow. Like I said, it was my first feature film and I was a little naive. As I'm standing there with my pants at my feet the lighting guy is checking the amount of reflection off my ass. He's moving his light meter all over my naked lower torso, and I'm standing there like some kind of idiot. I'm a little nervous, so there is some shrinkage, and I just want to go home. It's then that I realize that the whole crew is standing on the far side of the set laughing their asses off. It seems that there is no sex scene for Sweenz, they're just having a good time at my expense. "Hey, let's take advantage of the new guy, he's never done a film, let's see if we can get him to drop his pants in front of the whole crew" hardee har har. There was no script revision, no sex scene no nothing. They got me. They got me good. It was quite the chucklefest.

I did a SAG Signatory film called *BZERK!* in '00 or '01. It drug on so long, I lose track. SAG Signatory means they have approval to use union actors; they just don't have to pay them union wages. The script was weird, and the writer was the director as well. Very finicky, he was an Iraqi dude named Soly. The story was about a group of real estate people that go on a scavenger hunt and get captured by some devil worship group, with a stop at a strip club in there somewhere. Like I said, weird. We shot in a real estate office, a strip club, a hotel room, in the car, in the desert, at Castaic Lake, a parking lot, a hotel lobby, on a mountain road at night and at a balloon race. I almost forgot about the balloon race; I don't think any of the balloon people knew what we were doing there. It was renegade film making, and I don't think we had permission to shoot there because it seemed like we were sneaking around to get the shots. There was a lot of hiding behind trees and cars trailers and asking people as they walk by if they want to be in a movie. That kind of thing.

This director also needed 15-20 takes of every scene. That was too much; 15 takes of me getting out of the car is unnecessary. The shoot would drag on endlessly and then he'd want to come back the next day and do these scenes again. After about five months of this we took a break for a month; just stop filming and come back next month. What the hell? Let's finish this mofo so we can all move on with our lives. Patience is starting to wear thin; too many locations, too many nights, too many delays and way too many takes. One of the actors quit, that's how bad it was. We came up with plenty of good suggestions etc., and he turned them all down. "No more input from the actors, just do the lines I've written." Most of my scenes were with another guy, "my buddy," and two girls who were traveling with us. One scene called for me to kiss this girl and feel her up a little while we're sitting in the car. We start rolling and I'm kissing her and start to move my hand up her blouse and she stops the scene, turns out the window towards Soly and asks, "now what's this for again?" I guess she was asking what the movie was for, maybe what kind of distribution he had planned etc. I'm not really sure why that occurred to her at that particular point. All of a sudden she wanted to make sure the movie was legitimate before she let me feel her breast. Soly comes over and goes over his little spiel about the movie and asks me if everything's ok. "You bet, I'll fuck her if I have to, you know me Soly, anything for the craft." I'm dedicated, see, I'll do what I have to do to make this movie right. We cut down on some of the physicality and finished the scene. I was glad too because she had McDonald's on her way to the shoot and tasted like onions and mustard.

My buddy and I, along with the girls, had to shoot some more scenes in the car, we didn't finish and had to go back a couple of weeks later to re-shoot. Well Ben, my partner, doesn't show up; he had quit and Soly wanted to continue on like before without acknowledging the fact that we're missing someone. He just starts shooting the scene like Ben's there. But he wasn't. It's just me and the girls even though when we pulled over, there were four us in the car. We had dialogue, for crying out loud, and now Ben's seat is empty. I suggested that we pretend I killed him and buried him in the desert, but Soly wouldn't have any of it and we shot the scene starting with Ben and finished without him, I guess he wanted the audience to figure it out on their own. Like I said, it was renegade film making.

And so it went for months and months. We had wrapped and were waiting for the final product when 9-11 happened and Soly disappeared, and we haven't heard from him since. He literally disappeared. Weird, wild. I wonder if he still has our movie.

CHAPTER 27
I GO SKIING

I got seriously into water skiing for a while in college. A buddy of mine had a boat, was an avid skier, and he taught me a great deal. Just the two of us would usually go. No one else would get up that early, so we'd have a driver and a skier- no spotter. It wasn't really that safe, but we lived like the wind; free and breezy. We used to ski on the Mississippi River in Cape Girardeau. Oh yeah, skiing on the river, I don't know what we were thinking. I never did like skiing on the river, too much debris floating around.

The river is where I first used trick skis. Trick skis are aptly named. There is no rudder on them, so they're hard to control. They're short and oval and just ramble all over the place. It also doesn't help trying to control them in a fast moving river. There are wakes from barges to deal with, the barges themselves, fish jumping, logs from trees, and dead animals floating. It's a cornucopia of flotsam and jetsam to trip or ski over and then take a tumble into that dark, churning concoction of mysterious river water. For some reason, I always picture a river as being full of bodies that have lodged underneath a log or something, just waiting for me to come by and break it loose, so the rotting corpse can float up out of the depths and scare the shit out of me. Rivers are spooky, aren't they? I'm not sure why I think rivers are full of bodies. I just do.

There's something else about skiing on a river; once you fall down, and you will, by the time you make it back to the surface, the current has carried you about 200 yards downstream from the boat, which is still going the other direction. With no spotter, it sometimes takes a minute for the driver to realize he's lost his skier. By the time he does notice, you're a mile down river and moving fast. I didn't like that feeling of moving so fast and having no control and being carried along by river current. I don't care how good of a swimmer you are, you can't fight the Mississippi. I wore a ski vest, of course, but it still feels weird moving that fast while floating. I'm flying past the markers on shore at 30 mph just trying to avoid tumbling into a corpse. Needless to say, we didn't ski on the river very often.

In my experience, men have to learn their lessons the hard way. Men don't know not to do something unless they, or someone they know, get hurt doing it the first time. Many times alcohol is involved. Maybe most of time. Hell, maybe every time. Apparently, men just don't get it. Watch *America's Funniest Videos* and you'll see dumb men day after day doing shit they shouldn't be doing and getting hurt doing it. Take ski jumping, for instance. No one in their right mind would try ski jumping; flying off a ramp behind a boat, going 50 mph, trying to get airborne. Oh, yeah, that sounds like a good idea. Here's a thought: Let's do it after drinking all day. So there I was, head full of Budweiser, in the water, on jump skis, no spotter in the boat, just the two of us. Getting ready to fly. Real safe.

Skiing on jump skis is no problem. They're very long, wide, and you pop right out of the water. But you don't just get to ski on them; you must jump with them. Since you fly over and off a wooden ramp, the rudders on the skis are short and stout, which of course, makes them hard to control. I love that phrase. Short and stout, here is my handle, here is my spout. Oh, that's where that comes from. I knew it sounded familiar. Oh, I forgot to mention that you have to wear a harness when you go ski jumping. The harness wraps around your torso and keeps your right arm tight to your body so the power from the boat doesn't pull you over when you're in the air. That right there should have been a red flag. "Being in the air" is just not a phrase that you associate with water skiing. Airborne indeed. The idea is to get up out of the water, get stable, cruise over to the right side of the boat, and I mean the right side. You're supposed to get almost all the way even with the driver and when he gives the signal, you turn your skis to the left and cut back hard with a burst of speed, shoot across the wake behind the boat, get your speed to around 50-55 mph. Yes; I said 50-55 mph. Hold on with all your might as you cut across the wake, hit the ramp, fly up and over the ramp, hit the water, stand up and ski on. Sounds good. Sounds simple. Let's give it a try.

The only real advice I get, the most important advice, is "don't look down." When you're in the air, that is. You have to look down when you're approaching the ramp. Just don't look down when you're in the air. "Keep your eyes on the tree line, not the water." That should help. I didn't realize how hard that was going to be. Don't look down. How the hell am I supposed to see where I'm going? The first instinct you have is to look down. It's human nature, looking down is what you do when you're flying off a ramp in a lake being pulled by a boat. Look down is all you can do. But I get ahead of myself.

The first run goes OK, at first. Again, let me remind you, we have no spotter; it's just the two of us. I yell "hit it," and the boat takes off and I come out of the water. It's a little after 1 p.m. on a Tuesday and it's cloudy, but the air is warm. The wind I've got blowing across my chest is just enough to harden my nipples. I've had my lunch and a couple of brews, and I'm cruising atop the water on skis that are about a foot wide and eight feet long. I'm feeling confident. I'm in control of these skis.

I'm a little shaky at first. I've never skied on boards this long, but I'm fine. I head to the right in preparation for my cutback. As I pull up even with the boat I can see the ramp up in the distance. That's when I realize this is wrong. I'm in way over my head- how am I going to get from this side of the boat to the other side of the boat and then hit the ramp dead center? There is no way I can get back to the other side. What was I thinking? I should just let go of the rope and call it a day. But I don't. I receive the signal to start my cutback. I start to turn back behind the boat, and I'm slowing down, just coasting, I'm keeping tension in the rope, but I'm still slowing down. I get to about 4 feet from the right side of the wake and the rope tightens and I'm hurled across the wake in a wide arc.

It's like cracking the whip and I'm the only one on the end. I don't just accelerate; I'm snapped across the wake. Once everything gets caught back up, I'm flying. I cut across that wake so fast I have tears in my eyes. I'm not sure if the tears are from moving so fast or fear, but I'm crying my ass off. I know now that the 50-55 mph was real. I get across the wake and I'm on the outside edge of the arc so my speed is maxed out. I think that was the time I was most frightened, waiting for my turn to hit that ramp. I'll never put on a life jacket again.

Things at this point are still going pretty good, the skis are slapping, water is spraying, then I hit the ramp. As soon as my skis hit that ramp I fell down. Keep in mind I'm going about 50 mph. Hitting a wet wooden ramp at that speed can lead to some interesting injuries, and that is what's going through my mind as I see the ramp speeding towards my face. The ramp is made out of plywood, so it has a little give. I hit that thing and bounced 15 feet in the air and straight over the top left corner of the ramp. I fell before I got parallel to the boat, so I'm literally flung to the outside. While I'm airborne I realize that I'm going to be killed. I hope it doesn't hurt.

Somehow, while in mid-air, I got spun around, so I hit the water upside down and backwards while still wearing the skis. This should be ugly. I plunged about eight feet deep, I looked to the left and through the murky depths, I see the Lady of the Lake, but she's not ready for me just yet. I pulled myself towards the light. The light of the sun, not the death light. I came up out of the water unscathed. It's a miracle. I've survived. I'll be a son of a bitch- I'm invincible! Instead of counting my blessings and going home, I decide to try again. If that first one didn't hurt me, nothing will.

So I kept trying and trying and trying. After about five attempts, I can now get over the ramp, but each time I get airborne and I think "don't look down," I would look down. When you put your eyes downward, that's where you go. I don't know why, it just happens. It's so weird. I look down, and then I crash. I look down, and then I crash. I find it almost impossible to keep my eyes up. I need to look down to see where I'm going. It's like jumping off a building and not looking down; tough to do. I keep flying off this ramp and trying to keep my eyes on the tree line, but I can't. I keep looking down, so I keep going face first into the lake. You'd think a boy would learn. I hit the water every way you can imagine and still keep trying. I finally get a jump in and land and ski off. It's an incredible feeling even though it took almost two hours of this nonsense to do it, but I ski jumped. It took almost a week before I could walk upright again. I didn't know you can bruise every muscle in your body, but it felt like I did. I never did go ski jumping again. It wasn't good stuff, and it wasn't good times.

There is tool out there called a boom bar. What to say about the boom bar? It was, like the ski jumping, a one-time deal. It didn't take much time on the boom bar to realize I wouldn't be doing that again. It seemed fun. Hell, it looked like fun. It's a training tool to help you learn how to ski barefooted. Skiing barefoot is not something I really felt the need to do. Plain old skiing had been good enough for me. I could ski on one ski and that was enough for me. Hey, that rhymes.

Some buddies and I were out on a boat, and one of them had recently acquired a boom bar, so we figured we'd give it a try. It's a 10 foot long pole that attaches to the side of the boat and sticks out over the water. The idea is: you enter the water and hold on to this pole with both hands while the boat takes off and pulls you up onto your stomach. Once you get to cruising speed, around 40 mph, you flip onto your back, curl your feet up, spin around on your butt, put your feet down, and bingo bango boingo, you're skiing barefoot. The directions made it seem so easy, but not so fast, buster. My trip on the boom bar wasn't all that simple.

Since no one else would do it, I went first. I got into the water and grabbed on to the pole. So far, so good, although the boat isn't even in gear yet. All is well. I'm in the water and holding on to the pole, and I give the word to go. We gently take off, and the gentleness quickly wears off. As we increase speed, things get less and less gentle. Things get mean, rough, and nasty, just like Proud Mary.

The problem with barefoot skiing is you have to be going fast. You can't do it at 20 mph. You need to go 40. As we went faster it got harder to hold on. The water crashes into your face, the drag increases, and my shorts slid to my knees. I had my legs spread out in the flying V formation to keep my shorts on while trying to protect my gonads from being battered into paste. Balls are precious and delicate things. I'm not sure having them smacked around at 40 mph is a good thing. This was the first water sport I'd done where a cup would've come in handy. Bruised and battered balls aren't going to do anyone any good.

I tried to keep my head above the water line so I didn't drown, and I held on for dear life as the water threatened to take me away. I battled all these things and had no idea what came next. How long do I have to hang on? When do I flip over? Will my shorts remain with me? Why am I doing this? What, pray tell is going to happen?

I held on with one hand while the other pulled my shorts back up, tucking my junk safely between my legs, holding on with one hand only made matters worse, because I started to wobble. I was weaving and wobbling, fighting off drowning or being sucked into the prop when the guys in the boat start yelling at me to flip over.

OK. That answered that question. I needed to flip over. So I did, and I was upside down, facing the sky, being pulled alongside a boat at 40 mph. You might think it would be easier, and you would be wrong. The water battered my ass cheeks. You might think, that doesn't seem so bad, almost like a water massage, but it wasn't like any water massage I've ever had. It was like being blasted with a fire hose. It was a full-on assault on my backside. I had bruises on my ass for a week and sat on a life jacket the rest of the day.

So there I was, hanging on to the bar, upside down. I think I finally got my shorts so they would stay up, and I'm in business. I hadn't broken anything yet, nothing had been dislocated, and everything seemed right. I curled my feet up tight to my chest and spun around on my butt. By the way, I'm not sure if I mentioned this, but to spin around with your legs in the proper position, you have to remove your left hand from the boom bar in order to let your legs through. Otherwise, your legs would be stuck on the outside of your arms and there's no way you can stand up. No, the arm must be removed first. The problem, of which there are many, is that once you let go with your left hand to let your legs through, the water pounds the shit out of you as it tries to pull you off the bar, so you have to do the transition quickly; move the arm, slide the legs, re-grab the pole.

I had two hands on the pole with my legs in the middle, holding on with every fiber of my being as the 40 mph water crashed into my nether regions. Slamming, pounding, bombarding and basically whaling on my privates while the water tried to force my fanny cheeks apart and make its way into uncharted territory. Yes, Virginia, that mean old water tried to work its way inside to tickle my innards, and it did. Water has its way because it's nature's way. Water will always find a way in. Unfortunately for me, it was trying to work its way in at 40 mph. That's just too much torque, I think. I've never had an enema, but I doubt it's applied at that speed. If I hadn't clamped down as tightly as I did, I may have felt it all the way to my larynx. No thank you, I'll pass.

So I'm curled in a ball, basically holding on to this pole with my legs in between my arms, knees to face, just skimming along the surface, with the water trying to rip my balls off. I'm not sure I really wanted to stand up. I was safe there, my ass clenched tight, and I was holding on with every fiber of my being, so why ruin that by trying to move? I could just ride it out for awhile, call it day and say I did the boom bar. I'd be satisfied with that. Who wouldn't be? However, it was not to be.

The boys start yelling at me to stand up. Stand up, they say. Stand up. So I tried. There is a great deal of feel in doing a task such as this. You have to have your feet at the just the right angle. You must slowly lower your feet until your heels are skimming the water lightly and then dig your heels in just a touch. Once you dig your heels in, a little wake comes up that just happens to hit you in the nuts. It's a solid wake, too, not big, but what it lacks in mass it makes up for in velocity and narrowness, and it's a straight shot on the boys; kind of like a small, high pressure hose right on the satchel. That, in itself, was motivation enough to stand up.

My heels dug in a little, and I found some purchase. At first I'm a little wobbly, and it's hard to keep my legs and feet on line- they have a tendency to meander. I'm back to the old weave and wobble, as I try to stand up. There are a lot of things going on in the duder's head right then. I had to stand up with complete balance, weight over my backside, gently pulling myself up, all the while keeping my feet in perfect alignment with the solar system. All the planets have to be aligned; it just doesn't work otherwise. The feet are the key; they must be perfect; the exact right amount of weight, the perfect angle, not too deep, not too shallow. The legs must be spread and balanced. They must be firm and sturdy. The upper body has to be upright and hearty, a solid base from which to maneuver. The arms must be steady and unfailing. They must hold the whole thing together. As I said, the planets have to aligned. All these things were going through my mind and I hadn't even tried to stand.

I was still in a semi-crouched position pondering my future, as my ass was gently skimming the water. I tried to stand. In ski jumping, you're told not to look down. In boom barring, you should be told not to let your toes go under the water. When I tried to stand, my feet leveled off and went under.

When this happens, your feet stop moving, but the rest of you doesn't because it's still holding on to the boom bar which is connected to the boat. Weird science, man. Once your feet go under, your legs are shot back behind you and you slam your front side right down onto the water. I didn't say "into" because you go "onto" the water. I wish I would have gone into, but at that speed you just get slapped down onto the water.

For some reason, I didn't let go. I could have, but I didn't. I was face down, the boat wake splashing me in the face, the speed trying to tug me off the bar. The water tries to tug my shorts off, and again, batters my balls. I am being beaten to death hanging from a metal pole connected to a speeding boat.

I flip over onto my back and start all over. I went through this nonsense for about twenty minutes before I finally got up and skied barefoot. Way overrated. It may be different using a rope behind the boat instead of a boom bar next to it, but I didn't see much difference. It was the most beat up I think I've ever been doing water sports.

Nobody tells you that it tears the shit out of your feet. The soles of my feet were never designed to bear the brunt of 40 mph water grinding them into hamburger. I had to wear slippers for three days.

CHAPTER 28
DOGS

When I first got to college, I moved into a house with a dude named Jimmy. When Sweet Lou came down he moved in with us as well. After several months at school, we each had a dog. Louie had a Great Dane/German Shepherd mix that weighed about 150 lbs.; his name was Chester, but we called him "Chester the Molester" for reasons that will be revealed soon. Jim had a female Irish Setter named Spike- great name for a female dog. I had a dog from a litter that Chester and Spike had, and his name was Avatar (from the movie *Wizards*). Spike was pregnant with a litter and was due any day. The night she went into labor, I was home alone. Granted, I was a grown man, but nonetheless, I was home alone.

I didn't realize what was going on at first, but she had dropped a puppy on the floor and my first thought was, "what the hell has she been eating?" It was then I saw that it was a puppy. Oh my goodness, we're having babies! I brought her down to the "birthing area" in the basement and wondered what to do. Spike is having pups and she's looking at me as if I have the answers, but all I wanted to tell her was, "I don't know nothing 'bout birthin' no babies." But since I'm the human, I'm in charge, so let's do it.

She lays down and starts pushing out pups, but after five she started breaching and needed help, and I guess I should help her, but I'm not sure how and I'm not sure about interrupting or intervening during this process. Spike is looking at me with that "how about a little help there, slugger" look on her face, so I started pulling puppies out. It's kind of an odd feeling. First of all, it's very messy, and I certainly didn't want to break anything. We kept banging them out until she dropped 14 puppies. What the hell are we going to do with 17 dogs in the house? It will be madness, but I'll tell you this much, when you go to the park with 14 puppies, you *will* meet girls. Women can't resist puppies; they will lay on the ground and let them climb all over. "Well, gee, I too, would like to climb all over you, and you and you."

The major problem with 14 puppies is that they leave a lot of poop. Each morning we would take turns going down to the basement and confronting the 40-50 piles of puppy poop. That brings up the second big problem: puppies don't have enough sense to leave the poop alone;

they have to play in it like it's no big deal. They're rolling, jumping and wrestling in their own droppings. Dumb dogs. So you'd have to bring them outside for the morning hose down and then do the floor, shoveling poop for an hour, then hosing and disinfecting the floor. For me, it was a total gag fest, so I started paying my roomies to do my work for me. There is nothing in the world like a pack of puppies, and sometimes you wonder, "why can't you just stay puppies?" I think that would be the ultimate job, just hanging around and playing with puppies all day, but after they're done weaning, it's almost a pleasure to see them go.

We lived out by the woods for a while. One day as we're sitting on the front porch, we see the dogs coming out of the woods, and they're dragging something. The three of us are trying to figure out what the hell they're dragging and Louie notices that it's a deer. Not actually the whole deer: he's missing his head, part of his shoulder and one of his legs. We're figuring there's no way these dogs killed a deer; are they that savage? Could these sweet little darlings run down, bring down and then tear apart a full-sized deer? No way, they must have found it by the side of the road and brought it back for a weekend cook out. We've got a picture of them standing over this deer carcass and they look so proud. We, of course, told everyone that they had killed the deer themselves, it just seemed to make a better story.

Chester was a cool dog. Big, blond and badass. Chester was the most independent dog I've ever known. That dog didn't need anyone; he did what he wanted when he wanted and to whomever he wanted. Chester would disappear for weeks, sometimes months, at a time. And then, out of the blue, you would come home and he'd be sitting on the porch like he'd just seen you that morning. He showed up back at home several times wearing a new collar. He had found a family, they "adopted" him, and when he was done with them, he'd leave. You have to love the spirit. We would always see other dogs that looked like Chester roaming around town. We thought he was out getting laid all the time and the town was full of his bastard children. That's where Chester the Molester came from. Oh, he was a dickens that one was. The problem with all the wandering is that he would get a lot of tickets from the dog pound because he would get picked up a lot. One day Louie got a notice that Chester was in the pound and his bail was $120.00, which to a working college student, was a lot of money.

The three of us were drinking at the Mule Lip (great name for a bar). The "Lip" was one of our favorites. A lot of great ideas were generated at the Mule Lip, this one included. We came to the conclusion that we should break Chester out of jail. Seems like a feasible, workable idea, doesn't it? Break a dog out of the pound. Yeah, what is this? Gunsmoke? But we worked out the details, and it did seem like it could work.

We'd all been there before, and we'd never send the same guy to pick Chester up because we didn't want them to know who he belonged to. I don't know that it made any difference, but it made us feel sneaky and that was good enough. One night around 2 a.m. we decided to put our plan into action. We parked about a half a mile away from the pound. The place was surrounded by corn and soy bean fields. The side we needed to attack was fronted by a soy bean field, and soy beans only grow about six inches tall, so they don't give much cover. The field butts up against a cyclone fence about 10 feet high, and on the other side is 10-footwide swath of gravel, then another fence about eight feet high, and on the other side of that fence are the cages.

The cages all have swinging doors so the dogs can go in and out. We're about 100 yards from the fence and figuring out our game plan. It had been raining for two days and everything and everyone were soaked. I had recently gotten out of the Marines and felt that I was best qualified to come up with plan. I said, "follow me," and took off running. We were all running and tucking and hitting the ground rolling and getting up and running and tucking and hitting the ground like we were dodging shots being fired from machine gun turret.

By the time we got to the fence, we were covered in mud and soy beans and laughing our asses off. Louie and I climbed the first fence, and as soon as we hit the gravel, the motion light went on and every dog in that place came running out and barking and braying and yelping and jumping up and down. I think every dog in there thought they were the ones being broken out. We would've liked to have taken all of them, but with the lights and noise, we didn't have much time. We're running up and down the gravel path calling, "Chester, Chester," and he's nowhere to be found. The other dogs are going crazy. There had to be 20 dogs going off at the top of their lungs, and we can't find our dog. At the end there's one cage that seems to be empty, so we go down and call Chester's name, and he comes strolling out like we're disturbing his sleep.

He looks at us and does that doggy stretch thing, and I'm thinking, "you ungrateful bastard." We're risking jail time and this mofo acts like he doesn't care where he sleeps. Louie and I climb the fence and grab Chester to throw him over the first fence. We pick him up and he doesn't get excited at all, very calm, very cool; I don't think he knew what was going on or even cared for that matter, so we toss him. It's only eight feet, so we get him over on the first try. He hits the gravel and it's chaos. Those other dogs are losing their minds. Now they all want out- it's like the end of a movie where everyone's trying to make the escape, but some don't.

Chester is running up and down the gravel path, he understands now, he knows what's happening and is ready to go home. Of course, we still have to get him over the big fence. Jim is on the other side getting ready to catch him. That's how you know alcohol was involved; he wants to catch a 150 lb dog that's just been thrown over a 10 foot tall fence. It takes us three attempts to get him over, but we do it. Chester was calm as can be, even looked like he was trying to reach over, God love him. We get him over, follow him, and hit the ground running. We didn't tuck and roll on the way back; we just made a beeline for the car. Chester was so excited that he kept running into us and knocking us down into the muddy soybean field. We got to the car and hit the gas and made our getaway. Jim's car was completely covered in mud inside and out, but we rescued our dog and never paid the $120.00. Good stuff, Good times.

CHAPTER 29
SOME PARTY STORIES

There is a time and place for everything. Acid and Disney World are such a time and place. I doubt that's what Walt had in mind at first design, but he created a haven of joy for recreational drug users. The sights, the sounds, the smells, the people; it's sensory fulfillment.

When I was eighteen, some friends and I ate some peyote while camping on the Colorado River. We watched the sun come up from a cliff 300 feet above the river. Doesn't get much finer. Every color of the spectrum was in the sky that morning, or at least it seemed that way; it could've been raining. We had the endless sky above us and the river meandering below us, lying on a bluff in the Arizona desert. Perfect. We had moments of pure clarity. We felt we could almost reach up and touch heaven. It's moments like that when you realize how insignificant humans are on the timeline of the universe. We may have actually wept. Now you take that same peyote and give to a guy driving a bus, and you're going to have a completely different experience. He's freaked, panicked, can't believe he's driving a bus, would really rather be at home, and a guy with three arms just got on the bus and doesn't have exact change. Different deal.

Acid and Disney World, that's the real deal. I was in Florida with my friend JoJo, and we took a road trip on a Monday, heading to Disney World. We got a room within walking distance of the park. You don't really drive well on acid because there are too many visual things going on. Acid and driving don't mix, and that's the problem with driving; it doesn't do well with any drugs. I think it takes too much focus away. Away from what I'm not sure. Sometimes it takes your focus off your driving; other times it takes the focus off the party. Either way, focus has been shifted. That was quite profound. *Focus has been shifted*. Wow, this guy is something. When I found out that driving doesn't mix well with anything was in high school. My friends and I were coming back from the movie *Wizards*, which is a great acid movie. It's a Ralph Bakshi animation. Animation is the best for acid people. I think that most of the animation done today is by drug people. It has to be. So we ate the acid, watched the movie and were on our way home in a Volkswagen Rabbit, a bright yellow sumbitch, and my buddy driving makes a huge swerve trying to avoid the "giant turtles," and that's when I knew not to drive on acid. I think the good Lord was watching out for our dumb asses that night.

So, now we're back in Disney World. We check in, eat the cid and hit the tram, the monorail. Nice ride, very peaceful, kind of like the quiet before the storm. Acid affects you slowly; you can always feel the subtle changes, a little trail here, a little splash of color there, just a little tingle and then the inevitable question, "are you getting off?" I'm not sure why that always happened, but it did. People you did drugs with always wanted to know if you were getting off. Do you feel anything yet? Can you tell? What do you feel like? What's happening? Is my hair growing? I can feel it doing so. Do you feel anything? Is it good stuff? I don't feel anything yet, do you? Are you getting off? Yes, by God I am.

Acid makes you grin like an inmate in an asylum. You can't stop grinning for any reason; that's why your face is sore the next day-you've grinned for 11 straight hours. You can't put your face through that much joy and not expect a little soreness. We wandered around that park all day not really doing anything, just walking and grinning, grinning and walking. Acid will make you have laughing spells as well. It's usually something so stupid, you normally wouldn't give it second notice, but on acid, it's just a riot. For example, we went into this building to watch a thing about animation. We were the first ones in line; it wasn't even a line really, just a big lobby. We're standing there just chit-chatting, I don't how long we stood there, maybe 30 minutes, totally oblivious to our surroundings, just in the moment full of happiness.

My compadre tells me to turn around, and when I do, I see that the lobby is full. There must be 300 people in there and we didn't hear one of them come in. I was still under the impression that we were by ourselves. I turn back around and JoJo is laughing so hard he's got tears running down his face, which naturally sets me off. The more we think about the fact that 300 people "snuck up" on us, the more we laugh, and now we're both shaking hard and have tears and snot running down our faces.

So we're standing there shaking and crying and snotting, praying the doors will open so we can get away from these sneaky bastards. How the hell did this many people sneak up on us? Are they all Ninjas? Can they all be wearing wrestling shoes that don't squeak? Have they all just been standing there and not talking? How the hell did 300 people fill up this lobby without us knowing it? Curious. The doors finally open and we grab our seats, we settle in, and we come to the conclusion that the "acid is pretty good."

We finished up our day by sitting in the parking lot staring at the big golf ball which is the Epcot Center. You can actually sit and watch stuff for a long time when doing acid. One night during the same week (it was one of those party weeks), we sat up until 4 a.m. watching trucks unload cars onto a dealership parking lot. We found it oh so interesting. That's the beautiful thing about the cid; you don't have to be doing anything to enjoy it.

I've been on dozens of canoe trips over the years. Trips being the key word here, I think. Mushrooms were always the choice on float trips; maybe it's the organic thing. Out in nature we would stick to the organic drugs. Mushrooms, contrary to popular belief, aren't that much of a hallucinogenic, at least in my experience. They're supposed to be, but I don't ever remember hallucinating from mushrooms. Mushrooms always made me laugh. I love the drug-induced laugh; it's not just a chuckle, it's an endless howling, that will make your sides and jaws hurt. That's the best, isn't it? Just laughing until it hurts. Maybe that's why I became a comedian. I love the sound of people laughing.

On one particular float, we had an odd number of people so Scott decided to float on an inner tube tied behind our canoe. It seemed like an OK idea at the time, but that was before the mushrooms kicked in. Things were going along swimmingly. Unfortunately, one of the side effects of mushrooms is that sometimes they make you poop. That was my side effect for the day. I had to stop and take care of "nature's business." Naturally we had no TP, so you have to make do with whatever you could find. On this occasion, I found these huge leaves with soft fuzz on them. I'm not kidding- big ass leaves with this downy fuzz covering the entire front side of the leaf. It was amazing, and it was just as comfortable as any store bought paper I've ever used. It was really something, exciting, new, maybe even a little alarming, something this soft and nice on my bum, growing wild next to the river. What crazy, remarkable thing will happen next? It turned out to be one of the most enjoyable outdoor movements I've ever had. I came out of the bushes, refreshed, awake, alive and clean as a whistle. What a beautiful day! The sun is bright, the air is warm and we're floating on the river. Could life be any sweeter? Is it the mushrooms that make me want to hug you all?

Here's an example of how much fun things are on mushrooms. As I was doing my business, the rest of the party were lounging in the water, and Louie was wearing day-glo green shorts that clung to his ass when wet. We're standing there and he farts, not that funny, but when he does fart, those shorts are clinging to his butt and an air bubble forms. As we're standing there we watch this air bubble move up the crack of his ass for almost five minutes, by the time this thing hits his waistband and dissipates, we're gone. The other four of us are on the ground. It is too funny. That phrase has been used before, but this truly was "too funny." We couldn't take it. I think Chris ran off into the woods to recover, and we laughed for almost fifteen minutes.

I remember just lying there on the gravel bed, rocks sticking to my face and body, curled up in a ball shaking with laughter. You're almost in your own world when you laugh like that, all these endorphins are being released, chemical things are happening, and you just lay there and laugh with your whole body. Very therapeutic. The best thing is, when we recall it later, we get another good round of laughs. Can't beat that, getting another round of hysterical laughter on a recall. We probably should've called someone. It may be hard to function after that; after all, we've just witnessed the funniest thing that has ever happened. Let's get back on the water.

Just under an hour later, the mushrooms are going full tilt, we're smiling from ear to ear, and the cold beers are going down sweetly. Tragedy was just around the corner. Tragedy may be a little strong, but it was almost tragic, for me at least. We're casually working our way down river and the current starts to pick up, and now we're heading into a sharp turn. In the middle of this turn is a huge tree laying smack dab in the middle of the river. The roots were facing us. How that son of a bitch got into the middle of the river is beyond me. It was lying on its side, like it had grown right out of the river and the current had finally knocked it over. I'd never seen anything like it. This thing had a root span of about eight feet and stood four feet out of the water, and that tree had to be 100 years old; it was huge. The current whips us into this turn, so I rudder hard and get to the outside of the turn and Scott, trailing behind us tied to our canoe on an inner tube, goes to the inside of the turn, so we straddle this root structure and the rope gets hung up it and stops us dead in our tracks. The canoe is on one side and the tube is on the other, and the current is cooking. All of a sudden, we see Scott cruise past the end of the tree stump on the other side and he's going about 20 mph, no life jacket, of course. The river is carrying him along like a cork, and he's high on mushrooms and looks scared as hell. This could be interesting. The other canoe pulls over and grabs Scott. He's cool now that he's on shore, but that was close call. Now that they're all on shore, it's funny; they're all getting a good laugh.

Meanwhile, my canoe is straddling this tree stump with a huge current trapping us. I can't pull the tube around from the other side because the water is moving too fast. I figure I'll get in the water and swim around to the other side and bring the tube back over. Apparently another side effect of mushrooms is poor judgment. I guess I wasn't thinking about the current. I'll tell you what though. I thought about it right after I jumped in; I thought about it hard. I slipped over the right side of the canoe and by the time my belly button hit the water, my legs were on the left side of our vessel. Suddenly, I realize, oops, I may have just screwed up.

I grabbed on to the side of the canoe as my legs were dragged underneath, so I stopped myself from being swept away, but as I'm holding on, it's pulling my body under and soon my arm is the only thing out of the water. I'm basically holding myself under the canoe, kind of tough to breathe that way. I figure I'll let go with my right arm, and as I come underneath the canoe to the left side, I'll reach up and grab hold of the side of the canoe and pull myself out. I would try to come up with another solution, but I'm starting to drown and there's not much time. So I let go of the right side, slide under the canoe and reach up for the left side. I grab hold and the current slams me into the tree then starts sucking my legs under the trunk, and I grab hold of the canoe with both hands and try to pull myself up.

You really can't climb into a canoe like that without capsizing it, plus the water is holding me down, so I stop to collect my thoughts. My girlfriend is starting to panic, but she's no help anyway, the shrooms have her. I hear my buddies over on the shore laughing. They said it was funny, how fast I got sucked under. Strangely enough, it didn't seem all that funny to me. I'm basically trapped between the canoe and this giant tree trying to figure out how to get to the other side of the tree and bring that tube over here. My solution was to go under, let the current bring me below the tree, surface on the other side, reach up, grab something, pull my way against the current, get the tube, bring it around the back of the stump- against the current mind you, and free us from this trap. I tell my girlfriend that and she starts to cry, she feels that I'll drown. I tell her that I'm Water Survival Qualified by the United States Marine Corps. That makes her feel better. I didn't tell her that we got tested in a pool with no current and no head full of mushrooms or even the fact that I was eighteen then.

So under I go. It tore up my back pretty good because I went under at quite a clip, but I grabbed a branch, pulled myself to the tube, freed it from the roots and got it back to the other side. It took ten minutes and most of the energy I had left, but by God, I did it. I survived the mission. We're free and we head to shore to regroup. As we're recovering from our brush with death and discussing how difficult and dangerous that mission was, Louie asks, "why didn't you just untie the rope?"

"What?"

"Why didn't you just untie the rope and let the tube go?"

I don't know which made me madder, the fact that I didn't think of that earlier or the fact that he waited until it was all over to suggest an easier way to do it. Maybe he could have mentioned that when I was fighting off death. It would've been a nice thought as he gave my eulogy. "I wish I would've mentioned untying the rope sooner."

Drinking and boating have always gone together, always. Just ask Capt. Hazelwood of the Exxon Valdez. The good Capt. is also another good example of what can happen if you don't use your head. You can crash an oil tanker into *land*. Boaters have always been drinkers. I think it's being near the water. Anybody that lives or plays near water seems to be a good partier. I could be wrong, but I have spent a good deal of my time in or near water, and these people like to have a good time. Times may come up where you have to decide whether to put gas in the boat or fill up the cooler, and the cooler will win most of the time. As long as you have beer, you can row the boat out. Or get a tow- "I have beer, but no gas, can we get a ten mile tow?" Absolutely.

I was in a boat wreck once. It was a Friday night, the 13th. I'm not superstitious; it's just a coincidence. Although...you never know. I tended bar for 12 years and every night that the moon was full was always a different kind of night; more fights, more weird activity, more everything. We had been out on the boat most of the day having some cocktails and other assorted fun in the sun. We ended up at our favorite lake bar. Everyone's got one, that bar you go drink in after you've been out all day drinking in the sun. I should have known the night was going to end badly when I dropped my shorts and dove naked into the lake in front of 100 people on the patio. Go home, Sweeney. I did get a little round of applause though. That was nice.

Things started winding down around midnight. We're talking to a friend of a friend kind of thing when he asks if we want to go for a ride in his new 32-foot Scarab, a nice little racing boat capable of going about 90 mph. That is quite quick on water. Hmmm, let's see, get into a stranger's fast boat on a Friday night at one a.m. after drinking beer all day and beer and Jagermeisters all night? Sounds good. What could possibly go wrong?

As it turns, a lot could go wrong. Louie, Mike and I get into this clown's boat and he takes off like he's been drinking and eating in Mexico and needs to get home before he loads up his shorts with Montezuma's revenge. He's doing figure eights and jumping wakes and flinging us around like beads in a baby's rattle. When the fire extinguisher came flying off the wall, we probably should have said something. When we got airborne, we really should have said something. Boats aren't supposed to leave the surface of the water. They are run with propellers, which strangely enough have to be in the water to work. Not that he could have heard us over the roar of boat and wind whipping by.

When he turns, and starts heading back to the dock, relief was felt by myself and my two friends. Thank God, we'll be off this boat in a minute. I look out and see a boat, a boat, hmm that's weird, there shouldn't be a boat out there, coming right at us, should there? Am I the only one who sees this boat barreling down on us, and us barreling down on him? Hello? Does anyone else see this? There's a boat coming, there's a boat coming. Is it a hallucination? How come I didn't see it a second ago? It's not a hallucination. I can hear it. I can see it pushing water.

The other driver said he had his lights on, but I don't believe him. If he had lights on, I think I would've seen lights. The only light I saw his boat in was our anchor light. It makes absolutely no difference now; I just wanted to clarify. So I see the boat, and apparently I'm the only one; everyone else is oblivious as to what's about to happen. Mike and Louie are just holding on for dear life, and the driver is...well, I don't know what he was doing, not watching the water, that's for sure. We're headed right at this boat and this boat is headed right towards us. I'm just about to scream out "look out for that boat" when we slam into the other boat, head-on at 30 mph. Granted, 30 mph doesn't seem like very fast until you take into account that the other boat is also going 30 and the fact there aren't any seatbelts in a boat, the only the thing that stops your body's forward motion is the dashboard.

The moments right after impact are gone, I have no idea what went on. There are about 90 seconds that I'll never get back. I got knocked out cold. When I come to, I'm lying in about six inches of water. It was just enough water to cover my ears and give you that feeling of being in one of those sensory deprivation tanks. I can't hear anything but muffled screaming. I can't see anything because someone was lying on top of me. I tried to stand up, but I was having trouble moving, and I still have no idea of what's going on.

Why am I wet? Why does my head hurt? Why does my chest hurt? Why does my shoulder feel weird? Why can't I breathe properly? Why? Why? What the hell is going on? Am I in heaven? Am I killed? Why is heaven full of water? I'm assuming, of course, that I'm in heaven and not hell. I could be wrong; I hope not. I finally stand up and now I'm standing in about ten inches of water, and I still can't figure it out. I guess my head was still a little cloudy, but I know I'm not dead. Why is our boat sinking? Then it hits me. Holy shit, we hit that boat, and it comes flooding back.

We were in a boat wreck. Wow, I've never known anyone who was in a boat wreck. I've heard of boat wrecks. I've even heard about people at our lake that were killed in boat wrecks, and now I'm in a boat wreck. Then I notice that we're sinking fast, and I can hear people on the other boat yelling at us to get off before it sinks. Get off? Into the water? I turn to Louie to see if he's alright. He had been sitting behind the driver's seat and apparently was not alright. He looks up and freaked the shit out of me. He had slammed his face into the back of the driver's seat and had split the upper left half of his face open. Uh Oh. That can't be good, and I can't tell what's really wrong with him because he's covered in blood down to his belly button.

Now the water is just about thigh deep, not a good sign for boaters, standing in your boat thigh deep in water. I started picturing the huge circle of suction that will pull us under when the boat sinks. I don't want to drown. In retrospect, I doubt a 32-foot boat would create that kind of pull, but you never know. I grab Louie and step off the boat. I try to swim over to the other boat and realize I've dislocated my shoulder. It is really hard to swim when your arm isn't in the shoulder socket, the ball of the shoulder has to be firmly planted in the socket for it to work properly.

I try to yell out to the other boat when I realize I've got broken ribs because it hurts when I expand my lungs. I'm holding on to Lou and now our boat is going down and with it the only light that I can see. I start to freak out. I thought we were going to drown. Louie has a bad head injury, so he's out of it, he's got no clue. I can't hold on to him and swim, and I can't tread water very well because I've got broken ribs. I have a hold of his collar with one hand, and my little legs are just kicking away trying to keep our heads above water and I can only take tiny little breaths. Of all the injuries I've had, the broken ribs were the biggest hassle- not the most pain, but he biggest hassle. There's really nothing they can do for you, there are no casts, etc. Just time. Yeah, about four months of no laughing, sneezing, coughing, burping, yelling, breathing deep, singing or sleeping on your side, and believe me that when you sleep with broken ribs and roll over on your side, you'll know.

So we're just trying not to drown, and suddenly a light hits us. It's the police helicopter. That was quick. Exactly how long have we been out here? The other boat throws us a life jacket and rope and they pull us in. We get pulled out of the water and see Mike, our other buddy. Apparently he jumped ship right after the collision and didn't see any reason to stay and help us. Quite a friend, that one was. He still hasn't heard the end of that. The driver I don't remember seeing again. Weird. I don't know if he was on the boat or not. The girls on the other boat seemed a little panicky after seeing the blood pouring down Louie's face. As their boat starts moving us back towards shore, you can see the lights of our boating dimly fading out of view as it sinks to the bottom.

It was really an odd feeling. We were just in that boat, and now it's on its way to a watery grave. They took us back to shore where three ambulances were waiting. They sat us down on the picnic tables for a quick look. They had to cut my sweatshirt off, and I'm not too happy about that as it is one of my favorites, but my wife tells them "go ahead and cut it up." She has never liked this particular sweatshirt because it was given to me by a previous girlfriend. Chicks. The guy confirms my suspicions of a dislocated shoulder and then tries to strap me down to a stretcher. This is the wrong plan for a dislocated shoulder. The only comfortable position is sitting up and leaning over, taking pressure off the shoulder. I inform the guy of this and he tells me that no one rides in the ambulance without being strapped down, so I tell him that I won't ride in the ambulance, and tells me that yes I will, and I say no I won't. So I ended up strapped down for a 20 minute ride to the hospital. A small, rural hospital, a hospital that is not ready for four seriously injured people at 2:30 am. As soon as we enter it's chaos, and as we arrive, I hear my wife say, "we don't have insurance, so treat him as cheaply as possible." How's that for love? The nurse informs her that they treat everyone the same and she reminds her again that we don't have any insurance. I think the Mrs. was suffering some shock; either that or the Rumplemintz was still in her system.

I'm wheeled into the corner so they can put a chest tube in Louie's collapsed lung. That's great and everything, but "CAN SOMEONE COME OVER HERE AND LET ME SIT UP?" No one comes, so I repeat my request, "HELLO. CAN SOMEONE LET ME UP PLEASE?" Again, no response. Now I'm getting pissed; all I want to do is sit up. So I figure if I tip the gurney over somebody will come over and see what the hell I want. The problem with that plan is that it really hurts a dislocated shoulder when you struggle against the straps of a stretcher. Owww. Finally, someone comes to attend to me. "What is it, sir?" the nurse asks. What is it, sir? I'm not sure I care for your tone. I'm over here in a great deal of agony and she's copping an attitude with me. Why if I wasn't strapped down, I'd get up and give you the why to's and the what for's. But you are Blanche; you are strapped down. It seems that my injuries didn't warrant immediate attention. Well for the love of St. Peter, all I want to do is sit up, and if not that, then how about a little shot of Demerol? That might take the edge off.

A little comment about Demerol; it's an absolutely wonderful drug, a little slice of heaven. Unfortunately, the only time I've had Demerol is when I was hurt in some fashion; you don't find it much as a recreational drug. Demerol will take your pain away, be it physical or mental. That pain is gone, toots. If you've had alcohol beforehand, it has a tendency to make you vomit, but it's worth it. I've had morphine too. It differs from Demerol in that with Demerol, the pain is gone, with morphine it's almost like you can still feel the pain, it's just that you don't care. That's special.

Back to the lake. As the evening progresses, we all get taken care of. I finally get my shot and pass out. I think that's probably why they gave it to me, just to get me to shut up. I wake up the next morning and have no idea where I am. That's happened before, but never in a hospital room. Uh oh. Sweenz, what have you done? Then I see my shoulder wrapped up, I've got lumps on my head, and I can't breathe. Oh yeah, the boat wreck. I realize that I'm still in my shorts from last night, but the lake water has been soaked up into the sheets. Lake water is not clear. It's kind of green and brown, so naturally, I think I've made a mess in my shorts, gross. What the hell was I drinking last night? I don't remember drinking Midori mudslides. I scooch (a slang term meaning to move closer to) over to the edge of the bed to go to the bathroom, and when my feet hit the floor, I fell down because my right ankle has swollen to the size of grapefruit. What the hell? I'm just lying there on the floor, I felt like someone came in overnight and beat me with a soap filled sock; my body was one big bruise. I'm going to sue this hospital for not watching out for me. I crawl to the bathroom dragging my IV pole and take care of business. Thank God I didn't soil myself. It turned out to be the one bright spot of the day. I ended up with a dislocated shoulder, a concussion, a bruised sternum and three broken ribs, but we all healed up eventually and I no longer ride in anyone else's boat.

Partying goes well in the desert too. We partied a lot when I was stationed in 29 Palms. We were young, foolish and in love. We were just kids. We used to play a board game called *Dealer McDope*. It was game about drug dealing. Fun stuff. We would also have a tendency to party while we played the game. Good, solid, rock hard partying. We lived in the BEQ's, which were the Bachelor Enlisted Quarters. Three guys to a room. On game days, we would sometimes have eight or nine guys in there, elbow to elbow, rib to rib, trying to play a board game.

One Sunday we had a half gallon of tequila to play with. Tequila used to be a fun friend to play with, but he can turn mean. He doesn't play well with others, he's not a mixer, he doesn't socialize well with others, and he doesn't like sharing his space. If you play with tequila, you should only play with tequila. Don't bring any other friends; it should be a solo affair. We had the tequila, but we couldn't just do shots all day; we had to mix it with something, we're just kids after all. Someone somehow found some pina colada mix and we made frozen pina coladas with tequila. If I remember correctly, it tasted like shit. Cuervo and coconut? Nice mixture. But what's a girl to do? So we drank Cuervo coladas all day.

Late in the afternoon we ran out of colada mix. I headed down to the soda machine to grab some sodas. I'm not sure what kind of soda I was looking for to mix with tequila, but off I went. Being Sunday night, the soda machine was empty except for strawberry soda. Yuck. I've never been a fan of strawberry soda, and now I'm buying the last few cans in the machine. I headed back to our shelter with my sodas. No one seems very excited about my find. What? What is this madness? You don't want to do shots of Cuervo and chase them down with strawberry soda? It's a classic mix, known throughout the ages as the elixir of the Gods. Tequila and strawberry soda. We're all trashed by now anyway, nothing makes much sense.

We've been playing this stupid board game for almost ten hours, and we're tired, groggy, weary, drunk, not necessarily stoned, but beautiful. And we're chasing shots of Cuervo with strawberry soda. Doesn't get much better. Sometime around 6 p.m. I decide it's time to lay down. I'm hungry. I don't remember eating today. Did I? I don't remember leaving this room. Is that possible? Have I been in this room with all these people...all day? Have I not seen the sun? Did we party so much we forgot to go outside? We forgot to eat? Doesn't matter, it's time to lay down. I doubt it was really sleep that I was doing, more like a complete body shutdown. "That's enough," my body seemed to say. I won't accept any more into my system today. I'm shutting down.

So I shut down for an hour or so when my buddy Brent burst into the room shouting about something. He seemed to need me to wake up and do something, and even if you held a gun to my head, I couldn't tell you what he wanted, but it was something. I bolt up in bed and understand that something's not right with me. I feel...well, I feel... let's say queasy. But it's a bad queasy. I don't even head to the bathroom. I bolt out the front door into the sand and rock. I leaned up against this boulder and got rid of all that Cuervo and strawberry soda, got rid of it right there in the sand. It took me a good 20 minutes to wrap things up. I must have been full. The bright spot was the strawberry soda. Puke isn't quite so unpleasant when flavored with strawberries. I did feel much better though and slept like a baby in swaddling clothes for the rest of the night. I was a little pekid for a few days, and I never, I never, and I mean never, drank strawberry soda again. That stuff will make you sick.

We had us some times at the Stumps. One day a buddy of ours left his camera in our room before we took off for the weekend. When we returned on Sunday night, the camera was gone. That's right, someone had stolen it. What we didn't know, was that the guy who lost his camera had called the MP's. We had no warning when the MP's knocked on our door. This was not good because we had things in the room we weren't supposed to have, like drugs and alcohol and stuff. My roommate had three hits of acid on him and when the MP's knocked on the door he freaked out because he knew they were going to strip search us and the room. I'm not sure why he thought we'd be strip searched. We'd been in trouble before and had never been strip searched. But that was the big fear. We didn't want to go to the brig and break rocks with 16 lb. sledge hammers all day. I'm too young to die. What in God's name are we going to do? The answer? Eat the acid.

This decision was reached in about four seconds. A total freak out. He panicked and so did we. The last thing we needed was the law rooting through our belongings, so we ate the cid and opened the door. Enter the MP's. They ask a few perfunctory questions, look around, take some notes and then tell us, "we need you fellas to come with us so we can take a formal statement." Uh oh, they want us to go with them; that can't be good. They didn't search us and they didn't search the room. Thanks, dude; we ate that shit for nothing. Now they want us to get in a car with them and go to the "office" to give statements after eating a hit of acid. This has all the markings of big trouble.

We piled into the car and head off. Going anywhere with the law isn't a good thing, but doing it while waiting for acid to take effect is a worse thing. We have no idea how long this will take or how long before we start getting off. By the time we each have a seat at a desk it's been almost 30 minutes since we ate the tabs and any second things are going to get dicey. They follow us in and the building has about four desks lined up on each side of an aisle. The lockup is off to the left, and you can see it right when you walk in. Holy shit, I hope they don't lock us up. That's a tough way to enjoy your drugs, sitting in a jail cell. I'm sitting at one desk, Brent is behind me at another desk, and Drew is across the aisle from me and one desk down so I can see him clearly. Drew and I are facing each other and our MP's each have their backs to each other. OK, that's good. I'm trying to be as brief as I can in my sentences. I don't want to speak too much for fear of giving away our little secret.

I don't know if you've ever sat down with Marine MP's while waiting for LSD to take hold of you, but it's unnerving and the anticipation is killing me. I'm ready to jump up and just run home. I want to end this thing and get the hell out of here. Wait, did that pencil just roll by itself? I can feel a ball of sweat forming on my forehead, and any minute it's going to roll down my face and it will be all over! This huge, monstrous ball of purple sweat rolling down my face is a dead giveaway. "I gots trouble coming boys, I gots trouble coming to town." Uh oh, things are starting to happen, it's just a feel, but it's there, it's palpable and it means bad things. There are subtle changes going on all over, visual, spiritual and metaphysical. We need the get the hell out of here. Too bad I can't just say, "look we're starting to trip, it's been fun, but we gots to go."

As I'm trying to focus on the task at hand, I glance over at Drew to see how he's doing and he's got this huge smile on his face that looks like it's threatening to jump off his face, slide to the floor and work its way towards me. He looks like he's having the time of his life. I've never seen him so happy. He's a black dude and has large teeth, and that's all I see when I look over, TEETH, just his huge gargantuan teeth, like dinosaur teeth. He looked like a caricature. I can't believe those monstrous teeth fit into his tiny little head. His smile was literally swallowing his whole face, and when I see that I start to laugh because I know he's getting off. I catch myself and hold it in check. I don't need an uncontrolled laugh attack while we're still in the company of the MP's. I glance over my shoulder and Brent is the same way, all smiles. Then he winks at me and I do one of those snort laughs, and this huge, worm-like snot rope flies out of my nose and onto my shirt. It was almost the final straw, I'm on the verge of a gut busting guffaw. I cannot believe I just blew this thing out of my face, what an inopportune time to do something like that. It was horrifying and hilarious at the same time. I somehow manage to hold on and smoothly clear the offending mess off my shirt with the back of my hand.

We need to get out of here soon or we're going to lose it. When you need to laugh, it's not good to hold it in. You could blow your brains out the back of your head if you hold it in too long. The tension is starting to mount, pupils are dilating, faces are getting flushed, and if I don't get to laugh soon, I'm going to anyway. I don't know how long we were there, but it was long enough to let the cid get going full bore. I don't know how we kept our shit together. When we walked out it was walking into a cloud. A cloud of love and relief. We get outside the door and all three of us break down in laughter. We're actually lying in the sand laughing our asses off. Then we realize that we're still in view of the MP's shack and it would be none too good to have them see us lying in a pile laughing like school girls. So we got up and headed home, trying to figure out what to do with the next eight hours on a Sunday night. Good stuff, good times.

CHAPTER 30
I'M A COMEDIAN

I wasn't always a comedian. I'd never thought about being a comedian for a job. I watched and enjoyed comedians on TV as a kid, but it never occurred to me that I could do it even though, oddly enough, I was your typical class clown. I was always the funniest guy in school and, later, at work. I enjoyed entertaining my classmates at every opportunity and giving my teachers the "back talk." I didn't understand that phrase, "back talk." How am I supposed to respond to your inquiries if I don't talk back, which is exactly the kind of question that got me in trouble. Then I come to find that talking back and back talking aren't the same thing. No, sir, not by a long shot; nobody wants the back talk, they don't want that at all. Back talk is smart-assy and unappreciated. So I had some conflicts with my educators. I didn't know at the time I could make a living with this kind of behavior. In my defense, I was a little kid; I wasn't thinking very deeply about a "career." I just wanted to play with my friends and make them laugh.

In December of 1988, I was tending bar at a place called Menage. I always worked in meat market type bars. I couldn't work in a tavern or someplace where the barkeep listens to people's problems. I worked to party and get laid. I didn't care about your problems. If you've got problems, see a shrink. One of the managers told me that he used to run a comedy club in Detroit and that I was funnier than most of the people he had paid to do comedy. The seed had been planted. I went up to the Westport Funny Bone in St. Louis to watch the open mic night. I sat in the back (as is my custom) and thought, "I could do this." So I started writing things down in my yellow legal pad. I'm not sure why I picked that particular venue for taking down notes and ideas, but that was my first notebook of comedy. I never used another one though. I went to the spiral notebooks after that, spiral notebooks filled with notations, thoughts, ramblings and a thousand bar napkins with scrawling all over. I never did get very organized.

I made my first and pretty much last New Year's resolution that year. I was going to get up on stage for open mic and do five minutes. Being that it was already mid-December and I was going on stage in January, I best get writing some material. I wrote up five or so pages of Christmas and family material and thought, "this isn't that hard." I practiced in front of the mirror for hours, speaking into a hairbrush. What a big boy you are, performing a show for yourself in the bathroom. I must have looked like an idiot.

I practiced and practiced and was ready to do my thing. I actually had a gig in the business world at this time as well. I had gotten my real estate license and was working at an office. The bartending gig was more fun and better money, and my heart was never in the real estate game. January 10, 1989, was the date I popped my comedy cherry. It was a Tuesday; Tuesday is open mic night at the Funny Bone. Everyone who worked at the bar with me had thought that this was a great idea, so I made them all come to the show. That way, if I died a horrible death, they could all watch and the story would become legend. I had about 30 friends come up and had taken up about eight tables stage left. I thought it might be helpful to pad the audience with people who already thought I was funny. It was.

The house was full, packed to the walls, yikes. The murmur of the crowd hung over their heads in a swirl of anticipation and cigarette smoke. Drinks were flowing and tension was mounting. The show's about to start, and I think I was about seventh in the lineup that night. Good spot. Not too early, not too late. I, of course, didn't know it at the time. That's something you learn later; still, at the time, it felt like a good spot. I had gone over my material a thousand times. I was going to talk about Christmas and being from a big family. I was ready, at least as ready as I was going to get. Then the lights in the showroom went off and we were about to begin. As soon as I heard that "Good evening ladies and gentlemen..." I almost shit my pants. To this day that was the most nervous I have ever been.

I was nervous that first night of boot camp, standing on those yellow foot prints, but at least I had a rough idea of what I was in for. That night at the Funny Bone, I had no idea what was going to happen. I was literally shaking. I felt like backing out; there is no way I can do this; go up on stage in a dark club and be funny. No way, it can't be done, at least not by me. This is for comedians, not for me. What was I thinking? This isn't being behind the bar and entertaining my fellow employees and customers, this is real shit, man. I scoot off to the men's room and I pee again, and then I poop again. My whole body is in a state of anxiety, so it's rebelling against the pressure I'm putting on it. My body doesn't want to do this; it wants to go home. What was I thinking? I need to just leave and forget this ever happened. I can't go out on stage by myself, I can't do it, I tell ya. It's too much. It's too nerve racking. Just leave me be. Then I hear, "hey dude, you're next." Uh oh. Time to do it. OK- let's go. Nothing I can do about it now, time to meet my maker. I'm standing in the aisle as I hear, "are you ready for the next act?" Holy shit, that's me, I'm now the "next act." I'll never forget the intro Craig Hawksley gave me "This next guy is a bartender at the sleazy nightclub Menage, and he gets more pussy than Frank Sinatra did in his heyday, please welcome Mark Sweeney." Now that's a great intro. It may have been the best intro I've ever had.

I don't remember what was going through my head on stage. I was nervous as hell and I remember my leg shaking the entire time. I hurried through it as quick as I could even though I was doing really well. I got a lot of laughs and it felt good. I do remember walking off the stage and thinking, "this is what I'm going to do for the rest of my life." No shit, I'm not lying. I remember thinking that distinctly. I knew at that moment I would become a comedian. It was my second epiphany.

I had just left the stage and was walking back into the crowd through the applause and the darkness and I knew, I just knew. It was that good, plus I killed, MY FIRST TIME! I must be a natural, a gifted comedian, maybe I'm a savant. That's possible, isn't it? A comedic savant? I've never been on stage before, and I killed. I wonder if that's ever happened before? I was flying high. It was the most exhilarating experience I'd ever had. I had found my niche. I need to get on stage again. I've always loved making people laugh, but this was something different. I don't know what's different about it, but it's different than making people at work crack up. For some reason this was more rewarding, gave me more of a sense of accomplishment, like I had done something special, made an impact, whatever. I just know it felt good, and I wanted more, I wanted a lot more. I had broken through to a new world and I was going to be a comedian. I had questions, many questions. Craig Hawksley was the emcee of open mic back then and he was like the comedy guru of Westport. We'd hang around after the show and hang on every word he said, absorbing information and constantly asking questions, and Craig would answer. I learned quite a bit from Hawksley during those times, most of us did. Thanks, Craig. Of course there is only so much you can learn off the stage; most of the learning comes on the stage. It's very much an On-The-Job training type of thing.

My first line of business was to quit my job. That's right, one open mic night and I quit my job, not my bartending job of course, but the real estate gig was finito. I actually went into see the boss and told him I was quitting to become a comedian. He told me good luck. He said he could tell I wasn't going to last long anyway. I couldn't have been happier now that I knew what I was going to do for a living. I'm going to be a comedian. I didn't really know how long it would take to be actually making a living as a comedian, but that's what I was going to do.

My second open mic went a little differently than my first. I didn't do the same material. I thought after my first set worked, it was time to do some new stuff. How's that for being clueless? Get some laughs, OK, that material is good to go, time to move on. The second night I did a five minute joke. That is to say, one thought that was expanded to a five minute bit. I did a five minute driving bit. A five minute driving bit! What cojones! What makes you think you can come up with five minutes of material about people getting in your way on the road? It was a total nightmare. All I could think of was, "I wonder if I can get my job back?" I was sweating like Albert Brooks in *Broadcast News*. I couldn't believe I'm not funny. Last week I was a king, I killed, I slayed, I destroyed, I was fantastic, I was a comedian. This night, I was dung. "This guy sucks. Who's next? Is there anyone else coming on?" I was mortified. I got through though. I quickly found out that not everything you write is funny.

I wasn't really going after a style or type of comedy. I was of course influenced heavily by Cosby, Pryor and Carlin. When I was about ten, I got Bill Cosby's *When I was a Kid* album and listened to that thing until I could recite the entire album, which I did frequently. Oh sure, it caused some problems in class because I would do it at "inopportune" times. Such is the beginning of a comedian. But I didn't know what kind of comedian I would be; I just wanted them to laugh. After my second open mic night I was asking this guy some questions and he pointed me in the direction of Steve "The Scream" Pollard who told me of a show on Thursday over in Illinois. I went over with my few minutes of material and the host tells me I need to do 15 minutes. That's fine except I don't have 15 minutes; I've got almost five. He might as well have told me to do an hour. I told him I don't have 15 and he said "well you can't go on then."

Pollard told me to just talk about anything, so I went on and talked about going on family vacations and it was pretty funny. Nothing prepared, just telling stories. I may have found my "comedy stylings." I can just talk about stuff I did and have done. Cosby did it, Pryor did it, you know, not making stuff up, just talking personal experience, now maybe I can do it. We'll see.

Open mics were a blast. At the time there may have been 30 guys showing up to do a set. The manager of the Bone at the time was Al Canal, a famous man in St. Louis, or at least up at the Funny Bone, and he would put pieces of paper in a hat and you drew for a spot. If you got a number, that's the spot you got, if you didn't get a number, tough titty, come back next week. I usually got on the list even if I didn't get a number because I always brought a bunch of people and they would drink and spend money. Management likes that. Plus, I was one of those guys who hung around the club all time, watching the pros. Canal liked that and would throw me a scrap once in a while, "you can do ten minutes on Thursday night." Getting those spotlights was incredible, getting to do a regular show, not an open mic night, but an actual paying crowd during the week! I felt like hot shit.

I do have a very hard time watching those videos from the early days, though. I looked like I was trying too hard. I was very much trying to fit the "comedian" mold, and it's embarrassing to watch, but we all have to start somewhere. Watching professional comedians was actually a good way to learn. There were no handbooks or guidebooks or anything that told you how to be a comedian, so I watched how other people did it and went from there. Strangely enough, that's how I learned to snow ski as well.

I didn't really have a plan or anything when I started. I didn't know how to set comedy goals or anything of that nature. I just wanted to be a comedian. I even tried dressing the part, jeans with white high top tennis shoes, t-shirt and a sport coat with the sleeves rolled half way up. Hey- that's what I saw the other guys doing. That outfit, fortunately, didn't last long. It's important what you wear on stage, at least I think it is. First impressions are key, at least that's what I think. I'm not sure of any of this, I'm just making speculations. All these statements are purely my opinion. It's just what I've learned from doing this. If you go up wearing torn up clothes and look like shit, that's what they'll expect from you. Torn up and shitty comedy. If you don't care about what you look like, why would you care about your comedy? I could never wear a suit or be too dressed up because that's just not sweet poppa. Some of the worst shows I've ever done were done wearing a suit. It's just not a comfortable feel for me. I could never wear a hat either. When you wear a hat on stage, it gives out a certain persona that has to mesh with your material. Is that true? Your clothes have to mesh with your material? Yes, I think it is true, but I don't know. You play around with it until you find your proper outfit. Then you have your "persona." Now I'm ready to be a comedian. All I need are some gigs. That's great, how do I get a gig? Is there a signup list?

When you start this comedy thing, you'll do a gig any place at any time just to get some experience. That's the only way to get better, to be on stage. You can practice in front of your bathroom mirror for days, but you won't become a better comedian until you get on stage night after night. We used to do this one place in the summer called the French Quarter. It was a bar in St. Charles, Missouri, just across the river. It was a jazz bar downstairs, and if went through the club, there's a door in back and it opened on to a staircase that led to a room upstairs with a mic and a stage. It was a wobbly stage with an unsteady folding wall, but it worked for us. The top of the stairs ended at the end of stage right, so whenever someone opened the door, the music would slither up the stairs and drown out anyone who was on the stage at the time. If an audience member had had enough, they would leave, but when they left they would have to walk right past you and head down the stairs, so not only were they walking out on you, they did it so everyone else could see. Not that the other twelve people would have noticed anyway, but it was a nice little reminder of your place in the world.

Myself, Pollard, Steve Smith, Cedric the Entertainer and a bunch of others used to go up on Sunday nights and get paid in draft beer. That was the deal: free draft beer and we could do as much time as we wanted. That was the real kicker, we could do time, not just five minutes like open mic, but twenty or thirty or forty. No one did forty because I don't think any of us had that much material, but it was a great work out and it made you try new shit every time we went. It was hosted by a guy name Desi Arnez, not Lucy's husband, but that was the name he used. He was a large man with a huge handlebar mustache and he was a "heavy breather." He'd always breathe heavily into the mic. One guy said listening to Desi was like listening to a five minute obscene phone call. I always remembered that. Desi was infamous for using other people's material. I didn't know that at the time because I wasn't that familiar with other comedians' work, but found it out later. I'd be watching Night at the Improv and someone would do a bit that I recognized as Desi's, which of course wasn't true. The TV guys weren't stealing Desi's material, it was the other way around. He even did the whole Superman bit from Seinfeld's act. Desi never did anything more than open mics, so I guess it doesn't matter.

When I started open mic, there were around 30-40 guys that would show up every Tuesday for a while, and after a couple of years, Steve Smith, Pollard and I were the only ones still doing it and now it's just me and Smith and Cedric. Every one of those guys that started with us is doing something else now, so I've got that going for me. After a month or so of open mics, Pollard asked me if I wanted to go on the road with him and do some one nighters. We packed up our shit and off went. I was about to experience "the road."

ONE NIGHTERS

The term one nighters brings back different memories for different people. To anyone who has frequented a bar, worked at a bar, built a bar, cleaned a bar, heard of a bar, or even driven by a bar, the one nighter brings back memories of drunken, sloppy sex with a stranger, often in the back seat of a car. Good stuff, Good times.

All comedians start off doing one nighters. It's like prep school; you've got to get out and do them. You can't escape it, you can't skip over it, you must do it. I can't possibly think of any comedian who never worked a one nighter. It's just part of the program. There's nothing quite like them, especially early in your career. You've never handled an unsupervised room of drunken yahoos in a tavern in southern Arkansas, but you're about to. It's all new; your job, your clothes, what you're about to do, you're on the road doing comedy. You're a comedian, and you're getting paid for this show. It's only $25 and all the draft beer you can drink, but you're still getting paid. It's only fifteen minutes; surely nothing can go wrong in 15 minutes, can it? Yes, things can go wrong in 15 minutes. As you take the stage, butterflies are tickling the insides, you've got to pee, you're wondering if the pee mark in the front of your pants from earlier is gone, and oops, I think I have to take a dump as well. Oh yes, the live performance. "Good evening," I say. "Fuck you," is the reply. Goody, we're off. That is such an odd thing to hear just because you take the stage, who says "Fuck you" when hearing "Good evening?" What a strange world.

I had the benefit of being taken under someone's wing shortly after I started. A road dog extraordinaire, Steve "The Scream" Pollard. He was a true road dog. This dude could do a show for anyone, at any time, under any circumstances. We did a show on a bus once. A retirement home was taking the residents to a flag dedication at a new nursing home and they took a bus and had us do a show. Me, Pollard and thirty seniors on the bus, most of them had walkers and tripods with wheels to carry their intravenous meds, along with various other implements of the old. I don't remember getting many laughs, but it's hard to make people suffering from dementia laugh; they've got other things on the mind. Weird, wacky. After five open mics, I'm going on the road. First stop, the Silver Star Lounge in Ft. Leonard Wood, Mo. A biker/army bar, on the outskirts of town. Where else but on the "outskirts?" Is there any positive vibe that comes to mind when you think "the outskirts of town? No, there aren't. It's just thoughts of fields and ditches and body dumps. That's the outskirts. Twenty-five dollars and draft beer, again. I can't believe how many gigs I did where the pay was $25 and draft beer. They never offered bottled beer, only draft, the cheap bastards. I'm riding down with Pollard and Smith and the headliner was to meet us there. Five minutes outside of town, I'm informed that I'm the emcee. Bullshit, is my reply, I don't know anything about hosting a show.

"Well, it's time you learned," Pollard told me; everyone has to know how to host a show. So now I'm the emcee. The stage is a dance floor, big enough for five hundred dancers, and I'm standing in the corner with a train light in my face scorching the back of my retinas. It was some old theater light that was used to light actors up, like somewhere from 1000 yards away, and now it's sitting two feet from the edge of the stage where this light can sear its image into the back of my skull. There are twenty people there, all trashed on beer and shots. Jack Daniels, in particular, and I'm not sure what it is about JD, but it makes people ornery, not to mention disinterested.

These people are yelling shit through my entire show, so I'm just staring into this light, eating a huge turd and plugging onward. I did every single bit in my act at the time and I fulfilled my time obligation, so good, now it's someone else's turn. The last couple of minutes were a bit vague, but I didn't have any more material. I mean for God's sake, I had only done open mic five times. That was it, I don't have any more. After watching two of my companions suffer somewhat similar fates, I didn't feel so bad; apparently I'm not the only one who sucks.

Next, the headliner hits the stage. He gets about 20 minutes into his 45 and he's struggling hard, then he slams down the mic and tells the crowd of drunken bikers and army boys that they're too stupid to understand his material. Then he walks off the stage, leaves the building, gets into his car and drives off. We're standing there going, "what the fuck?" UH OH. A couple of the bikers stand up and start moving in our direction, and then a couple of the army boys joined them and it didn't look like they were coming over to say "good show, we enjoyed your performance." It looked like they were coming over to show who's who about who's too stupid.

We're debating whether to say fuck it and just run for our lives, but we haven't gotten paid yet. I guess the headliner didn't care about his money. Strange set of priorities, $25 or my life, hmmm, I pick the money. I can't believe we're going to get shanked in this bar. I didn't see any, but I'll bet these mofo's had some type of weaponry up a sleeve. I just started doing comedy and I'm going to be killed in Ft. Leonard Wood, Missouri. This sucks. Fortunately the owner knew these fellers and simmered things down. Then the owner comes up to us and says that we owe him 20 more minutes and no one is getting paid until he gets his full show. I'm stunned; these people hated us for the last hour and then were ready to skin us, and this jolly nuts wants his full show. My mentor, for lack of a better word, tells me that as the emcee, it's my responsibility to do the rest of the time. That should be some accomplishment considering I ran out of material an hour ago. Tough shit, get up there. So back I go, and to my surprise, Richard Pryor, George Carlin, and Bill Cosby all suck at the Silver Star Lounge too.

Later, The Scream had us pull into this parking lot where the only business open was Domino's. Chris and I are leaning against the car shooting the breeze when Pollard enters the store. Pollard is inside talking to the pizza guy, when all of a sudden he comes bolting out carrying a pizza and disappears around the corner of the building. The Pizza man comes out and says, "your buddy just stole a pizza and I called the cops."

"What?"

"I had a pizza on the counter for delivery and he grabbed it and took off, so I called the cops."

Again, for the second time tonight, uh oh. Our first thought was to deny knowing him but since there's only one other car in the lot, I doubt we would've been believed. With no other alternative, we hop in the car and take off, and we catch up with his dumb ass on the entrance ramp to the highway, so we pull over, he jumps in, and we bolt. He told us that he thought the pizza was a delivery mistake and that it was free. We took turns beating him until we reached the state line. My first paying gig, and I end up on the run from the pizza police. Good stuff, Good times.

Pollard took me on a lot of gigs and I learned fast- you have to. By the end of the first year, I started getting gigs in actual comedy clubs. I was moving up in the world. I got some spots on Thursdays or Sundays at the Bone in St. Louis and started going on the road. I couldn't believe it, I was going "on the road" to do comedy. The road is where you're first introduced to the "comedy condo." In all the years I stayed in "the condo" I never once stayed in one that I would classify as a condo. They were apartments, at best. Most of the time they were dumps, shitty little dumps, dumpy little shitty dumps. It was just a cheap apartment that three different comedians stayed in each week. They would leave on Sunday or Monday, and by Wednesday the new group was getting settled. They were usually cleaned by one of the staff who never really seemed to give a shit how clean it got. I knew instinctively not to use any condiments in the condo. I don't know why, I just knew, long before you heard stories of guys sticking their dicks into the mayo. I don't know why anyone would do that, boredom perhaps. At first you don't mind the condos because you're on the road, you're doing comedy and you're staying with other comedians. Life is pretty sweet. You talk a lot about comedy. There is a lot of comedy discussion; that's all you really talk about as a new guy. Comedy. There were a lot of "how to" sessions and many nights spent drinking to the wee hours, chasing girls and sleeping until noon. After a few years, the condos aren't so sweet and the comedy talk bores you. The last thing you want to do is sit around and talk comedy with the new guys. By the time I started headlining, I realized why all those headliners I shared a condo with were always in their rooms. It wasn't too long before that's where I was spending my time.

One nighters don't vary much either. I pulled up to one in Tennessee that had a sign out front that said, Tonite (many of the one nighters use the tonite spelling, apparently there are plenty of e's but not enough g's or h's) Tonite: Turkey shoot and live comedy. I tell you, that will make you feel special, being on the same bill as a turkey shoot. It's a little intimidating anyway, a bunch of guys standing around with shotguns blasting away at a little board. Whoever gets a piece of buckshot closest to the center, wins a turkey. I know, I know, I thought they actually shot at a turkey too. But this way seemed easier than sitting in the damp bushes all day.

Now the shoot is done. "All right you sons of bitches, let's get inside and watch this here comedian- you funny, son?" (Shit, I hope so.) We head into the bar and start the show, and it goes from slow to bad to hellish. There's only about seven guys in there and they would rather talk about "the shoot" than listen to me. The verbal abuse continues for about 20 minutes and then a fight breaks out. That's right- there are seven guys in this bar and two of them start a brawl. Hilarious. They called the show after that; I guess they figured it would be unfair for me to follow a fight. The guy gave me the $50 and off I went into the wild unknown. It was the one and only time I had a turkey shoot as my opener.

When you're starting out, you will literally go anywhere, anytime, anyplace for a gig. I went out once for sixteen straight weeks. I never did that again. Sixteen weeks is a long time to be gone. Most of the work you're doing takes place Wednesday-Saturday. Sometimes the other nights would fill up, but mostly no. Now you've got a couple of nights off with nowhere to go, nowhere to be and no money to do anything about it. When you're making $250 a week, the money doesn't go far. I don't know how many nights I've slept in my car over the years, but there's been a few.

One week I was up in northern Wisconsin in April with a couple of days off, so I thought I would do some camping. I had no camping gear whatsoever, so it was more like me sleeping in my car in the woods, but I called it camping. I still had my lawn chair in the car because I was in Florida the week before. That's what you call finding out about routing the hard way. One week in Ft. Lauderdale, the next in Heywood, Wisconsin. Well done, young Skywalker.

I pulled off into the woods and set up a little camp. I pulled my lawn chair out, started a fire and made some sandwiches with the leftover meat I had in the cooler. All the ice had melted so the meat was a little wet. I don't know why that's so gross, wet, cold cuts of meat, but it is. I towel dried my lunch meat and chowed down. I had a six pack, and I just sat there in the woods with my fire, my sandwiches and my beer. I was on the road doing comedy and I couldn't have been happier. I make the decision to sleep outside that night; it's been a beautiful day and it looks like a beautiful night coming my way. As I start to get sleepy, I drag out my pillow and sleeping bag, pull my hat down over my face and call it a night. About three hours later I wake up, the fire is out, it's dark and cold and I've got almost four inches of snow on me. What the hell? How many months have I been asleep? It was 62* yesterday and now I'm covered in snow and freezing my ass off. It took me a second to gather my thoughts and figure out where the hell I was and what I was doing. I slept the rest of the night in the front seat, very comfy. By the time it was done, it had snowed almost eight inches. I got up, cleaned off the car and hit the road. I'm off to another gig, it's not until tomorrow though. I wonder where I'll stay tonight. I wonder.

YOU'RE FIRED

Pollard and I had booked this gig at a car dealership. They were having a special sale and had a tent set up with a band and all the trimmings. Our job was to do a little comedy while people took breaks from shopping for cars. Pollard goes up first and does about ten minutes then it's my turn. The setup and the crowd were not exactly conducive to good comedy; a lot of people milling around, eating, talking and not really paying attention to the show. The dealer had a special on the Suzuki Samurai and this was right after they had several rollover problems with this particular vehicle. I said something about how they "stop on a dime and roll over on a nickel." That didn't go over very well. All of a sudden I see the manager running towards me. He grabs the mic and says, "that's the show, folks." He drags us into the office and starts going off on us. I wasn't really paying attention though. There was a lot of cussing and telling us they were trying to sell these vehicles and it didn't help reminding the buyer that they flip over easily. Well whoop de do, it was a joke, man. He didn't get it and we had to stand there and take his abuse because he hadn't paid us our

$50 yet. When he finished, he gave us our cash and requested that we leave the premises as our services were no longer needed. Next time don't hire comedians to sell your product.

One night I had this gig on a riverboat on the Missouri river. It was in my first year so I was still learning. There were about 25 people in the crowd. The crowd was made up of mostly seniors and a handful of nuns. Doing a show with nuns watching you is disturbing. There wasn't a spotlight; the whole room was lit, so you could see everyone, which means you can see them not laughing. It's bad enough when you can hear that they're not laughing, but seeing them not laughing is the pits. I got to the stage just as it was leaving the dock. When the engines increased in rpm's you could feel the whole boat vibrate, and I said, "I bet that vibration makes you old people have to pee." All of a sudden most of the seniors get up and walk out. I'm thirty seconds into my show and I just walked 90% of the crowd. I'm not sure where they were going since it was a boat after all, but they were pissed off enough to leave the showroom. With the room all lit up there was no hiding the fact that these people were walking out on me. Nice. I've still got 25 minutes left and it's just me and the nuns. Then I did this joke about skid marks in underwear and lost a couple of the nuns. Any longer and it will just be me in the room. I could see the seniors because they were right outside the window. That was weird, doing a show for six nuns while having the people who walked out on you staring through the window. I finished the show with few, if any laughs, but I learned something, and that's what counts, isn't it?

My next boat show wasn't for another ten years. This one was for a group of realtors on a river boat on Lake of the Ozarks. It was a two-story boat and the show was on the bottom floor. They had a bar at one end and me at the other. I knew it would be a hell gig right from the start. The cruise was supposed to be about an hour. I figured I'd do 30 minutes on the way out and 30 on the way back in. Everyone is at the bar and they have tables set up, but only a few people were sitting there; the rest of them are at the bar and talking shop. As I'm getting ready to start my show, the boat leaves the dock. I'm standing on top of the trap doors that lead to the engine, so when the engine revs, the whole floor shakes and the noise is unbearable. You can't hear a thing. I have a mic and speaker and even I can't hear me. The whole bottom floor of the boat is shaking to the point that it's making me itch.

Everyone is still at the bar with their backs to me and I'm yelling my act at the top of my lungs. The people who are sitting down four feet in front of me can't hear a word I'm saying. I kept looking out the window waiting for the boat to turn around and let me know we're almost done, but it just keeps moving in the same direction. I just keep plowing through and I am finally ready to wrap things up when the boat starts turning around. Holy shit! I'm almost done and the trip is only half over. How did time fly by so fast? I tried to work the crowd but that didn't go very well. It's hard to talk to people when all they can hear is the roar of diesel engines. I hemmed and hawed for another ten minutes and called it a day. I'm not sure if anyone noticed or not. I could've just stood there and moved my lips and I would have received the same response. I knew right then that I would never do another riverboat.

A BAD GIG

About two years into this comedy thing, I booked a corporate gig during the Christmas Season. It was for a car dealership and their managers and family. I had been doing comedy over a year and thought I could fulfill the obligation of a 45 minute set. To begin with, I was wearing a suit because it was my first corporate gig and I thought you were supposed to wear a suit. It was a Christmas party, so I thought everyone would be in a good mood. If they were, I certainly couldn't tell. It was at a private country club and they had me set up behind a podium, which of course is the worst possible set up. Being behind a podium is not conducive to comedy. People behind a podium aren't funny; they're giving a speech. The sound was bad as well, there were speakers in the ceiling, so you know they weren't very good. The speakers were in the ceiling, which was about 30 feet above me.

I'm introduced and I take the mic out of the podium stand so I can at least stand with the mic in my hand. The cord is only about three feet long, so I can't get too far away from the podium, about a foot or so, but at least I'm out there. After 20 minutes, I haven't gotten a laugh and the sweat is running down my face. I don't ever remember wanting to get out of a place so badly. Those people hated me. I was totally lost; I didn't know what to do. I've still got 25 minutes left, I'm almost out of material, and I'm waiting for someone to come take the mic from me and say, "Ok, that's enough" and put all of us out of our misery. But no one came, they just stared at me. I started to do material from my friends, Dan Chopin, Kathleen Madigan, Buzz Sutherland, Dan O'Sullivan etc, etc. That didn't help either.

I sucked no matter whose material I did. I don't do material that wasn't written by me, but in those early years I made exceptions from time to time in desperate situations. I was willing to try anything to get these people to laugh. No go, I finally wrap it up, put the mic back in the podium stand and RUN! It's hard to describe the feeling of being booked to do a gig as a comedian and do the show for no laughs, 45 minutes of nothing but me standing there waiting expectantly for the chuckles that don't come. Ouch. It's lonely alright. Nobody comes to save you. It's you by your lonesome.

I head to the bathroom to try and dry off some of the sweat, and when I look in the mirror, I'm soaked to the nipples. My shirt is soaking wet halfway down. I try to loosen my tie and it's so wet I can't get it undone. Fuck it, I'll go get a fork. I return to the bathroom with a fork and work to get the knot undone. I finally do and the tie is soaking wet as well. I have got to get my check and get out of here. I almost told them to keep their money but decided that they had put me through hell, so I'm taking the check. I got my check and was heading for the door when I hear, "hey, Sweeney" Oh no.

Someone knows me, it was a guy named Dave Baumann who I went to boot camp with. He was one of the three of us that day that had joined the Marines. I hadn't seen him since boot and he wants to catch up on old times. So now I've got to stand there and talk to him while everyone else walks around, getting drinks etc., and taking peeks at me and pointing. "There's the comedian." It was humiliating. I sucked hard and now I'm standing around for the second round of scrutiny, I felt every eye in the place boring into my back; I really felt the desperate need to boogie on out of town. I finally get out and hitting that cold December air was a refreshing blast of newness. It's over, bro, that show is over and it's time to move on. The next day I got a call from the lady that booked it asking how it went. I told her and she said, "you comedians are always so critical of yourselves, let me call the contact and find out what they thought, and I'll call you right back." I never heard from her again. Oh well, at least I'm a comedian.

I love being a comedian. It's a good job for people who don't want to live their lives as mature, responsible adults. It's kind of a childish job. You're only responsible for about 45 minutes a night, 90 on the weekend. The rest of the time no one gives a shit what you're doing.

That's nice. You can go outside and play all day, take a nap and then go to work. I don't mean to say that it isn't work because there's a lot involved in the process. For one, you have to write. Without material, it's really hard to get booked. Secondly, you have to find work. The clubs don't come looking for you; you have to look for them. Rejection is a huge part of this job. Not everyone wants you. Some of them adamantly don't want you. I also like the fact that I didn't really have a boss or anyone to answer to. That's pretty sweet. No one is looking over your shoulder critiquing your work. No *one* is the key word here. There's a lot more than just one critiquing you. I didn't think about that at first. I couldn't do a "day job" because I didn't want to be judged or analyzed, so I pick a job that is judged and analyzed by every crowd you stand in front of. If they laugh, your critique is good; if they don't, you suck. You're shitty at your job and we, the crowd, will let you know. It ended up being a much more analyzed job than I had before. It also happens constantly, like every time you go to work. The people, they just stare and judge and critique. Oh well, at least I'm a comedian. A real one. Not like the ones you see doing commentary on VH-1 or any other show that has commentary about video clips or whatever. They always put "comedian" under these peoples' names. Look them up, not one is a comedian. I'm not sure what they are, but they're not comedians. An interviewer once asked me to define a comedian. "Someone who makes a living doing stand-up," that's a comedian. No one else. If you're not paying bills by doing comedy, you're not a comedian. That sums it up pretty well.

THE EPILEPSY GIG

One day I did this show at Clinton Community College in Clinton, Iowa. The show was being held in a secondary building behind the rec center. It was a one story building and the show was in one of the basement rooms. The room itself was weird; it looked like a kindergarten classroom with painted hands on paper all over the wall, but it had grown-up books on the shelves and three couches. I'm not sure what it was used for. There are exactly eight people in this crowd, and six of them are family. Really, the whole family came. I'm standing at one end of the room and there is a couch on the left and right, both facing the center, but the third couch has its back to me and it's also facing the center. So I'm standing behind this couch and there are two people sitting on it, both with their backs to me; I can't tell you how strange that was.

The couches are too heavy to be moved, so I ask them if they'd like to move to the other couches so they can see. "No, we're fine." So they're going to sit through the entire show facing away from me. OK, fine, let's move on. I'm doing my thing and it's not going very well. None of the eight seem to think I'm funny and two of them are huddled over in secrecy. I can't get over the fact these people are facing the wrong way, and I ask again if they'd like to move and they still don't. Am I that hideous that they don't want to look at me? I don't understand why they would rather watch the show facing the back wall. What the hell is wrong with you people?

I continue my struggle and about 25 minutes in, one of the ladies falls off the couch and hits the floor. Finally! I got them laughing; this lady is laughing so hard she fell off the couch. I've heard of falling off the chair, but the couch? Unheard of. Then I realize the rest of the family has gathered around her on the floor. "She's having an epileptic seizure" one of them tells us. Us being me and my contact. My contact calls for an ambulance, "it's on its way." Cool, all is well. I'm still standing on my little spot behind the couch while a couple of the family hold her down and one tries to keep her from swallowing her tongue. She's thrashing around and making un-nerving sounds, sounds that I'm unfamiliar with. Scary. I ask if I can do anything, like I'm going to be some kind of help to this poor woman, and they inform me that she "does this all the time." The ambulance arrives and they put her on the gurney, and as they take her out, everyone follows. Everyone; even the two people who weren't family and my contact. Now I'm standing all alone, still behind the couch. And as they move down the hall in their medical caravan, I yell after them "Thanks for coming, I hope you enjoyed the show."

HELL GIGS

Every comedian has had hell gigs. It's just part of the process. When you're starting out, hell gigs are many. First of all, you're doing comedy whenever and wherever you can. Secondly, you're not that funny. You may think you're funny, but you're not. You're getting funnier, but you're not quite there. Give it another five years.

One night I did this show in a sports bar in Tupelo, Mississippi. The room was divided into two sections, one being the sitting, drinking area, and the other had about 25 pool tables. The World Series between the Braves and Indians was on TV. I remember this because every TV in the place was on. The TV's over the bar still had the volume on. I'm actually *watching* the World Series while doing the show. There are about 20 people sitting in the chairs in front of the stage, about 40 people playing pool, and the rest were huddled around the bar cheering on the Braves. There was so much noise, I could barely hear myself. I've got the bar on my left full of people, and on my right I've got people playing pool, and I mean there's a pool table four feet from the stage and I'm in the middle of this crescendo of noise, trying to do a little comedy. I'm getting nothing, nothing, I tell you, but people yelling at the TV and the crashing of pool balls ringing in my head. People sitting three feet in front of me kept yelling at me to speak up. Hey numb nuts, I'm speaking into a microphone that's hooked up to an amplifier. Maybe, just maybe, if they wanted to have a comedy show, they should shut down the pool tables and turn down the TV? Huh? What about that, huh? I never did make it back to Tupelo, but what a game.

ROUGH NIGHT IN IOWA

I was doing a show at Penguins in Cedar Rapids, Iowa, one weekend and had an interesting night. During the first show the emcee was getting heckled a little by some drunk douchebag and he wasn't handling it very well. After the middle act finished, the emcee went back up to introduce me and the heckler starts in on him again. The room isn't really policed very well, no door men, no men period. It was just the girls, so the heckling went on. The emcee was being abused by this guy and the tension is starting to mount and you can see people squirming in their seats. I'm standing in the back mentally pleading for this guy to just bring me up and I'll take over. But no, he just keeps trying to get the best of the heckler and is losing unmercifully. By now the tension in the room is palpable, people are uncomfortable and it's going downhill. He starts to tell the heckler he's an asshole etc. and the heckler starts talking about kicking the emcee's ass. That's nice, threatening the acts with physical attacks. Just when things can't get any worse the emcee says "fuck you, let's bring up your headliner."

He introduces me and I hit the stage to complete silence; everybody is on edge, and they don't even applaud when I walk up. Now I realize not many people are in jobs where they receive applause just for showing up for work, but I do, and when it's not there, it makes for an unsettling moment. Right away this guy starts in on me, so I stop everything and explain to him that his behavior wouldn't be tolerated. Then he asks me "what are you going to do about it?" So I made a deal with him and told him if he'd shut up for the rest of the show, I would gladly go out and throw hands with him after the show. If he wants a brawl, I'll give him one, AFTER I finish with work. This seems to satisfy him temporarily.

When he starts in again, I have to stop and mention the fact that he will be escorted out if he doesn't behave. He asks, "who's going to throw me out?" Then this guy at a table in front stands up and he's so big, he blocks out the spotlight. He's sitting with three other guys who turned out to be football players at Iowa, and he looks over at the guy and says, "we will." So I look at him and say, "they will." The heckler actually stood up and looked at the table and then sat back down and shut up. Unbeknownst to me, one of the bartenders had called the police. I continue on and this guy is still noisy, and I'm about to deal with him again when I see the cops walk over to his table and drag his ass out; he's struggling with them and I almost expected to see the pepper spray or taser. They're dragging him out and everyone starts cheering and clapping. How's that for a clue that people don't want you around? They cheer and applaud when you leave. Once he's gone, the show took a 180, the tension was gone and everyone had a splendid time.

I did have a little talk with the emcee about handling hecklers-mostly don't get them riled up, pissed off and then give the show to someone else. We found out later the guy took a swing at one of the cops and they hauled him off to jail. Dumb ass. The second show that night was much better for the crowd, not so good for me. Within five minutes of taking the stage this chick sitting front row dead center leans her head down and pukes all over herself and then just sat there! At first I thought I must have been wrong, but I wasn't. She puked all down her shirt, partly on her pants and the rest on the floor, and then didn't do anything about it. I was mortified, horrified and terrified at what I saw. How can the other people at her table not see this? How can they sit there and not notice? Did nobody notice this girl throwing up all over herself? Am I the only one? How can that be? But be it was.

She sat through the entire show with puke all over her, and I'm trying to be cool and not say anything. It was hard, though, not looking at the vomitus. You know that's true; it's hard to look away from puke. It's even harder when you're trying to do a show. How am I supposed to concentrate when I've got this puke-covered chick sitting right in front of me with a puke pile at her feet? How, I ask you, how? The most amazing thing is that nobody in her group even noticed. Maybe they were trashed too. I thought about telling her it's ok to get up and use the ladies room, but she didn't seem to mind all that much. That, and I didn't want to embarrass her. If you can throw up all over yourself and pretend it didn't happen, more power to you. That's some serious denial.

ROUGH NIGHT IN WICHITA

I was at The Loony Bin in Wichita, Kansas, and some girl's phone goes off. Since the audience is asked before the show to turn off cell phones, I say something to her about her importance in the world. She's on the phone so she doesn't really hear me, I thought. I turn and face the other way and out of the corner of my eye, I see her walk up on stage. I've never had this happen before, so I'm dumbfounded. Did this chick really just step on the stage? I've been heckled before and had verbal confrontations with people, but I've never had anyone climb on stage. I don' t even know what to say at first. I'm still asking myself if this chick is really up here? Yes, she was, and she's got her phone in her hand and gets right up into my face.

"Do you have a cell phone? Do you have a cell phone?" Having a stranger so close to your face is uncomfortable, isn't it? I don't know you and you're invading my breathing space, so back your ass up, lady. So I ask her what the hell she's doing up here and she gets even closer, I mean, she's nose to nose with me asking over and over "Do you have a cell phone, do you have a cell phone, do you have a cell phone?" Yes, I do, you stupid bitch, but it's in the car; it's not attached to my hip like a tumor, now get off the stage. Then I see a couple of doormen coming and they escort her off the stage and bring her back to her seat.

Well, this should be interesting because now she's cast a weird pall over the crowd because the whole thing was a little surreal. I try to continue on but she's all in a tizzy and starts mouthing off about me being a dick, etc. I say something about the rudeness of people and their cell phones, and she says, "Fuck you." Really? Fuck me? I don't think so, sister. It's time for you to go, so I tell the doorman to toss her ass and she stands up and pulls up her sweater, I'm not sure why, maybe some kind of flashing gesture or something, I didn't really understand the move.

When she pulls up her sweater she reveals this bra that goes from mid belly to mid chest, I mean this thing is huge. It's the longest north to south span of bra material I've ever seen. She wasn't big breasted, either; it was just a lot of bra. When I saw it I said "Nice bra, where did you get it? From your grandmother?" Well, she loses it then, boy. She flips me off with both hands going, "Fuck you, fuck you, fuck you." Wow, she's pissed. She's got three other people with her and they have no idea what to do. They're just sitting there watching this whole thing unfold. One guy is her husband and they're with another couple. She's flipping me off and I'm laughing at her because of her dramatic response, because I feel she's blown this thing way out of proportion. The doorman grabs her and she starts struggling, the whole crowd is stretching and craning trying to get a look at this nut job, and she's still going off, yelling and flipping me off. The door guys have literally picked her up so her feet are off the ground and as they drag her towards the back she's still flipping me off with both hands and yelling, "fuck you, fuck you."

By this time, I'm laughing my ass off. I can't believe what I'm seeing. I have never elicited this kind of passion in anyone before. When they hit the back of the room there is a metal swinging door that leads to the club next door and as they're pushing her through, she uses both feet to kick open the door. There's this huge boom and you can see her in the doorway light kicking this door open while leaning back, flipping me off and saying, "fuck you," one more time. It was like watching a mental patient being hauled off for treatment. The rest of her table is just sitting there, so I ask her old man if he's going after her and he says "not yet, dude, not yet." Who could blame him?

SHOWS THE WEEK OF 9-11
September of 2001, what a week eh? I was in Atlanta, headed down to Uncle Funnies in Davie, FL. I had a three-day layover at my buddy Dave's house in Atlanta. The morning of 9-11, I was sound asleep when Dave comes busting through the door yelling about a plane hitting the World Trade Center. We turn on the tube and sat in front of it until almost 2 a.m. That's a lot of television, and the only reason I left was I had to get to Davie on September 12, and I still had almost 700 miles to go. During that whole day I don't think I displayed

any emotion at all outside of numbness. It was so much to digest, emotion didn't really play a part yet.

About 2:30 a.m. I was on the road south of Atlanta and decided I had enough news etc. about the attacks and had to take a break. It had been almost 18 hours of constant pictures and videos and reports, and I was worn out. I turned off the radio and then started thinking. That was my downfall, the silence. My mind started to think about everything I had seen that day, the plane hitting Tower 2, the fires, the people trapped inside, people leaping to their deaths, it hit me all at once, and I started bawling. I couldn't help myself. I thought of all those people and their families and everyone and everything and I lost it. I had to get off the road.

I pulled over at the next exit and strangely enough, there was an abandoned gas station right there. It was a rural road exit so it was dark and deserted. I pulled over, shut off the car and bawled for about ten minutes. I don't know that I've ever cried like that. The jag finally ended and I got back on the road. The thinking thing got to me for a while, and each time I thought of those people it would wreck me. I made it to the club and was informed that we were indeed having a show that night. They had a private party booked and really didn't know what to do. I don't think anyone really knew what to do after that. What was the protocol? No one knew. The show that night had 12 people. That was all that showed up from the private party.

We did the show, and I had to mention the attack- it was a huge albatross hanging around everyone's neck. It put a weird pall on the room. People wanted to laugh, they just weren't sure if they should. I honestly wasn't sure if I was supposed to be doing comedy. 9-11 happened yesterday, and today I'm on stage being a smart ass? Is that right? No one knew. Thursday was a little better and Friday was better than that. During the second show on Friday, I mentioned something to the audience about keeping the victims and their families in their thoughts, and some lady starts walking up towards the stage. I can see she's crying a little and I start to panic because I know she's going to set me off.

It was incredibly difficult to be funny after spending all day watching them sift through the remains of the Towers. I felt guilty in a way, like I was still alive, etc. It was weird. I was talking about slapping my balls on the water while water skiing, and in the back of mind I see people hitting the sidewalks after leaping from 40 floors up. Hard to focus.

So anyway, this lady comes up on stage in tears, hugs me and says, "Thank you." This, of course, sets me off, and now she's got me crying; thanks a lot, lady. I'm barely able to focus and now I'm on stage crying-sweet. But I wasn't the only one; I saw a few others with teary looks and then people started to applaud. It was surreal, people applauding at this particular moment. It was kind of a release for me from the feelings of guilt. I realized that people *wanted* to laugh, they *needed* to laugh. And since I was a comedian, it was OK for me to be doing this. The Saturday night shows were packed to the gills; both of them had people standing in the back. After four solid days of 9-11 news, everyone wanted a break and they came out in droves for some laughter therapy. It was a really sad and rewarding week to be a comedian.

CHAPTER 31
SOME ROAD STORIES

I've always been kind of a nomad. I moved around a lot as a kid and I never really stopped. Fun things can happen when you travel. If you're gone from home for more than a few days, there is a different feeling about. You're out and about; you're traveling. When I travel, I drive, plain as that, and when I drive, I control. By control I mean the music, the speed, the stops and the temp. It's only fair; I'm driving, and my comfort is the most important thing. I don't trust anyone else the way I trust me. I'm a road dog, a driver extraordinaire, and your lives are safe with me. I don't easily trust someone with my life. These are my friends, I know these people, and by God, I don't trust them. When you're out driving around, I can't shake the feeling that "I'm the best driver out here." I always feel that way. Oh well.

I had left L.A. and was back on the road. There are just too many people in L.A. and most of them want the same job. You can't just get in the car and go somewhere; it's a huge production to deal with traffic every time you want to drive. It's madness; madness, I tell you. I'd rather be doing comedy. So I went back to doing it. I did comedy in L.A. but it was all showcase gigs where you only do seven minutes. Every time I stood in the back waiting for my 11 p.m. spot at the Improv I couldn't help thinking, "This is bullshit, I can a make living doing this." I decided to go back to being a full time comedian. That is what I wanted. To be on the road. Doing comedy. I'm a comedian, and I'm doing what comedians do; they do comedy on the road. Go from gig to gig, and do a little comedy. For the people, do a little comedy for the people. In L.A. it's hard to get work every week, and now I'm working as much as I want to. On the road, doing comedy. How soon I forgot February in Northern Minnesota.

Apparently, in my time away I've lost some sense, or I've lost whatever it is that tells you not to drive to Minnesota in February. But I'm working, and that's what I want to do. Doing comedy, for the people. On the road. The problem, unfortunately, is the road. It's covered with a sheet of ice- not glazed with ice, covered with ice. With a nice snow compacted layer on top. Then, like a fine northern desert, covered again, with a layer of ice. Let's drive, shall we? So we've got this white, clear layered thing going. I haven't been road-dogging for almost six years, and winter is when I decide to pick up again. Well done, Master.

WINTER GIGS

The gigs that will really kill you are the ones way up north. A 1000 mile drive for 14 people and the owner's kid. The owner, of course, would rather you didn't use any foul language in front of his 12-year-old daughter who is sitting in the front row. Well, get the bitch out of here because I just spent 18 hours in the car and I'm a little on edge. I was in Sault Ste. Marie, in Michigan's Upper Peninsula one year in January and these two guys who had been pounding beer and vodka shots during the entire show approach me and ask if I want to go out and party. Party? What do mean by "party?" I wanted to make sure I wasn't being invited to some kind of man orgy. I mean, I know it's cold up here, but a man has to know his limitations. "Well, it's not actually a party; we're going out on Lake Superior with an automobile hood chained to the back of a truck and pull each other around the lake." (Big pause for effect.) "I'm sorry, what?" Yeah, they wanted to go out and ride around a frozen lake behind a truck pulling a car hood. It's 12:30 in the blessed a.m., it's about -10 outside and, I didn't bring any mittens. Plus, I'd like to see my next birthday. He didn't have any of the answers I was looking for either.

"How fast do you go?"

"About 80."

"80? As in 80 miles an hour?"

"Oh sure," is the reply.

Eighty mph across a frozen lake in the middle of the night, in the middle of winter, in the middle of nowhere. "What happens if you crash through the ice?"

"It's too thick, won't happen." He tells me.

"Oh, I know, but what if it does?" I replied.

"We'd probably drown."

And I'm thinking; probably? Shit, with these clothes on and this water temp, yeah, we'd drown, and pretty quickly I might add. Thanks anyway, fellas; it sounds like a nice little adventure, but I'm not really into setting broken bones and suturing wounds out in the middle of Lake Superior in the middle of the bleedin' night. And by the way, isn't this near where the *Edmund Fitzgerald* went down? Yes, yes it is. "And Superior, they said, never gives up her dead."

Thirty minutes later, I'm lying on this car hood with a guy named Gooney (I'm not sure if that was his nickname or given name, and I didn't ask) on Lake Superior a little after 1 o'clock in the morning getting ready to get pulled around behind a truck on a frozen lake. Exactly what the hell I was thinking was beyond me. We start to move and Gooney says, "hold on and don't let your hands get under the hood." OK- I won't. Sounds like good advice. The surface is smoother than I thought it would be because of the snow layer, it was actually kind of cool. I could use a little more light on the subject; it's kind of dark and you can't see very well. You can look under the truck and see the headlights, but that's it. The chain is only about 20 feet long, which to me, seems short. Then Gooney tells me if the chain is too long, the whip gets too long and the speed gets too high. OK, I'm thinking "at least they're safety conscious." I certainly don't want the whip too long or the speed too high. Then we start to move and I'm enjoying it.

It's fun. We're only going about five mph at this point, which is just to get me used to being on this thing, I guess. I'm comfortable at this speed, to be quite honest with you. We could go this fast all night and I wouldn't have a problem with it. Well, Gooney and his buddy Randy would have a problem with it, so we start to speed up. I'm not sure how fast we ended up going, but I've never been more terrified in my life. All I could picture is me sliding off this thing on to the ice and rolling head over heels for about a mile. Mr. Tumbler, tumbling across the ice pack like a plastic bag blowing across the tundra. I bet it would've hurt too. Ice is hard, I am soft. Bad things man, bad things. What happened to Sweeney? "He died riding behind a truck on Lake Superior in the middle of the night." I did think about dying too. It's hard not to under those circumstances. Horrible thoughts were racing through my head. How bad would I be scarred up if I slid on my face? Would I break all the bones in my body or just the big ones? Are there any holes out here? Could I fall off and slide into a Lake Superior death hole? I don't know, I'm not from these parts. Death and warmth are all the thoughts I could muster.

Now we're flying across the ice, the wind is tearing up my eyes so I'm having trouble seeing, we're bouncing a little, not much, just enough to be concerned about bouncing off, and the wind is whipping through my clothes and into my marrow. I long for home, I long for a woman's embrace, a warm kiss, I long for a cup of hot chocolate, I long for sunlight, I long for, for, for...life. I want to live, damn you! Get me off this fucking thing before we're killed! I just wanted to reach over and hold on to Gooney, and say, "hold me, my ice warrior, don't let me slide off into oblivion." But I didn't. I'm not sure what Gooney would've thought if I had reached over and wrapped myself up in his arms, but I doubt it would've been good thoughts. So I held on myself and flew across the ice for about 15 minutes, which, by the way, was plenty. As I got up, I realized I wouldn't have fallen off. I had peed in my pants and it had frozen me to the car hood. I was fastened on baby, one with the hood, we had to take lighters to my britches to unfreeze me. Oh, it was exhilarating, not something I would do again, but it was an interesting way to spend a Friday night in northern Michigan.

I'm on a winter string of mainly one-nighters. Getting there wasn't the problem; getting out was the deal. The last shows were in St. Cloud, MN. Friday and Saturday night. Friday it snows about two feet; not two inches, two feet. Saturday during day, it sleets, covering everything with an inch of ice. Nice, very nice. Saturday it snows another ten inches. Even snowmobiles are getting stuck. OK, the week's over, let's get on the road.

I normally leave for home after the last show of the week. It sometimes means starting after midnight. Lone wolf is also a night owl, but since the snow is piled up to my window in the hotel room, I decide to wait until morning. Morning comes, what a pleasant feeling, morning has come, which means I didn't perish in the night. I hop into the car, not actually hopping, more of a gingerly glide. Any hopping done on a slick, icy surface can only lead to tragedy. I pull out of my space, turn for the exit and get stuck in the three feet of snow the plows have left in the entranceway to the hotel. Fabulous, I've been on the road for all of 12 seconds and I've run in to my first obstacle. With a borrowed shovel from the hotel, I dig my way out of the pile. I'm so afraid to stop I left the shovel stuck in the snow bank. I can't risk bringing it back to the office. I had to get a running start as it is to get through the snow pile that is left. I scoot across the street for gas and coffee.

Now, as I leave my oasis of warmth, the smell of coffee and cinnamon rolls, I'm ready to face the 825 mile drive home. Of course, I get stuck coming out in the pile that the plow left in the driveway of the store. Are you shitting me? I'm stuck again? Is this some kind of mind fuck? A little foreshadowing of the trip to come? I just got up an hour ago and I've been stuck in the snow twice, in less than 200 yards? What in the bloody Sam Hill is going on? I ran back across the street to the hotel and grab their shovel, which is still stuck in the snow pile, and dig myself out again. This time, screw the shovel, anyone that wants it can have it. I'm moving. Turns out, I should've just taken it with me.

Highway 10 across Minnesota can be a nightmare. The road apparently isn't on the map of roads to be plowed, which is going to fit into my travel plans quite nicely. Well, at least I'm on the road, doing comedy, on the road. Eight hours later, I've gone 120 miles. Yeah, it took me eight hours to go 120 miles. About every 20-25 miles I would reach a dry patch of road and take off, now I'm flying. Then I hit a patch of ice, do a little slide, do a little dance, do a little shitting in my pants. This apparently doesn't teach me anything, as I'm in a snow blind mind eraser mode, and nothing is sticking in my head. I hit another patch of dry road and take off. Then I see a "Bridges may be Icy" sign. We've all seen the sign, but how many actually slow down when they see it? Not me, I just keep cruising. Oops. Well now I know.

I hit this bridge going 65 mph, it's covered in ice and I immediately go into a spin. I'm literally doing full circles across this bridge. The only thing I'm thinking is what we learned in drivers ed: "turn *into* the skid, turn *into* the skid." It's great advice, but unfortunately, what I realize is: "I can't find the skid, I can't find the skid." The direction of the skid is easy to find if you're going four mph, at highway speed, the skid can never be found. You may find Jesus, but you won't find the skid direction. It's incredibly hard to focus on which way you turn the wheel when you're just hoping not to die. Turn into the skid? For the love of Mike, just keep me out of the river. Turn into the skid, oh that's rich. All I'm doing is spinning and screaming. Screaming like a little girl. I can almost see it in a dialogue bubble over my head "Aaieeeeeee, heeeeelllpppp meeeee." Oh sweet savior come to my rescue. At about this time, I get over the bridge, hit a patch of dry pavement and end up in the right lane, going the right direction. It takes me second to understand what just happened then; "Holy Crap, I'm a driving son of a bitch." The other drivers are eyeing me with admiration. Oh sure sir, nothing to it. That kind of thing happens all the time. I like spinning in circles over an icy bridge and lock it all back into place on the other side. Because, I sir, am a road dog. Bouts of pure idiocy, followed by moments of driving excellence, yes indeedy, that's me.

By the time I get to Minneapolis, the roads seem all right, so I keep going, past the hotels, restaurants, people, and safety, I just keep rolling. I'm going to make up some time. Twenty miles south of big Minny, Interstate 35 is closed down. Come on! This is Minnesota, you're used to snow- you can't close down a major highway! Yes, they can. I pulled off into a little highway oasis with about 600 other cars. This shouldn't be too much of a hassle. A thousand people all crammed into this one hotel, this one eatery, this one stop hell hole. I got out the map and decide I'm not going to let this stop me, there's got to be a way around. Eureka, there is, let's motor. I'll take a side road for about 25 miles, pick up highway 80 west and continue on.

Now, the problem with side roads is that they are rarely plowed, and along with the 40 mph wind, it can lead to some intimidating snow drifts. You can only cruise about 10 mph because you can't see through the blowing snow. It was periods of whiteout followed by sliding, followed by more whiteouts, followed by more sliding. Frequently, I'd have to pull over to let another car come by from the other direction because only ¼ of the road is open. I finally realize that I have to put on chains. I pull around a four-foot-high snow bank and prepare to brave the outdoors. Outside it's about -25 with the wind chill. Not a whole lot of outside work behind done at those temps. It's also fair to note that you can't put chains on while wearing gloves. It's a bare handed job. Ten minutes to get that first chain on. Now I'm back in the car looking for warmth. My frozen hands don't feel that good. Something's wrong, I've crippled myself, no, maybe they're just cold. Then it dawns on me that I'm basically sitting in the middle of the road with one chain on, one chain off, no deep cold clothes, 600 miles to go, and I begin to weep. But at least I'm on the road, doing comedy, for the people, out on the road. I finally just got a room and finished up the next day with the promise of never going back up there again in the winter. I did, of course, because I'm an idiot. Good stuff, Good times.

WINTER STORM '93

Winter storm '93. Do you remember where you were? I do. Philadelphia, Big Philly. South Philly in March. It was spring and it was beautiful. I wandered around the city, taking in the sights, sucking up the history. I had set a tee time up for Friday morning when the sun was shining on Thursday and we were having good shows. I had the condo to myself and all was right with the world. It started snowing

Thursday night and didn't stop until Sunday night. I was amazed. The entire city shut down. The highways were closed, the airports, the entire East coast was covered in snow and ice. My girlfriend at the time and her friend were on their way home from Florida and spent two days in a shelter north of Atlanta.

I was paralyzed. The shows had been canceled for Saturday night, and I had been paid but couldn't leave town. Nowhere to go. They had four feet of snow in the street. The streets of South Philly are very narrow, so no plows could get through. Not that those streets were much of a priority, considering the major interstates were closed. If it weren't for some mom and pop place on the corner, I would've starved to death. No stores in that part of town, no restaurants open, and mom and pop were only open because they lived upstairs from the store. On Monday, I decided to try and dig my car out because the snow is up to bottom of the window. I didn't have the proper attire for a blizzard and subsequent freeze, so I wrapped my hands with socks and off I go. I wished I had some bread baggies to wrap my feet in, just like the old days; when the kids didn't have a pair of snow boots to play in, you just had the four layers of socks covered in bread baggies and wrapped up by a pair of Converse All Stars, or a pair of Chuck Taylors. I can't believe the Chuck Taylors have made a comeback; there's absolutely no padding in those things. It's almost like going barefoot. You can feel every step you take vibrate up your bones until it rattles your inner ear. Or maybe that's just the way it feels like now. I honestly don't remember feeling sore at all as a kid. So I headed to the car with sock covered hands, and I'm ready to go to work. I was going to get that car out of there if it's the last thing I ever accomplish. Oh, I was leaving town, I'd been stuck in that condo for three days with nothing to do. I was antsy, aggravated, and ready to motor. Let's dig it out and hit the road, jack.

I was back at the condo in ten minutes. There was nothing I could do. I don't have anything to move snow with and there are feet and feet of it surrounding my car. There is no thing and no one moving. It was eerie, like some "after the apocalypse" movie. I was in downtown Philadelphia and there was no movement, no sound. I scurried back upstairs to rethink my position. I wonder if everyone's dead? Could the snow have been treated with some kind of chemical that kills? Am I immune to said chemical? Is that why I'm still alive? What in God's name is going on? Where are all the people? Oh wait, mom and pop are alive. I haven't seen anyone else in the store though. Is that the key? Is the store a haven? A sanctuary from whatever madness is happening? I better get my supplies together along with my thoughts. I'll need all my skills to ensure my safety. Everything's at stake now, baby. Wait...the TV is on. There are people on it. Is this what going mad feels like? Have I been cooped up too long? Maybe I'll go outside and try the car again. Maybe there will be people out. Maybe. One can only hope.

There are still no people around. Interesting. I'll take a walk, survey the area in case I have to escape from the undead. I'll need several escape plans, and since I have no weapon, I'll have to run. I can't fight off swarms of the zombies by my lonesome. I head out to plan my escape and around the corner and down the Avenue, I find a hotel. It's an old one, snuggled in between a couple of antique apartment buildings, the old, dark, stone buildings you find in the heart of a city that's been around for over 200 years. The hotel had the green awning out front and the two little signs that say "PARKING FOR REGISTRATION ONLY." I'm sure it would be classified as quaint.

Leaning against the wall in the entry way is a shovel. A shovel! The secret ingredient to my successful burrowing. I need a shovel, and I need one now. I hope it's real. I'll try to find the owner and see if I can borrow it. The doorman is inside by the fire; perhaps he will help this stranger, this vagabond, this shovel-less man. The doorman is an older black guy, in his seventies, wearing the traditional green topcoat and hat. He looks regal, refined and important. I approached and ask him about the shovel. He informs me that it's his and that he's brought it from home and it's a special shovel. I didn't ask about why it was special; he seemed like the kind of guy who would actually tell you the story and make a production out of it, so I let the comment pass. We discussed me borrowing his shovel for at least ten minutes. I couldn't believe it. This guy was actually interviewing me to use his shovel. Where was I staying? For how long? What am I doing in town? Is there a number there that I can be reached? How old are you? Have you used a shovel before? If so, can I see your license? This was just a snow shovel mind you; it wasn't encrusted with gold or jewels; it was just a snow shovel.

After much discussion and my assurances that I will bring his shovel back in better shape than I found it, he let me take the shovel. I pick it up and headed for the door. There were two screws missing out of the back and the shovel is wobbling all over. The edge is bent and curled up on both sides, the shaft is cracked, it's got rust all over it, and the handle has been taped, glued and nailed. I started to crack up. It was the kind of shovel you would find in the dumpster. This guy grilled me like I was banging his daughter and the shovel is a piece of shit. That's rich. But wait, maybe it had some kind of sentimental value. That was probably it; it may have been the first shovel he ever owned, or maybe it was the shovel his deceased wife had given him the first winter they were married. It didn't really matter, the shovel obviously meant a great deal to him and I will defend it with my life. No matter what happens my friend, I will find you and I *will* return your implement of snow removal. I'll let someone take this shovel when they can pry it out of my cold, dead fingers. There, it's out there. I said it. Now let's dig.

I got back to my car and realize I left my gloves/socks upstairs. I lean the shovel against the car and headed up to the condo. I returned less than three minutes later and the shovel is gone. The shovel is gone! The fucking shovel is gone! How in God's name did that happen? All I did was go upstairs. I didn't make any calls, I didn't visit the commode. I went up and came back down. My head is on a swivel. I'm trying figure out if the shovel was ever really there. Has the cold and the isolation taken its toll? Am I slipping into dementia, and if I am, will I know it? Has the chemically treated snow started to seep into my brain? Am I on the way to becoming...one of them? Am I experiencing the final, fleeting moments of clarity? Is this what it feels like to have your last cognizant thoughts? Did I, or did I not, just borrow a shovel from the doorman of that hotel, walk over and lean it against my car? I did, I know I did.

Look there. There is a slot in the snow where I stuck it in, proof. I did do it. I did borrow the shovel. Great, I'm not demented. Well, maybe, but not because of this. Now what the hell happened to it? How am I going to face that old man and tell him his shovel has been misappropriated? He trusted me. He trusted me with his shovel of sentimental value, and I let him down. That's the worst part; I let him down; I promised him I would take care of his shovel and I blew it. Because I can't just not go back. I have to tell him that I lost his shovel, face to face. I can't imagine the heartbreak I'm going to cause this poor man. Replacing the shovel is not going to make it better. He wanted **that** shovel.

Now, I'm pissed. Whoever took that shovel is going to make me look bad. Like my word is no good. I'm going to beat someone down. I'm starting to rage. If I find who took this, I'm going to rip them a new asshole. The balls. That's when I noticed the footprints. There, in the snow. Footprints. Leading away from me. Away from my car! Away from the shovel! Holy Shit! Those are the footprints of the mofo that stole my shovel. They have to be. So I start to track. Wasn't that hard really, there were no other footprints out. I just followed them around the corner, down the street, around another corner, and I must have gone six blocks when I hear the scraping of a shovel on concrete. The footprints turn the corner and there he is. The guy who stole my shovel. His shovel. **The** shovel. I've got him. Red-handed. If I have to kick this guys ass to get this shovel back, I'll do it, I don't care, I'm that fired up. I start to look for a weapon, but I find none. It will just be the two of us, in the middle of the street, in the middle of a dead city, in the middle of Winter Storm '93. A fight to the death. A fight for the shovel. Mano a mano, a cage match for the ages. There is no escape; you can't run in snow that's three feet deep. But wait, Batman, he's got the shovel. Well, I'll disarm him with charm and then go in for the attack. I approached.

"Excuse me, did you get that shovel from over on 2nd street?"

"Uh huh" he says.

"I need it back" I explain.

"Is it yours?" he retorts.

Is it mine? Is that what he asked? How is that relevant? Is it mine? I was about to tell him the whole story, but when I thought about the fact that he just walked off with, I decided an explanation wasn't necessary, he was going to give me that shovel, and he was going to give it to me right now. "Yes, it is mine, I'm in a hurry and I want it back now." I think he could tell I was serious and was in no mood to be trifled with. I was literally ready to go to blows with this dude. He'd gotten my dander up. Normally, I would've just let him finish; after all, the driveways in the city are only about three feet long, but the fact that he just took it and caused me upset and anguish made me take a step forward and reach out. "Fine, take it"

I took the shovel and retreated carefully. I didn't want him pulling a sneak attack once my defenses were down. I got back to the car, spent almost three hours getting my car free. I returned the shovel as promised and the old man smiled when he saw me; he was, I think, beaming. He seemed genuinely glad and relieved to see me and the shovel again. He just shook my hand and said, "Thank you." It really must have been some special shovel.

NOVEMBER 1980

One fall, Louie and I took a road trip from Cherry Point Marine Corps Air Station in Havelock, North Carolina, to St. Louis. We were stationed out there and made frequent road trips across the country. On several occasions we did it over a regular weekend. That's 2200 miles round trip over two days. We would take off Friday after work, get into St. Louis about 8 a.m., catch a z and then hook up with our friends for a little partying, go to sleep and get up Sunday and drive back to North Carolina. If I remember correctly, there might have been some speed involved, both physical and chemical. Why did we do it you ask? "Because the road was there," I reply. We were always looking for something to do.

On this particular trip, we had partied pretty good the night before at the Crabtree Lounge. It was a beach bar full of locals. Louie and I didn't hang with too many jarheads; we were trying to ease our way back into civilian life by hanging with beach people. Many of the beach people didn't really hang with military folk, but we were cool, and we always had money to spend, drugs to share, and we were fun, so we'd eventually grow on people. It's true. I wouldn't lie about that. So, we'd go to the Crabtree and drink 50 cent draft beer all night. Now when you mix a lot of draft beer with black beauties (which were speeders), it wreaks havoc on your digestive tract. No regular type of business if you catch my drift; it basically liquefies your insides. It happened every time, so no worries. A little touch of the runs was worth a good time.

The next morning we took off. We've both got some gastro problems, but it turns out mine were worse. We were sitting at an intersection in Winston-Salem, North Carolina, and I pass a little gas. I know right away it's potent. Naturally, I don't say anything. Louie gets a hit of it, kind of gags, says, "Jesus Christ," opens the passenger door and throws up in the street. Right there in the middle of the intersection, he's tossing what's left in his tummy right on to the pavement. I start laughing so hard I think I pooped in my pants a little.

I've got tears running down my face, I'm trying to keep my insides from leaking into my shorts, and Louie is still leaning out the door. The guy behind us honks because the light has changed and I start moving;

Lou's still got the door open and showing some reluctance about pulling his head back into the car. I didn't blame him really. It doesn't really matter how bad the gas is, the person who released it is never bothered. I know it's a stereotype, but people do like the smell of their own farts, at least the people I know. I crawled through the intersection and tried to get over, Louie still has the door open because he's not done, so I'm trying not to bash in to anything and slam the door on his head. I pulled into a gas station and skidaddle into the men's room before I have myself an accident. I return to find Louie beet red, bloodshot eyes, and tears on his cheeks. Naturally this sets me off on another laughing rampage. To think that my little fart did that to a grown man, made me proud. At that moment, it was the funniest thing I'd ever seen. Good times.

The rest of the trip went downhill. Hard to believe a trip that started with such jocularity could go bad, but it did. I had packed some peanut butter and bologna sandwiches for the drive. It's not as gross as it sounds. My dad turned us on to them when we were kids. My brother Phil and I are the only ones who really took to them. I still eat them on occasion. Somewhere in Tennessee I could tell something's going wrong in my stomach. It's gurgling. Not a hunger pain gurgle, I mean- it was a "I've got food in my stomach and it's fighting with someone gurgle." I had never had food poisoning before, so I didn't know what was going on. Either the peanut butter, the bologna, the nacho cheesy Doritos, or the sweet tea had some kind of a germ on its ass. Louie is asleep in the back and I'm driving through Nashville at 80 mph throwing up in a Doritos bag. That finally wakes him up, and he's cranky. After that trip I'm surprised we stayed friends. I make him puke with a fart and then he has to listen to me puking into a chip bag.

"Are you OK?" is what I thought I might hear, but, "what the fuck are you doing?" is what I heard. He takes over the driving tasks as I laid in the back seat and dry heaved into the cooler for the next six hours. More good times.

There wasn't much to salvage out of that weekend. By the time we got rested and feeling better, it was time to go. Time to go get stuck in snow storm in the Blue Ridge mountains. We didn't go back to St. Louis for awhile.

I'm going to make a bold statement. Food poisoning is a bummer. I'm not talking about E. coli poisoning, like when you die; I'm just talking about good old-fashioned food poisoning. A little puking, a little runs, a little dehydration and top it off with complete loss of muscle control. Oh yeah, fun stuff, especially if you're some place that's not convenient for puking and diarrhea, like in the car.

My worst case of the poisons was in Cincinnati, Ohio. I went to a Dairy Mart at 1 a.m. and had a double chili cheeseburger. To this day, I don't know what the hell I was thinking. It wasn't just a double chili cheeseburger, mind you; it was a radar double chili cheeseburger. I sure know how to treat a lady. So, I ate that thing and woke up about 4:30, and I realize I've been awakened by my stomach growling. I felt OK, but my stomach was making so much noise it disturbed my slumber. Then the contents of my stomach start moving around. Uh Oh. This isn't going to be pretty. I toss and turn for about two hours and then get up and head to Cleveland for a showcase at the Improv.

As soon as I got on the road, it hits me. I need to go potty. I used a gas station and then another gas station and then another and so on. I hadn't even gotten out of downtown Cincinnati and it took me an hour. I had to stop every ten minutes. So I decide to blow off the showcase, I'll never make it to Cleveland. I turn around and headed home. I finally gave up on using normal facilities, by then I was just pulling on to the shoulder of Interstate 75, hiding behind the passenger door with my pants around my ankles and trying not to poop or puke on my shoes. It went pretty well until I got to Lexington, Kentucky, then I got stuck in rush hour traffic. Nice, very nice. Now I'm hiding behind the passenger door with traffic crawling by and everyone getting a nice big eyeful of the pooping, puking Sweenz. "Oh, I'm fine, don't worry about me, I'm a comedian." I just waved and wished everyone a safe drive home. I finally made it home and to this day, I have never had another radar double chili cheeseburger from the Dairy Mart. That wasn't good times.

OUR FIRST ROAD TRIP

When my wife and I moved to L.A., we drove. The idea behind this was that we could split up the driving to make it easier on everyone. Unbeknownst to me, my wife couldn't stay awake more than 30 minutes in the car. It's like traveling with an infant; as soon as I strap her in the car seat, she's asleep. So I ended up driving the 2020 miles and she drove the 40. Thanks, baby. It's been refreshing.

The hardest she has ever made me laugh was on this trip. We had stopped to eat lunch in Oklahoma City. I don't remember where we ate or what she had, but it disagreed with her. It made her a little gassy, if you will. Or, as my grandmother would say, "she's got a touch of the winds." We're about an hour past lunch and I'm driving and she's sleeping. Oh, the surprise. I've got the widows rolled up, radio down and I'm keeping things quiet in consideration of her well-earned rest. We all know how exhausting eating can be, and it just plumb tuckered her out. We're cruising along and I hear this little squeak, which confuses me because I can't identify it. It was one of those little girly farts. It's a fart, yes, but it can almost be called petite, if petite can describe a fart, which I do believe it can. Since I can't tell what it is, I move on. About a minute later I hear it again, another squeak. "What the hell is that?" I ask of no one. I'm checking the visor, the glove box and anything else that may be the cause of the squeak. Another 30 seconds rolls by and I receive another one, this one hits me and, "Eureka!" I realize what it is: my wife is passing gas! Oh, man, I knew I would figure it out. It's a fart, by God, I knew it wouldn't escape me forever.

Now that I've figured out where the squeak is coming from, I think that she's really awake and she's playing me for a fool, thinking she can mess with me and feign sleep. I lean over and she's out cold. Her hat is on sideways, she's drooling, she's asleep. That in itself makes the whole thing funnier. She's passing gas in her sleep. What a riot. I don't know that I've ever really wondered if people farted in their sleep, I know dogs do, so why shouldn't people? It's just not something I ever thought about.

Here she is, my bride, my woman, my wife, fast asleep with the wind touching her like a hurricane. The pace has now picked up, and every 20-30 seconds, I'm getting another squeak, and each time she does, I start laughing. I'm having a great time, but problems are arising. Each time she does it, I start to laugh, even though I haven't finished the previous laugh, so it's building and building until I'm having trouble catching my breath. I'm weaving all over the highway, tears are streaming down my cheeks, and I'm having the laugh of my life, but it's getting out of control, and   we're in danger of going off the road. I crack her on the ass and I say, "woman, wake up you're killing me." She wakes up, takes a deep inhale, makes a face, and says "Oh my God, you are such a pig." Oh, yeah, there you go, honey, here I am, a grown man, sitting in the car laughing my ass off at my own farts. You certainly have me pegged.

SUMMER 2003

What a summer. I hit two deer. That's right, two deer. I actually only hit one of them; the other one hit me. The first one was in April. I was heading to St. Louis from Pittsburgh. I had participated in a "Comedy Competition" in Pittsburgh. I've done dozens of these over the years, and the funniest guy never won. Not to say that I was the funniest, but amongst the comics, the guy we thought should have won never did. I got knocked out in the second round and was heading home.

Going from Pennsylvania to Ohio, you have to cross about 20 miles of West Virginia. As I hit the border, I see the infamous deer crossing sign. It's a helpful sign, I suppose; it makes you take a little more notice. Some signs are more helpful than others, "PRISON AREA-DON'T PICK UP HITCHHIKERS," that's a helpful sign, "ROAD COVERED IN WATER," that's another helpful one. "BRIDGES FREEZE BEFORE ROADS," that's one I never paid attention to until after I had the incident. I was looking for deer the best I could. I'd seen four or five on the side of the road already, so I knew I was entering a war zone. It looked like a serious battle had taken place. Deer carcasses all over, but it wasn't a massacre, I suppose, because some of the deer had headlight glass embedded in them and I think I saw some smears of paint, so they did some damage as well. They remind me of Kamikaze pilots, these ballsy deer are on a suicide mission. I can't believe they don't realize they can't win. No way. We have superior firepower; we're smarter, faster, can drive and have opposable thumbs. Let it go, you dumbasses, to continue on is futile.

But they don't give up. They keep flinging themselves onto the roadway. The timing involved is quite intricate. Cars are averaging 70 mph, and these fools have to time their leaps precisely. I don't get it: don't they realize that the lights coming down the road bring death? EVERY TIME. You think deer legend would tell tales of the lights on the hard path. The stories of the brave souls before them who had tried to take on the lights and lost. I mean, what do deer talk about around the campfire? Salt licks? Boring. Foraging? Again, boring. You think somewhere along the lines one of these idiots would speak up and talk about the "lights of death." Fools. Plus, don't they realize that there isn't shit on that side of the highway that isn't on this side? Look around, morons.

I was coming down this hill and as I get to the bottom, a semi passes me. He was haulin.' He gets about a cab length ahead of me and this deer darts on the road. Somehow, someway, the truck misses the deer and I plow straight into it. Before I could hit my brakes, I've got deer guts and all that is held in deer guts, splattered all over my windshield. When I hit this deer, my large cup of lukewarm coffee falls and splashes the back of my legs, which immediately, I take to be deer shit. I gagged and almost puked until I realized there's no way that deer shit made it through my ventilation system, circled around behind my passenger seat and splashed my legs. Whew, that was close.

Having a windshield covered in deer shit is a nice look. I don't want to use my wipers for obvious reasons, so I'm peeking out of an uncluttered spot in the top left of the windshield, almost on my tippy toes. About five miles down the road, I pulled over into a truck washing facility and take a peek at my car. It ain't pretty. The headlights on the left side are busted, the hood is bent up, the grille is mashed, there are tendrils of some un-Godly origin hanging from a jagged piece of headlight casing, and to top it off there's about five pounds of deer shit and entrails on my hood and windshield. It's 3:45 in the a.m. and I'm somewhere in West Virginia. As I'm standing there, this guy from the truck wash comes out for a visit. As far as I can see, he's the only one around. I don't want to be stereotypical, but he was a little country, a little backwoods, a little Deliverance. He made me uneasy.

"Hit a deer?" He says.

What I wanted to say was, "No, it was actually a turtle." But I didn't. I thought if I did, I may have to explain that it was just a joke. Maybe he wouldn't have thought it funny and called some of his friends, and they would have some kind of party with me in an abandoned slaughterhouse, deep in the West Virginia woods, where my screams would go unanswered, so I said "yes, I did."

"Looks messy."

"Yes, it does."

"You're gonna have to clean that off."

"Yes, I am."

"Whew, that is a mess."

This clever banter went on for a few minutes. I then asked him if I could use a hose or something, to clean off the innards. He told me he didn't have a hose, but for $25, he could wash it off for me. Considering the time, the place, the circumstances, I thought it best not to haggle. "$25, is fine, hose this puppy off." Twenty minutes later, I'm back on the road, the ride doesn't look so good, but I was traveling and back on the road.

I went the next four weeks deer free. Then I hit another one. No shit. Actually, this one hit me. I was in Indiana driving in a biblical rainstorm. A blinding rain, a blizzard of rain, a torrent of rain, a wall of rain, it was raining hard. The kind of rain that makes people pull over under a bridge overpass, which by the way is dangerous as hell. I was glad to see them go. Get the hell out of my way, you pussies, we've got a real driver here. Clear the way, sweet poppa is coming through.

As I was crossing over a small bridge, I see what looks like a deer standing the left lane of this bridge. Have you ever seen such a thing? A deer...on a bridge? What the hell is wrong with you? I slow down to go by him, and I was down to about 20 mph, just crawling by, and as I approach he lowers his head and charges my car. He caught me in the left front quarter panel, rolls down the side of my car, snaps off my mirror and radio antenna as he's putting dents in the side the whole way back. I was stunned, shocked, mortified and horrified. How in the hell did that just happen? Did it happen? Was it real? Could I have just imagined it? A hallucination maybe? No, my mirror is gone- it was real. I'll be damned, that son of a bitch just crashed into my car. If it wasn't raining, I'd stop, go back and beat the crap out of him, just pull my 5 iron out of my golf bag and then bash his brains in, right there on the side of the highway. That will teach him. Don't mess with me, bro. I'll kill you with a golf club. But it was raining. Did I mention that? So I don't want to get wet just to make my point to a deer that may or may not be still alive. Perhaps I should have realized that this particular deer wasn't right when I saw he was wearing a helmet and orthopedic shoes.

A DESERT TRIP

A couple of weeks after I moved to L.A., I had to return to St. Louis to retrieve my car. I had set it up so that I would go on the road for a few weeks, pick up some cash and work my way back to L.A. Seemed like a delightful little plan. Upon execution though, not so delightful. My last gig was in Tampa. Now, I've got to drive from Tampa to L.A. Oh, did I mention that my air condition had blown its compressor?

Yes, that makes the story so much tastier. Did I also mention it's July? If I'm not mistaken, that's the hottest month of the year, and I'm going on a 3000 mile drive in the summer with no a.c., apparently there is something wrong with me. And if not now, then by the end of the trip, I shall certainly have some screws loose.

Driving through Florida wasn't too bad. Entering Alabama wasn't overly uncomfortable. Cruising through Mississippi was muggy, but sufferable. Things got a little testy going through Louisiana, the bayou holds the heat. By the time I hit Texas I knew what heat was. Texas is too big. I know the Texans like it that way, but come on. You can't even drive across it in one day. That's too big. Most of it is sand, and by most, I mean about 86%. All day long it sucks up the heat and then slides it across the highway in glimmering sheets of molten air. It heats your lungs that in turn heat your insides, so you're getting it from both sides. It's almost like being micro-waved. Holding your head out the window doesn't help either. Being slapped in the face with 110* air at 70 mph doesn't really refresh like you think it would. I was soaking towels in the cooler and hanging them on my head. It was quite the cure. Before too long the water in the towel would heat up and ruin everything, but for a few moments I really had something. I even took some pictures of myself. I look miserable. It's pretty funny. Money was tight, so I slept in the car. One night in West Texas, I was at a truck stop and saw a group of Mexicans run across the highway into the U.S. It was eerie in a way, watching these people sneak into the country. They even have signs on the highway in some areas. It's an illegal's crossing sign that has a couple of people holding hands and running, they're pulling a child who's feet aren't even on the ground, so it looks like they're going at a pretty good clip. Hilarious.

JULY 1994

My buddy JoJo and I are booked for a couple of weeks of work on the East Coast. We're driving. Well, I'm driving. He has a college gig a couple of nights before and they're paying to fly him, so I'm going to meet him in North Carolina in two days. I'll be taking his wife's car. Why? I don't remember why we were taking it. I just know that we were. He had taken the car to have the oil changed before the trip. He didn't completely trust the oil changers, so he decided to check it himself before we left. Since we were outside in the garage anyway, we sparked one up, just a little doobie before I depart. The plan is for me to leave at 11 p.m. and drive all night. He checks the oil and finds it to his satisfaction, slams the hood of the car, and I'm all set. I didn't notice that he hadn't put the oil cap back on. It was just sitting on top, unsecured, loose, unbound, just waiting to be utilized. I wished I would've known; I would have put it back on and saved myself some hassle.

I departed. About 10 minutes later as I'm getting on the highway, I hear something rumbling in the engine area and then stop. It sounded just like an oil cap bouncing around the engine cavity before falling to the roadway. Since the noise stops, I think, "well, the problem's gone," and I keep keepin' on. As I'm crossing the Mississippi, I smell oil, not necessarily burning oil, just oil. I naturally assume it's the smell of the refineries in East St. Louis. But no, it strangely doesn't smell like East St. Louis. It doesn't smell like Sauget, which is a town of strip clubs, liquor stores, gas refineries and nothing else. Seriously, that's all that's in the town. But this isn't Sauget I'm smelling, this is like...well, it's like fresh oil. Hmmm. I wonder if it has anything to do with us checking the oil? Could it? Then I see the smoke. Uh oh, there's smoke coming out from underneath the hood! That can't be good. I must get the car pulled over. One problem, I'm in East St. Louis.

For those unfamiliar with East St. Louis, it's a rather poor area of town that has very few white people. Ok, there are no white people. There is, however, poverty, and poverty leads to crime. A friend of mine from high school was murdered in East St. Louis- how's that for a happy story? Anyway, I need to pull over and do so at the next exit. I saw lights and I headed for them. It happens to be a Shell station. Something familiar. I don't know why that made me feel more secure than say Ed's Gas and Tires, but it did. I'm saved, I'm saved and I'm safe. Praise the Lord.

I pulled into the station, and to say it's "run down" would not paint the proper picture. It was the kind of oily, seedy, full of weeds in the cracks kind of place. Exactly the kind of place where cops find bodies on *The First 48*. Perfect. I scan the area apprehensively, checking my surroundings, finding out what I've got to work with. Is there an escape lane? Will I run someone down if necessary? Would I? Could I? I shut off the car, pop the hood and go take a look. The inside of the engine compartment is covered in oil. Since the oil cap was gone, there was nothing keeping the oil in. It had sprayed out everywhere and was dripping over everything. What a mess, I think to myself.

I checked the oil level and was down almost two quarts, good thing I pulled over when I did. I need more oil. I also need an oil cap, hmm, I wonder where I can get an oil cap at 11:45 on a Tuesday night? I went into the station and the owner is a Pakistani dude with his wife and three kids with him. Why he has his kids with him is beyond me; maybe they're safer at the gas station. Believe it or not, this guy had a pretty good supply of stuff. I bought some oil, a funnel, a circular clamp, a screwdriver and a soda. I can use the soda can as a new gas cap and the screwdriver to tighten the clamp. I go back to the car and begin. I dumped the soda, punched a hole in the side and then tore it in half. I was going to use the bottom half as an oil cap. There is enough of a flange at the top of the opening to clamp the can to. Clamp the can to, that's sounds funny. Say it. Now say it faster. Lots of fun. So I got the can over the opening on the cylinder head, and as I'm screwing it tight, the lights go off. What the hell? Is there a problem? Are we under attack? I see the owner shuffling out the door with his family in tow.

"What happened to the lights" I inquire.

"We're closed" is his reply

"Can you turn them back on for a few minutes? I can't see what I'm doing"

He says he can't, that it's midnight and he needs to get his family home. Under normal circumstances, there would be lights from other stores or gas stations or Quicktrips or anything. But no...I have to choose the one exit that has NO other source of lights, not a twinkle, not a glimmer. Thank God I'm almost done. I get the can pushed down and tightened up and I'm ready to go start the car and see if my fix works when I notice the cans of oil sitting next to the car.

The cans of oil that have not yet been opened. The cans of oil I DID NOT put into the engine BEFORE I put the can and clamp on. Are you shitting me? I went through all that hassle without filling the engine with oil first? Is this guy a dumbass or what? Now I'm standing in the lot of a totally dark, deserted Shell station all by my lonesome in East St. Louis after midnight with full oil cans in one hand and my dick in the other. Not literally, it's a figure of expression. I wasn't actually standing there with my dick in my hand. There is a time and place for everything, and this isn't it. This is the time and place to get the fuck out of. Something I've failed to mention is that while leaning over the engine trying to engineer an oil cap, all the oil that had collected on the hood has now dripped all over my head, shoulders and back. I quite literally had a quart of oil running down my neck. It's hot and sticky and I'm starting to panic. Now I've got to wrangle this "modified" oil cap off the mount, put the oil in and then put the cap back on. The whole time I'm keeping an eye out for intruders or anybody up to mischief.

It's now almost 12:30, it's taken me almost 45 minutes to complete this simple chore. I fill up, try to clean up and hit the road. I traveled all the way to North Carolina with oil dripping off my hair and down my neck. I had never been so sick of the smell of oil in my life. All the oil that is coating the inside of the engine compartment is heating up and cooking right where it sits and then filtering it's way into the car. It collected in my ears and in every nook and cranny of my torso. I'm quite sure I've never been this miserable. The trip was long, the trip was tedious. I never thought I would get the oil off of me. I finally did reach my destination, knocked on JoJo's room, and he's sleeping in the dark, cold room and looks as comfortable as anyone I've ever seen. He sees me standing there in the light of the afternoon, covered with oil, which as now collected packs of dust, anything that floats by clings to me, so now I'm oily and dirty, and he gets quite a kick out of that. But I'm here and I need a shower. I threw my clothes away. There are some things you don't want memories of; that was one of them. God, how I love the road.

CHAPTER 32
GONE FISHIN'

My dad used to take us to stocked lakes for a day of fishing when we were kids. You can't go wrong with a stocked lake. Nowhere for the fish to go. They're trapped. They're hungry and we've got food. You can't escape this tasty glob of stink bait on the end of this delicious hook, can you, Mr. Bullhead? Stink bait. Stink bait may be the most appropriately named item on the planet. My mom wouldn't let us keep it in the refrigerator; she said it would contaminate the people food. Stink bait does stink. I don't know what's in it, and you can actually make your own, but we never went that far. You'd have to be some kind of special to make your own stink bait. I think there are some kind of innards in there. I don't have access to innards. Never have, hope I never do. My dad would take us to the stocked lake to fish for bullheads, which are some kind of catfish. We would go there and sit in the sun for hours and hours and catch fish like mad. Sometimes we would catch stringers full and you couldn't throw fish back into the lake, you had to keep them. We never brought them home though, we always gave them to someone else who was there fishing for food. We just fished for fun, and my dad told us some of the other people there needed them more than we did, so we always gave up our hard earned catch, not to mention the fact that my mom doesn't clean fish. No Sir. Doesn't clean fish. Will not, cannot. There was also no way my dad was going to clean 30 fish, so giving them away benefited everyone.

We had some great pics from those days. Everyone had on their Chuck Taylors, and in one picture I'm wearing a green dress shirt and American flag jean shorts. Who the hell was dressing me? I looked like an acid trip gone bohemian. A green dress shirt! Long sleeves as well. Classic.

One trip took us to visit some strip mines in Pittsburgh, Kansas. Big gouges in the land where mining operations had taken place and later filled up with water. We used to go fishing there. I shouldn't say used to go, we went once. It turns out once was enough. My dad, me, Jimmy and Phil. We packed up the car with our gear to go fishing. Very exciting. My dad was famous for his station wagon packing skills. Just the right amount on the roof, just the right amount in the back. Very scientific, very well planned. My dad's mantra about trips was, "better to take it and not need it, then to need it and not have it." We took everything my mom would let us strip out of the house. "Dad, stop it, we don't need the lawnmower."

One year, before our annual family vacation to the lake, we had packed the car the night before while the car was in the garage. We had that thing stuffed to the gills- just enough room left over for the kids. We had it wrapped up in tarp in case of rain, wrapped in rope and then duct taped closed. There was no way anything was getting in there. It stood on top of the car like a cowboy riding a bull to certain victory. It had to be ten feet tall. "Good job, boys, let's call it a day."

The next morning we gather our thoughts and the final touches are applied to the process that goes in to getting a family of eight on the road. A lot of last minute peeing, pooping and general pain in the ass activities. As soon as you'd get two or three kids in the car, two more would take off for God knows what, then two or three more would come back but the others were gone. It took hours to get all the people in the car and ready to go, hours. In the old days when someone went on vacation, the neighbors would all gather on the street and driveway to say adios. Sometimes there would be 10-15 people standing around while the car is prepped for departure. They said their goodbyes, gave best wishes for a fun time and a "we'll keep an eye on the house." I miss that. It was nice. We're all in the driveway waiting for my father to back the car out of the garage. But wait! Are you sure it's going to clear? It looks a little tall. That's really something that has to be taken into account before the packing process begins. Oh yes, we've packed it too tall. My dad can't get the car out of the garage. It took us over an hour to unpack, move the car outside and repack, because the whole process of getting everyone ready had to start all over. Everyone had to pee again, etc. I thought we would never leave. We all voted to leave the tarp and all that stuff off, but that wasn't going to happen. We packed it up the way it was and off we go. Years later there was a scene in *National Lampoon's Vacation*, where Chevy Chase did the same thing. I think of my father every time I see that.

We had almost as much stuff for the trip with just the four of us. We headed out on Friday night and were to come back on Sunday. We head to the mines and set up our camp. There is always something comical about setting up a tent. I don't know why. It just never seems to go smoothly. Of course, this was in 1971 and all tents were heavy canvas with many poles of various shapes and sizes, with ropes and clips and springs and stakes and loops and such. It was all made more confusing because we had no directions. The tent had belonged to my grandfather and the directions had been lost long ago. Trying to put a six-man tent together with three boys under the age of 12 is no easy task, but we managed to get it up, and we had our site staked out. We had set the tent up on the side of one of the mines. There wasn't really any flat ground around, so we were kind of slanted. No big deal, we thought. We did a little fishing, had some supper and called it a night.

Sometime during the night it started raining. It must have been raining pretty hard because there was enough rain running through the tent to wake us up. That's an exciting way to wake up, with six inches of rain water rambling over your feet. I don't remember who woke up first, but soon all of us were up trying to figure out why the *inside* of the tent was wet. "What's going on in here? Where is this water coming from?" We scrambled around for a flashlight, clicked it on and saw the river of water coming through the tent; we're all looking for something dry to put on, but there's nothing left. Everything is soaked. This tent was a six man size, but when there were four of us in there trying to salvage dry clothing it was chaotic. Everyone was scurrying around under the glow of one flashlight with a scratched up lens, trying to hold stuff over our heads. We managed to get pants and shoes on when my dad goes outside to take a peek. The sun hadn't come up yet, so it still a little dusky.

My dad must have seen something because he pops his back inside the tent and says, "everybody out right now." He said it with a certain sense of urgency, so we bolted outside. We look up the hill and we can make out what seems to be a wall of water at least two feet high coming down the hill. Granted, two feet may not actually be "a wall," but it seemed like it at the time, you know, given the circumstances. There we were, the four of us standing there in a deluge of biblical proportions, mud up to the lower shin area, watching our tent slowly get knocked down by this mini river. It took about five minutes, but just as the sun was cresting the hill, the tent came down and was swept away. I can still see the look on our faces as we watched our tent slide down the hill, a look of complete dismay. I'm not sure kids that young understood dismay, but that was our look. Utter dismay. The rain continued to pound on us with no shelter and nowhere to go.

The rain finally stopped and the sun came out. The temperature immediately shoots up into the low 90's, so the humidity was jungle like. We decided to try and collect some of our stuff. As soon as I took a step my boot came off, so now that's gone and I'm down to one shoe. I was down on my knees for ten minutes trying to dig that boot out, and I was covered in mud from ankles to neck by the time I was done, and then heat started to harden the mud to my clothes. At this juncture, this is the most uncomfortable I'd ever felt in my life. We started to gather our things, along with the tent. It all ended up at the bottom of the hill. I say all, but we lost some stuff. We didn't fold or anything, we just want to get out of there. Everything is soaked and covered in mud so we just crammed, jammed and stuffed everything we could find into the back of the wagon. Great, let's go. The road leading down the hill is fairly narrow, about three feet of clearance on either side of the car. It goes downhill at about 35 degrees, pretty steep. The bottom of the hill goes right between two strip mines, it's narrow, and there's water on both sides. I'm sitting in the back seat on the passenger side. The car stinks, the smell of mud, dampness, wet canvas and maybe, just maybe, a little bit of tears.

We're about three quarters of the way down the hill when we start to slide. I hear my dad say, "oh shit." This took me by surprise because my father doesn't swear. Never has. I've heard him swear twice in his life. He always told me that swearing was the sign of an ignorant man who doesn't have the vocabulary to express what he feels so he uses swear words. Holy shit, dad, that's heavy. So when my father does swear, there is something looming large. I looked out my window and all I see is water, "well that can't be good," is my thought. I should be seeing ground, not water. Is this how it's going to end? Sliding off a hill of mud into a strip mine filled with water? What the hell? I haven't even gotten laid yet and it's over for me. This sucks. Suddenly we start to slide in the other direction. "Yeah!" We're going to make it, dad's a great driver, we're saved. Then to we start to slide back the other way, and now we're fishtailing down this mud slicked hill. Uh, Oh. We're all going to die. Damn. I have so much to live for. How can this...wait, we're going back to the other side. We did this a couple of more times and then made it to the other side. My dad stops the car and gives up one of those nervous laughs that come out when you narrowly escape some type of tragedy. "Is everyone alright?" Everyone was. Well, now what to do? Let's count our blessings and head home. Good plan.

About 30 minutes later, as we're driving down a back road in rural Kansas, my dad says "I think there's a lake around here."

"What? Are you crazy?" After all this, the guy is still thinking about going fishing? I think my brothers and I were about ready to go home, the car stench is getting worse, we're hot, wet, crabby, and we're starting to grow fungus. Please, for the love of God, take us home. But he's rubber-necking the area and saying stuff like, "I remember seeing it on a map," or, "doesn't this area look like there would be a lake around here?" or, "I've got a good feeling about this area." Then he pulls over! "This looks like the spot." At first I don't think we thought he was serious until he turns off the car and starts grabbing gear. He is serious! So we grab our gear and start hiking through the woods. We must have gone a mile and we're starting to get a little crabby and tired, I mean, after all, we're just children, when all of a sudden, bam, there's a little lake.

Well, a lake may be pushing it, it was more like a pond. "Oh yeah" my dad says, "this looks like a honey hole." The excitement starts, a honey hole, that's what he called it, that's got to be good. We started to fish. Nothing. Not a bite, not a nibble. I don't think that water was more than two feet deep. We're on the bank and the sun is beating us into soft, wet piles of little boys. After an hour or so we decided we've had enough. Our clothes are still wet and now they are covered in burrs, the day is getting hotter and more humid, and we begin our trek back to the car. We didn't find out about the chiggers for about 30 minutes.

Everybody starts itching around the armpits, ankles and waistline. We figured we had walked through poison ivy or something. By the time we pull into the driveway we are all in quite a pickle. The chiggers that had attacked us are in full boring mode and working their way into our systems along squiggly red lines. We get inside, strip off our clothes and see red welts all over. We've got red welts all around our armpits, our ankles have bites all over them, and we've all got a belt of red chigger bites around our waists. We ended up with the biblical rains, the flood, we've got the near death experience driving out of the mines, the forced march through unfamiliar and treacherous woods, we've got chigger bites all over us, rashes and chafe marks from the wet clothes, and I do believe mold was growing on us somewhere. Now that's a memorable fishing trip.

I had some experience with chiggers again, later in life. When I first moved to St. Louis I had a friend named Ron. He had a lake behind his house and we used to camp out and fish for catfish, who like to feed at night. We had little bells attached to our rods and if a fish got on, the bell would ring and excitement commenced. One afternoon we decided to do a little fishing. We sat on the bank in waist high weeds and just enjoyed the day. We sat there for an hour and a half with very little action, and then I headed home.

On the bike ride home, I started to sweat and then started to itch. Hmm, that's odd. By the time I get home I'm in full itch aggravation. I go upstairs to the bathroom to take a look. I've got chigger bites all over, and I mean all over. Chiggers like to go to the warm places on the bod. Armpits, waist, and...yes, the crotch. I had a full belt of red welts around my waist, I mean this red ring went *all* the way around. My pits are lined with them sumbitches, and I'm afraid to even check my crotch.

They're all over my sack. I know, I know, freaky and just a little uncomfortable to think about. I could not believe how many bites I had, so I started counting. Perhaps that's a little weird to some, but I had to know. There were well over a hundred. I can't remember exactly, but I distinctly remember going over 100, I want to say like 120, 125; that's kind of what sticks in my mind. I was rotten with them. I had never thought something like that was possible. Imagine, if you will, a 15 year-old boy standing there with a one inch thick belt of chigger bites around his waist, imagine, if you will, his armpits encircled in the red welts of the chigger and his friends, running amok, creating havoc, burrowing deeper and deeper into the darkness of my being. That's what chiggers do: they burrow; that's why the welts get longer, they're burrowing. Nice thought. Now, imagine what's going on downstairs, where it's warmest! I was riddled with those bastards. I literally had 20 chigger bites on my boys. Twenty! Is that hard to believe or what? To paraphrase, "I WAS IN HELL, SIR!"

I think my mom cried when she saw me. She made me sit in a bath of Epsom salts for awhile. Remember those? Epsom salts? They used to cure everything, eh? Fever? Epsom salt bath. Headache? Epsom salt bath. Broken leg? Epsom salt bath, then a trip to the hospital, of course. Let's not be ridiculous- they can't fix broken bones. I'm not sure Epsom salt was the cure for chigger bites. I didn't itch when I was in there, but the bath doesn't kill them, and that's what you have to do to make the itching stop. KILL THEM! Just mass murder them. Total annihilation, extinction, baby, you've got to take their lives in order to save yours. The secret, and this comes from experience, is to cover up the air holes, if they can't breathe, they can't burrow. So my mom and I spent almost an hour putting on chigger-aid, it's like finger nail polish and it suffocates them. The process is slow because you have to cover each hole individually, and when there's over 100, it takes some time. I took care of the ones on my crotch of course, but mom helped with the rest.

Another problem with chigger bites is that each time you move it aggravates them and they itch. A lot of itching going on and you can't scratch because that makes it worse. There are many mental games going on with this sort of thing. Don't scratch and don't move, so I laid there on the couch tried to remain immobile. That of course is impossible. Have you ever tried to remain completely motionless? You think it would be easy, but even the slightest movement of your arm in turn created movement in your armpit and then off you go. You can't walk because that aggravates the bites on your balls. Plus everyone wanted me to stand up so they could see my back and armpits. Oh, I was like sideshow attraction. How many chigger bites can one boy stand without losing his mind? I actually stayed home for school for two days. I just couldn't move without going into a scratching fit like some loony in a padded room. It reminded me of that Cheech and Chong movie where Cheech is in a padded room wearing a strait-jacket and he just wants someone to scratch his balls. To this day, I've never again sat in high weeds and gone fishing. Lesson learned.

Over the years my dad would take us places to go fishing. Then, we started getting older and doing other things. After I enlisted in the Marines, my dad wanted to go on another fishing trip. This time... Canada, the place my dad had gone with his father-in-law on several trips. I can remember, as a kid, my dad leaving on these trips. He'd be gone for a week. We thought that was the coolest thing ever. Being gone for a week! Fishing in Canada for a week, the ultimate trip. My dad traveled a lot on business when we were kids but never for a whole week and never on a fishing trip. I'm not sure why we thought that was so cool. Maybe the idea of being in Canada was impressive to us. That or the fact they slept in a tent for the whole time. As a kid, sleeping in a tent was awesome. Even if it was just in the backyard, if you were in a tent things were alright with the world. I think it was the whole thing of sleeping outside; it's just too much for a kid to pass up. WE GET TO SLEEP OUTSIDE! The possibilities were endless. We can get out of the tent and walk around. Just tooling around the neighborhood. That, of course, can lead to trouble for many reasons; first of all, none of your other friends are out, they're all in bed sleeping. Suckers. Unless, of course, they got to sleep outside too, then meetings and rendezvous were definitely on the agenda. Bad news there, kids. Eight or ten fourth graders hanging out after dark in the creek behind the Hy-Vee. No good can come of that. But I digress. Sleeping in a tent was a big deal. Until you have to do it for a week as an adult, then the sleeping in a tent doesn't seem so special anymore.

So my dad scheduled the trip. We're only going to the Canada/US boundary waters, so we drove. Me, my dad, my brother Phil, my Uncle Larry, my cousin and a friend of my brother Jimmy's. It turned out to be a great trip. We didn't catch that many fish, but we had fun. My cousin caught the biggest fish of the week- a 20 pound Northern Pike. We had all these elaborate lures, the top of line gear and whatnot and my cousin is rooting around in his tackle box and finds a piece of nylon rope with some hooks stuck in it. We had been having a slow day fish-wise, and when you're in a boat for twelve hours fishing and the fishing sucks, boredom can be a killer. Your mind can wander. You may try anything different. Hmmm, maybe if go whammalamma fish pajamas each time I cast, I'll catch something. Maybe I'll put this lure on backwards and fish left handed. Maybe I'll only fish off the right side of the boat; there's probably no fish on the left side. Maybe if I pee in the water right here, it will attract some fishes. Like I said, the mind wanders.

So Danny decided to try fishing with this piece of rope. We get a pretty good laugh from it because it's all curled up and twisted and dirty and nappy. It's got oil and dirt on it, and if I'm not mistaken, some stray hairs. I don't know why I had to classify them as "stray hairs." If they weren't "stray hairs," they'd probably still be in somebody's head. But he tied it up anyway and casts away. It's not very aerodynamic, so he can only cast it about 15 feet. When he casts it, it sails like you would think an eight inch piece of nylon rope with hooks hanging off it would sail. After a few casts he gets a hit and lands the biggest pike of the week. We were flabbergasted; there's no way you caught that thing on a piece of rope. I've got $200 worth of lures here and haven't gotten shit, and now you're going to fish with a piece of rope? Now, of course being the fishermen we are, everyone's now rooting through their tackle boxes looking for pieces of nylon rope with hooks hanging off it. Weird thing about fishermen, or fisher people if you prefer, they're very superstitious. Every fisherman in the world has his "lucky lure," or his "lucky hat," or his "lucky rod," or his "lucky thermos," or his "lucky knot." Yes, I've fished with someone (my father) who had a lucky knot. "This knot has never let me down," and "this knot is the greatest knot known to the world," or "every time I use this knot, I catch a great fish." Weird dudes, man.

One night the boys decided to go out and fish after dinner. My dad and uncle just wanted to stay around camp, so Ronny, Phil, Danny and I loaded up the boats and headed out. After an hour of unsuccessfully hunting for lunkers, we headed back to camp. The sun had set and was it was pretty dark when we got back. It seemed that my dad and uncle had retired for the evening for the camp was silent. That's one thing about the woods up there, it can get quiet. Quiet like I've never heard. Quiet, man, quiet. Did I mention that it was quiet up there? After sundown, it gets damn quiet. Not a peep, not a pop. Just quiet.

Ronny and I were tying up the boats as Danny and Phil headed up the hill. It may have been 40 yards between lakeside and camp. As Ronny and I approached the crest of our little hill, Danny and Phil are standing there, frozen, not moving, statuesque. "What are you guys doing?" "Shhhh" is the reply. They are obviously listening to something. I wonder what it is? Are dad and Larry talking about us? What's going on? What are you listening to? Then we heard it...a growl. A fucking growl. There was a growl coming from the woods. We knew there were bears up there; we hadn't seen any, but we had been told about the precautions. We couldn't see if my dad and uncle had tied the food up to the tree, but we couldn't imagine them forgetting that. You can't forget stuff like because, well, bears can come and kill you. The four of us are standing there listening to this bear growling in the woods and wondering what to do. What should we do? Scream? Try to frighten the bear in some fashion? Should we just stand still and hope he goes away? Should we charge and attack? You know, kill, before you get killed? Somehow, that didn't seem like a very viable solution, we didn't know where he was, much less how big or mean he was. There were too many unknown variables to attack. Someone come up with another plan, and do it quick. Then we realize that my uncle and father are sound asleep in the tent. Should we yell out to wake them and risk pissing off the bear? Maybe hearing our voices will send him into a rage resulting in human slaughter. Who knows? We don't. How long can we stand here? Hours? Minutes? Can we outwait and outwit this bear? This carnivore? This man-eater? This boy-eater?

Then we hear a growl followed by a snort and that was all it took, the four of us turn and ran down the hill and jump in the boats. The bear is attacking, get to the water! Bears, of course, can swim, so we start paddling for our lives. Deep, powerful, maddening strokes. We know we've got to outrun this bear if he's coming after us. Stroke, stroke, you bastards, get us out of here. Then it dawns on us...we left dad and Larry asleep in the tent with a bear in camp. Holy crap! They could be torn to shreds and never know it. We could be stuck here. Nobody knows where the hell we are. My dad can get us out, he knows the way, but we don't, if he gets eaten by a bear, we're screwed.

Now what? The camp was on a little peninsula, so we started the engines and motored around the point and get another look at camp. We had dropped our flashlights when we turn and ran to the boats, so we couldn't see much on shore anyway. Danny did have some matches, but they didn't really light up the shore line well enough to see. All that did was spotlight us to the bear, so now he can sight us in with a scope and put our heads on the wall of his den. We had to try and get a better look. We must have circled around that point for 30 minutes before shoring the boats to take another look for the bear. As we're approaching the camp, we hear it again. Growling. Deep bear growling. Death growls. You could almost see his snout, with pieces of his last kill hanging in bloody shreds from his huge, sharp, rotting, broken, tarter-covered fangs. Death is coming, boys, let's prepare like men. If it's our time, by God, it's our time. Just kids, that's all we were. Kids. I was the oldest at a fresh-faced eighteen; we're too young to die. Too young to be torn apart by this savage beast unleashed from Satan's sanctuary. God have mercy on our souls. There we stand, the four us, preparing to die, or least preparing to find the remains of my dad and my uncle, then I notice it. "Wait, sshhhhh."

"What is it?" the others inquire. "Listen." So we listen. We listen hard. I'm not sure we could have listened any harder. It was the hardest I've ever listened. I notice it, yes, there it is. It's rhythmic. The growling is rhythmic, it's got a cadence. But wait, bears don't growl rhythmically, do they? They growl like... well, like bears growl. They certainly don't growl the same way each time, with the same tone and same duration.

"What the hell is that?" Then it hits me.

It's snoring. Dad and Larry are in there snoring. Son of a bitch. It's snoring. It's not a bear. It's snoring. Holy shit, that was close. Snoring, it's fucking snoring. We're out there scared out of our minds, completely freaking out, terrified for our lives and the lives of friends and family, trying to escape death by getting in the boats and effectively giving dad and Larry up for sacrifice to save ourselves. Then to come back, risking life and limb to save someone dear to us and those guys are in there snoring their asses off. Ain't that something? I can't believe we just spent an hour of our lives on this little incident. It was. It was just about an hour between start and finish. Unbelievable. We thought it was a bear. A bear. We had thought those two snoring was a bear. Not just me either, it was all of us. I wasn't the only one running down the hill and trying to escape by water. A bear. The next morning, my dad and Larry thought that was the funniest thing they'd ever heard. They had quite the little giggle. I don't think they understood the gravity of the situation. They did, however, appreciate the fact that we had left them for dead when we escaped to the boats. Ha, ha, fellas, hardy har. Good times.

I've been on several memorable trips to the great land to the north. We keep going further and further north. By 1992 we were up in the Northwest Territories. That's a long way up there. We'd usually fly to Saskatoon or Yellowknife and then take a float plane the rest of the way. Yellowknife was amazing. It's basically where the roads in North America end. And it does like the edge of the world. I think the only reason the town exists is because they discovered diamonds there in the fifties, and where there's money to be made, they will build a town. Float planes are a trip in themselves.

Takeoffs in a float plane are fun. It's a bumpy ride, to say the least. Some of it depends on the size of the plane. I've been on ones that hold twenty people, and I've been on ones that hold five. The smaller ones are a rougher ride, especially if there is any wind at all because, of course, wind makes ripples on the water and ripples roughen up the surface of the water. The very water we're trying to take off on. So wind = ripples = rough surface = rough ride. We move away from the dock and turn into the wind, we throttle up and head out, and we're slamming against the water and bouncing and weaving, and you can almost feel the nuts and bolts falling off the plane and raining down upon the countryside.

On the larger planes there is a little curtain separating you from the pilot. On the small planes, one of us sits shotgun. When you're sitting in the pilot's lap, there's not much going that you're not aware of, and there is a lot going on to get one of these planes off the water and airborne. Our pilot is young, nineteen, which seems young to be flying float planes, but no, he's been doing it for almost five years. Crazy Canucks, they start 'em early. So we fire up and head into the wind and this guy is turning wheels and adjusting knobs and rotating dials and pushing buttons and he's doing it all over the place, above his head, to this left, to his right, on the control panel and even some knob behind his seat, no shit, behind his seat! Not to mention the fact he's working a couple of pedals on the floor, playing with the throttle and working a huge yoke that's mounted to the floor. I want to ask what all this stuff does, but it's such a flurry of arm movements, I don't want to distract him.

He's working all this stuff at once and we're banging across the water and it's so loud you can't hear anything but the engines screaming in your ear and the incessant crashing of the plane into the waves, and everything is shaking, and you just hold on and hope for the best. You look out the front window and you seem to be running out of water and there are trees coming up and it doesn't look like we're going to make it. Let's just go back and start over and see if we can't get some more speed generated. It's like organized chaos in this cockpit; there is a flurry of activity going on, his arms are flailing, he's moving the knobs and yanking on the yoke (which is something you don't get to say everyday), and the trees are upon us and I know we're going to fly straight into them. I just want to yell, "Abort, abort." He's starts pulling on this yoke like he's a Yale oarsman and finally we leave the surface, we missed the trees, everyone is OK and it gets a little quieter...we're airborne. Praise the Lord.

A few years later, we went on another trip, this one inside the 60th parallel, not too far from the Arctic Circle, baby. The North Country. The land up yonder. We're going fishing. Why go that far to fish, you ask. Because we can, that's why. If you've been up there once, you'll go back again. It is absolutely the most pristine, beautiful place I've ever been. One solid week of no cell phones, no TV, no radio, no chatter, no traffic, no people, no noise, no animosity, no intolerance, no hatred, no war. It could be classified as Nirvana, not the band, the place. At least during the summer, it's like that. You will die up there in the fall, winter and spring, but the summer is a delight.

We picked up our float plane in Stony Rapids, Canada. Stony Rapids is about a two hour flight north of Saskatoon and has a population of 500 not including "the ones who live in the bush." I thought that was great phrase, "the ones who live in the bush." Sounds like the name of a horror movie. The nightmare continues as the search goes on for the "ones who live in the bush." A group of serial killers. I doubt Canada even has serial killers; it just doesn't seem like that kind of country. I mean, I'm sure they do, but it's not a country known for its violence. Anyway, I won't go into longitude and latitude, but it's a long way up there. Stony Rapids was on fire.

I'd never seen a forest fire before. I found it to be a little unsettling, especially since it was burning on the other side of the river that we were taking off from. The fires were started by lighting, and no one puts them out. According to the folks up north, "it's nature's way, eh?" I love the way the Canadians talk. I asked him about them being put out and he said the snows will do it. The snows? It's freakin' July. I'd hate to have to "wait for the snows" to put out my forest fire. Maybe someone should grab a hose and water pump and start dousing these things. Nobody up there seemed to care, so we didn't. So, we're ready for another float plane flight. As we're standing on the dock, I do a little pre-flight check of the plane. I notice there's a piece of duct tape on the left wing. Hmm, that's curious, I'm sure it's not actually necessary, someone must have just stuck it on there for whatever reason. It *can't* actually be holding the plane together. When I mentioned it to the pilot he replies;

"It's covering up a hole in the wing."

"What do you mean, a hole in the wing?"

"There's a small hole in the wing and the tape keeps the wind from getting inside and tearing the wing apart."

I didn't even know what to say- our lives are depending on duct tape? Is that really possible? Yes, it is, Virginia. I inquire further;

"So the duct is the only thing between us and death?"

"No, we super glued it too"

Oh well, now I can rest assured; there's duct tape *and* super glue, we should be fine. The view from a float plane over northern Canada can hardly be described with words, it's like being a bird flying over heaven, at least to me. Nothing but wilderness as far as you can see.

Yummy. Landing in a float plane is just about like taking off in one, except reversed. When you get close and the pilot is slowing the engines, and he starts in with all the knob and lever adjustments. It's pretty wild descending onto water. It's usually the last thing you want to do in an airplane- land in the water. You can see it rushing up and it takes your breath away for a second then you splash down and all is well.

We're at the camp. We're ready to unload our gear and get this fishing trip started. But first we have to unload our gear, unload supplies for the week, and then load up the gear of the guys going home. Now, we're ready, except no fishing today. We have to get settled, go through orientation about the boats and motors, the transducers and depth finder, the emergency power, the communications system in case "something happens" to our camp manager, and various other things about generators and power amplifiers and battery hookups etc, etc. I hope someone else was paying attention. I'd hate to be in charge of calling in a rescue mission when I didn't pay attention to the orientation. Someone could be dying and I'd be in there trying to figure out how to turn the satellite phone on. Hmm, that didn't work. What did he say about the connection?

We got through orientation and decided we were all hungry. "There's a bag of hot dogs in the one fridge" says Jason, our camp manager, who by the way was a great guy and great manager. I'd like to think that we were his favorite group of all year. At least the best group in July. We did have a good group, if I must say so myself. We had two groups in our party: my father and I along with my brother Phil and his buddy Joe Ward, and the other part was my dad's buddy Phil Lutkemeyer, his son Jaime and his son-in-law John. Great people.

My brother and I fire up the grill, grab the bag of hot dogs and cook up about 30 of them. We're really hungry, you see. No buns, so we just put them on pieces of bread. We're roughing it, after all. Someone says something about the size and taste of these particular brand of wieners when Jason comes in and asks us why we're eating all the breakfast sausage. Sausage wieners?! No wonder they taste funny and are very small. We all had a good laugh and decided to go to bed before we got hungry again.

Our first morning in camp we were up by 5:30, it doesn't get dark up there during summer, so by 2 a.m. the sun is coming up already. 5:30 in the morning and we're ready to go fishing. Breakfast every day was up to us. Nothing special. We did have something called Red River a couple of times. Red River is northern Canada's version of oatmeal. I think oatmeal has more flavor. Red River may be the plainest taste I've ever encountered. It sticks to the ribs, don't get me wrong, it also keeps you full for a while. Red River also had the reputation of either loosening up your digestive tract or binding you up for days. It affects different people different ways. I'm more of a binder, while my dad is a loosener. I don't know if loosener is a word, but that's what I'm using.

Being in the boat with a loosener can create problems, especially if he's 72. No matter how many times my dad went in to "take care of business" he always had to do it one more time during the day. Totally understandable. The problem is the short warning span. When I hear "uh oh" I usually had less than two minutes to find a place to put the boat so he can get off and "take care of business." Two minutes to find a place on shore to pull up. You may not think that would be any big deal, but the lakes in northern Canada are full of rocks. Lots of rocks, there are rocks everywhere. You can't escape them, you can be cruising along in 80 feet of water and then come upon a reef that is two feet under the surface. Nice. Full of rocks, not just rocks, but big rocks, the kind of rocks that will rip a boat open like a Christmas turkey. There are rocks upon rocks; did I mention there are a lot of rocks up there? So, finding a place quickly became a very important part of my day. Once you get the boat close to shore you have to pull the motor out of the water so you don't scrape on the rocks. Did I tell you about the rocks? There are rocks everywhere. Then I use the oars to get us in the rest of the way with my dad leaning over my shoulder urging me to, "go faster." Oh, we had some times.

Getting him back in the boat was an adventure in itself. My father's balance isn't what it used to be, and he's very tentative when it comes to "leaping back into the boat." He informed me that there will be no leaping going on, so we had 5-10 minute discussions on how to gently lower his ass back into the boat seat. Hilarious. It was precision work.

I'm not sure if I mentioned rocks, but there are lots of rocks up there. My dad and I got stuck on the rocks three different times. Sometimes the shallow water hides rocks that you can't see because of the other rocks in front of them. There are rocks hiding behind rocks. Sometimes I could swear that they were moving over to get in my way. The first time it took us almost 15 minutes to get free of the damn thing. The wind was blowing up a storm and we were just pivoting on this rock, just spinning in circles. The rain and wind were pelting us into submission. The temperature was dropping rapidly, and being wet wasn't helping. We had rain suits on, of course, but the wind just blows the water under your hood and down your chest and back. It's really quite uncomfortable. All we really wanted to do was to curl up in a little ball in the bottom of the boat and wait for the sun. We couldn't use the motor without tearing up the prop, so we tried to oar our way off, and I'm pushing one way, my dad's pushing us the other way, but the wind keeps changing and blowing us the opposite way of whatever way we were pushing. Almost comical if you're not the one in the boat, we must've looked ridiculous. Now we're just standing there looking at each other as our boat spins in circles, trying to figure out what to do next without getting dizzy. We finally disembark from this particular stone after much cussing and discussion.

The final rock incident was the day before we went home; you would think that after seven days of dodging rocks, you would get better at it. You would be wrong. This time though there was some panic involved. We're on a rock in less than two feet of water and the wind is blowing us right into an island that is surrounded by ROCKS! If we don't get out of here soon, we'll be stuck for sure. I've got the prop just barely in the water trying to pull us backward and I'm freaking out because we can't get going in the right direction because of the wind. I look back at my dad and he's sitting down, gently pushing the oar through the water like he's on a casual float down a babbling brook. I snap at him to push off the bottom and he informs me he can't reach the bottom and not to snap at him again because it's not his fault I drove us onto the rocks. OK, good point, I'm just getting a little panicked back here. We eventually start crawling backwards and now there is a rock in Wignes Lake that has a long silver scratch along its back. I don't like rocks anymore.

During a heat wave, northern pike, at least big ones, are hard to find. The hot weather messes up their minds. It messes with you too. The temp can go from 90 down to 50 in about 20 minutes. It's blazing when the sun's out, then drops 15* when a cloud passes, then it drops another 15* when the wind picks up, then it goes back up to 90* when the cloud's gone, and then 20 minutes later, it's dropped to 50* and it's pouring. We changed clothes 10-15 times a day. We were told about the heat and fish behavior every day by Jason, who, by the way, works for the government in the off-season, studying fish, so he knows from where he speaks. Didn't matter to us though. We were set on catching pike no matter what we were told, then complained that we weren't catching any big pike. Stubborn bastards.

Trolling for big lake trout was the way to go. Most of our guys didn't like trolling. You just sit there while the boat drags your lure through the water. Boring to some, fishing to others. I finally got my dad to agree on a morning of trolling. You just find a deep hole and cruise back and forth over it. It was a windy day, big surprise, and off we go. Jason had let me borrow his personal rod and reel, so I'm being extra careful. Trolling in the wind is hard because the lines have a tendency to get tangled on the turn around. Jason tells me a little trick about turning the boat 180* right away instead of making a loop turn and we'll be OK. It worked for the first ten turns and then the wind caught us. Or I should say, caught my line. All of a sudden line starts flying off my reel with a wweeeeeeeeeiiinnnnnggggg sound. Like that scene in *Jaws,* when the shark takes off with the bait, I damn near became a "loosener."

It scared the crap out of me. I know I've got the fish of a lifetime. My heart is pounding, and I can feel the tingle in my blood- this is going to be unbelievable. I calmly put the motor in neutral as I prepare to do battle with this monster fish. When I put the motor in neutral the line stops coming off my reel; hmmm, that's weird. I look down over the back of the boat and see my line going into the water...right above the prop. Curious. I pull the motor out of the water and see my line wrapped around the prop about 10,000 times. So it wasn't the fish of a life time, it was an Evinrude outboard motor. Much easier to catch.

Things don't look good. I spent ten minutes trying to cut the line off and decide I need to take the propeller off. Again, another adventure begins. In calm water it can be tricky, and in three foot swells, it's damn right ticklish. So I'm leaning out over the water from the waist up, holding on to the top of the engine with one hand while undoing cotter pins, bolts and washers with the other. I pull back a couple of times to avoid a swell and notice that my dad is facing the front of the boat. "What are you doing" I inquire. "I can't bear to watch," he says. Well perhaps you can watch in case I go overboard, you know, just as a safety kind of thing. I'd hate for him to glance back and find that I've been gone for five minutes. So, I get the prop cleaned up, put back on the shaft and all the torn up line back into the reel. I figure I'd lighten things up a bit when I return this stuff to Jason. "Hey, can you fix this?" As I give him a reel with a monstrous bird's nest. Ha ha.

The whole week went without incident until the last day. We got to fish until 3:30, then back to camp, pack up and catch ze plane. Jason went out to look for the Lutkemeyer party about four and couldn't find them, which believe it or not, is a big deal. Not being able to found. They could be lost, but that's unlikely since we had GPS equipment in each boat, which means they've broken down somewhere, and that can't be good. God knows where the wind will take you; they could be on their way back to Saskatoon.

We called in a float plane search and they found them stranded on some rocks with a broken lower unit and most of their clothes on fire. Yes, they were burning clothes to attract attention, burning clothes and a life jacket. I wish I could've been there for that. Dousing a life jacket in gas and torching it up. The boys said it was worthless because it burned up in about a minute. They spent a total of five hours stranded on a pile of rocks in the middle of the lake watching our boats pass them by all day. We cruised by them twice and didn't see a thing. They must have been pissed. "What the hell is wrong with those guys, we're swinging oars in the air, burning anything flammable and they just keep boating by." Just one more adventure above the 60th. We fished 10-12 hours a day for seven days. Even avid fisherman get a little tired of fishing after that kind of schedule. Jason cooked dinner for us every night so we could fish until 9 p.m., then usually a cigar, and off to bed. I couldn't believe how early I went to bed every night. Fishing is very tiring, I guess. All in all it was another great trip to the north woods. We got to see the northern lights for the first time, surprising at that time of year. I felt ready to go home until we hit the Minneapolis airport; it was full of people yapping on cell phones. Put me back on a float plane.

CHAPTER 33
I GO SKYDIVING

I fell out of a plane once. It was on my 45th birthday. I was working in Vegas and decided to celebrate by going skydiving. I've always wanted to do it, but for one reason or another it never transpired. I was scheduled to go twice when I was in Okinawa, Japan, but due to the whole "restricted to barracks" thing, my opportunities passed me by.

A few words about Vegas. First of all, I was there in July. As we all know, the summer is warm. The week I was there it got over 110 every day. 110 degrees, that's toasty. "It's a dry heat though," yes, well so is a kiln but you still don't want to be running around in it. The week after, I was in Laughlin, NV. Laughlin, wow. A thousand people living in the middle of the Mojave. It was over 120 degrees every day I was there. Can you really imagine 120 degrees? When the water in the pool is too hot to get into, it's too fucking hot outside. At night it got down to 92, on Tuesday, I think. You could still see heat waves coming off the sidewalk at 3 a.m. What the hell? You spend the whole day going from air conditioning to air conditioning, all the while trying to stay in the shade. A difficult task indeed. It's an amazing sight, watching thousands of people walking around Vegas in weather that is fit for gila monsters and other types of leathery lizards.

When you hear the word "tourist," the people walking around Vegas is what you picture. Strolling through the desert heat with huge rings of perspiration around their necks and bellies, which are also carrying the infamous "fanny pack." For the love of God, put the fanny packs away. Granted, they are convenient, but come on, how many guys need to carry that much shit with them? At one point, you may as well start carrying a purse. A man just doesn't need that many supplies for an afternoon stroll down the strip. Then there's the water, everyone has their water. We can't leave without our water. In Vegas in July it's mandatory, but it's still adorable to watch everyone you see carrying their bottles of water around like it's their juicy-juice. Just strolling and sweating and gawking and drinking out of their sippy cups. Ooh aah. Look at the big Lion. (Which by the way, is the largest bronze statue in North America.) Snapping pictures of everything, oh, look, a strip club, what are the chances?

A few years ago, Vegas started this new ad campaign, toting itself as a "family vacation" spot. Oh, for the love of Mike. A family vacation spot? OK, let's see, it was started by gangsters to launder money made from drugs, loan sharking, mayhem and murder. It grew because of gambling, drinking and whoring. People go there to experience debauchery, to do the things they wouldn't do at home. "Let's go play blackjack for a while, hang in the bar, get hammered, and then go find some hookers." Too bad the kids aren't here.

Just because you put in a roller coaster and a GameWorks doesn't make it Six Flags. Look around, nimrods, this place isn't for kids. There are guys on every corner passing out flyers advertising strip clubs and escort services. Every bus has an ad with a half-naked girl on the side, and she's selling something to do with sex. Sweet. And if your kids somehow miss the flyers and the buses, they can look down and see titties and g-strings on the flyers on the ground. "What's this, daddy? Can we go here?" Sure Daddy would like to go, but he's got the wife and kids with him and they're on "vacation" in Vegas. Titties, drinking, gambling, depravity; keep the kids at home man. There has to be a place that's just for adults. There has to be. After a couple of years they've gone back to "what happens here, stays here." That's better. That's how it should be. I like that, having a place to go where you can use your location as an excuse to be an idiot.

"What the hell did you do that for?"

"Well..."It's Vegas."

Like that explains everything. Drink too much, gamble too much and certainly, eat too much.

"Hey how was your day?"

"My day? My day was fine, I ate six buffets." Nothing makes people bigger pigs then an unlimited food supply. Let's see, I'll have a little ham, maybe some beef, I think I'll take a hot dog, ooh maybe a brat too, hmm, I think I want some macaroni and cheese (because you can't just get a delicacy like that at home) maybe some fried taters, oh, a roll, grab a couple of those rolls, what else do we need? Let's see, how about a chicken fried steak? Oh yeah, now we're talking, lots of gravy, I need some cheese, "has anyone seen the cheese?" Wait, there's noodles over there, maybe I'll make up a little stroganoff, I'll have to find beef chunks, you know what? I think I want a taco too, no, put some more of that cheese sauce on it, oh yeah, that's looking good, Billy Ray, let's see, is that everything? Nope, I forgot bacon, I need to head back to the front. Not all the way to the front, just far enough back to get what you need, and that usually requires cutting in front of someone, but since you've already been through, it seems OK.

"Hey, no cuts, man."

"Oh, it's OK, I've been through the line already and just forgot some things. I'll just be a minute while I pile my plate so high I can barely hold it with one hand." Why do we do that? Put so much food on our plates that we can barely transport the food back to our table? It's a buffet for crying out loud, you can go back and get more. You don't have to pile your food so high it's in danger of toppling over. Then comes the dessert; even if you're full, there's still room for dessert. I have to have some pie, maybe a little, just a little piece of cake, that cheesecake is looking pretty good; of course you can't have pie without ice cream, and the cake may need a little splash as well. Oooh, you know what would go good with this? Reece's pieces, or some colored sprinkles or Oreo crumbles, and last but not least, a nice layer of jelly beans. Bon appetit. After a meal like that, there's only one way to finish it off; a nap. It's Vegas, baby.

There's also some type of optical illusion in Vegas. It looks like a walking town. When you can see something, it looks like you can walk to it. You can't. You can try, but by the time you've gone a mile and the place you were heading to isn't getting any closer, you realize, it's time for a bus or the tram or a cab because it's too fucking far to walk. How come we're not getting any closer? I can see New York, New York from my hotel room, why can't I walk there in an hour? Are the sidewalks secret treadmills? I know my feet are moving me in the right direction; I've gone through twelve intersections, why is my destination not getting any closer?

I like to play blackjack. But sometimes I don't like the people who play, especially the older ones, or the people who play all the time. They always want to give advice: "you may want to split those son." Or, "I'd double down if I were you."

"Hey, shut up, old man, I'll show you how to play, let's go ahead and hit my 19."

Even the dealer will speak up, "Sir, you have 19."

"And I want 21, give me a card, Chauncey," then throws me a five, I'm busted, but the guy giving me advice is sitting next to me with 15, looking at that five and going, "What are you doing? That's my five."

"Well, apparently not, sir, I paid for it, you enjoy that nine, now leave me alone or I will fuck up every hand at this table." I'm sorry if I can't add up five and nine as quickly as Einstein, and don't even get me started on Aces. "Oh great, now I have to figure out two hands, one for eleven and another for one, it's too much adding, I'm drinking, I can't think, I need out, aaaaaaiiiiieeeeeee." That's why I don't really gamble. I don't like doing shit like that with strangers. I can play cards with my friends, but sitting at a table in Vegas with people I don't know? Terrifying. I never feel like I'm qualified to be doing this. Is that stupid? It's not rocket science, its cards. I'm just a little leery of gambling because I got burned once in Twenty-nine Palms.

We were playing a game called "in between." Two cards were laid down and you bet on whether or not the next card would be "in between" the two. I had an ace and a three, so I bet the pot of $250 and pulled a deuce. I just sat there and looked at that two. I don't think I've hated a number before or since. That deuce killed me. Everyone was screaming and jumping up and down and I was dumbfounded. I even had to borrow about $40 to cover the debt. There goes my money for the next two weeks. It was an entire paycheck gone in an instant and I've never really gambled much since.

I went skydiving in Vegas, me and my pa. My folks were actually in Vegas that week, so my father joined me. Much to my mother's chagrin. We had two options, tandem jump after a ten minute class, which considering what we were about to do, I personally thought, could have been a little longer, or jump solo after an eight hour class. Well, I'm not spending eight hours in training just to plummet to the ground alone. If I'm going, I'm taking someone with me. Plus, I don't think I wanted the responsibility that comes along with parachuting. Most of the time, I don't want to count on anyone, but this time I passed the torch. If I've got someone strapped to my back, I know he's going to do everything to save his neck, which means, I'm saved too. Yeah. So we took the ten minute class and jumped tandem. I'm not going to make any jokes about having a man strapped to my back. I've had guys tell me, "I'd do it, but I don't want another man that close to me." Well too bad for you, homophobe. I'm going jumping. Plus, once you leave the confines of the plane, having a man strapped to your back is the last thing on your mind. I could've had a naked Boy George strapped to me and I wouldn't have noticed. There are way too many things to occupy your mind- like dying.

On the ride from the strip to the airport, which wasn't really an airport as much as tin shack with a runway in the yard, we filled out our paperwork. About ten pages worth of paper work and each page had the words "DANGER/DEATH" in the background in red ink. That's nice. "DANGER/DEATH." I guess they wanted to make sure we knew that we could die from this little excursion. It was rather amusing because it was on *every* page, front and back.

They also didn't take responsibility for anything, not the weather, not acts of God, not pilot error, not mechanical error, not instructor error, nothing, nada. They didn't take responsibility for a thing. It was amazing. There was even a clause in there that said if we tried to sue them, we had to pay for their legal expenses. I'm thinking, "what the hell? Are we going to die today?" Those thoughts do go through your mind, what it would be like plummeting to the ground from 15,000 feet. Would it hurt? Would it be scary? Would I poop in my pants? Yes, is the response to all those questions. I don't know if it would really hurt though, the heart attack would probably kill you first. It would be a wild way to die wouldn't it? Splat, man, splat.

We filled out our forms, signed the line and agreed to the fact that we could die today. All-righty then. Let's get to the class. I call it a class only because they did. It wasn't so much a class as a "meeting." The instructor had us watch a video, show him our "arc" and we were ready to jump. Ten minutes and we're ready to jump. Talk about a hurry-up society. My dad and I were the third group to go up. I saw my father getting a little nervous when he sees how high up the plane is. "You can barely see it" he says. "It's just a little dot." I just said that it was a small plane and just seemed smaller in the air. I didn't really know what else to say. These could be our final moments together and I wanted to reassure him, but by God, that plane does look way up there. He's just staring up at the plane and not saying anything. Then the group in front of us starts jumping. They are so small, they are barely seeable. You can just faintly see movement and my dad says "oh, boy, is that them?"

"I do believe it is."

"Oh my, they are way up there."

"Yup, they sure are."

"We should be all right shouldn't we?"

"We should be, yes."

"This will be fun."

"Yes, I think it will."

"Plane's coming back."

"Thank you Tattoo."

"Who?"

"Never mind."

"Boy they are way up there."

"They have to be Dad, if you want to free fall."

"Freefall...I don't like the way that sounds."

"But that's the best part."

"We should be OK, right?"

"Sure Dad, we'll be fine."

"OK, the plane's here."

"Yes, it is, it's our turn."

"I guess we're next."

"I guess so."

The plane lands and we headed to the door. A word about the equipment. We were issued a jump suit. Mine was orange, just like at "work camp." I'm sure originally it was a nice outfit, but now it's in tatters. When you jump tandem, you land by sliding in on your butt. After many butt landings the seat of the jump suit had completely worn through. The seat of the pants are literally hanging there in threads. It's either from wearing out or the fact that so many have shit their pants when they jumped, the back had rotted out from so many washings. We were also issued elbow and knee pads along with a vintage WWII flying helmet. I'm not sure why we were issued knee and elbow pads; if anything goes wrong, my elbows and knees will be the least of my concerns. I guess I could try to land on all fours, like a cat. Somehow I doubt I'd have the presence of mind to try and land on my elbows and knees, but it gave me something else to think about. That would be funny though, a guy who's parachute didn't open trying to land on his elbows and knees, talk about balance. The helmet was a helmet in description only. It was a leather helmet with the ribs of padding along the top. I say WWII flying cap but an old time football helmet would be a better description. This helmet might have helped if someone was throwing tennis balls at our heads, but outside of that, I didn't see much benefit in wearing it. I don't know why anyone would be throwing tennis balls at the heads of other humans, but if they were, we had the helmets for it. When I asked my jump partner if the stuff would do us any good in case of an emergency, he just shook his head no. It seems it was just policy.

We were ready, the plane has landed, and we began to load up. My jump guy has a camcorder so we can capture these moments for posterity. He then asked me if I have any last words. "Last words?" Oh I get it, he's a comedian. How about this for last words? "If anything happens, I hope I take a big poop on you," how's that for last words? Smart ass. Once you get in the plane, everyone squeezes together and "your man" straps himself to your back. It took 20 minutes for the plane to reach 15,000 feet. When we first got on the plane, it was noisy and full of excitement, there was a lot of chattering going on, but the higher we got, the quieter it got. By the time we were at altitude, there wasn't a peep out of anyone. Strange. It's almost like everyone realized these may be the last faces we ever see. This could be it. Could be. Would be? Would you be my, could you be my, won't you be ... my neighbor? "It's time," says the pilot. The skooching towards the door begins. My guy and I were the last two out. What amazed me is how quickly people got sucked out once they got close to the door. I kept trying to watch someone go out, but if you blink your eyes, they're gone. Whooooooosh. Gone, man. My Dad was two groups in front of me. I saw him at the door, he turned to say something to me and in a flash, he was gone. I'm not sure what he was trying to say, but he had been sucked out of the plane before he could get his words out. Happy trails, Dad.

I was making wise cracks to the camera and have this little thing planned where I'm yawning and mugging for the camera on the way down. I'm going to do a little comedy for the camera as I skydive for the first time. Nice plan. It never really came to fruition though. As soon as I put my feet outside of the plane, all I can do is look out in wonderment. I also noticed the noise, going 140 mph is noisy. I'm sticking my head out of the plane and just enjoying the view when I look down, it dawns on me what the hell I'm doing. The ground looks far away, which means we're pretty high up and the next thing I know, we're out. It only took a split second and we were gone.

I hate to use the phrase "the first step is a doozy" but this moment is exactly what they're talking about. The second you're out the door, it sucks the breath out of you, your stomach plunges to the top of your body cavity, everything from the colon on up gets radically shifted up into your chest cavity. Your lungs try to wedge themselves into your throat and your brain is trying to bust its way out of the back of your head. It's a very strange feeling. I was gasping for breath because it was like having the wind knocked out of you, the adrenaline is coursing through me at high speed, the wind is roaring in my ears, I can't hear a thing, and my cheeks are blowing back into my face and flapping around like a St. Bernard's. My heart is about ready to break through my breastbone, and I see the ground rushing towards me and we're falling at somewhere around 150 mph. Although it feels faster, it's hard to gauge the speed because my eyes are tearing up and I can't see.

Somehow, in all this, I forget to do my little comedy act. As it turns out, there is no comedy when you're crying. Strangely enough, as your body plummets to the earth, closer and closer to death, being the clown doesn't enter into the equation. No sir. I don't think comedy crossed my mind again for the rest of the day. I think I tried screaming, but couldn't get the air out of my lungs. They advertised this jump as one where you could "see the strip, Mt. Charleston, Hoover Dam!" But all I saw was the ground. I didn't even think about looking around. I don't know many people who would have the presence of mind to sightsee while they fall towards earth. All you can do is look down. It's impossible to look at anything but the ground. I mean, for God's sake I was plummeting towards earth. I've never plummeted before.

I liked it. It was liberating, I didn't think we would die but I started wondering when he was going to pull the cord. I liked the free falling, but still, I had to wonder. If this guy has a heart attack, I won't know it until it's too late. I keep waiting for his arms to drape over me in a death wilt, and then quickly realize that the force of the wind will push his arms back and I'll never see the death wilt. I'll never know until just before we hit the globe. Godspeed, little one. We free fell for about 40 seconds then the chute gets pulled, and with it, the harness you're wearing. Cool, he didn't die, we're going to be all right. That's nice.

Did I mention the harness? It is a harness in all senses of the word. To begin with, you step *into* it. That is not a good sign- any occasion you have to step into something with canvas straps, politely decline, no good will come of it. I realize the strapping in is necessary, but damn. When you go from 150 mph down to 20 mph up, those straps have nowhere to go but up, problem there is: I'm going down. The straps grab me like I've never been grabbed before, but since I've been rappelling before, I knew to put my testes up and out of the way. If you

257

don't pull those puppies up and out of the way, you'll have a stomach ache all day. Testicles are gentle animals; there's no reason for them to go through that type of trauma. I reminded my father of that as well, so he pulled his to the inside and made sure everything was tucked safely away. Once we get settled, it's a gentle float to the ground. The thing I noticed most after the chute opened was the quiet. It was completely silent. It was fantastic. That's all I can say; except for the strap giving me a good why-to and what-for, it was an incredible experience, and the most amazing adrenaline rush I've ever had. By the time I got on the ground, my dad was just sitting there on the ground with nobody around him. I walked over and asked if he was alright and he replied "I'm not doing that again." It's OK, dad, you don't have to.

CHAPTER 34
ROAD TRIPPING - THEN AND NOW

I have been on dozens of road trips over the years, many memorable, some not. I've had some excellent ones with my friends. There's something special about loading up the boys in the car, filling the cooler and off you go. When my buddies and I went on our first spring break in 1977, we had so much fun we made a semi-pact to come back again, maybe a 25 year reunion. As it turns out, we attended more than that. A group of us decided to go on one after we turned 40. We'd leave the wives and kids, etc. at home and just cut loose for a week. Ha. After so many vacations over the years, I've noticed a distinct change in the drive itself, as well as the activities that are participated in. In your twenties, the cooler is stuffed to the rim with beer and ice, not a second thought is even given to food. Food? What the hell do we need food for? It's only 1100 miles. We can eat when we get there. As we get older, the beer gets less and less room, and things like, sandwiches and snacks take over, along with a large supply of soda and water. Hey- don't forget your vitamins either. Water, for God's sake, did anyone even think of bringing water in our younger days? Water was something you used to brush your teeth, not to get you through a road trip. Karl, don't forget to take your Metamucil, we promised your wife we'd make sure you took your one good poop a day.

In your twenties, you drove straight through, only stopping for gas. It was about the only time you got to pee in a toilet; the rest of the trip, you peed in a bottle and then stashed it somewhere to be tossed later. Something we learned about that, don't put them back in the cooler. You know, just in case. The later road trips take an extra day or so because of all the stopping and grazing, it's like being on the road with a group of pregnant women; what with all the pee breaks. You make 30 stops before the Florida state line, what? Do you people all have enlarged prostates? It's either that or everyone's bladder has shrunk to the size of a plum. Nobody pees fast anymore either. It can take almost three days now to reach our destination because we're spending the nights at hotels instead of driving. Oops, it's 10 o'clock, time for all good boys to get to bed. What a bunch of pussies. "I'm not staying at a Motel 6, I need a posturepedic mattress or I'll be wrecked for a week."

On vacation in your twenties, you drink until 5 a.m., get up at 7, feel terrific and have a bloody mary for breakfast. Now, we're in bed at 10 p.m., up at 8, and having a full breakfast so "it doesn't screw up my metabolism." I found that as you get older, the earlier you start drinking, the earlier you're going to bed. If the elders start drinking at noon, it's "goodnight sweetheart" by ten. Not even a wet t-shirt contest will keep you up. "I've seen titties, I'm going to bed." That, my friends is a sad day in a man's life; when he realizes that he's not getting out of bed to see titties. "Just shoot me where I'm laying man, because it's over. Toss my dead ass over the balcony and let maintenance clean me up in the morning."

You eat better when you're on a road trip when you get older as well, and I suppose it's because you have more money. In your twenties, you don't spend more than $25 to eat for a week. We can eat when we get home, I need drinking money. It's usually a lot of sandwiches and happy hour bar food, which is actually a great little meal after a day of drinking at the beach. A pile of fried cheese sticks, fried ravioli, fried chicken wings, fried meatballs, fried zucchini (your veggies) all dunked in a hearty ranch dressing. Maybe a side of monstrous cheese cubes, and if you're lucky, and I mean very lucky, barbeque cocktail weenies. Ooh, la, la, a meal fit for a king. Now, you can't possibly think about eating all that fried food without thinking that you're giving yourself a heart attack. You can almost picture the grease wrapping itself around a piece of Swiss cheese and lodging in your aorta.

I've had a few memorable trips with my buddy Karl. One time we were going on a weekend float trip and five or six of us were taking a van. I'm not sure why we had a van, it belonged to someone, but I'm just not sure who. After three or four days down in the woods, everything on the way home smelled a little musty. It was pretty rank, or so we thought. Then Karl took off his shoes. It was like a bio-weapon of mass destruction. We didn't even know what it was at first, a fart? No, not even a fart stinks that bad. Did we hit a skunk? No, no skunks. Did we run over a bag of decomposing chicken parts that had been lying in the road in the hot sun all day? That could be it, but the driver insists he didn't run over anything, so it's not the chicken parts. What then? Did someone shit their pants? Or did they shit them yesterday and we're just now noticing? No, it's not really a shit smell. What in God's name is it?

We're going through everything in this van trying to track down this odor so we can kill it and move on with our lives. We're literally being gagged into submission. It's like nothing my olfactory has ever experienced. I don't even have something to compare it to. It's like...well, it was like an old, hot, urine soaked blanket, mixed with the odor of a sweaty, unwashed crotch/ass area thing mixed in with just a touch of dirty, fungus-infested feet. Feet...wait a minute, that's it! Karl just took off his shoes, maybe that's where the smell is coming from. And it was; the aromatic death that was strangling us and trying to prevent any of us from having children was coming from his tennis shoes. Since they were fairly new shoes, he didn't want to throw them away as per our suggestion, so we hung them on the outside door handle. There was a small residual fog that lingered behind for a short time, but we drove the last three hours with his shoes banging against the door as a constant reminder of the death gas that was just waiting to be invited back in.

On the return from a ski trip one week, one of my friends wanted to fly home. We were in Colorado and he had been a little crabby for a few days and was ready for home. He pleaded for us to take him to the Denver airport for a flight home. No way, pussycat; we drove out here together, we're riding home together. If one gets dropped off, they'll all want to be dropped off. I don't care if we don't see each other for six months, we're in this until the end. We are all on this train to hell. I'm not sure I totally blamed him; Karl was on that trip too, except now, his feet were older and, therefore, more pungent. We made him keep his shoes on for the entire drive home. We'd been down that road.

I've also found your tolerance level with your friends decreases with age. I guess it's because we expect more of them when they get older. I don't know why, you've known these knuckleheads for anywhere from 5-25 years, and none of them have changed. In your twenties, you could cram six or seven of your friends in a car built for four, and hit the road, and still be getting along at the end. Now, you would consider taking two cars instead of being "uncomfortable." Or, maybe we should rent a Winnebago; that would be nice. The kids can get braces next year- Daddy wants to travel in comfort. I'm not sitting in the middle of the back seat for anyone. We seem to place a much higher value on comfort as we age. Even going so far as to pay cash money to get what you want. "I don't care if it's an extra $100, I want the big pillow."

Vacations are exhausting. When did that happen? When did having fun become so tiring? What happened to "I don't want to leave" when it was time to go. Now, when the week's over, it's, "I'm ready to go." And by God; you are ready. It **is** time to go. I need to get home and rest from my vacation. We might even leave a day early. Hmm, that's a thought. Whew. I'm pooped. The recuperation process takes longer too. After you got home from a road trip then, you were ready to rock. "When is the next road trip? Maybe I shouldn't even unpack. Now, it's all you can do to make the drive home. You just want to take a shower and sleep on a bed that's not full of sand and beer. Using a clean bathroom, with clean, dry towels that smell like Bounce dryer sheets. I never want to leave again.

My first spring break was in 1977. I had just graduated from high school, I had enlisted in the Marines, and I was 17. It was a very good year when I was 17. Mike and Louie and I drove down in Mike's red Cutlass Supreme. Red, with a white vinyl top. It was a bitchin' ride in 1977. Both of those guys were already 18, so I was the only one underage. We drove straight through. I don't think anything could have stopped us. We were on a mission. Our first spring break! I honestly don't remember hearing of any legendary spring breaks before us. People went on spring breaks, sure, but I just don't think they were like they are now. Spring breaks now are insane, anything goes and it's always a drunken, rowdy party full of nudity and debauchery. I'm jealous. We missed out on that shit. Spring breaks in the seventies were fun, but they weren't filming videos of it.

I still remember driving across the Florida border. It was right after dawn and the sun was just out and the temperature was perfect and everything was all right with the world. There's just something about driving into Florida, something changes in you. You're in FLORIDA mofo and it's time to party. This of course doesn't apply to people who live in Florida. If you reside there, I'm sure the excitement doesn't apply. But for the flatlanders, it's a world of wonderment. Sunshine and beaches, beaches and babes, babes in tiny swim suits, tiny swim suits and a beer with small tendrils of ice running down the side. Florida. Ahhhhh. Don't get me wrong, I could never live in Florida. It's too hot and muggy, plus they have hurricanes, but to vacation there is a joy. To this day, when I drive across the Florida border, I *feel* different; it's Florida, damn it, and things are good.

We hit the border, the three amigos, on our way to Ft. Lauderdale. That's what sucks about feeling that way after crossing the border-Lauderdale is still eight hours away. We're in Florida, everybody is happy, "Hey, let's burn one in celebration." That gets passed unanimously and we burn. Later, as we gaze in euphoria out at the Florida greenery, we've got tunes cranking and well-being in the air. We pull in about three, check in and ten minutes later we're at the beach. Can you imagine? Eighteen hours in the car and we head to the beach. Kids.

We had a blast every day. We spent time poolside, drinking, then we'd spend some beach time drinking, then we'd go back to the pool. We met a ton of people and drank with all of them. We met this guy in his thirties who let us drive his Corvette around town. What the hell? How cool are we? Driving around in a white convertible Corvette. He had a Scarab too, so we went out on that as well. See why I love Florida? Vodka shots were the rage of the week. Not vanilla or orange or cherry or whatever the fuck they flavor vodka with today. It was vodka, Smirnoff vodka, we drank it warm, we drank it straight, and we had a good time doing it. For the most part I didn't have any difficulty getting into bars. Either Mike or Louie would somehow pass me their I.D. and no one seemed to notice. Crazy kids.

One of the major reasons to go on spring break is girls. Girls like Florida too. Girls come from all over America for spring break in Florida. About three days into this trip we met this group of seven girls, they were at the pool and we started hanging out with them. After a couple of cocktails, you can talk to anyone. None of us were the suave, cool, debonair kind of guys who could just pick up girls on a whim. But, none of us were trolls, and we gots personality. Walkin' personality, talkin' personality. Oh yeah.

We figured with seven of them and three of us, someone's going to get laid. Oooh la la. And get this; they're from St. Louis. There are 50,000 girls down here and we hook up with some that live 20 miles away, go figure. We go out partying with them that night, things go well but nothing special, we do a little dancing, do a little drinking. Nobody hooks up with anyone. Next day the girls find out there's been a mistake in their reservation and they have to be out by noon. They still have two days left and nowhere to stay. Oh yeah, come to poppa.

We invited them to stay with us. We're thinking brilliant, great strategy, we'll get these guys into our rooms yet. This will be great! We're going to have seven girls staying with us in our room! Halleluiah. There is a God and he just dropped a huge gift on us. It's going to be two days of drinking and nakedness and madness the likes of which we've never dreamed of, much less seen. This is going to be legendary.

Two days later, we couldn't have been happier to see them leave. It was unbelievable. The room looked someone dropped a K-Mart on it. Girls have a lot of stuff. Lots of stuff. There was shit hanging from everything that stuck out of the wall. "Oh, here's a protruding nail head, let me hang something on it." Our dream was slowly dissipating. I think it took five minutes after they moved in that we realized we weren't going to get any lovin' from this group. First of all, there was no privacy; with ten people in a four-person room, things are snug. Before, we took turns getting to have a bed to ourselves, and on the other nights, you shared with your buddy.

Guys don't like to share beds with their buddies. I don't think it's homophobia per se, but it just seems weird to share a bed with your friend. Women do it without a second thought. I think maybe it's because when guys picture women sleeping with women, we think that maybe they'll kiss or something. So, sleeping with your buddy just doesn't seem comfortable. For some reason it makes you giddy. All of a sudden you're ten years old on a sleepover. On a float trip once, we got a room after a long day on the river. Forrest (who we called Trees) and Scott and I and Louie worked together and were pretty good friends. Scott and I were in one bed and Forrest was in the other bed and Louie was still in the bathroom.

The three of us are just lying there in the semi darkness, reminiscing about the day and chuckling about the amusing things that happened. After a long day of drinking and floating and sunning, you're a little tuckered out and get a little silly. As Louie comes out of the bathroom, there have been several moments of quiet, you know, just before everyone nods off and Louie says, "Trees, I hope you don't mind, but I sleep in the nude." That, my friend, may be the funniest thing I'd ever heard, and we started laughing, and laughing hard and laughing long. It had to have been ten minutes before we started to settle down. It was amazing, we could not stop. It was contagious. Each time we would simmer down a little, someone would start to laugh again and the whole process would start over. I finally got up and went outside just to get away and clear my head. My sides hurt and I was giving myself a headache from the laughter. I finally got settled down and am about to go back in when I hear those guys start up again, and off I go. I'm glad nobody happened on by while I was out there in my shorts laughing like a hyena with tears rolling down my cheeks. I may have even tinkled in my pants a wee bit. All in all it took 30 minutes to get everyone ready for sleep again. We had a couple of start-ups, but nothing got out of control again.

Back to Spring Break with the seven girls in our room; even if we put three to a bed, there's still four people left. We had people sleeping all over. Seven girls make a huge mess. There, I said it. Girls are messy. The process of getting ready was really something to behold, watching seven girls getting ready for a night on the town. Wow. The bathroom looked like a makeup display counter. It was just unreal, the whole thing. We actually started looking for other girls to hook up with so we didn't have to sleep in our room. It was two days of chaos. We did get some making out done, nothing too heavy though; keep in mind this was 1977 and it was a bit more conservative sexually than it is now. Girls Gone Wild hadn't started yet. So they spent a couple of days with us, and overall it was fun. We learned a lot about women. That was the good thing. At that age you don't know shit about girls, so it was a nice education.

CHAPTER 35
DRUGS

I like drugs. I always have. I am not alone. Drugs are an integral part of our lives. All of our lives. Everyone uses drugs. There are drug stores on every corner. Grocery stores have aisles full of drugs. If you get a note from your doctor, you can get really good drugs. For legal reasons, you need a note from your doctor to get the good stuff. A note from your mom or buddy doesn't cut it. You need a special note. Once you have your special note, you can head to the back of the store, where, hidden in the corner is the secret place where they dispense the DRUGS. You've always had to get your drugs out back, deals don't go down out front, illegal or otherwise, drugs are always something you go to the back for. The so-called "legal drugs," the drugs our government thinks us worthy of having. The Physician's Desk Reference has over 4,000 drugs in it that our people in charge have OK'd. More than 4,000 and yet they've decided that there's a group of about 20 that they don't want us to have. Why? Because they said so, that's why.

Alcohol and nicotine kill more people each year than **all** of the illegal drugs combined, with plenty to spare. Alcohol has ruined more lives and families, nicotine is one of the most addictive drugs known to man, but you can get all the liquor and smokes you want, no one gives a rat's ass. But smoke a joint and by God, people are up in arms. "The demon weed," if you will. Pot has ruined...no lives. If you let it, pot will un-motivate you, but only if you let it. The only lives ruined by pot are the lives of the family members of people who are in jail for selling pot. Don't get me wrong, you can hurt yourself and other people if you don't use your "drug sense." You can't load up your head with acid and "take a drive," or eat a handful of mushrooms and decide to go out and "do a little shooting." Drug sense has to play a big part of drug use. To quote Clint, "a man has to know his limitations." Exactly.

The United States has spent $300 billion+ fighting the drug war. Nice waste of money there. If they want to win the drug war, they should stop fighting it- it can't be won. If they want to work on the drug problem, as they see it, they should work on the demand, not the supply. You can do whatever you want with the supply, but if the demand is still there, there will still be drug users. This is America, we're free, and we want to do whatever we want to do. It's part of the package. I can't believe no one in this government learned anything from Prohibition. Americans don't like to be told what to do, especially when it comes to recreation. No drinking. Are you shitting me? Did they really expect that to work? So what happened? Nothing really. People just kept drinking because they were adults and wanted to make their own decisions. Prohibition only gave rise to gangsters. Well done, douche bags.

Gangsters and various other branches of organized crime got their start from selling illegal booze. Why? Even though it was illegal, people wanted to drink. Prohibition is gone, but gangs are still here. What are the gangs today selling? Illegal drugs. Again, nice move. Legalize drugs, good bye gangs. It's just that simple. No, it really is. The prisons empty out except for the malcontents and wackos that really need to be there, and the drug people go home. I know; I should be in charge. Humans are going to inebriate themselves in one way or the other, legal or not, it's going to happen. Imagine how fast we could pay down our national debt if we manufactured and taxed recreational drugs. Mind blowing, I agree. Our government makes a ton off of liquor tax, I wonder what they would make taxing pot, coke, meth, barbs, bennies, mushrooms, etc. Pot and mushrooms grow out of the ground, for crying out loud. Like corn and cabbage.

Legalizing drugs is a radical move for sure. But does it really matter? This is America, by God, land of the free, home of the brave. If a crackhead wants to smoke themselves to death, let them. It's their choice. If they want help kicking the pipe, let them go get some. It's the same for junkies, cokers, hop heads, crankers, trippers, x heads, and all the other dopers out there. Stop telling us what drugs we can do and what ones we can't. There must be more pressing affairs to attend to. Maybe some of that money should be spent on insuring that everyone has a job, a place to work and some insurance. Hmm.

Creative people have always used drugs, still do. Straight people can't imagine shit like that. You think *Shrek* was conceived by some guy wearing a suit sitting in an office daydreaming that shit or some guy on a float trip drifting down a river with a head full of mushrooms? Seeing trolls and various other creatures, like, say for instance, an ogre or a talking donkey. Anybody that comes up with talking animals was doing some kind of drugs. It's no secret that creative people use drugs. A lot of drug users and a lot of drinkers. Yes indeedy. I think that's what helps the creative juices flow sometimes- you look at things from a different perspective on drugs, that's the whole point. Lewis Carroll, who wrote *Alice in Wonderland,* was a huge acid user. If you know the story, the acid angle isn't hard to believe. A chick falls down a hole and finds a whole other universe with giant talking chess pieces and an invisible cat that shows his teeth when he smiles; no, no drugs working there. That story should have been called *Acid in Wonderland.*

I think maybe Dr. Suess dabbled a little in the recreational pharmaceutical department. I mean, think about some of his books. *Cat in the Hat*? I remember having scary dreams about that giant cat knocking on our front door in the middle of the night wearing that striped hat. To this day, when I see stripes like that, it gives me a chill; isn't that something? The kiddie book scared me. *Green Eggs and Ham* was another classic. I don't know what kind of creature Sam was, but he was creepy. I'm not sure what either one of them were. They looked like animals but stood upright. They were furry like animals, but they talked and had facial expressions, exactly what kind of mutants was the good "doctor" seeing from his seat at the typewriter? The eggs aren't green doc, it's the mescaline. My all-time favorite is *Horton Hears a Who.* I love Horton- how can you not? But come on; he finds the one dandelion in a monstrous field of dandelions, and on this dandelion, he finds a whole civilization of Who people who live on this dandelion and have buildings and parks and stores and sewer systems. On a dandelion! I don't know what kind of Doctor the Suess was, but my guess is a pharmacist.

Strangely enough, some of the best drugs I've ever done were in the hospital, which is ironic, because I don't think that as an adult, I've ever gone to the hospital unless I was involved in some drug or alcohol related mishap. All completely legal drugs, good drugs, some seriously good drugs. Drugs so good, after they give them to you, they can cut your body open... and you don't care. Rip your body open from sternum to belly button, and you come through it fine. A little scarred up maybe, but they've got drugs for that too.

One night at somewhere around 3 a.m. coming from a bar, Louie and I got into a little scrape with these four young skinheads in downtown St. Louis. It was on the on-ramp to the highway, as a matter of fact. This car had stopped halfway up the on-ramp. These skinheads were having words with a couple of black kids in the car in front of us while standing on the entrance ramp. Well, we had some cocktails in us, and I told Louie that I wasn't going to sit here long. Then he says, "don't do anything, I don't feel like fighting, I'm tired." We were about 30 at the time. I assured him of calm unless things escalate. A couple of minutes go by and nothing happens, these dumbshits are all talk, so I flash my brights at them to indicate I'm ready to go. Dipshit # 1 comes back and kicks the side of my car.

OK, that's enough right there, I'm out of the car. Dipshit #1 is standing there and says, "Don't mess with me; I just got out of prison." So I walked up and punched him square him in the face. He wasn't ready, but that's not my problem. If you're going to talk shit, be ready. After I hit him, he starts to fall back onto the guard rail, which is all that's keeping him from falling 60 feet onto the pavement below. I reached out and grabbed his shirt to keep him from going over; I wanted to teach him a lesson, not kill him. As I had a hold of his shirt, his buddy tries to tackle me. I let go of dipshit #1 because now I've got dipshit #2 with his arms wrapped around me. I grabbed the back of his belt with my left hand and went to grab his hair with my right. I was going use his momentum and give him a good toss. Since he has no hair, my hand finds no purchase and when I move to throw him, he's got my left arm pinned to my side and I as I pivot, my body turns but my arm doesn't and it dislocates my left shoulder.

I know right away something is amiss because my arm is dangling in a weird way and my shoulder hurts like a mofo. I then did the only thing I could think of and called "time." By then Louie was out of the car to assist me, and the funny thing was when I called "time," everyone stops for a second, just like it had been ingrained in us as kids. "Time" works. And when everybody stops, I scurried back to my car because I've got some problems and am in no condition to be fighting on a highway on ramp in the early hours of the morn. I've got to get out of here and seek medical attention. Within the next few minutes, there is some tension, but now there are about 15 people standing around on this entrance ramp trying to settle things down. I'm already sitting in the car doors locked, ready to go. I'm done fighting, I need to go.

Since you can't drive a stick shift with a dislocated shoulder, I got in the passenger seat and Louie drove to the hospital after we dropped Danielle off. She was 21, just a wee lass and worked with us at the club. She was quite traumatized by the whole thing, so we dropped her at her car before going to the hospital. After I checked in, they give me a shot of Demerol on top of several pitchers of beer and a pound of chicken wings. They didn't serve the beer and wings at the hospital; I had them at Boomers- they just piled the Demerol on top of all that. I was standing in front of the X-ray box when I feel the beer and wings getting ready to move. Thank God they have a lot of things you can deposit your vomitus in. I felt no pain that night. Alcohol and Demerol, quite a mix.

That was my first of six shoulder dislocations, and they've always had a hard time getting it back in, which sucks. It's very uncomfortable, you know, having your shoulder ball cut loose of the socket. The first time, they couldn't put it back the normal way so they rolled me onto my belly and hung 20 lbs of sandbags off my wrist to slowly pull it back in. It's time consuming, but thanks to the Demerol, you don't care. Unfortunately, your hand swells up like a Cornish game hen due to the sandbags cutting off your circulation. One time the sandbags didn't work and the Dr. was squatting next to the gurney looking at this contraption and going, "hmmmm."

That never comforts a patient, does it? A Dr. going, "hmmmm." It means he's baffled, oh shit. If he's going, "hmmmm," he doesn't know what to do. Either that or he's going over other options, none of which I want to be a part of. Then he says, "I want to try one more thing." And I'm thinking "one more thing?" that's all that's left? Just one more option? Shit man, we've only tried like three different ways, there has to be more than four ways to put a shoulder back in. "Well, the drugs aren't loosening you up like I want." Which was weird because my shoulder hurts and I was feeling pretty buzzed. Then he says, "this next one is kind of a last resort." Wow, "a last resort." I'm telling you, Doc, you've got some serious bedside manner. A last resort, Jesus, where are we, deep in the bowels of Mongolia? Isn't this the U. S. of A? Haven't we come a long way in medical technology? I was dying to see what the last resort was.

I stayed on my stomach with my left arm dangling off the side of the gurney. The nurse brings out four thick-ass straps and starts strapping me down across my back. Uh oh, this isn't starting off like I thought it would. I thought, first of all, I was going to get my meds replenished, I didn't know I was done with my shots. Then they grab another nurse and she mounts the gurney, straddles my lower back and puts her hands on my shoulder blades and pushes them down. The strapping nurse gets on her knees and grabs a hold of my right arm. So I'm strapped and straddled and being pulled down on one side and I'm getting a little nervous. All of I can think of is, "Is it safe?" I don't fucking know. Then the Doc gets on his knees next to me on my left side and asks "are you ready?' Ready? Ready for what? What are you going to do?

He wanted me to take a deep breath and exhale all the way and when I do, he's going to "yank your shoulder into place." Hmm. It seems he's going to yank on it hard enough and with enough weight for me to be requiring straps and straddles. I take my breath and exhale and yank on it he does. The whole gurney tilted a little bit, I thought for a second we were going to tip over. The pain he caused by doing that was incredible but short. It was like a lightning bolt shot out of the shoulder joint, down and across my back and then rifled down my legs and out my feet...and then it was gone. As soon as that ball gets back in the cup, it gives you a pee chill. Instant gratification. It was all worth it just for this feeling here. It was my first experience with instant pain relief. Ahh! My shoulder is back in place, delightful. Let's dance. That's the kind of joy it brought you; it made you want to embrace life and thank God for every breath and makes you want to sing and dance and prance and leap. You wanted to hug and kiss everyone and say, "thank you for being you." You just wanted to wrap the sun up in a blanket and bring a little love with you wherever you went. Or maybe it was the Demerol, one of the two.

Cough syrup is an interesting buzz. It's actually hard to explain. For those in the know, it's like tripping on acid and being really drunk. There is no other buzz like it. We used to use Robitussin DM. We called it Delta Mike or wearing the robe.

"What are you guys doing this weekend?"

"I think we're going to wear the robe."

Or, "I'm going to be hanging out with Delta Mike." Oh, we were clever tykes. Unfortunately, the type of syrup you need is no longer available at your neighborhood drug store, they make it differently now, probably a good thing. We used to buy it from the PX. It wasn't in stock for very long. When you stood in the cough syrup aisle, you could tell where Delta Mike was because it was the only cough syrup that was sold out. There were literally dozens of cough syrups available, but there was always an empty hole where Mike was or rather, were Mike should be. We would send someone out to check every couple of days, kind of a reconnaissance mission and when Mike was delivered, we'd ramble up to the PX and load up. We only bought two at a time, you know, so we wouldn't raise any suspicions; as if nine guys standing in line with two bottles each of Robitussin weren't suspicious. Idiots. Within days the Robe would be sold out again. Curious.

The first time you do the Robe, you only drink half of a 10 oz. bottle. According to the crafty Robe veterans, that's all you need to start. You just chug it down and wait. There were no worries; it went down smooth and easy. Thirty minutes later there is usually a battle with a bout of nausea, and battle through you must, for if you hurl it out, you've defeated the purpose entirely. You walk it off, lay down if you feel the need, but keep it in. DO NOT THROW UP! That is the golden rule of wearing the robe. It wants to come out, it needs to come out, your body realizes that it doesn't need that much cough syrup under any circumstances and tries to repel it from whence came, but you must not let it win. Be strong, be a man, beat the robe, for if you do, you will be rewarded. You will truly be rewarded.

The first few times you wore the Robe, you only needed a half of a bottle. Then you had to start increasing your dosage, it also got harder and harder to drink the shit. The taste started to get to you. The first time, you just chug it down, but by the fifth or sixth time, you'd take a swallow, have a 7-up chaser, take a swallow, have a chaser. By the time it was all said and done, it may take you an hour or more to get a whole bottle down. After about eight or nine times, you were done, it was over. Wearing the Robe was finished, playing with Delta Mike was done. All good trips must come to an end, and so it was with the Robe. You finally reached a point where you absolutely could not take another drink of it. The sight of it made you gag. The very smell of it made you gag. Trying to drink it? Totally gag fest. The buzz wasn't worth the hour of choking and gagging it required to get the bottle down. Until you reached that point however, the buzz was a good one.

We used to play a lot of board games in Okinawa. That was interesting, trying to play Monopoly under those circumstances; sometimes it seemed that everyone was on something else. Some were drinking, some were getting stoned, some were playing with Delta Mike and even others were on blues, which were like Valiums. Quite an eclectic group of personalities on an eclectic group of drugs. You know kids. Getting all those guys together to focus on a board game was quite a trick in itself. We'd play Risk and Monopoly the most. We'd always have guys getting up and wandering off in the middle of a game, then someone would have to look for him and then he'd disappear and we'd send someone after the second guy and the first guy would return, alone, without the second guy. This went on and on each time we'd play. It's amazing we ever finished a game.

The first time I did the Robe, we were playing Monopoly, and as we're playing, I feel my head start to itch. I casually stroke my scalp. I don't want to draw any attention to the fact that I can feel it. I'm "getting off" as they say. This goes on for about ten minutes; I'm trying to be cool, trying to be the crafty drug veteran, but my head itches like a mofo and scratching it feels so damn good. For some reason, I don't want to let these guys know that I'm starting to get off. I'm not sure why, I think it's because I'm the new guy and this is my first time working with the Delta Mike Project. Maybe I was afraid of them taking advantage of me and stealing my Monopoly properties. Maybe I didn't want to seem like a lightweight. I don't know why thinking that getting off after drinking a half of a bottle of cough syrup would be considered "lightweight," but maybe I did. I was, after all, just a boy. All I know for certain is: *I don't want them to know.* I felt that everything in my life hinged on whether or not I can keep this to myself. I cannot, I simply cannot let these guys know I'm getting off. Which was really stupid, the whole point of taking drugs was to get off, why fight it? Enjoy, embrace. I really can't think of any reason I wanted to keep this a secret. But my head is starting to itch pretty good, and finally I can't take it anymore and excuse myself to use the men's room.

I walk around the corner and assault my head with all ten fingers. I'm scratching and itching and itching and scratching to my heart's content. I was in absolute heaven; it was the single greatest feeling I've ever had. It was a step away from ecstasy. All I'm doing is scratching my head with everything I've got, and I was never happier. I don't know how long I was doing that, but when I stop and look up my playing partners are all standing there staring at me with these huge, shit-eating grins on their faces. I have never seen such a happy group. "Are you getting off?" they ask. Well, I think so. I may have just come in my pants from scratching my head. Is that normal? "Yes" they reply "it is." Awesome. I feel good. I felt part of the group now, I've crossed over a bridge to embrace Delta Mike with my new friends. Yeti then says, "listen to this," and starts singing Crimson and Clover through a giant fan. I may have stood there for 30 minutes I was so mesmerized.

I couldn't walk away; my buddy singing through the fan blades was the coolest thing I'd ever heard, or maybe it was the Robe.

Weird stuff happens on the Robe. Examples? OK. One night we went to the movies to see *Alien*. We choked down some Robe and headed to the theater. We were sitting there and I remember the lights dimming and the curtain opening; all of sudden the curtain starts to close and the lights came on. Everyone starts getting up to leave. Curious that I may have missed a fire alarm or something, I inquire as to where everyone was going. The movie is over I'm told. "What?" I reply. "The movie has been going on for two hours and now it's over, we're leaving, let's go." I was dumbfounded. I just had two hours go by in about fifteen seconds. I may have to rethink this Robe shit if I'm not going to remember anything that happened. I had to go see the movie again.

Not everyone enjoyed the Robe; some had what we would call a "bad trip." I'm not sure why, but some just didn't take to the Robe. Some guys would just throw up and then the trip is over. Some guys just had a bad reaction to it. I don't think the body was designed to hold that much cold medicine. One was a guy named Chuck. Chuck was a good guy, just didn't do much partying. Chuck was huge, somewhere around 6'5." You would think a guy that size could hold his party supplies. Well one night Chuck does the Robe. He gets through the nausea OK, but after he starts getting off, things start to happen. He starts to seem a little disoriented, a little distracted, and quite frankly, he was giving us a good scare.

We were trying to convince him that it's OK, everything is alright, no worries mate, just relax and ride the Robe. That didn't work. Chuck wants to talk to an officer. We tell him that talking to an officer would lead to unpleasant things. Much more unpleasant than what he's going through now. I'm not sure that drinking cough syrup was against the law or anything; I just don't think our superior officers would condone such behavior. And trust me when I say that talking to authority with a head full of Robitussin is not where you want to be. As a matter of fact, talking to authority is always the last place you want to be. As we're trying to talk to Chuck, he takes off his clothes and climbs on to top of his wall locker. The top of this locker is about eight feet off the ground and Chuck is on top of it, wearing nothing but his boots yelling at us to call his mom. I'm not sure why he wanted us to call his mom, but that wasn't going to happen. Even if we did manage to get a hold of her, I'm not sure that she would've been happy to talk to her son under these conditions. "Hi, mom, it's me, your son, Chuck. I'm not sure why I'm calling, but I'm naked on top of my wall locker, I drank too much cough syrup and I need you to come and get me." How would a mom handle that? Especially at 3 o' clock in the morning. He stayed up there for over an hour, and we just got some chairs and played in his cube for awhile until he eventually climbed down. I'm not sure, but I don't think Chuck ever did the Robe again. Poor bastard.

Cocaine, there's another one. Oh the demon dust. I never really liked coke; the whole three years I was doing it. That is the biggest problem with coke, it doesn't care if you like it or not, all it says to you is "let's do some more." I understand how people get addicted to it. I shouldn't say I understand because I don't. Doing drugs is choice; if you want to do it, then do it, and if you want to stop, then stop. I don't care much for the "I'm addicted and can't stop routine." I've always felt that was a weak excuse, it's just easier that's all. It takes some balls to quit something you enjoy, but you can do it. But coke will make you want more. Cocaine will make you go with people you don't know to places you shouldn't be. Pulling up to some dudes house at 4:35 a.m. with some guy you met four hours ago, and he tells you "be cool around this guy, he's a freak; stay by the door and don't move around, don't look directly at him even if he's crying, he likes knives, liquor and coke, but not white people, so be on your toes and if things get weird, meet me back here at the car." And you're sitting there going "OK." To quote Martha Stewart- "that's not a good thing."

Cocaine was always too intense for me. I'm a pretty laid-back guy. I didn't do the whole disco and coke thing because I was in the Marines at the time, but we never went out dancing on coke. We stayed in the house with the doors locked and shades drawn, sitting around the coffee table for 15 hours talking about absolutely nothing. Those grinding jaws, those clenched teeth, the tiny pupils, the utter intensity, the sheer paranoia, lots of fun. It sucks. The problem is, even though it sucks, you want another bump. You always want another bump, always. Even after 15 hours of hell, the crusty, bloody nose being dabbed with kleenex, you still say "let's do another line; what? We're out? Well, we better call somebody!" There are very few things in life that are uglier than someone after two days of cocaine use. Coke will ugly a person up in a matter of hours.

When they do shows about drugs, coke is always made out to be the drug of the beautiful people; people are out dancing and singing, drinking champagne, living the good life. Bullshit. Even when we were out at a club doing blow, it wasn't this glamorous party. It was a group of people sitting at a table in the back, away from everybody, taking turns going to the bathroom for a bump. Everyone would sit around and try and talk into each other's ears about shit that doesn't matter. Oh yes, very glamorous. Sex and coke can mix, but you've got a very small window of opportunity. You can be all worked up and ready to go and decide to do one more line, uh oh, there it goes. Just had to do one more, didn't you? I could be getting laid right now, but no, that last line just killed your dick. There's no way that thing is going to work now. Might as well cut another line.

Drinking. What the heck fire can you say about drinking? I'm not sure where to even start on this one. Many people do it. Some people do it all the time. Some people are good at it. Some people aren't. Drinking is fun. Drinking can be a nightmare. Drinking can make you feel good. Drinking can make you feel like dying. I never understood why something that makes you so happy at night can make you feel so bad the next day. Weird dichotomy, don't you think? Are there any other things you do for pleasure that have such horrible physical consequences the next day? I don't think so. Drinking is social. Drinking is anti-social. People drink because they're happy. People drink because they're sad. Drinking can make you funny. Drinking can turn you into an asshole. People drink at weddings. People drink at funerals. Drinking makes you suave. Drinking makes you a dribbling slob. Drinking can make a genius a moron. Drinking can make a moron a genius (even if it's only according to his even drunker friends). Drinking is cool. Drinking can be uncool. Drinking can be heaven. Drinking can be hell.

Drinking is all those things and more. Oh yes, so much more. Drinking is the reason behind every stupid thing you've ever done. If not all the stupid things, then at least a good majority of them. The reason behind the stupidity is judgment, or actually, lack thereof. Alcohol takes away your judgment, and judgment, it turns out, is an important thing to have. It will save your life, just like lack of it will kill you. It is a precious thing and we take it for granted. What douchebags. Alcohol takes your judgment, wipes its ass with it and tosses it aside with a carelessness that is hard to grasp. How many times have you said "I'm fine, I can drive?" Two hundred? Three hundred? More? I don't have an actual count for myself, but it was way more than I care to admit. Drinking will make you express your love for complete strangers, some of whom may not want your love. You don't care, you love them, and, by God, you're going to let everyone know. Only when you're drinking will you make that late night phone call to an ex so you can tell her you still love her. That is such a smooth move. The only thing that will make it worse is if her new "male companion" answers the phone. Judgment, man, judgment.

On Memorial Day 1994 I borrowed my friends' jeep. There were five of us doing a little bar-hopping, and we were hitting the road again. As we loaded in, I reminded Sweet Lou to put his seat belt on. Many reasons for that request. First of all, we're in a jeep with no doors. Then there's the fact we've been drinking all day, we've got five people in the jeep, the vehicle is registered to someone else, it's a Holiday weekend, etc. Well, he refuses; he says he'll "hold on" if something happens. Oh that's rich, he'll hold to something as we're rolling down an embankment. Like I said, judgment.

As we're sitting at a red light, I remind him again to buckle up, but to no avail. The light turns green and I make my left turn onto a four lane road. As I straighten out my turn, I said something to Louie, when I get no response, I turn and realize he's gone. Apparently the three in the back realize it too and someone says, "Louie fell out." That's right, boys and girls, he fell out of a jeep going three mph. I pulled over to the right, look back and he's lying in the middle of the turning lane, flat on his back with his arms straight out to the sides. He looked crucified. We ran out into the street and circled around him. He's not moving so we're kind of freaked out. We don't want to move him either, in case he's really hurt, but we're in the middle of a busy street with cars and plenty of opportunities for police to come by. We are in no condition to be talking to the police. He was just lying there with this glassy look in his eyes, and he's not blinking or anything. I'm yelling his name, and after about 60 seconds he looks at me, sits up and gets off the road. We kept asking him if he's alright but he won't answer. He seemed pretty shaken up. Everybody was quiet; there was a very odd vibe going on. We were just walking and looking at Louie He still hadn't said anything; he just walked back to the jeep, got in and put his seatbelt on. I think that's called "a lesson learned."

One night Louie and I were about 45 miles from home drinking with some girls we met in Florida and it was time to head home. Sweet Lou was too drunk to drive, but insisted on doing it anyway. We had a little argument about it and I finally relented. We hadn't gone two miles when he drifted to the left and ended up straddling a traffic median. Apparently it was narrow enough to fit between the wheels, except now we're stuck on this thing going 40 mph. We clipped a speed limit sign, snapped it off and it crashed through the top half of the windshield and sprayed glass all over the inside of the car. He yanks the wheel to the right, climbs over the median, crosses the street, but he crossed the street too far and ended up going down the ditch, up the incline and onto a shopping mall parking lot and then over a parking block, which, strangely enough, rips off the oil pan and breaks the axle. That, of course, brings us to a stop.

At least ten seconds roll by and then he says, "OK, you can drive." Well, it's a little late for that, don't you think? As a matter of fact, I think we've been disabled. The problem now is that we're both underage, fairly drunk, a long way from home and we've got pot. What to do? What to do? Well, let's see, it's 3:25 a.m., we're going to have to call somebody. So we called his dad, who wasn't happy to be talking to his drunk son in the middle of the night. Nonetheless, he came to get us. We rolled up the last of the pot, which was more than we thought, and had quite the little party. Yes, sir, sitting there in the parking lot, 3:00 in the blessed a.m., smoking a joint, drunk, young, happy and leaning up against a blue Pontiac with a broken axle and a torn off oil pan. Good times.

Picture this. A crisp, clear, fall day in the Midwest. Gorgeous. Spectacular. God-like. A celebration is called for. A celebration indeed. How about a trip to the wineries? Many people don't think Missouri when they think wine. But we've got some nice wineries just outside St. Louis. You drive out, have some wine, drive back. Ideally. The group we went with was our work/party group. We do both things together. But this group tended to overdo things, just like many young, foolish, laugh in the face of death type people.

We headed to the wineries and do a little drinking on a Sunday afternoon, just about four hours' worth. Four hours of drinking may not seem like a long spell of drinking, but it's wine. Wine, wine, lots of wine. We had done our thing all afternoon and they were closing shop.

You can buy warm wine to go, so we did; about six bottles. Since we were drinking people, someone had a big bucket with ice in it. What the hell he had a bucket of ice for, I don't know, but it turned out to be just what we needed. You put the bottles in the ice, spin them around for about ten minutes and you've got cold wine. So there we were, the bunch of us, just standing in a circle around that bucket of wine, passing bottles around. We had three or four different kinds. Just passing them around the circle. Classy. What a classy bunch of drinkers.

Eventually, it was time to go. Let's get in our cars and drive. Or better yet, let's race back to the highway. Yeah, let's do that, let's race. Dipshits. We headed to the Funny Bone, I don't know why, it just seemed like a place to go. Well, we got thrown out. That's not too embarrassing, is it? Being thrown out of your own club. We were ready for a party anyway. Let's go to a party. We left the Bone and that's the last thing I remembered. That is definitely a bad sign. It's only happened once, the blackout thing. I hope to never have it happen again. It's very unsettling; not being able to remember what you did, or where you went. Apparently we had quite a time. I woke up at home about 5:30 a.m. with the TV blaring, sprawled out on the living room floor. I also happened to have a full Flintstones glass of wine on the table. I don't know where it came from or where I got it. But it was full, to the top, there wasn't more than 1/8 of an inch of room in that glass, which is actually something I was proud of. The fact I drove home almost 30 miles with a completely full glass of wine in my lap and didn't spill a drop. Quite an accomplishment, let me alert the Academy. I found out later, I got the wine and the glass from some party we were at. I don't think I ever got drunk on wine again. That was the second time, and both times were not good.

The first time I got drunk on wine was in Okinawa. You could buy a gallon of it for about $3, good bargain. Well, once you drink a half gallon of red wine, you never do it again. I was sick for four days. You've got to do some serious drinking to feel like shit for four days when you're eighteen. I guess it was the sugar. We had some good drinking nights in Okinawa. Not much else to do on some days. When you put forty Marines in one big room, leave them unsupervised in a foreign country, things are going to happen. Sometimes; bad, crazy things. Things you don't tell anyone later in life. Like your wife. Boys will do things.

We could get Absinthe over there too. Yikes. This stuff had an opium base, so it was pretty potent. You could only do about two shots, anything more and you were in trouble because it can be hallucinogenic. Wild, wild stuff man. We didn't do the whole dripping it over a flaming sugar cube ritual; I think we bought it already prepared for consumption. One night; that sounds ominous doesn't it? One night... how many bad stories start off...One night. Anyway, one night my Oki buddies and I were sitting around playing board games again. We were playing and doing shots and a guy named Green had done about four shots of this stuff. We knew he wasn't really with us anymore because we kept catching him staring off into space. We were playing, and Green announces he has to go the john. We continue on. We play and play and forgot all about Green.

Everyone eventually retired, and the next morning we realize that he never came back from the toilet, his bunk is empty and un-slept in. A group of us go on a reconnaissance mission to track down our missing Marine. We file into the head and there he is, buck naked on the floor of the stall with the door locked. It seems he sat down to do his business, passed out and fell off the toilet and then slept on the floor of the stall all night with his pants around his ankles. Nice job, big boy. He never did drink the Absinthe again. Absinthe made a lot of guys never drink it again. Mr. Ackerman got drunk on it one night and then proceeded to throw up all over the inside of his mosquito net. In Okinawa you had to have mosquito nets because there are no screens, no AC, and plenty of mosquitoes, so you need the netting. Well, one morning we got up and Ackerman's asleep and there's this two-foot-wide big smear of something on the inside of his net, there are three or four of us standing there, staring at it, trying figure out what the hell he's got on the inside of his netting. Well, Mikey sticks his nose close, recoils and announces, "it's puke, man, he puked on the inside of his net," which means he went right back to sleep. Or maybe he didn't even know it and almost pulled a Jimi Hendrix. Good times.

Okinawa was like that on a lot of nights. If we weren't drinking on BC Street, we were drinking in the barracks. The problem with drinking in the barracks was that it was verboten. No drinking in the barracks? What kind of rule is that? No drinking? Are you serious? We're 18 years old, thousands and thousands of miles away from home and...we're Marines. Young Marines to boot. That means only one thing. We didn't follow the rules. We drank in the barracks. Sometimes we would do it out on the roof. You got on the roof from the stairs. Good place to hide, unless someone was looking for you. If we drank inside you had to keep your eyes peeled, if someone of authority came into the squad bay, someone would yell, "lifer on deck," which was a little obvious, but it worked. You had to be a little discreet, of course; you can't just walk up and scream it out- you'd turn your head or cover your mouth and alert the boys. Everyone would stash their stuff, stand there and whistle until the coast was clear, then right back to drinking. It was beautiful. Oh we were some sly devils.

The weekends on the rock were something. Not everyone partied, but most of us did. Everyone also had stereos. I mean STEREOS. It was insane. The Far East has a lot of electronic equipment. A lot of it. We could go to the PX and get $5,000 worth of stereo equipment for $1,000. We actually had to build cabinets in our cube in the barracks to hold our sound systems. Each barracks were broken down into cubes, five on a side. We used our wall lockers and stereo storage lockers that we built as walls. No protection from sound, of course, but it gave you and your cube mates a little privacy. Four guys to a cube, so things were a little snug. It was constant noise during the weekend; everyone rocking out and partying down, good place to get some rest. The goal was to have the biggest, loudest, most powerful stereo- that way, you could rule the night.

The weekend I got discharged from the Marines I headed up to spend a few days with my buddy Mikey who lived in Pennsylvania. We were going up to his Dad's hunting cabin in northern Pennsylvania. Mikey had gotten out earlier in the year and was working as a prison guard in State College, PA. He seemed to like the gig. We headed to the camp in his jeep, which in my opinion had seen better days. Tears in the roof, broken windows, and since the windows were made of plastic, they had been repaired with duct tape. Strangely enough, the tape prevents you from seeing out the window. We headed up in a nor'easter. I'm not sure if they have nor'easters in that part of the country, but that's what if felt like, a total deluge of cold, wet, windy, wet, cold, windy water slashing at us from all angles. The holes in the roof didn't help much, and the duct tape on the windows made it so we could only see out the front. If a wall of rock slid down a hill, we wouldn't know it until it hit the vehicle. Too late then, amigo. It's over the precipice we go. Happy trails.

We eventually made it to the camp. Mikey had brought along a bag of pot for us and had it stashed in this skiivies, his underwear, if you will. His father was there with a couple of his cronies and Mikey didn't want it to fall out of his pocket. I guess he forgot about it when he went up the hill to use the outhouse because when he came back he had a look on his face that didn't exude happy thoughts. It looked like something had gone wrong. Horribly and inexplicably wrong. He told me that when he dropped his pants to sit in the outhouse, the bag of pot had fallen into the outhouse. That's right, you heard me. The bag fell out of his undies and down into hell. This wasn't a commercial type of privy. It was old school, a ten foot deep hole dug in the ground with a wooden covering. I asked him if he was sure, and he said, "Yes, you can see it sitting on top of the poo pile." Ah yes, the poo pile. You don't often come across a poo pile, but the phrase "poo pile" does it justice. We went back up the hill to take a look and sure enough, our dope was sitting in the baggie, right on the top of the poo pile. Right there on top, like an M&M sitting on a cupcake, almost like it been set there by some unseen entity that was challenging us to retrieve our meds.

We stood there about ten minutes, not saying anything, just looking at our pot sitting in the bottom of an outhouse. You could almost hear the wheels turning. The two of us trying to figure out how to get our shit out of the shit. It was coming up on dinner time, so we headed back to the cabin to sup. Throughout the entire meal we were trying to figure out how to do this and praying that none of the other guys at the cabin had to have a movement. That's all we needed was for one his dad's friends to "make the trip up the hill" and make our retrieval plan worthless. Not that we had a retrieval plan at this point, but still, we didn't need anyone piling on, so to speak.

We came up with some ideas; none really stuck though. We thought of lowering one of us down, but that was gross. Before you think poorly of me, the "containment area" wasn't wet, the outhouse wasn't used frequently, and it's made from dirt so it wasn't a wet pile, but it was still a pile of poo, just not like a porta potty. The lowering idea didn't seem feasible; we'd need a sturdy rope and one of us to go down. Then we thought of going into town and finding some kid we could use, and you know, give him a couple of bucks and let us lower him into the shit pit. That didn't pan out because his dad would've wanted to know where we were going at night in the middle of the woods.

We finally had a Eureka moment. It wasn't that deep. We could use a stick and drag it up the side. That would work. Wouldn't it? Yes, it would, was our consensus. Now we had to figure out how to do it without alerting our cabin mates as to what we were up to. They may have already wondered what the two of us were doing standing in the doorway of the privy, staring into its depths. Planning, that's what we were doing, my friends, planning. We headed back to the cabin to prepare our tools. We had to wait for the old men to go to bed. If they saw us flashing a light into the bottom of the outhouse, it may have raised suspicions.

We just kept pouring the old boys shots until they had all passed out, and then we went to work. We had found a fairly sturdy stick, had a flashlight and a new baggie to put our pot in. You can't keep your smoke in a baggie that has been in the bottom of an outhouse very well, now can you? We snake our way up the hill to the privy. Mikey reaches down with the stick and it's too short. We have to make an extension with another stick and some duct tape. (Is there anything duct tape can't do?) We make the stick long enough, put it in the hole and shine the light down. The baggie is gone. What? How could that be? It was down there before dinner and now it's gone? Did one of the old men take it? How could he have? Then we shine the light around and realize the baggie hasn't been removed, it's been shat upon.

One of those bastards snuck off and took a dump without us knowing. Now, there's a new pile of poo covering our bag. How much more are supposed to take? Did I mention that we really wanted to get high? We decided to go ahead with our plan. Mikey was the smaller of us, so he has to do the stick work. Why was smaller better? Because you have to lean in to the hole in order to reach the bottom, that's why. The other guy has to hold the light and the back of the leaner's belt to insure that he doesn't do a header into the pile of poo. So there we were, two grown men, former Marines, in a slight drizzle in northern Pennsylvania, in the dark of night, trying to retrieve our bag of pot from the bottom of an outhouse. That's real nice, fellas, real nice.

I'm holding the light and Mikey's belt while he leans down into the hole. He drags the baggie near the wall, adjusts his position and starts to drag it up the wall. I'm not sure if we had a plan on how to get it once it got to the top of the wall, because it would still be three or four feet away, but we'll cross that bridge when we come to it. Let's get it up the wall first. Off the bat it seemed to work pretty good, the bag was easily dragged up half the way, the second half proved to more tedious. He dropped the baggie six or seven times before finally getting it to the top and holding his position. I'm glad no one in the cabin woke up saw the two of us in the privy, one down in the hole, the other holding his belt and a flashlight. There might have been some 'splaining to do. Once he got it pinched to the wall, I reached down and around him and grabbed it. We got it! We are freakin' awesome. A lot of people would have given up, but not us. We stayed the course and completed our task. We changed baggies, threw the dirty one back and danced around in a circle. We may have been drinking as well. We won! We won! We rolled up a fatty and sat behind that outhouse and had ourselves a much deserved break. I'm telling you once again, Good times and Good shit.

CHAPTER 36
IRAQ

From My Diary.

Dear Diary:

I just got through security at the airport. I can't believe I feel so guilty going through there. I'm not trying to smuggle or sneak anything on, so why do I feel like it? "Here's my shoes, my belt, my loose change, my hat, the entire contents of my pockets and the skivvies I've been wearing for a week." Ha ha, I hope they're ripe.

"What are these?" I'm asked as he searches through my bag.

"Those? Those are the scissors I use to trim my balls, why don't you put them back in my bag or hold them by the handles?" Nimrod.

Now I'm in Memphis. I don't know why they give the little safety spiel at the beginning of the flight. No one pays attention. Yes, yes, we know how to fasten a safety belt, thank you though. Will you please just shut up and let me read, you're breaking my concentration. If you really want to save my life, don't crash the plane. How's that for a safety plan? No crashing. Seems like the best idea to me.

People are idiots. Why do they have to get on the phone as soon as we land and the seat belt sign has been turned off? The freakin' second we land, dozens of them are on the phone "I'm here, I'm here, Hi, I'm here, I'm here, Hi, it's me, I'm here." Hey, dumbass, shut your pie hole, we're all here. Can't you wait the five minutes it takes to de-board and then make your call? Do you have to irritate the shit out of everyone within the range of your voice, just because the plane lands? I wish they issued us tasers when we got on board. Not the police ones, just teeny tiny tasers, just enough to let them know to stop their present behavior. At least that would give them something interesting to say. "I'm here, I'm here," zzzzzap, "Aarggh, I'm here and I've just been tasered, it hurts and I'm dropping to my knees. I'll call you when I get to baggage claim." That should do it.

Just got on the plane to Amsterdam. It's a big plane. It's a nine hour flight, I hope they put enough gas in. Maybe I'll listen to the safety talk this time, especially the part about flotation devices. Yeah, maybe I'll listen to that one.

We've been in the air for two hours. I don't know where I am. Had the pasta for dinner. It was some kind of special. We were watching this thing on the movie screen about how to make homemade baby food. I don't know what's going on. First it was a documentary about Jack Nicklaus, then the baby food thing, now it's a special about Johnny Cash, quite the eclectic selection. What's next? How to survive a volcanic eruption? How to construct papier-mâché masks?

12:30 in the a.m. Most of the plane is asleep; the guy across from me is spread out on the floor. I forsee a lot of sore necks upon landing. I sleep for about 20 minutes at a time. My prediction? Tiredness. I bought a book of puzzles and word games but can't do any because they're too hard. Is that possible? Am I getting too stupid to do Megafun puzzles? Maybe I'm just tired. That's it, I'm not dumb, I'm just tired.

I'm awake again, we're about two hours outside of Amsterdam, and I must have been snoring because the chick in the burka is staring me down. Easy, princess. Just look away, sister, just look away. The clouds look like sand dunes. Either that or the delusions have started.

3:15 in the a.m. We've gone seven hours into the future. Breakfast is served. It took me three minutes to eat. I must've been hungry. Now I have to go have a sitdown. Sitdown is another phrase for taking a poop. Just so you know. I've never taken a sitdown on an airplane before. You know the whole "having your testicles sucked out the bottom" thing has always made me a little nervous. I've always timed it correctly. Maybe I'll wait awhile, you know, to see what happens. We've landed. We're stuck on the tarmac because we're a little early and someone is in our gate. Morons. I still have to poop.

Dear Diary:
We had a five hour layover in Amsterdam, it's now around 7 p.m. and we're somewhere south of the Netherlands and north of Kuwait. We sat around the airport and had some Heinekens, and now I'm a little tipsy. Had chicken curry for dinner; now there's a meal that will stay with you. Curry. I can't get that taste to go away. Why? Why eat the curry? Have you learned nothing over the years? We're watching Zorro in Arabic with English subtitles, kooky, crazy stuff. I should've gotten more Xanax.

I've slept in 20 minute intervals for two days.

286

They passed out newspapers, but they're in Arabic. Ha ha, got me. I don't read Arabic. Alert, we're over Bucharest and heading out over the Black Sea. I look out the window and its black alright. We land in Kuwait at midnight. I'm ready to get off the plane. It's been almost 20 hours in the air. I'm getting crabby.

I am tired. Yes, definitely tired. We got to bed around 2 a.m. We're staying at the lovely Swiss Inn in downtown Kuwait. Hmm. The Swiss Inn? What kind of authentic Kuwaiti Hotel is that? The Swiss Inn, oh for the love of Mike. We had an interesting breakfast downstairs. Tried something called foul masamas, and it lived up to its name. I'm not even sure what it was. I ended up having cereal and some fruit. The milk was warm. Apparently they don't use ice in Kuwait. There's not even an ice machine in the hotel. You think living in the desert would make people appreciate ice, but you'd think wrong. I guess they figure they've gone without it for thousands of years, why change what works?

Dear Diary:

We went out in town for a little while to do some shopping. The boys spent 30 minutes looking through movies to buy. I guess buying DVD's over here is some kind of bargain. All I bought was a Coke and a bottle of water. Hey...somebody put a leash on me. You have to drink bottled water. You can shave, shower and brush your teeth with the water; you're just not supposed to drink it. Yeah, well if I can't drink it, I'm not brushing my teeth with it. I guess they don't want you getting the runs while on a helicopter. Off to Camp Virginia.

A couple of great shows. The first one was an impromtu show. The Captain was giving us tour and then says "Oh, let's go in here." It's called lockdown and it's full of Marines going home. They're all watching *Braveheart*. Funny. The Captain walks up, turns off the TV and says "We're going to do a comedy show now, please welcome Jeff Capri." These guys are just staring at her; she's not even a Marine Captain, she's Air Force, and they're just staring. Well, Jeff's not here yet, it's muddy outside, so he has plastic Subway bags on his feet to keep his little Southern California beach shoes clean and is still tip-toeing through the mud. What joy that brought us.

There had to have been a 100 Marines standing around waiting to go somewhere and here comes Capri, hair down to his shoulders, huge white plastic bags on his feet, trying to negotiate muddy puddles, all the while trying not to spill his coffee. We're all standing at the door going, "please Jeff, hurry up, they're waiting and staring and we need you to come up here and eat this bullet." He walks in, removes his bags and does his shit. It turned out to be quite pleasant. These guys are all going home soon and are in good moods. We could've been making balloon animals and they wouldn't have cared.

Then it was off to chow. Had the steak and lobster. I'm not kidding. I spent four years in the Marines and never had steak and lobster once. We've been on this base now for over five hours and still haven't done the show we were scheduled for. It's getting closer though, I can feel it.

We're getting ready to start my first official show of the tour, and I'm psyched, I'm primed, I'm ready to go, I'm chomping at the bit, so get me to the stage, boys, I'm ready to spit fire and crap thunder. Then I find I'm going last. That's OK, I'll bring this baby home. I didn't realize of course that will be 80 minutes away. Damn, now I've got to kill another 80 minutes. I hope I still have the energy because I'm tired, really tired.

Had to use the porta potty again. Things were a little different this time though. It was at night, and at night there are no lights. Hmm. No light while sitting in a porta potty, how the hell am I supposed to know when I'm finished? I mean I know when I'm finished, but what about after? How do you know when it's time to pull up your britches and move on? I'm holding paper up to the vents at the top trying to catch a little light from the moon to highlight this paper and let me know it's OK to move on. Wacky stuff, man. I didn't like pooping in the dark.

Tomorrow we get our helmets and body armor and head into Iraq. Cool. Until you think about why you're wearing them. Hmm. Not so cool now is it big boy? Yes, it's still cool. Body armor, it even sounds cool.

Had chow again. We've eaten like pigs since we've been here. Had to use the porta potty again. I don't know what's going on. I've been here three days and have had 22 sitdowns. I hope I don't have dysentery. We've received our helmets and body armor. It's heavy, man, really heavy. We're flying on a C-130 troop carrying plane. It's snug. Elbow to elbow, knee to knee. You get to know your neighbor during the two hour flight. I hope I don't have to poop. Nobody wants to poop on a C-130 because the commode just hangs from the wall of the plane. There's no privacy, it's just there. So it's you at the back of the plane sitting on the toilet with 150 people looking at you. It's not for the timid.

Dear Diary:

We're finally in Iraq. Camp Al Asad. Here everyone is armed. Everyone. They wouldn't issue me a weapon though. There are bunkers everywhere so you have someplace to go in case of a mortar attack. Concertina wire is covering everything and huge blocks of concrete reinforce every wall. It looks like a damn war zone. Hmm. Things seem a little more real here. Well, enough sightseeing, I'm hungry, where's the chow hall? We checked into our billeting. Nice digs. The five of us and two Army escorts. CWO 5 Pace and Sgt First class Foley. Good dudes. They were there to escort us around under armed guard and make sure nothing happened to us. Nothing did.

We all stayed in the same room; the sheets I was issued seemed a little damp and just a touch musty. I opted for a sleeping bag and a towel. I had to make my own pillow out of dirty clothes. That was nice, sleeping with the smell of ass and dirty feet in my nostrils. Sweet, sweet bouquet. War **is** hell. This is so far, one of the greatest trips of my life. I'm already thinking about my next trip over here.

Last night I slept for all of two hours. Now I'm tired. I wish I could've been this tired last night. They don't stop flying into Al Asad just because the "talent" are trying to sleep. The gall. Comedians need our beauty sleep. Since we've been here there has been a lot said of "hydrating." We're supposed to drink three gallons of water a day. Well... that's a lot of water. But I did it, and last night it came back to haunt me. I must have gotten up to pee 15 times, it was ridiculous; no wonder I couldn't sleep, my body was afraid to shut down for fear I'll wet my bed. The latrine is too far of a walk in the middle of the night in the pitch blackness, so we all had to use "pee bottles," empty water bottles into which you pee at night. Priceless. Standing outside the billeting area at two o'clock in the morning, complete darkness, helicopters flying overhead, fog in the area, a damp chill runs through you as you try to pee into a water bottle without going all over your hands. This is what it's all about. This place is fantastic. This is being alive. I love it here.

The Lieutenant brought us over to the chow hall this morning. We had breakfast and then he asked us to walk around and talk to the troops. You know; just mingle around their tables and be funny. What?

289

What do you want us to do? Walk around and do improv at 6:30 in the morning? Who are we, Robin Williams? Shecky Greene? First of all, that shit's hard to do, just walk around and be funny; second of all, these guys have no idea who we are. If we were bigger names that everyone knew, it would be a different story. To them we're a five pack of civilians interrupting some of the only quiet time they get.

"Hi, where are you from?"

"Um, hey man, I'm right in the middle of my oatmeal. Now please go away." But we did it. We didn't put anyone on the floor with belly laughs, but surprisingly enough, we got some chuckles.

Dear Diary:

Wow. What a day. Our first helicopter ride. A Marine helicopter, our only day with Marine pilots, the rest of the time it was in Blackhawks with Army pilots. I don't know if that makes a difference to anyone, but I wrote it down and now it's being transcribed, so there you have it.

On the way to the flight deck, the first driver pulls off the road and gets stuck in the mud. We spent 20 minutes rocking that thing and finally got it out, I say "we" but it was just me and the Chief. The other boys decided to just watch and run the video camera. As we're rocking this vehicle, it starts moving forward, grabs terra firma and scoots out. Well, I'm still pushing as it takes purchase and when it takes off, I'm still pushing, but of course, there is nothing left to push. The vehicle is gone and I can't stop pushing, I'm not actually pushing anything though, the truck is gone, I'm pushing air and the weight of the flak jacket keeps my forward momentum going. Yes, it keeps it going all the way to the ground, I go down to my knees and then went forehead first into the mud. Oh, everyone had a good laugh. A really good laugh. Of course Bob got it all on tape and when watching it later, it really was funnier than shit. What was also funny is the way which people we showed it to laughed. Everyone got a huge chuckle from it, so in the end it was worth it. I mean, we're here to make people laugh, right? I didn't really hurt myself, so what's a minor concussion if it's for a gewd cawz, I axe yu, am I rite or em I rigt?

We flew into Korea Village, there are no Koreans there, but there used to be. Saddam had the Koreans who were building the highway living there. It was a Marine base, all jarheads, goody. We saw some insurgents upon landing. They were standing at the edge of the flight deck waiting to chopper out. They were blindfolded and handcuffed, but we couldn't take pictures of them, so you'll just have to believe me. We asked if we could, but they told us, "No, sir, you can't take pictures standing alongside these handcuffed, blindfolded insurgents." It would've made a great pic though. These guys were out in the boonies, nothing but desert for hundreds of square miles. Heavy. We did the show on a makeshift stage in front of a couple of tanks. Pretty cool. Most of them stood for the entire show. We took a tour of the base as well. Dusty is a word I would use to describe Korea Village. There was a layer of dirt on everything. This place was nothing like Al Asad. These guys were conducting a lot of their business in tents. Tough duty. Remind me to send them some stuff.

On the flight deck for another chopper ride. Everyone's got their helmets and body armor on. We're adorable. Just like little soldiers and Marines, waiting for our Blackhawk ride. You feel pretty safe wearing body armor. Not so much with the helmet though, I wasn't so sure those things could stop a bullet back when I was in, and I'm still not sure they could. They are good for banging your head around the inside of a tank, though. If you think about it, your body's not what needs armor in a helicopter, it's your ass. If you're taking incoming fire in a chopper, it's not coming from the side, it's coming from underneath. We shouldn't be wearing them, we should be sitting on them. Especially on Valentine's Day, you don't want to get your boys blown off on Valentine's Day.

The machine gunners on the choppers are serious. I'm thinking they're not going to take us anywhere dangerous. I mean, we're civilians for God's sake. They won't take us somewhere where we could get shot down. Would they? Yes, they would. I think I realized it when I saw them sweeping the ground with the machine gun fire. Hmm. But hey, if we get shot down in a helicopter in Iraq on the way to do shows for the troops, we'll be comedy legends. So we had that going for us.

Dear Diary:
Camp Poliwoda. Holy shit. This place is fortified. The choppers land and someone on the flight deck is motioning to us in a somewhat frantic manner. We casually stroll out of the chopper and the guy is waving us on, again in a frantic manner. A little confusion at first, what's going on? Why he is so spastic? Are we late for the show? What else could it be? The chow hall must be full and they're anxiously

awaiting our arrival. No. He wants us the hell off the chopper so it can get out of here. If the birds stay on the ground more than a couple of minutes, the base becomes a mortar target. Oh well, then let's skeedaddle shall we? By the time we put our shit down, the choppers were taking off. Windy. Yes, very windy, standing under the blade wash of a couple of large helicopters as they soar into the sky. Now we're all dirty again. Why bother washing? We've been covered in a layer of dust for three days. Cowboys, that's who we are. We're Cowboys. Yippe Kay Yay.

Everything here is covered in sand bags and huge concrete blocks. You have to wear your body armor everywhere. That was fun, trying to sit in a porta potty wearing a bullet proof vest when it's well over 100*. It gets warm inside a porta potty in that kind of heat. By the time you close the door and turn around, the sweat is running in rivers. No breeze in a porta potty, no sir, no breeze at all. Comfy. Cozy. It was kind of scary knowing these guys had to live like this, basically underground. Not one square inch of that place was uncovered. We were the first entertainment to come out there, just like at Korea Village. I liked that. I liked being the first people to come to these FOB's, which is a Forwarding Operating Base, in case I haven't told you. They enjoyed having us out there. We had the show in the chow hall because it's the most secure building there. Everybody rocked and it was off to Camp Wilson. Another FOB.

We choppered in, got settled, took a small tour, and hit the firing range. Andy and I were the only ones who went, and it was awesome. We got to sit on the top of a humvee and fire a machine gun. That's a feeling of power by God. Slinging out thousands of rounds of ammunition a minute. Just laying it down, baby, a wall of lead, the metal blanket, the sheet of death, the steel curtain, no man's land. It felt good tearing up that trash barrel. I'm sure word will spread through the barrel community that I am not a man to be trifled with. I riddled that puppy full of holes with my machine gun. Rat tat tat tat tat tat tat tat tat tat tat tat tat.

I'm Machine Gun Marky. Don't be messin' with me. Wouldn't that be great? To have a machine gun turret on the top of your car? You know, just in case? Cool. Then we got to fire the M-14 rifle, which is sort of like the M-16 in weight and feel, but it has a lot of accessories. Infrared, grenade launcher, a scope, the whole nine yards, the complete package, the whole kit and kaboodle, all the fixins'. It was righteous.

Don't me wrong, I'm not a gun freak or anything, but damn, it's fun. It's a great feel and I love the smell of cordite. Nothing smells quite like a rifle range. It's intoxicating, I want more, I want more because, of course, to get that smell, you have to fire more weapons. Can I fire the pistol? Oh, please let me fire your sidearm, sir. Bang, bang. Yes, please let me go, bang, bang. I just want to shoot some more. So we fired the M-9 pistol for a while. They had somebody taping this whole thing and she's supposed to send us a copy. It was a fun way to spend Valentine's Day. Now it's off to chow and the show. Good thing, because I'm starving. Where's the porta potty? I have to poop.

These guys slept in bomb shelters- most of them were underground. I asked some PFC how it felt sleeping in a bunker and he said "secure." Point taken. It was odd watching people popping up from holes in the ground to scurry over to the chow hall for some comedy, reminded me of that Whack-a-mole game. Another great show. Again, we were the first entertainment they've had. Everyone was incredibly cool and good times were had by all.

Originally, they had us all in the same room. There was a slight problem with the beds. They were so worn out and beat up that when you reclined on it, the middle sagged almost to the floor, and you were wrapped like a giant burrito. It was almost comical, the five of us laying down on these racks all sunken down in the middle, struggling and grappling to rise out the depths of tortilla hell. OK, we're going to have to do something about this. They got us some cots, but only three, so Bob and I grabbed a couple of them and headed across the hall to the conference room. The other room is getting kind of small, what with all the moving going on. Stacking two mattresses on top of each other in the hopes that it will support the weight of a grown man. Shuffling, figuring etc, it all became just too much. Bob and I set up our stuff and we gots room baby, we gots plenty of room. It's a conference room, and it's just us. But first, a shower.

This place was a FOB, so they don't have any amenities. The shower is indoors, but you have to go outside to get to the "shower trailer." There's not very good drainage in the trailer so the whole place is soaked all the time. Everything that comes near the floor absorbs moisture like a sponge. It's not easy to get to either; the land in Iraq doesn't drain water off when it rains; it just sits there until it evaporates. That makes it muddy all the time, and there's a huge trough of mud around the shower trailer, so it's a tip toe job. Not an easy task to accomplish wearing shower shoes. Everything in the shower trailer is dripping wet and after drying off, I dropped my new, clean, dry skivvies into a puddle. I don't care how quick you are, you can't catch a dropped pair of skivvies before they hit the ground. Boom, splash, one less clean pair of shorts for this trip. I accidentally left my t-shirt full of dirty clothes (my pillow) in the conference room when we departed. Now Camp Wilson has a memento from me, my pillow full of laundry. Cherish, my friends, cherish.

Dear Diary:
We're supposed to go to three different FOB'S today but got rained in. Choppers won't fly in the rain. They will, but the pilots won't. Apparently they don't like to fly if they can't see the ground. Seems reasonable. We slept in until nine. They all got a good chuckle when someone suggested we go by road. "Ha ha, sir, that's a good one. Take the road. Oh, that's very good, sir." I actually felt bad that we were missing some shows, especially since we were going to places that were out in the sticks, but damn, it felt good to sleep for a while. By the time the weather cleared and we got a chance to take off, the whole day was blown. We missed every show today, and it was guilt mixed with some relief from the pace. Yin and Yang, sweet and sour, tai and chi, you get my meaning.
We headed to LSA Anaconda. It's a huge base and receives mortar attacks from time to time. As we were walking to the PX, the Captain was telling us what to do in case we hear the alarm for incoming mortars. I asked if it was a siren or whistle or something like that and he said, no, the guy will come on the base intercom and say "incoming." OK, no mistaking that warning. That's when you head for a "hard building." The buildings we slept in were not "hard buildings," so in case of attack we had to run outside and find a bunker, or a "hard building." Most of the mortar attacks occur at night. Needless to say, I didn't use ear plugs that night. You don't want to sleep through certain things, and a warning for a mortar attack is one of them.
We got to sleep in a bed though, in our own private room. We shared a latrine with one other guy, but it was indoors. Indoor plumbing, our first on this trip. Ooh la la. We were living large. I was

asleep by 9:30. I was sleeping soundly and dreaming pleasantly when I waken to a boom, followed by a few seconds of silence then I hear about nine booms. Then nothing. Hmm, should I peek outside and see what's going on? The booms sounded far away, but they still sounded like mortars. I didn't hear anything else, and heard no one stirring, so back to bed, my weary comedian. If they get closer, I'll check it out, but right now, I'm tired. Plus, if there's something going down, they'll come and get me, won't they? Big day tomorrow, three shows I think.

Dear Diary:
We were scheduled to do three shows but ended up with five. We took tours and met people and had some chow and met some people and took tours and did a show and took a tour and had some chow and met some people and did a show and took a tour and met some people and did a show and met some people and took a tour and took a drive and met some people and did a show and met some people and took a tour and had some chow and met some more people and then did another show.

It was a rambunctious day, to say the least. After morning chow we headed over to the hospital to take a tour and meet the Dr's and maybe mingle with some wounded. Honestly, I wasn't looking forward to mingling and trying to brighten the spirits of wounded troops because I'm a puss and I get choked up easily. I could envision myself walking around bawling like a baby going, "hey, where you from?" Good job, man, you've been a real bright spot. Thanks for livening up my day, if I wanted this kind of reaction, I would've had my mom come over. Fortunately, there were only a couple of guys in there and they had minor injuries. Whew. We did meet all the docs who went into great detail about what they could do in that tent. "Anything a regular hospital can do." It was amazing. Full surgical capabilities. Then we did an impromptu show for some of the staff and a couple of wounded guys. We did it in the little room they had set up for the chow hall. A couple of tables and us. Just standing at the edge of the hospital tent, weaving our magic. Well, it can't get much tougher than this.

Later...
We're in a huge metal hangar standing on the back of a big truck with F-16's taking off outside and doing a show for Special Forces guys. Not big laughers, the Special Forces guys. It is surreal. You can't hear shit when those jets take off, it literally rattles the walls. The jets took

off about every five minutes and when they did, everyone would just stand there and wait for it to get quiet again, we'd stare down at them on the hangar floor and they'd stare up at us standing in the back of the truck. It would take almost a minute for the jets to get far enough away so we could hear again. The Special Forces guys laughed, but it wasn't big laughs. Or maybe we just aren't that funny. Surely I jest. Maybe it was because they had to stand the whole time. Or maybe it was because they were Special Forces and they just don't chuckle like the rest of us. Who knows, we came, we conquered and we moved on.

Let's take a tour. Let's take one more tour and then let's eat. I'm starving. I came here eating twice a day. Now, after eating three times a day, I'm hungry two hours after eating. I need to eat. I'm starving. Did I say that already? Because I am. Let's eat. We've got a show coming up. I may have to poop again too. I mean, what the hell? I'm here aren't I?

The next show has maybe 200 people in a gymnasium. Not the best acoustics, but if you talked slow, it sounded OK. As the show approaches the halfway mark the Captain comes in and asks us if we'd do another show after the next one. What? Do you mean one more after the next one? Um, OK. I don't know how were supposed to say no. I mean, it's for the medical staff that never gets time off to do stuff like this. Yes, of course we'll do one more show. So, now after this show, we go over to the movie theater, do the "big show," then head over another hospital and do a show at 11 o'clock. Super. I'm not tired anyway, but I am hungry. And I do believe I need another sit down.

We do the "big show," about 600 people for this one. We had two generals sitting in the front row. I'm not military anymore, but I still know that I have no business being in the company of generals. Generals for God's sake. Generals. So we do the show and it rocks. Can't go wrong with 600 people in the audience. We do the meet and greet and take somewhere in the neighborhood of a hundred pictures, wrap it up and head over to the hospital to do our 2300 show. Groovy.

Another surreal event. Two doctors, five nurses, two patients...and the chaplain. All of us snuggled together in the employee break room. Very informal. Hard to actually "do" material when you're standing in front of a refrigerator with ten people sitting around, you have to be a little more conversational. It actually went very well, we got laughs. I made fun of the chaplain and a nurse who had chapstick in a holster and everyone had a good time. Are we done now? Can we go home?

We've been bopping around for almost 19 hours. Is it time for bed yet? I'm hungry, and I think I need to poop.

The next morning we took another chopper ride. Went to Camp Duke for another chow hall show. Another tough crowd. Great lodging, even though it was only for a couple of hours. Took some pics with some Iraqi civilians. They like having their pics taken with Americans, or at least they seem to. This one guy gives me this brown plastic bag to hold during the picture. I, of course, ask about its contents.

"This isn't a shit bag or anything, is it?

"No, it's my lunch bag." He says.

I hold it up for the picture and the guy who gives me the bag is behind me and goes "one, two, three...boom." All the Iraqi's are laughing their asses off. Oh, yeah, ha ha, you got us on that one. It's good to know they've got a sense of humor. Well, we'd love to chat, but we've got a chopper waiting. I don't know where we're going. I do know that I'm hungry. Is there someplace I can have a sitdown before we go?

Dear Diary:

Now we're at Camp Mahmudiyah. I fell asleep on the chopper on the way over. What's going on here? We're flying over hostile territory on an armed Blackhawk helicopter and I'm nodding off. Have I become that complacent? Are my worries so few that I can sleep in this situation? Apparently. They were pretty excited to see us at Mahmudiyah. They didn't believe anyone would come to their camp. It was not in good shape. The First Sgt told us the blown-up chicken plant was the highlight of the base. After the chopper engines ceased their fluttering the First Sgt said "I'd give you a tour, but this is pretty much it." They had a "special lunch" lined up so the soldiers could "eat lunch with the comedians." Unfortunately, they had lost a comrade earlier that day so spirits weren't the best and they just wanted to eat and go about their business. On small FOB's like that, everyone knows everybody, and when they lose somebody they're all down, so there wasn't much goofing around during lunch. They did all come to the show though. Great group. Another show in a hangar. Another show where they all stood. Shook some hands and took some pics and soon we're off to somewhere else. As we were leaving, a patrol was heading out and the First Sgt says, "don't get blowed up," to each vehicle as it leaves. Sound advice from a crafty veteran. Is the chow hall still open?

Dear Diary:

Well, it's over. We did our last show tonight. Camp Rustimiyah. We did it outside in a boxing ring. It had to be 40* outside. Chilly. We're in Baghdad now. We flew in by chopper to one of Saddam's palaces. We flew in complete darkness. It was kind of eerie. You can't use lights at night or we could get shot down. That would be a bummer. Baghdad has a lot going on, and none of it is good for us. The palace was amazing. Reminded me of how Liberace decorated. Saddam was lacking in taste. Gawdy is not a taste. It was very Vegas-like. There were three bathrooms for our room. We all shared a room on the last night. The slumber parties were coming to a close and we wanted to get in our last moments in together. Tomorrow it's back to Kuwait and then take off on Monday. "I'm so glad we had this time together, just to have a laugh or sing a song..." You get the picture.

We had a great time. I'll probably wait a little while before coming back though. I'll need some time to regroup. We took thousands of pictures, hours of video, had 40 chopper rides, flew on two C-130's, fired machine guns, did around 25 shows, met hundreds of our nations' military, ate like pigs, pooped like animals and slept like insomniacs. Ta ra for now, my sweet prince. Come back soon.

CHAPTER 37
I GO TO AFGHANISTAN

From My Diary.

Dear Diary:

Well, I'm off to Afghanistan. I thought I was going to Iraq, but I was wrong. Things change. I got home from Déjà Vu in Columbia, MO, around 2 a.m. My cab came at five, three hours of sleep. That should be plenty. I'm rested and ready to travel. My cab driver was a former Marine and somewhat of a conspiracy theorist. He covered everything from the Kennedy assassination to the Israeli Mossad. He had thoughts on everything, and after 15 minutes my head was spinning, I don't even think I said anything but "uh huh." That's just too much info at five in the morning. I can't think that fast. I'm not even sure he took a breath.

I rented a car in L.A. I got a Prius battery car. It took me ten minutes to figure out how to start it. I had to use the driver's manual. The motor doesn't turn on until you start moving. You just put it in gear and go. Bizarre. It shuts off when you stop too, so I was confused. I know it's economical, but I'd like to at least know my motor is running. My flight to Frankfurt, Germany, is at 6:30 p.m. I showed up at two. If you've ever flown out of LAX, you know to get there early. It took about 90 minutes to get through the line and check in. Then you have to go stand in line to put your luggage through security. I happened to snag an exit row seat for my 11 hour flight to Germany, I thought I had hit the motherload; I'll have plenty of room to stretch myself out. I was wrong again. The exit row is right next to the bathroom, so everyone that waits for the bathroom stands right in front of me. That area, also unbeknownst to me, was the stretching area. Super. Fifteen minutes after we take off, the seat belt lights go off and at least 50 people get up and start moving around the plane. Fifteen minutes into an 11 hour flight and it's a mad scramble of movement. I thought they were giving away free ice cream or something. Then there is a steady stream of people invading my area doing stretching exercises. Jesus, people, we've been in air for 15 minutes, sit your ass down and get out of my aisle. Of course this went on for the next 11 hours. I won't take this row again.

Dear Diary:

My traveling companions are Rick Kunkler, Sandy Brown and Jentle Phoenix. We landed in Frankfurt, Germany, and got picked up by Pete, an Air Force dude, taking us to Ramstein Air Base. We stayed in VIP housing, so that was nice. It would be the last time for two weeks we would have our own rooms. There is no a.c., so it's a good thing the weather's nice. I wonder what it's going to be like in Afghanistan? The jet lag thing isn't bothering me at all. I'm special, or so I thought. I went to bed at eight p.m. thinking I'll sleep like a baby all night. It's now one a.m. and I'm wide awake, up watching German television. Not an easy thing to do because they're speaking German; and it's like they have a different word for everything. I go back to bed around 4:30 and flip and flop until 6:30. Now it's time to get up, go to chow and get ready to fly to Manas, Kyrgyzstan. I'm tired. I guess I'm not special, jet lag affects me too. Who'd a thought?

Dear Diary:

We're in Incirlik, Turkey. Why? That's just the way they do things. We had to stop and get fuel, etc. Spent over two hours in Turkey, but we couldn't leave so I didn't see much of Incirlik. We were there long enough for me to have a sitdown. This foreign travel is affecting my bowels again, just like my trip to Iraq. What the hell is it with me and pooping during worldwide travel? I won't cover that topic again, but if you want, you can go read about my Iraq trip and get all the info you need.

We land in Manas, Kyrgyzstan around 3:30 a.m.; little did I know there would be so much night travel. As we're getting ready to depart, we're informed that the plane has to be towed to a more secure area. We deplane, get on a bus and head to a debriefing; why, as civilians, we have to be debriefed, is beyond me, but we do. Apparently there are many rules, etc. that apply to us as we stay in beautiful Manas. We debrief, head to chow and get ready for a nap. It's now almost eight in the morning and I'm lying down for my nighttime sleep. This could mess with a boy.

It's noon and I'm up. Time for chow. We're going to end up doing a lot of this, sleep and chow. You never know when you're going to get another chance to do either. I knew that from Iraq, sleep and eat when you can. Our flight isn't until eight tomorrow morning. Of course, due to the military philosophy of "hurry up and wait," we have a roll call at midnight. We show up to the PAX terminal at midnight, hear our names called and now we're excited, we're getting on a plane to Bagram, Afghanistan.

"We're here, we're here" we call out.

"That's great sir, just have a seat."

"When's our flight?"

"0800, sir"

"You mean tomorrow morning?"

"Yes, sir, just have a seat, we'll let you know when it's time to board."

"Well, what are we supposed to do for the next eight hours?"

"Just hang loose sir, just hang loose."

So we sat there for eight hours waiting on our flight; we did a lot of that, waiting for our flights. We got used to killing time. We drank a lot of fluids, some of it due to boredom: "hey, what do you want to do? Do you want to get some more water?" That, of course, led to many potty breaks, all just a vicious cycle. You also learn how to sleep sitting up, leaning over, lying on chairs, lying on the floors, etc. Good times. Just like hobos, grabbing z's whenever you could. I miss lying down for my slumber. Seems like something weird to miss eh? Sleeping while lying down. Odd, the things you take for granted.

Dear Diary:

Well, it's now almost nine a.m. and we're airborne. We're flying on a C-17 cargo plane. We just flew over the Himalayas; that was cool. I've never seen them before. I was doing a little video-taping and somehow got my camera strap wrapped around the door latch and as I was backing away I almost opened the door at 30,000 feet. That was close; fortunately, it takes four other latches to get the door open. It still freaked me out for a second. I'd hate to be sucked out of an airplane from that height. Tough fall.

We land in Bagram, Afghanistan, in the early afternoon, I think. The days are already starting to bleed into one. I think it's Friday, but that would be the 17th, I think. I'm not sure. Who are you? Where are you from? It's either Thursday or Friday, where am I? Who am I? Where did this cake come from? We're in Bagram, and it's a little hotter here. I'm starting to sweat, nothing drastic, just a little damp. We're being weighed for our flight to FOB Fenty, near Jalalabad. They can't put too much weight on the prop plane we're taking or it could go down. Don't want that. I'm starting to get tired. We've been up since eleven last night and I think it's around two in the afternoon now. A prop plane flying through the Afghanistan mountains is not what you would call "a smooth ride." There seem to be many updrafts and downdrafts, and yes, maybe, even some sideways drafts. So we bounce and roll and swerve for about 15 minutes before we land.

We land at Nangahar Airport, and Rick gets off the plane snapping pictures and taking video until I point out the big sign that says "no flight line photography." Rick had no video camera though, he used his phone. Which I thought was priceless. Video- taping the entire trip on his phone. He did it though, never wavered, never questioned his decision; that, by God, was dedication.

As we disembark, I notice the heat. It's warmer here, like 30* warmer. I ask the forklift driver how hot it is, "hot" he says. I believed him. Found out shortly it was 118*. Nice. I don't think the heavy sweating will start for a while though. By the time we had walked across the flight line, and yes, we walked across the line, there is a green/red light that lets you know it's safe to cross, but we did cross right where the planes landed. We get to the gate and I'm soaked. I'm wet from head to mid thigh. Uh oh. I may be in trouble, this is hot.

Dear Diary:
We're here and we're finally going to do a show. It took a cab, a rental car, two commercial planes, a military plane, a crop duster and a bus to get here, but we've made it. We're off to our lodging. The girls are lodged in a hard building with air conditioning, nice racks and a microwave, not bad for a FOB. Ricky and I are in a tent. That's OK with us. We're here to do shows for the troops not stay in nice comfy beds. We're in a tent. It's a big tent, but it's a tent. OK, cool, we've done the tent thing before. Of course, I've never stayed in a tent in the Afghani desert when it's 118* outside. The sun heats up the tent. I know, I know, it's a brilliant observation. It's simple physics, really: the sun transfers the heat to the tent top, which releases it into the tent "body." It had to be at least 100 in there, and I'm being generous. It was obvious there will be no naps in this mofo. You can't take a nap in those kinds of conditions. I don't care how tired you are. The heat tires you out too; I didn't think of that. No wonder I'm sleepy. The tent did have a.c., but it only cooled the bottom twelve inches of the tent. Hilarious actually. I put my mattress on the floor and just stayed low. If

you were lying down and decided to sit up, it was unbelievable, a difference of 40* or more. Once, when I sat up, I started a rain storm. Wild, wacky stuff. I've got a headache. When do we eat?

So we hydrated and hydrated and then hydrated some more. In the first couple of hours we were at Fenty I drank three gallons of fluids; I'm not shitting you, and only peed once. How's that for some sweat? They actually have charts in the latrine asking what color your urine is. If it's dark, you're dehydrated, drink more water. If it's this color drink more water. Even if it's clear, you're hydrated but they want you to drink more water. I don't think I could've put any more fluids in me.

About an hour before the show, Rick heads to medical. He needs an I.V. It seems he's lost more fluids than he's replaced. The boy needs to be hydrated even more. We're not sure he's going to make the show, so the girls and I are planning on going without him. He's on death's door, he's been taken down, out, there's no way he can go on. The talk is of a medivac flight back to Bagram. He may be suffering from kidney damage. We're not sure how long the lad can hold on. He's already been fighting for his life for over an hour. Has he received brain damage? Will he survive? And if he does, will he still be the same Ricky Kunkler that we've come to know? God in heaven give us the strength to deal with...what? He's here? Oh, well then never mind, he's OK and ready to do the show. What a trooper. The show went very well, fun had by all. Then I was off to the shower, we've been up almost 24 hours and I'm ready for sleep, but I can smell myself and I've got a couple layers of salt dried on my skin. I don't want to ruin the sheets on the mattress. Oh wait, we have no sheets or bed coverings or a pillow. Now I can make my famous pillowcase out of a t-shirt and dirty clothes. Just like in Iraq, sleeping with the smell of ass and dirty socks in my face. War is hell.

Dear Diary:
I know I skipped a day in there somewhere, but we went into the future getting here, so it seems right to skip a day or lose a day or whatever. I'm confused. We'll call it the 18th and leave it at that, OK? OK. It's 120*, groovy. It's not even a dry heat; there is a small river nearby and it puts out just enough moisture to make even 120* seem uncomfortable. We mosey around all day, try and nap, get some chow, try to nap, grab some more chow and head out on a road convoy. I

didn't think they'd really take us on the road outside the wire, but here we are, and there we go. On the road in a military convoy of humvee's riding through Jalalabad. That's why we signed those release forms letting them know it's OK if we get killed. Out of sight, man. I didn't really worry about getting blown up though. I figure if God's going to take me out in an IED blast, what can I do about it? If it's Allah's will, then it's Allah's will. Let's party. We're on our way to a FOB called a PRT. It's reconstruction camp that helps the locals get shit done. The other half of the camp hunts the bad guys. It's a nice synergy. Rebuild, hunt, hunt, rebuild.

We took a tour of the base and there were trees there. Apparently, most of the FOB's don't have any trees. Perhaps that's why it's so hot, no shade. Well, the PRT did have shade and it was lovely. Hard to believe standing in the shade was again a 30-40* difference in temp. Give me some more please sir. I'd like some more shade. We did two shows at the PRT because they couldn't fit everyone in the chow hall at the same time. So we did one, turned the room, and five minutes later we're into the second show. Efficient indeed.

When it's time to go back to Fenty for the night, we have to go through a "briefing" about our journey. We were supposed to be gone by nightfall but didn't make it, and now these guys are uptight and a little stern. We're standing in nothing but the headlights of the humvee, wearing our body armor listening to stuff like, "if we get hit by an IED, we'll radio for help and be evaced from where we get hit, and if we take an RPG or small arms fire, we'll confront the enemy and then move back here for any medivac that is necessary."

As comedians, we're all looking for some comedy in this, but there doesn't seem to be much there. I want to give some clever comment about what he's saying, but he seems so serious, I thought twice about that. Then he tells us, "We're on the lookout for any taxis or a white corolla that is known to belong to an insurgent." As he's giving out the license plate number, I'm reaching for a pen, I want to take down this number and keep my eyes peeled. I'm ready to help out, let me take a weapon and sit up top. "That won't be necessary, sir, we've got you covered."

As we're leaving the gate the Afghani who is manning the post is taking too much time lifting the gate and our driver yells at him, "hurry up mofo, you're making us a target." Wait... what did he say? Making us a target? Was that it? Making us a target for what? That doesn't sound too good. Making us a target? Should I be concerned? Should I do something? What am I looking for? I don't want to be "made a target." I'm not sure anyone does. Can we get moving please? Nothing happened though, it was a nice, short ride. We stayed off the hard roads the whole way back, we took to the fields. Bumpy. Next thing we know, we're on base. Praise the Lord. I'm still tired and I'm still hungry and I'm still hot and I'm still sticky, and I still have to poop. I love it here.

Dear Diary:

It's 0800 and already over 105*. Eight o'clock in the blessed a.m. and it's already hot. You can't really bring enough baby powder for a trip to Afghanistan in August. I've been dusting my balls about a dozen times a day. It's all you can do, just keep dusting. Keep a fine layer of powder all over, so you don't chafe yourself raw. I've got so much powder on me, every time I take a step; clouds of baby powder come poofing out of my shorts. Yes, I said "poofing." I'm not sure if it's a word, but you know exactly what I mean. I looked like that Pigpen character from Charlie Brown, just walking around with my haze of baby powder crystals surrounding me. I smell baby fresh, for just about ten minutes. I better get some fluids. Pee bottles were utilized in Afghanistan as well, and by now I knew to always use a wide mouth bottle. Ricky had the record: he filled up six bottles one night. That's a lot, six pee bottles. I guess he had some fluids today. That was usually the first chore you saw the men do each morning, walking to the trash can with their collection of pee bottles in their arms. Classic, simple. I woke up last night about three a.m. and never made it back to sleep. We're taking malaria pills and they give you these wild, intense, vivid dreams. A couple have even been disturbing, and I'm not a man who disturbs easily.

Last night Ricky had a little rash "downtown" from all the sweating we've been doing. I must not have been paying attention because he mentions something about "hand sanitizer will help jock rash, won't it?" Next thing I know he's on his bunk with legs in the air wailing about "it burns, it burns." I guess he put some of that 90% alcohol hand sanitizer on his balls. We had a good laugh about that, one of those I'm so tired I can't stop laughing moments; we went on and on over that one. It was pretty funny, and strangely enough, it seemed to help.

I realized this morning that I still have a headache. It's been two days and my head still hurts. It must be the heat. It can't be from lack of fluids. That seems like all we do, consume fluids and then go pee. Fluids, pee, fluids, pee. The girls skipped breakfast and lunch today and were reminded rather sternly by Lt. Kodrin that if you don't eat or drink out here you will die. They made it for dinner.

We can't get to our next gig tonight; it's too dangerous. The base we were supposed to go to got attacked last night, so no comedians. I guess they're serious about not getting us killed. So now, we're doing another show here at Fenty. I hope we get a different crowd. Ha ha, get it? A different crowd on the same base. Oh that's rich.

Had "surf and turf" for chow tonight; once a week they have surf and turf nights. We had steak and crab legs. Nice. One problem though, the silverware is made of plastic and doesn't open up crab very well. I'm not sure if you've ever tried opening crab legs with your bare hands, but it hurts. It hurts and it's messy as hell. By the time dinner was done, I had open gashes on my palms and one halfway up my wrist from a slipped grip. Next time, I'm getting macaroni and cheese.

Dear Diary:
A day off today, no show, no travel. We just hung out, drank fluids, peed and ate. That was it for the day. Today was the Afghani Independence day so we went across the airfield to where the Afghani Security Forces stay. They work with the Americans to fight the Taliban. We had some traditional Afghani food, which I, of course, was going to pass on. I'm a picky eater and won't eat just anything, especially food that has been prepared in the mountains of Afghanistan. Unfortunately, if you don't eat what they've prepared, it's considered an insult. Well, far be it from me to start an international incident because I didn't eat goat meat or camels' feet or yak balls or whatever the hell it was. I didn't ask, I just ate. It was actually quite tasty. See felt? Do you see what you get when you try something new? Do you see?

Afterwards we stayed and did some traditional Afghani dancing. I danced and danced and danced, I felt I could dance the night away; I danced until I couldn't plum dance no more. Just about ten minutes. There is much leaping and prancing and jumping about. I just don't have that kind of energy. After five minutes, I, again, am soaked with sweat from neck to knees. Very attractive. Not that it mattered, for outside our girls and a couple from the camp, there were no women there. The Afghanis don't party with their women. They have a whole different outlook on the female persuasion, which I won't go into. It was just the men folk, dancing their little hearts out.

We took many pics, the Afghanis love to look at the pictures once they've been taken. It's an amazing thing, these guys are mesmerized over the ability to take a picture and then be able to look at it. Rick and I also have a pic with Major Houzman, the head of the Afghani Force. What an intense dude. You can see by looking at him that he's a no nonsense s.o.b. I found myself just staring at him. He intrigued the hell out of me. LT told us he's been fighting the Taliban for years. He also was leading the charge against the Russians when they invaded. His platoon, of course, were on horseback and they were attacking Russian tanks. Now that is some wild shit, attacking tanks on horseback. The dude has been around. So we're taking pics and taking more pics. We also soon realized that we were the only four left and each time we took a pic, there would be 20-30 Afghani soldiers swarming us, or the girls actually. That's when the LT. said, "we've got to go right now." You don't have to tell me twice, let's boogie. It was a great experience. It was the first time in my life I've gone dancing with the Afghani Security Forces. Adios, my new friends, perhaps we'll be able to dance together on the next full moon.

Dear Diary:
We're now back at Bagram. We're waiting on a flight to Kandahar. It's now noon and our flight is at 1:30 a.m. We've got some time to kill. We met the Catholic priest named Father O'Brien. This guy was a card, from upstate New York, chain-smoked and had a grizzled, gravelly voice and sounded like a drill instructor. Hilarious. He was telling us about the "shit pools" in Kandahar. And yes, he used the term shit pools. I even asked him.

"Father, can you say shit pools?"

"I can say anything I want, it's war."

OK, gotcha. The Shit Pools are a group of four sewage treatment pools that sit at the edge of the base and when it gets hot (which is everyday we're there) you can smell them as soon as you get off the plane. We got in at three a.m. so we didn't get to smell them as it was only 85*. I'm not sure why I used the term "get to smell them" like it's something to look forward to, but we didn't smell them at all- that night.

We've got a 2 p.m. flight to a FOB in Qalat, Afghanistan, so before we leave Capt. Tucker takes us by the shit pools. I'm not sure why, but I think we just wanted to experience them. I mean, what's the point of going to Kandahar if you don't get to smell the pools? He drives us over and then says to open the windows. We do. Wow. What can I say? I started to gag and the Capt. is laughing his ass off, so I take another breath and throw up in his lap. That will teach him. Words can't give this aroma justice so I won't try. It's raw sewage, it's 122* and there is no wind and they have the aerators going full blast, bringing that sludge up and shooting it out in a five foot wide spray of brown water. It was like a fountain in hell. That is all I can say.

We're flying to Qalat in a Blackhawk helicopter. The pilot wants to know if we'd like to fly with the doors open. I've ridden in a lot of choppers, but never with the door open, so I convince my compadres to agree. Yes. Yes we would, let the gentle breeze float over us and chill our overheated cores. Well, that was a mistake I shant make again.

I sat in the back row, facing the front. All I can say was that it was like being slapped in the face by three people for 45 minutes. Not knock out slaps, just ones that fall just short of stinging. I was totally miserable. I wish someone would've said, "don't sit back there, it's a little windy." It was advice I could've used. The straps from my helmet, my body armor, my hat, my shirt, my camera bag, everything that wasn't secured down is whipping me about my face and neck. I can barely look out the open door, not only do I have helicopter blade wash attacking me, but the wind is over 120* and it is launching a non-stop assault upon my tender face. It was my worst helicopter ride...ever. I finally take my helmet off and cover my face. I got used and abused. I won't do that again.

Dear Diary:
Great show last night in the chow hall in Qalat, FOB Lagman. Great group. We took some pics on humvees, holding weapons, etc. The motor pool guys showed us a bunch of pics of what goes on around there. I can't share it with you because I took a pledge of silence. They also had a collection of dead camel spiders tacked to the wall. I don't like spiders anyway and camel spiders are especially creepy. First of all they can get to the size of a trash can lid and they're fast as shit. Not a

good mix; even the thought of them gives me the willies. When some of the guys get bored they have fighting matches between scorpions and small camel spiders, then they pin the losers to the wall. That was a little creepy too, watching spiders and scorpions battle in a death match. Yucky.

Ricky and I shared a tent that was right next to the place where they stored the explosives they find on the roads etc. I wish we would've known that beforehand. There is also a pallet of acetylene canisters right outside our door. That's a lot of explosive shit right next to sleeping quarters. If a mortar comes in anywhere near us, I do believe that Rick and I are toast.

Dear Diary:
We took another road convoy to a PRT in Qalat. That's always a trip. They ride right down the middle of the road telling people to get out of the way. Then we stop because "there is something up in the road" and they have to check it out. I'm confused. You're getting out of the humvee to check something out and we're left here on our own to die? Oh, sir, you won't be alone- the machine gunner is still with you. Comforting, that's what that was, having a machine gun watch over you is...comforting. Then I asked the driver, "don't you have people to do that? People that come out and check out weird shit on the road?" Then he tells me, "yes, sir, that would be us." Oh, I get it, well carry on. We get to the PRT and have some chow, very casual. We were just sitting on the ground and eating some grub. Not too bad, it's actually kind of comfortable, almost like a picnic, albeit a dirty, dusty picnic. The sun is going down and we're in Qalat enjoying a nice little supper. There is a puppy running around and we start to play with him. He's adorable as hell and we can't help ourselves. I've got him in my lap and the First Sgt. tells me.

"I wouldn't be playing with that dog too much."

"Why not?" I reply.

"Because she's a wild Afghani dog with no owner who roams around with no shots, and if she bites or scratches you, there's no telling what kind of disease you could end up with."

"Okey doke," I say as I gently put her back on the ground.

You don't have to tell me twice. Seemed like sound reasoning. The last thing I need is some type of intestinal parasite from the pooch. Or distemper or rabies or scurvy or the flu or botulism or chicken pox or some other type of weird middle eastern disease that hasn't been seen in humans for two hundred years. What if I get the Black Death? I bet they still have it over here. The girls didn't care though; they were carrying her around all night.

We did the show in DFAC (chow hall) with no lights or sound. Just us standing there in front of the crowd. I use the term crowd loosely. There were only 60 people on this FOB and most of them were Romanians. They didn't speak any English, but they came to the show anyway. Trust me when I say there wasn't anything else to do. They didn't laugh much, but they seemed to enjoy the physical hijinx. The generator ran out of fuel half way through Sandy's set, so we held our little flashlights on her until the genny came back on. It went pretty well considering the circumstances.

Dear Diary:
We're back in Kandahar. The shit pools greeted us home like a long lost lover. Open arms enveloping us in a putrid cloud of revulsion. Welcoming, beckoning us home. A warm, wet embrace if you will, one that you hope doesn't become too clingy. That's not something you want hanging off your clothes, the odor of the shit pools, no sir, that's not something you want a'tall. "You're back," the pools seemed to say; "we've missed you." Then someone asks "Who's hungry?" Turns out we all are. Let's go get chow. Even the pools can't stop the hunger. We've eaten three times a day since we've gotten here. Unreal. I'm talking full meals too baby, not just some snacking going on. We're eating some damn food. Even the girls ended up grubbing down on a regular basis. Well, it's either that or die. Let's eat.

We've got a show tonight at the outside pavilion. Huge place, the biggest so far. We're excited. We have to be back at 7:30 for a sound check. Maybe we should go get some chow. You know, while we're waiting. Ricky and I show up for the sound check, and the girls over slept their nap and are running a little behind. Ricky and I handled it pretty well. Fifteen minutes before the show, there were about five people in this huge pavilion. Five, that's it. We're in deep trouble here bro, there's room for 1000+ in this mug and we've got five. Airy. Plenty of room to stretch out. Plenty of room to stand. Plenty of room to throw a football. Hell, there's plenty of room to hit a five iron. There's space open, man, there's space open. Grab a little, sit right down, we're doing a comedy show. For the love of the sweet Savior, somebody come to the show. What the hell is going on around here? This is the biggest venue we've played and nobody's here. Then Capt. Tucker tells us there was a comedy show here last week and it was packed. Well that's just super. Here we thought we were something special. Turns out they have shows all the time, bands, comedians etc. They even had the Buffalo Jill's Cheerleaders out there a couple of weeks ago and had lines a mile long. Now we're here and there are five people here. Well tra la la la la la.

While we're having this explained to us, Rick is doing an on-camera interview with AFEES, which is military programming. But while he's doing this interview, he keeps asking me the questions the interviewer was asking him because he couldn't remember. It was priceless. The camera is on him and he's looking off camera going, "Hey, Mark, where have we gone? What have we done?" So I'm answering him and then he relates my answer to the camera. It was just more good times. Now it's five minutes to showtime and I haven't been paying attention to the crowd. I turn around and there are about 400 people out there. Where the hell did they come from? How did I not notice that the place was filling up? Are they all Special Forces? Are they so sneaky, they can fill up a pavilion, without the people on stage noticing? Whatever the case, we had a great show. Up in the mountains of Afghanistan, in the dark of night, on stage with the sound of gunfire and mortars periodically sounding off in the night; a 105* breeze, so gentle, it's like a baby's kiss- bringing with it, in a soft cradle, the smell of the shit pools. Man, it doesn't get any better than this.

Now we're on our way back to Bagram, one more show, then it's on the way home. We couldn't get a regular flight out, so the Capt. hooked us up with a friend of his who flew prop planes. He told us off the bat that it was windy in the mountains today and it may be a bumpy ride. It was. One of girls starts scrambling for an air sick bag, fills it up and starts looking for another- that was a panic. Nothing like the pressure of finding a sick bag for someone who's in the process of throwing up. It was a rough ride. We flew high, we flew low, we flew sideways, and I shit you not, at times we were so low the mountains were all we could see. No sky. I've been in a lot of planes in my day, from military cargo planes down to float planes in northern Canada, but I've never been in a plane when you couldn't see sky. There has always been sky somewhere; somehow you've always been able to see the sky. Not this time, Jack. No sky out the side, no sky out the back, no sky out the front. I'm not sure how that was possible, but it was a small plane, you could see out the front and I swear, I didn't see any sky, just brown. Unsettling, you ask? You bet your ass. I didn't even point it out to my fellow passengers; I thought I should just keep this between me, George and Rob; and Brad too, he noticed, he's a Special Forces dude and he was standing up in the aisle, looking out the front, so I'm assuming he knew how low we were. I bet we could've jumped out of the plane and not been killed; now that's flying a'low. We do some maneuvering and twisting and turning and he gets us back in one piece. Thank you, George. Thank you, Rob.

We attended a fallen warrior procession tonight. A sobering experience. You know you're doing comedy in a war zone and you know people get hurt and die, but to see it first hand was powerful. They told us it was happening around midnight; just head to the main road, you can't miss it. About 11:45 we headed out. There was a strong wind blowing and the air was so full of dust it made halos around the light fixtures. There didn't seem to be many people about and we thought we had missed it, so we just kept heading south. We found the road and followed the lead of those already there and took our places on the shoulder. Within the next ten minutes another 1000 people had joined us, they poured out from everywhere and soon we were shoulder to shoulder on the side of the road with the brown air swirling around us. You could see about ½ mile down the road to where the emergency lights flashed and we waited. Like all things military; hurry up and wait still applies. The small motorcade finally starts moving toward us, the dusty air has left it's thick residue in our hair and eyelashes as well as filling our ears with grit. There were two fallen warriors that night in the procession. A pick-up truck with flashing lights rolls by followed by two trucks carrying the caskets. Everyone salutes as it passes by. Even though I didn't know these boys, it made me cry. I felt that I knew them that night and it hurt to see them gone. It was an incredibly sad moment. It made me think of their friends and family and it hit me hard. A minute later they turned on to the flight line and we lost sight of them. Without a word, everyone dispersed and headed back to our hooches. There really wasn't anything to say.

Dear Diary:
We're on our way back to Kyrgyzstan tomorrow, then to Germany, then to L.A. I'm pooped, I'm down to my last pair of socks, I'm ready to

sleep laying down, I'm ready to take more than a two minute shower. I'm ready to shower without a puddle of mud forming at my feet. I'm ready for my Q-tips to come out of my ears clean. I'm ready for 100* heat, so I can laugh in its face. I'm ready to decrease my daily fluid intake to one gallon. I'm ready to forget the smell of the Kandahar shit pools, I'm ready to stop flying for awhile, but strangely enough, I'm not ready to leave.

I was awakened at 0330 by Jennifer, our MWR contact at Bagram. We can't go to Kyrgyzstan and then Germany because they're not flying out of Kyrgyzstan for almost a week. We're going to send you to Kuwait and hope you get a flight out of there. Then she leaves. I'm lying in my bunk. "What did she just say?" I was sound asleep. She shakes my leg, lays this riff on me and bolts. I'm not sure what's going on. Something about Kuwait instead of Germany? No way, I'm not getting stuck in Kuwait and having to buy a ticket home. We're confused, bewildered and still half asleep. Rick's up and we start bitching about it. I thought we had learned some patience from this trip, I mean with all the "hurry up and wait" the military still seems to love so well, but no; as soon as someone messes with our plans, "this is bullshit" starts and the "we're classified as GS-15's" nonsense. We bitch about it then fall back asleep.

We wake up to some confusion. We're told we're on a flight to Kuwait and it leaves in two hours, so get ready, you're leaving. They allay our fears about being in a foreign country without knowing anybody, we'll be on a military base and we'll be taken care of. We get to Kuwait and it's 130*. Seriously, I've never been in that kind of heat before; you can feel your skin burn. It's a weird feeling. Your skin burning. It feels warm in your lungs too. It's like opening the oven and taking a deep breath. So we sweat and lug our bags and clear up the confusion of trying to check in and hearing "who are you now?" They don't have a record of us, etc., but they put us in VIP billeting which was a tent just like everyone else, but it was pretty sweet. The a.c. worked splendidly, cooled all the air, not just the bottom, it was only set at 75*, but since it was 130* outside, it felt like a fridge.

Well...it's chow time again. We haven't eaten in almost five hours and we're famished. By the end, every time we went somewhere the first question we asked was "when's the DFAC open?" Chow hounds. Yummy. So we ate, bummed around, those guys did laundry, which I couldn't see because we're going home tomorrow; why get some clean clothes all mashed up and mixed up with dirty ones. We should be dirty coming back from all this dirt.

We've got a 9:45 a.m. roll call for a flight to Dallas. After that, we're on our own. We pack our trash, line up our bags in the Dallas line and we're set. We're ready, we're lined up and ready to go sir; count us in, we're here. Well, not so fast there, sonny. The Dallas flight has been canceled, so you're now going to Atlanta. Be back here at 12:45. When's the flight? Ten p.m. OK sounds good, that will give us...let's see nine hours and fifteen minutes to be ready. That should do it. I don't think we'll need any more time than that. Well, let's head back to chow.

It's hot again, surprise. The thermometer says 132*, and it's in the shade. This may have been a hallucination, but I swore I saw a camel blowing on his balls. That's how hot it is here. Thank God for powder. I may share some with my camel friend.

We're back in line for roll call. We're called, instructed and informed. We have to start going through customs, one by one. There are about 300 of us going and we all have to go through customs. We go in and dump everything out of all our bags, and I mean everything. They go through each item you have individually and then put it aside, and once that's done, you take it over to another table and re-pack. A hassle? Of course, but the way I pack, I was done quickly, good thing all my clothes were dirty. We go to another hooch and do another roll call, this time, bring your stuff. Now we're all in formation, civilians included. It's been a long time since I stood in a military formation, but there we were. Little soldiers, of all us, well, three little soldiers and one Marine. The formation turns and heads towards the buses. We get on the bus with our backpacks in front so we can sit down in the seat. We're headed to the Kuwait airport. I'm not sure how long I thought the drive would be, but I didn't expect an hour. I've been to Kuwait before and swore I saw the airport 45 minutes before we got there. But we got to the airport, got on a plane and now we're heading to Ireland to refuel, etc. We had a Guinness at the airport bar. That was cool, having a Guinness in Ireland. Then the Colonel came up and said the no drinking thing included us. Good thing I was already finished.

So, that's my trip to Afghanistan. I wish everyone could take a trip like that to see what it's really like. Not like what you get from the news but what it's really like. I wish everyone knew what our men and women are doing over there. What they're doing to get by, what they're putting up with on a daily basis. What they miss about home, who they miss at home. War sucks, it always has, and unfortunately as humans, we haven't figured out a better way to get along with other humans. I think if people really knew what our people are coping with over there, they may never again bitch about anything they put up with here in the states. Don't forget them, they haven't forgotten us.

Good night, sleep tight and don't forget to take your malaria pills.

CHAPTER 38
BACK IN IRAQ

From My Diary.

Dear Diary:
Well, I'm off to Iraq. I'm sitting in a plane in Washington D. C. I've been hanging around the airport for almost five hours and I'm ready to go. I'm in the economy seats but I'm not fretting; I should have plenty of room. I'm picturing a plane about half full. I mean how many people can be going from D.C. to Kuwait? As it turns out... a lot. What the hell? Are you people all really going to Kuwait? Why? What's going on there that you need to be a part of? The plane is packed.

I'm sitting behind a little kid who seems to be about four. As soon as the plane takes off, he slams his seat back. Seriously? You little shit, do you need that extra room? I don't think he does, so my job now is to distract him on the right so I can reach up with my left hand and push his button in. I need to get this kid's seat back up or I'm going to lose it. I'm not going to spend the next 14 hours jammed up because someone showed this little knucklehead how to put his seat back. I just don't feel that a kid that small needs all that room. His feet barely hang off the seat edge, what does he need extra leg room for? Maybe I can slip a little "kiddie doze" into his apple juice and get him to fall asleep, then bam, I make my move and get his seat back in the upright position. Very stealth. And let me just say, I don't know what "kidde doze" is and I certainly don't want anyone to think I carry around a supply of children's tranquilizers on hand "just in case," I'm just saying I wish.

Then, a couple of rows up another kid starts chiming in, "I want my mommy, I want my mommy," over and over. Oh man, come on, let's not do this. This isn't a movie man; it's not a comedy about a traveler stuck on a plane with a bunch of whiny kids, this is real life, my life. Don't tax my mental firmness by hitting me with all this before I even leave the freakin' ground. I can't get out of here for the next 14 hours and I'm being tested now? Holy Christ, what's going on? Then a kid at the rear starts in, and I'm stunned into silence. I'm sitting there with my eyes closed, just listening, concentrating on the sound and I start to laugh. It sounds like madcap chaos. I'm listening to babies crying, four-year-olds whining, seven and eight-year-old brothers going at each other, parents trying to reprimand their kids in public without causing a scene, I'm hearing overhead bins slamming, people talking way too loud for such close quarters, I hear four different languages, maybe five; what the hell is going on in this plane? I start to look around and there are a *bunch* of kids on this flight. Why? I don't know, I don't even know why they let kids fly. They shouldn't. Kids should be on a separate flight; that's fair isn't it? If you're this tall, you can't get on the ride. If it works for roller coasters, it should work on planes. Why should we all suffer because Julie and Omar want to bring the kids to Kuwait? We shouldn't, that's why. That's just the way it should be; kids under ten don't get to fly. If you need to go to Kuwait with your kids, take a ship.

Halfway through the meal, Scott comes back and tells Phillip and I that we can move up to Business Class with him. Hallelujah! Business Class, now that's the way to go. Plenty of room, the seats can go almost prone and it is a little slice of heaven compared to cattle car coach. Things are looking up. When we started I was crammed in, no leg room, no breathing room, no room to do shit. Now I'm sipping beverages while lying down, wrapped up in a blankie. Life is a joy again. Good night, sweet prince.

Dear Diary:
Kuwait. We made it, yeah. On my time, it's like 7 a.m., but Kuwati time is almost 5 p.m. We lost a day. I guess that happens when you go into the future. We get on base at Camp Arifjan, get settled, have some chow and prepare for slumber. It's only 8 p.m. but I'm pooped, wiped out, exhausted and plum tuckered out, I should sleep like a baby.

2:45 in the a.m. and I'm wide awake. I slept great for about five hours and now I'm awake and ready to start my day. The only problem is that it's 2:45 and there's not shit going on. It's too early to start a day unless you're a gravedigger or a cook at Waffle House, so what am I to do? I'm bored. I wonder what Scott and Phillip are doing?

I read for a couple of hours, did some puzzles, a couple of crosswords and a sodoku. When's chow? I hope I don't have the gastro problems I've had on previous trips over here. So far so good.

I'm back from chow and ready for a nap. Nap's over and now it's time for lunch and then off to Ali Al Saleem for our first show of the trip. Still, so far so good on the bathroom breaks.

The show rocked; we had about 300 people in an auditorium type place. We signed a lot of autograph cards, shook a lot of hands and posed for a lot of pictures. It was a nice ice breaker. I had three sitdowns before the show, and so it begins.

Dear Diary:
Went to bed at 10, it's now 2:30 and it looks like I'm up for the day again; what the hell? I need a sitdown. Who needs to poop at two in the morning? I do, that's who. At least here, we do not have to use the porta potties yet, we've got indoor plumbing; the portas are coming though, you know that, my friends, they're coming. I will say this: after last night's excursions in the men's room, I'm not having biscuits and gravy today. It's a shame though, B's and G's are delightfully delicious, but it wrecks my internals. I'm sorry about the discussions of bathroom breaks, but it's a huge part of life over here. Eating, sleeping and pooping, the cycle of life, if you will. Much importance is placed on these things, and not just with us, these things are important to everyone here. It's how you know you're alive. You need that stuff to look forward to, the next meal, the next nap, the next good bowel movement. Without those things to look forward to, what is the purpose of life? That's the question to ponder here my friends, without those things to look forward to in our lives; what's the point?

We're taking off at 8 a.m. for Ali Al Saleem; we have to catch a flight to Iraq. We're hanging at the PAX terminal (airport) waiting for a C-17 that will take us up north. After three trips to the portas, we're ready to load up the bus. The bus is full of soldiers heading up range, so it's tight quarters. We get halfway to the flight line when we're called upon to return because of a mechanical problem with the plane, and thank God they found it now as opposed to an in-flight discovery. We head back to the PAX and wait. Another two sitdowns and I'm getting chapped. The paper in porta potties isn't what you would call "top shelf." It's definitely from the discount pile. Rough, coarse and un-yielding, just what you want on a sensitive bum. It's been raining for two days and it's humid and clammy, not ideal weather for sitting in a porta pottie. You don't sweat like you do in the summer heat, but it's just enough sweat to make things uncomfortable and damp. Plus we have our body armor now, another 20 lbs of gear to carry around.

The flight to Ali Al Saleem was uneventful. I fell asleep right when I heard the announcement "We'll be landing in 15 minutes." Perfect, I'll get 15 minutes of shut eye, that should rejuvenate me just fine.

We did about five tours today. We did a long one at the hospital. I never did feel comfortable walking around talking to the wounded. I don't handle it very well and seeing injured soldiers is heartbreaking. Most of the injured weren't hurt too badly, but they're still all patched up and heavily medicated. We did what we can though and we did it without breaking down, so that was a plus. We finish our tours and head back for some chow and a shower. We're in the DVQ barracks (Distinguished Visitor Quarters). I'm in the exact same room I was in during the 2006 tour. I mean the exact same room, and last time I was here we got mortared, so I hope this night brings more quiet. I don't feel like sleeping in a bunker tonight. I've been up almost 22 hours and I'm starting to wind down. This place used to be called Camp Anaconda, but the Air Force took it over and changed the name to JBB or Joint Base Balad. Clever. The show was great- there were about 600 people in a huge movie theater. This was the biggest show of the last tour as well. It will be the last show we do like this. Tomorrow we head to the FOB's. (Forward Operating Base) I'm totally wiped, call time is 0600. I hope I can sleep past two in the blessed a.m.

Dear Diary:
We started out the day with a chopper flight to Camp Paliwoda. I had been there in 2006 and it was being mortared on a daily basis. It was the Camp where we had to run out of the choppers, get into a bunker and wait for the birds to take off. That really sucked, having to run with all your armor on and dragging your bags along. This is too much weight to run with. I came here to do comedy, not train for the Ironman. Isn't there a bell hop on this chopper? No, there isn't. Get your shit and boogie. This time it was a little more serene. We gently strolled off the bird on a clear, cloudless day. No rush, no panic, just a stroll. Sweet. They've actually got Iraqis guarding the compound; progress in full view. We had a great little show for about 40 guys; it's welcome back to the FOB's, boys, no more 600 seat theaters packed to the gills; back to doing shows for a handful of people in a tent or dirty courtyard with the aroma of overheated porta potties gently caressing your face. Ahh, back in Iraq.

Court Jester

Now we're at FOB Brassfield-Mora and I'm back in the porta. I don't know what it is about coming over here, but it wreaks havoc on my system. I'm not eating weird food or anything, but none of it stays with me very long. What gives? Huh? What gives? I'm eating twice as much as I normally do, but it shouldn't cause this, should it? I've noticed that there isn't much dawdling in a porta, you don't bring anything to read in there, it's all business and then move on, and business is brisk. The welcoming crew had a little sandwich buffet lined up for us, but only one light in the room worked and I admit, I was a little hesitant, what with my problems previously mentioned. The last thing I needed was to eat something else that would play "hurry up and get out" with my lower tract. I don't like eating in the dark.

The room was dark and the table was set up in the very furthest recesses of the room. It was cast in shadows and the beam of light that was reaching out, was full of dust, sand and other microscopic blots of unknown origin. I'm straining my eyes because I need to see what I'm looking at before I put any of it on my plate. It's just how I roll. It turned out to be delicious and I had two big sandwiches, a bag of chips, two apples, two gatorades, a cookie, a banana, an orange, a chewy granola bar and a cupcake. Hey, maybe that's why I spend so much time sitting in a plastic pooping box.

The crowd is light. It's Sunday, so there's no lunch being served, so no one really showed up for the show. It was MRE day, which are meals in a bag, not a big draw, so there were about 15 people scattered around the chow hall. And I mean scattered. If a grenade landed anywhere in the room, it would've only taken out one, maybe two people. Now, that's scattered. We didn't generate much energy, you know, 15 people in a room the size of a gymnasium. But we got through it; we're done and ready to hit the choppers, but wait. A group of guys that didn't come to show want us to come over and say hi and join in their barbecue. Even though we just ate, there we are, eating brats and a burger, along with two sodas, another apple and another bag of chips. I can't believe I'm still eating. It's not like I'm burning up thousands of calories; why am I eating like I'm storing fat up for winter? I'm full now, and I need a sitdown. I wonder what's up with that?

Now we're at FOB McHenry near Hawijah and there's nobody there. Two guys came out to greet us and informed us that there had been a "skirmish" and the rest of the camp had left to assist. I asked the

320

Capt. about the "skirmish," and he said, "Sorry, that's classified." When I asked what made the info classified, he replied, "that is classified as well." So I knew the camp comedian had been left behind. We sat in the VIP shack for about 70 minutes, then the choppers came back to get us. No show at McHenry.

Now the choppers are taking us to Camp Speicher and the fellas decided to have a little fun with us. Midway through the flight, we drop from 1000 feet to about 200 feet in seconds and the machine gunners open up on both sides. They wanted us to think that we were under attack, ha, ha. When we dropped like that I thought we *were* crashing, and it wasn't a pleasant feeling. I do admit, for a second there, I thought we were going down, I thought we had been hit and the chopper was crashing, I actually lifted my feet up so no rounds would come through the bottom of the chopper and blow my legs off. It had the zero gravity thing working like on a roller coaster, but the waiting to hit the ground was what I didn't care for. There really didn't seem to be time for my life to flash in front of me, all I remember thinking was, "fuck, we're going to crash." I was surprised at how calm I felt, I had actually accepted the fact that this was it, I was going to die. I hope I'm that calm when it's really time.

Then we made some sharp turns and my stomach was flying all over, I'm dodging brass from the machine gun, it's flying all over and I'm sitting in the ejection path. Then one flew down my sweatshirt, and yes, it's hot, they're hitting me in the face, on the neck and I'm just holding on for dear life. I think that's when I realized they were just flying around, playing. Ok, that's cool, we're fine, no worries, I'm not going to die, whew, ok, cool, everything's cool, it's all ok, we're not crashing, it's all good, ok, we're fine, I'm fine, he's fine, you're fine, we're all fine, I need to hug someone. Then I noticed Phillip screaming at the top of his lungs.

The noise inside a chopper is deafening, which is why you have to wear ear plugs. The engines were screaming, the machine guns are pumping out rounds and suddenly, all I could hear was Phillip screaming. I couldn't believe I could hear him over all that noise. Then I glanced his way and noticed he had a little green tinge to him and it looked like he was holding back from spraying the inside of the helicopter with vomitus. As we're into our 40th second of defensive maneuvers I'm having a blast. I like the feeling of having your stomach in your chest cavity. It's cool. I'd never been sideways in a helicopter, but it's an interesting feeling. Thank God we were wearing seat belts. I'm like a kid at an amusement park: I want it to go on. Phillip didn't feel that way, he's just staring at the floor, trying to hold on to his insides. I would've laughed if he hadn't looked so terrified. He had even stopped video- taping, so I know he was close to losing it. Then he started with the "I'm going to puke" look and we leveled out. The pilots thought it was hilarious, and I must admit, I was enjoying their antics as well. But all good things must come to an end and now we're approaching the landing pad, I'm hoping they do a combat landing, because you really get tossed around doing those, but sympathy for Flip prevented them from doing any other fancy moves. No one wants puke in the helicopter, too many crannies.

We've arrived at our lodging for the night and it is sweet. It's called Freedom Base and it's usually used for soldiers who need a couple of days off from battle. We've got individual rooms and a.c. That's all a girl really needs, isn't it? Just a room and some air conditioning. There's food available 24 hours a day, sweet. We get back from chow, I enter my room and all I can smell is feet. Not everyone's feet, just mine. I've got my dirty socks in a separate bag, but the bag apparently doesn't hold in odor. I'm using plenty of powder on my tootsies but my room still reeks of sweaty feet. I may have to turn the a.c. down to chill the smell. Does that work? Make it too cold to stink? I don't know, but I'm trying it.

We did an impromtu show for the some of the pilots on base. It wasn't scheduled, but they're just sitting there, why not do a show? I am out of juice, I'm totally wiped out and can't wait to hit the rack, and I'm going to sleep like a baby tonight, my friends. I am so looking forward to crashing tonight, I'm going to shower, wipe the dust off and sleep the sleep of a thousand dreams.

It's now 2:30 in the a.m. and I'm still awake. I finished one book and got halfway through another. I don't get this. I'm tired as hell but can't get my mind to shut down. I finally took a pill and slept like a rock from 3-6 a.m. Hell, three hours is all I really need, isn't it?

Dear Diary:
My sleeping meds haven't worn off yet, so now I'm groggy- perfect. This day is going to be about 20 hours long and I can barely keep my eyes open. Glad I'm not piloting. As we're sitting in the PAX terminal waiting for our choppers, a soldier approached me and asked if I was in

Milwaukee last week. I was, and he had seen me at Jokerz comedy club there. How's that for a small world? Friday night he sees me in Milwaukee, and the next week he sees me in Tikrit, Iraq. We were wearing different clothes, but it was us. That was cool.

We're off to FOB Doria, a mud soaked, sand wall enclosed camp that had no amenities. They didn't even have a proper shower; they would go out to a shed with a washcloth, a bar of soap and a couple of water bottles. Remind me not to complain about anything again. The place was a mud pit, and when we arrived they were trying to spread gravel around so they could move vehicles. Most of the camp was out on patrol, so we only had about 20 for the show, which is better than none for the show. This camp still had pee tubes, which are plastic pvc pipes shoved into the ground and you pee into them. Crude? Sure, but with no plumbing, you have to make due. Or doo doo.

Now we're back on the birds heading to FOB Summerall, outside Bayji, Iraq. We're doing this show in the DFAC (dining facility) and it's huge. I usually find these shows to be the worst of the bunch. The room is too big, people are eating and unaware that there's a show coming up, and it's just too much distraction. People are sitting down, facing away from you, talking, etc., but we're here to do a show and by God, that's what we're going to do. We blaze through the show and pulled it off. It wasn't the best show of the trip, but we got some laughs, and that's what matters isn't it?

Now we're off to Kirkuk and Camp Warrior. The four of us, the three comedians and our escort Kenny are all bunking together. It's just like camp. I mean, I guess it is; I never went to camp myself.

The show went pretty well, it was in an outdoor courtyard type of setting with the fast food joints surrounding us. Sometimes people would have to wait for their food and when it was ready it would be announced over the loudspeaker. Every 20-30 seconds you would hear "number 217, your order's ready" and it was loud enough to drown us out. You would have to stop each time you heard the click of the intercom. I guess things can't always go smoothly in a war zone.

Dear Diary:
I finally slept through the night. Well, not all the way through, I had to get up twice and use my pee bottle, but it was in all other ways a good night's sleep. It only took five days. We're leaving Kirkuk and headed to Korea Village to do a show for the Marines. I was at KV in

2006 and it was pretty bleak, so I'm not expecting much. We're riding in a Chinook helicopter and sometimes it can be a little bumpier than the Blackhawk. I've got my iPod working, and *Stranglehold* by Ted Nugent starts to play and it's amazing. I've heard the song a million times since high school, but listening to it while in a Chinook flying over Iraq was the best. It seemed fitting.

The flight to Korea Village is about an hour. There are only eight people on this flight and 15 minutes into the flight, Phillip looks a little green again, I see him lean over and say something to Scott, who then makes the puking gesture. That means Phillip is getting sick and needs a barf bag which they don't really carry on helicopters. I look up at the machine gunners and make the puking signal and I've never seen machine gunners move so fast; they were tearing apart everything and anything to find a barf bag. When none can be found one of them grabs the fire bucket and starts to pass it back when the other one empties out an MRE bag and passes it back, and just in the nick of time too.

Phillip grabs the bag and lets loose. I felt bad for him; no one likes to puke, especially on a helicopter. It was the one incident that I didn't capture on film. I just didn't think he'd want a picture of himself heaving into plastic bag while trying to keep in his seat. He puked off and on for almost 40 minutes, poor little slugger. I could tell in his face that he was expecting to land any minute, but alas, no, there is still some flying to do.

We finally get on the ground, and along with his gear, he has to bring his little barf bag with him to dispose of properly. We get settled into our quarters, which was just a plywood building, but it's got floors and walls, and that's what really matters. The Marines ask us if we want to hit the range and, of course, we do. We haven't gotten to fire any weapons on this trip, and that's always a highlight. Scott and I have done quite a bit of shooting, not so with Phillip. I don't think I've been around anyone who's never fired a weapon since I was in boot camp and I'm sure it's going to be interesting. We go through a little safety talk because no one wants to get shot by the comedians. Scott and I go first just to let Phillip get a feel for the action and then it's his turn. He fired the M-4 rifle first and it was the funniest thing we saw all week, until he fired the pistol. He did ok with the rifle until they put it on burst, which fires three rounds each time you pull the trigger and he was kicking up dirt ten yards in front of him. He unleashed a full clip into the dirt and Sgt Alvarado called him "one badass worm killer." We had a good chuckle over that, and then came the 9 mm pistol firing. We thought the rifle was funny, but I'd never seen Marines scatter like that when he opened up with that pistol. The rounds are flying everywhere; anyone lying on the ground would have been toast. Anyone standing in front of the target would've been fine. By the time he was done, there was a straight line of people directly behind him, no one wanted to stand off to the side in case he ricocheted one off the rocks. It may have been the biggest laugh we had all week. Thank you, Phillip.

As we head back to our hooches, the wind starts picking up and you can feel something in the air. By the time we got back, the wind was blowing about 50 mph and there is a sandstorm coming. This trip has been one of the dustiest and it doesn't look like it's going to get any better. As we look north east, you can see a dark brown/reddish wall coming at us. I asked what it was and was told, "sandstorm." Really? A sandstorm? I'm going to get my camcorder. As I'm standing outside the rooms, you can feel the sand start to hit you; it's about the color of dusk out even though it's four in the afternoon. I stayed out as long as possible, but when you're getting sandblasted, it's hard to maintain your place in the out of doors. I can feel the skin peeling off my arms and the exposed parts of my face and Phillip is screaming, "get in, get inside, come on." It reminded me of all of Bill Paxton's lines in *Twister*. That's all he said during the entire movie "come on, let's go, get of there, come on, let's go." Great writing.

I've eaten four times today and am back to regular sitdowns. The portas at KV were the cleanest ones I've ever been in, and I found out why. The locals on base clean them every two hours, and if you're in there, they start anyway. They'll knock on the door and I'll say "occupado" because I can communicate with anyone, and they start on the outside. The outside is cleaned with a sprayer and they go top to bottom, but there are vents at the top that don't stop the water from getting in, so you get a nice little shower of porta pottie disinfectant. Thanks, Hadji, maybe you could wait three minutes for me to finish up in here, or maybe start on the next one etc.

The show was great. We had to move indoors though. They wanted to do it outside, but you can't do a show with a sand monsoon blowing at your ass. When we got back to our hooch, the place was covered in dust. I slapped my pillow and it billowed red and brown dust. I had a mini Mount St. Helens going on in my room. I had to put a t-shirt over my pillow so I wouldn't wake up muddy. I went to take a shower and once again, I had mud puddles at my feet upon completion.

Dear Diary:
We're at the PAX terminal waiting for a 10 a.m. flight to Ramadi. There is a dust storm at Al Asad so they've been delayed. No flights take off in "red air." Sit tight and wait. We have a 7 p.m. show for the Marines in Ramadi. At 5 p.m. our choppers still aren't here. We may miss a show because of it. At 6 p.m. our flight arrives, and they can't get to Ramadi, so it's back to Al Asad for some late chow and back to Arifjan for a day off before we head back to the states. We're taking a C-130 cargo plane back to Al Asad, and when it picks us up at the VIP pad, there are only the three of us on the plane. We had this entire cargo plane to ourselves. They asked if we wanted to sit up in the cockpit and Phillip went up. Scott and I had been up there before so we declined; I needed a nap. When I woke up Scott told me that they let Phillip fly the plane. That's right, actually sit in the pilot's seat and take the controls. Oh well. He screamed on one chopper, puked on another and shot the shit out of the dirt, but he got to fly the plane. I guess it all works out in the end, eh? We've got an overnight here then back to Kuwait.

Dear Diary:
We had the night off last night and went to the movies. We saw *Push,* and I have no idea what the movie was about. It had something to do with watchers, shadowers, pushers, movers, etc. I couldn't write up a synopsis if I had too, but thank goodness I don't. We're sitting in the Kuwait airport waiting on our 11 p.m. flight to DC. Fourteen hours, that should be fun.

I got an exit row seat, and I know I said I would never take an exit row seat on an international flight again because it turns into the stretching, waiting for the bathroom, chatting area, but I needed the leg and elbow room. I slept like a baby for three hours, and then it was time to "kill time." I finished one book, started another, did some puzzles and then watched a few movies. I saw *Yes Man* with Jim Carrey, and that was ok, *The Express* was pretty good, something with Daniel Craig about Jews escaping the Germans, and *Marley and Me.* Marley and Me was a story of "the world's worst dog." It wasn't though; what it was really about is the world's worst pack leaders. This Grogan guy and his wife are obviously too stupid to own a dog, they should've stuck with a cat or maybe some fish. They have no control over their dog, how sad. Get a clue, watch the *Dog Whisperer* or something. I felt bad for the dog; he just wanted a pack leader to boss him around, and instead, he got these morons.

Are we there yet? I can't bear to look at my watch. We have to be at least 10 or 11 hours into this flight, don't we? I checked the map, and no, we're still only 1/3 of the way across the Atlantic. I keep glancing out the window looking for the sunrise and it's not coming. We finally get to DC and cruise through customs. We only have about 2 hours between flights, so there is a small sense of urgency. I get to my gate in plenty of time for my departure. Four hours later, my flight is ready. I don't know what the delay was, I just kept repeating, "serenity now, serenity now."

Going to Iraq or Afghanistan always changes my perspective when I return. Nothing is that bad or that urgent. Just relax, nimrod. No problem I have in the states can compare to what the guys and gals over there confront on a regular basis. Just keep your cool. They just announced that the flight will be here by 9. Then 9:30, then 10. Allright, you mofos, get your shit together and learn how to fly in the rain. Yes, it's damp and wet, and I don't give a shit; just do your jobs. Oops, "serenity now, serenity now." At 10:45 my plane arrives, I'll be home soon, and Iraq will be another memory. Until next time.

CHAPTER 39
I GOT DIVORCED

I'm divorced. Another loser. Not a loser at life- that may be a bit dramatic, just a loser at marriage, and as it turns out, I'm not the only one. Why does everyone think, "It won't happen to us?" That's a crock; it does happen to us; it happens to us all over the place. It happens every day. Thousands of them. According to recent stats, it's up to about 52% of marriages now end in divorce. That's a wild and wacky stat when you think about it. 52% of marriages end in divorce. Wow. Why even bother?

It's not like the old days when people stayed together no matter what. There would be no separation, no divorce; people stayed together until they slowly drove each other insane, maybe finish it off with a murder/suicide. Simple. Direct.

I had an amicable divorce, so that was cool. I know a lot of people who don't get along with their exes, and that's a shame. You're not married to them anymore, make nice. We just decided we wanted different things. She's still thinks highly of me, not highly enough to stay married, but still. She decided that her life should go in a different direction than the one we were headed in. Oh well. Adios, muchacho. Happy trails.

When my wife told me she wanted a divorce, she said she wanted to keep the house too. No way, I told her. This is your divorce, it's what you wanted, it's all about you. I told her I pay the bills, the mortgage and everything else, so I'm going to keep the house and I put my foot down; obviously I had no idea what I was talking about. Then I moved in with my brother.

I distinctly remember driving away with my stuff in a borrowed pickup truck. When I say "all my stuff" that's exactly what I meant, it was literally "all my stuff." I was in my forties and driving away with everything I owned in the back of a pick-up truck. How sad is that? A whole lifetime of stuff, fitting in the back of a pickup. Ok, it didn't fill the pickup, it filled up half the pickup, which is even sadder. At least it wasn't one of those mini-trucks. Filling up half a mini-truck may have been more than I could bear. Where did all my stuff go? Well, dumbass, you don't have any stuff. I guess that's part of being a nomad: you don't collect many things because you just have to keep moving them. If you live light, you can travel light. I just don't think I ever noticed how light I was traveling. I had no furniture, no big items at all. It was mostly clothes and books. Easy to move though, so I had that going for me. I moved a lot during my life; let's see if we can recall every move.

I started in DeKalb, Illinois, (which is also the birth place of one Cindy Crawford, we were even born in the same hospital). My dad was in college after leaving the Army, and I was born in couples housing on campus. Then came a few moves that I don't recall. All on the south side of Chicago. LaGrange, Bellwood and Tinley Park. I'm not even two yet and I'm on my fourth dwelling; I feel a trend coming on. I'm not sure if we were on the run from someone or something, but we were ramblers. I'm glad I don't remember all these moves. I might've felt rootless. I remember the ones that followed though. Off to Milwaukee, then to Cedar Rapids, IA then Overland Park, KS then back to the Chicago 'burbs. The town of Hoffman Estates.

I'm now in 8th grade and have moved seven times. No moss grew on my ass, that's for sure. I know I'm off on a tangent, but this is where this chapter has taken me, so I'm going to finish these thoughts. After Hoffman it was onward to St. Louis, move #8. I'm counting every place I was in long enough to get mail. That's a sign you're at least a little settled. Move #9 was to boot camp (I got mail), next move was to 29 Palms where we went from the barracks to the BEQ's and then off to Okinawa Japan, then to the Cherry Point BEQ's, and then out to Atlantic Beach with Sweet Lou.

That's now 14 moves in 18 years. I'm cruising. I moved back home after I got out of the Marines for a few months before I went to school. Then I moved to Cape and in with Jim and Louie near the park and then out by the golf course, so that's 17. Oh yeah, I'm just a ramblin' guy. Then I met Erin and moved in with her into that barn burner of an apartment; it was like living in an oven, so we moved, 18 and 19. She ended up moving back to California and I moved in with Charlie and Carla. Then I moved into a house with Louie and Ted over by the hospital, 20 and 21. Then Ted, Louie and I got a house on William St., and I was there for a while.

After school, I moved in with John in Schoettler Village and then moved to South County because of a girl. I think that's 24 moves we're up to now and I'm only 26. My brother Phil moved down south too and we got a place right off of 55 and Tesson Ferry. It was one of those places where there was almost no natural light. It faced North East and never saw the sun. That was the place where Jimmy K lived in the kitchen pantry while he and his wife were divorcing. We had a pretty big pantry and he tossed down a sleeping bag and stayed with us for months. It was really quite roomy. He had little shelves set up for his alarm and personal items, so it worked out nicely. Like a nice-sized cell, but you can get up and leave. No complaints. Move #26 came when we hauled our shit to St Charles and found an apartment above a bicycle shop in old town. It had 20 foot ceilings and a huge patio that overlooked the river; it was the coolest place we ever had.

We had to climb three flights of stairs to enter the back, which is what we had to do when moving. I noticed the size of the boxes decreases as I've gotten older. We used to haul these monster boxes all over and now...not so much. We're also not taking more than one box any more, hmm. I imagine, in another five moves, I'll be packing my shit in shoe boxes. So now it's me, my brother Phil and Jimmy K, who was no longer sleeping in the pantry - he had his own room. After that, move #27 came when Phil, me and Louie got a house over in West County, and that was a good time. I laughed more living with those two than anyone else. Then I started doing comedy and moved (#28) down off McCausland, on the outskirts of the city. That was the one room studio right about the bus stop. We called it "the ghetto." Move #29 was when my girlfriend and I got an apartment before we got married. Then we moved in with her mother for a few months before we moved to L.A.

The move to Redondo Beach was #31. We lived in the 300 block of Ave G. Nice place, three blocks from the beach, we were there for about three years before we moved again, but this time we moved two buildings down. How's that for a move? Two buildings. We carried most of our shit by hand and used shopping carts. Totally hillbilly, but it seemed the most logical thing to do. That was #32; 33 came when we left L.A. and headed to St. Louis. By the time we left Los Angeles, we were pretty broke, so we moved in with her mom again until we could buy a place. That took a year. Move #34 was moving in the place in St. Charles off of 94. Then I got divorced, and move #35 was in with my brother again. I then realized more than half of my life I've lived with my brother. Strange. Move #36 was buying a place in West County, St. Louis, and that's where I am presently. After writing all these down, I actually thought there would be more; it seemed like there would be more. It felt like it was more. I don't like moving. Never did. Check that, I don't like the process of moving. I did enjoy starting in a new place; it's a fresh start in a new home, cool. The old habits, etc, come back quickly, but for a few moments there, it's like having a clean slate. Everything is neat and clean and everything gets put in its special place, for now. So there you have it, 36 moves so far in my life. That's a lot of moving. No wonder my back hurts sometimes. I travel light for obvious reasons. At least if there's an Apocalypse and we have to get mobile, I'll be able to carry all my shit with me.

So now I'm out here again. That's where I was. Single. In my forties and single. I'm shitting my pants. Exactly what goes on out here? I've been out of the loop for a while. I'm freaking out. How does one go about getting laid in this day and age? Last time I was single, you hung out with people you knew, did some drinking and then ended up in someone's bed. It was a lot of good times. Of course, I was in the bar business, and that life doesn't really reflect single life for civilians. Bar people are different. We were night people. Many times we didn't hook up until dawn was breaking. I liked that, out drinking after work and getting naked as the sun's coming up. Good stuff, good times.

I'm paranoid about sex with strangers, which is new to me. I was never paranoid before, and it was awesome. We rarely, if ever, even used condoms. Can you imagine that now? Going in unwrapped? It's like Russian Roulette. There could be a bullet in any chamber. Bang, you're dead, all from getting laid. Nice world, thanks to whoever caused it. I remember a time when there was just syphilis, gonorrhea and crabs; that was it. Maybe a case of warts would occur, but not very often. Gonorrhea was about the only one you heard about, the clap, the drip, and it was usually fixed up with a shot. No worries. Syphilis was unheard of; the last guy we knew who had syphilis was Al Capone. I fortunately, never had to face that trauma, I guess I was lucky. It seemed like we were all so clean, it was beautiful. Then the nineties hit and there was an explosion of STD's. What happened? Why and when did people get so dirty? By then AIDS was huge, you still had gonorrhea and crabs, but now people were actually contracting syphilis. What? Are we in the roaring twenties? Syphilis is back? Well done. But then there was also chlamydia and herpes, you've got BV and LVG, you've got HPV and PID, there's Nongonococcal Urethritis and Granuloma and Lymphoganuloma, sometimes people get Molluscum Contagiosum or Candidiasis and to top it off you've got

Trichomoniasis. What the fuck happened? It used to be fun and carefree and now you have to worry about being killed from sex.

Even in Okinawa, STD's never really seemed to be a problem. Sure, a few of the guys got a little something, something from time to time. One day a guy in our barracks discovered crabs; that caused plenty of panic and paranoia. Crabs spread easily so we ran yellow duct tape down the center of the barracks and no one from the infected side could cross over the yellow line. They didn't all have crabs, but we weren't taking any chances. Most of us had never seen one and we wanted to. A bunch of us went into the head and were standing around the stainless steel ledge underneath the mirror and the crabs host put one of those little buggers on the ledge. There were five of us leaning over and peering at this tiny little brown dot and marveling at its size when it launches itself straight up into the air and disappeared. You would've thought someone was dropping huge turds on us the way we ran out of that place. Five grown ass men, Marines no less, scattering and screaming as we ran down the hall, trying to escape from the crab. Good stuff, Good times.

When I was married, I thought a lot of single people had some kind of cooties. Now that I'm single again, it's back to "she looks clean." That's nice. "She looks clean?" What kind of thing is that? I wonder if I'm the only one who thinks that? Who thinks he can tell by looking at someone whether or not they've got an STD? Who am I kidding? Get real, numb nuts. That's a good way to get your dick rotted off. That is no way to start your new single life, is it? "Hi, I like you, but my dick's gone, I thought I saw a woman who was clean and I was wrong and now my dick has rotted away and fallen off, what's your sign?"

It reminds me of Okinawa when we were warned about the "black syph." A horrible, horrible type of syphilis that was found only in the Far East, it was incurable and if you caught it, you could never leave Asia. You would be quarantined on the island forever. They couldn't take the chance of it spreading in the U.S. That's some pretty serious shit there man. That's some heavy info to have laid on you the first day. The symptoms were easy to spot, so there would no mistaking it. First your dick starts to rot, then it turns black and eventually falls off. A little while later, you die, which, I guess, is a good thing because once your pecker is gone, what reason is there to continue on? That pretty much sums up black syph. They told us this in an orientation meeting we went to upon arrival on the rock. To this day I've never forgotten it and still don't know if it's true.

So I got divorced and moved in with my brother Phil for almost two years (thanks bro), and then I finally got my own place and was living by myself. It had been a while since I'd lived alone. I grew up with a large family, then went into the Marines where I lived in the barracks or enlisted men's quarters, then off to college where I had roommates, and after college I lived with a high school buddy of mine. Now I was about 27 years old and had never lived alone. I met a girl who lived 30 miles away so I moved closer to her and had my own place. I was finally "on my own." Groovy. It was a one bedroom-cinder block walled palace. I had my own place.

That was where I was living when I decided to do comedy. The girl I moved out there for and I broke up; and since I had just quit my day job to do comedy, I moved to someplace more affordable. A $170 a month one room studio apartment, the one we referred to as "the ghetto." It wasn't really a ghetto, we just called it that because that's what it seemed like. Radiated heat that never worked so it was Russia-like cold in the winter and it also had no a.c. That was sweet in the 100* heat of a St. Louis summer. "It's not the heat, it's the humidity." Bullshit, it's the heat too. I still had a water bed at the time.

Remember those? Very popular for a long time. The first one I had was not baffled, what they called "free flow" and that was one sloshy sleep session. Try saying that fast three times, sloshy sleep session. You couldn't keep the bubbles out, so it was always noisy, and if someone else was sleeping with you, extreme care had to be taken upon entry or you could toss them over the side where they'd be wedged between the wall and frame never to be seen again. Or if you jumped in, you could fling her right into the wall hard enough to leave a dent in the drywall. I can't believe they even made water beds with no baffles, just sleeping on a giant baggie of water.

One time my heater went out at night in the middle of winter and by morning the water was so cold it chilled my bones. I mean it too, I was so cold my bones hurt, I didn't feel good for a week. My core temperature had dropped to what I felt was a dangerous levels. I never underestimated the water bed heater again. But in that studio apartment, I unplugged the heater in the summer to chill the water. It wouldn't get unhealthily cold because it was 90* in the apartment. I used to take a shower and lay down on the bed still wet with the fan blowing on me and hope I could fall asleep before the fan dried me off. Is this St. Louis or equatorial Africa? I didn't care though; I was doing comedy and living all alone in the big city. I felt like Marlo Thomas in *That Girl.* I just wanted to throw my hat in the air; like Mary Tyler Moore. I was living in a building where there were occasional overdoses and police visits.

One day three friends of mine and I had finished working the bar around 3 a.m., went drinking across the river and then played 18 holes of golf. We headed back to my house to do another party session and then we were going to the Chinese buffet for lunch. We had left the door open when this girl comes running down the hall screaming for help. We're all trashed so I doubt we're going to be much help, but she sees my door open and bolts inside in a panic. She's crying and screaming and we can't understand her. She finally gets it out that her boyfriend has committed suicide by hanging himself from in the shower. Wow, that's wild, man, a suicide? In this building? What are the chances? She's telling us that he drinks a lot and uses a lot of drugs and has been depressed lately and would we come down the hall and help him? We're obviously a little hesitant because the buffet closes at one and it's already 12:15, we don't want to miss lunch.

Someone picks up the phone and dials 911 and then disconnects when he realizes that we don't need the cops here- too much stuff around they might find. Crispy and I head down the hall to see what's what and the phone rings; it's 911 calling back, even then they had secret powers. It seems that if you call and hang up, they get suspicious and call you. The situation is explained and they tell us they're sending a unit over. Crispy and I walk down the hall and into this girls' apartment and sure enough, her boyfriend is hanging from the shower curtain rod with his belt wrapped around his neck. We can see he's not dead though. For starters, his feet are on the floor. You can't hang yourself with your feet on the floor, there has to be some clearance. Secondly, he's moving. That's another sure sign that someone's not dead, the movement.

He tried to hang himself, he just wasn't successful. He wrapped the belt around his neck and around the shower curtain rod, which of course ripped partially out of the wall when that much weight was put on it. I'm not sure I've ever heard of a shower curtain rod that could support the weight of a grown man. So he's not really hanging, he's actually standing there with one end of his belt around his neck and the other end wrapped around this bent, broken shower curtain rod. Sad sight indeed. It looks like he's still trying to choke himself though. He's just standing there, tugging on his belt He hasn't even started to turn blue, he does though look like he's going to pass out, so we took the belt off his neck, made him lay down on the floor, and then headed off to chow; our work here is done and we don't want to miss the buffet. As far as we're concerned, he's breathing, so he's OK. As we head back down the hall, the coppers show up and pass us in the hall, but we got out of there as quick as we could so we wouldn't have to answer any questions because as I said, the buffet closes at one. It's all about having your priorities in line.

I eventually had roommates again (my brother and Louie), but I had a good two-year stretch where I was on my own. And now I'm divorced and living alone. That can sound sad, but it's not. It's the freakin' best. I love living alone. Before, I never really appreciated it, but I do now. I'm in charge of everything that happens; if I drop a pair of britches on the floor, they'll stay there until I pick them up. Simple, profound. Nothing happens without my approval or my doing. For the first time in my life, I picked the paint colors, I picked the dish colors, I picked everything and from what I understand, none of it matches, and you know what? I don't care. I've got a Jeff Beck painting and a poster of Bob Dylan on the wall, and nobody's told me to take them down. How righteous is that? I know posters are old school, but I taped the edges and use the same tack holes for each showing, so it's not as primitive as it sounds. Or does it?

Do you know what the best part of being divorced is? Having complete and utter dominance of the remote. It's the best. I don't watch commercials, never did, never will. When the commercials come on, I start flipping and that's never gone over well with any woman. Why? I don't know. Woman don't want to switch channels for whatever reason. I try to convince her that commercials are written for stupid people, and we should refuse to be a part of it. But she doesn't want her focus shifted to another subject or story. I'm of the thought-do you actually think I'm going to buy your product because you made a television commercial? No, as a matter of fact, if the ad is irritating enough, I'll NEVER purchase your product. How's that for hardcore? It seems like a simple thing, controlling the remote, and it is simple, but it's also important to my overall happiness.

When you are a divorced man living alone, you don't have scheduled feeding times. I eat when I'm hungry. That's it; I eat when I'm hungry and I can have anything I want any time of day. You never hear, "Is that what you're having for breakfast? Reheated cheeseburgers from three days ago?" I reply "No, I'm going to have cake too." So I like living alone, and eventually I'll take another woman into my life, but for now, I'm enjoying every minute of the lonely boy, living alone. Yes indeed. Yes in goddamndeedy. Livin' the dream.

CPSIA information can be obtained at www.ICGtesting.com
Printed in the USA
LVOW060546020413

327122LV00001B/4/P